FORTH TO THE WILDERNESS

Forth to the Wilderness

THE FIRST AMERICAN FRONTIER

1754-1774

ช

DALE VAN EVERY

Quill

William Morrow

New York

Library of Congress Cataloging-in-Publication Data

Van Every, Dale, 1896–
    Forth to the wilderness.
    Reprint. Originally published: New York: Morrow, 1961.
    Bibliography: p.
    Includes index.
    1. Frontier and pioneer life—United States.
2. United States—History—Colonial period. ca. 1600–
1775. 3. Indians of North America—Wars—1750–1815.
I. Title.
E195.V3   1987   973.2   87-13948
ISBN 0-688-07522-3

Printed in the United States of America

First Quill Edition

1 2 3 4 5 6 7 8 9 10

Foreword

When, a few years ago, the august members of the American Historical Association named Francis Parkman and Frederick Jackson Turner as the nation's two most distinguished historians, they were responding to impulses deeply rooted in the American people. On the surface there was little resemblance between these two giants of scholarship; one wrote in the nineteenth-century tradition of the literary epic, the other in the twentieth-century medium of scientific analysis; one produced a whole shelf of stirring narratives, the other but one book and a score of essays during his lifetime. Yet each qualified for the posthumous honor conferred upon him by his particular emphasis on the most American phase of American history: the ever-moving frontier.

That the westward sweep should capture the imagination of past and present generations is readily understandable. From the days of James Fenimore Cooper's impeccably educated Indians to the modern onslaught of television "westerns," Americans have shown an inclination to escape from the humdrum of counting-house and factory into the great open spaces of the West. There they could find adventure and romance, true, but there also they could relive the story of their country's growth, the triumph of man in his never-ending struggle with hostile nature, and the oft-repeated rags-to-riches saga that is the dream of the humble and the pride of the self-made. Patriotism, victory over adversity, and material success—three basic impulses—all made their appeal through the reading of fact and fiction about the frontier.

Authors who would retell this story have long been tempted to embroider the truth, if only to cater to a demanding audience that panted for more thrilling adventure, more hair-raising excitement, more glamorous romance. Many, even among historians, succumbed to this lure and have been forgotten. Francis Parkman, virtually alone among his contemporaries, adhered closely to the facts of history, yet proved them so irresistibly colorful that his pages sparkle with life today as they did a century ago. Frederick Jackson Turner, too, saw the West not as a land of romantic fable but as a tangible force partially responsible for shaping the institutions and characteristics of the American people. Their concern with the truth won them acclaim from their own generations, and ours.

To the ranks of those who have found on America's frontiers the unadulterated facts needed to fashion a story of epic proportions can be added the name of Dale Van Every. Like Turner he sees the westward movement as a catalytic force helping create a distinctive civilization; like Parkman he tells his tale in a lyric prose that carries his readers into the hauntingly mysterious forests of the West, there to stand side by side with living men as they battle nature and each other. No addict of the television screen could hope for a more rousing story than that told in this book; no scientific historian should fail to be impressed by Dale Van Every's alertness to the truth about the past.

The fragment of history that he has chosen to retell in this volume admirably lends itself to his taste for apt characterization and meaningful generalization. His theme is a classic one in human annals: the conquest of a formidable obstacle, in this case the Appalachian Mountain barrier. In 1754, when his story begins, the frontier had been creeping westward for a century and a half before being brought to a halt by the 1300-mile-long range of underbrush-clogged peaks that barred the pioneer's path into the Mississippi Valley. Beyond the mountains lay a forbidden land already pre-empted by the trappers of New France and their Indian allies. The conquest of this barrier was a feat no less hazardous than the bridging of the Alps by Hannibal or the crossing of the English channel by Allied Troops fighting for their first beachhead in Hitler's Europe.

So the blundering Braddock found as he marched to his rendezvous with fate at Fort Duquesne. So John Forbes found when, three years later, he led the heroic expedition that planted the English flag at the Forks of the Ohio. Between these events, and afterward, the French and Indian War raged along the borderlands, and this war with all its savagery and heroism is the first of the subthemes stirringly described by Dale Van Every. His recipe for military history is temptingly palatable: a portion of broad strategy sketched in bold strokes of the pen, a leaven of strategic campaigns singled out for minute analysis with a fine eye to color and adventure, and a merciful omission of boring, insignificant detail.

Once the war was won in 1763, the British and Americans found themselves plunged into a new conflict by their own blundering and by the sense of destiny of a remarkable Indian named Pontiac. Realizing that the expulsion of the French left the red men at the mercy of the English, Pontiac struck a blow for his doomed people by launching a bitter attack on Fort Detroit, thus touching off a war that overnight flamed across the West. In his vivid descriptions of the campaigns and forest diplomacy that brought Pontiac to defeat, Dale Van Every soars to new heights. His pen endows the Battle of Bushy Run with an epic quality reminiscent of Parkman himself. This is frontier history at its best.

Pontiac was subdued, but still the Appalachian barrier held back the pioneers, guarded now by British ministers who were determined to halt the westward march lest it touch off new Indian wars. The Proclamation of 1763, defining the crest of the mountains as the western limit of lands open to settlement, was more of an annoyance than a deterrent, but it meant that the bold borderlanders who breached the barrier now had to dodge troops as well as Indians. Some did so in defiance of the law; others clamored for a shift of the Proclamation Line to open new lands beyond the mountains. Their allies in the long struggle that followed were speculators eager to engross great estates in the West against the day when the inevitable tide of homeseekers swept into the Mississippi Valley. The complicated story of the machinations of these jobbers, and of the gradual surrender of British ministries under their pressure, is wonderously simplified by Dale Van Every, whose flair for the significant and annoyance with the insignificant makes understandable a complex era.

He dwells, too, on the last pathetic attempt of the red men to hold their over-mountain domain, and on their defeat in Lord Dunmore's War. Now, in 1774, the Appalachian barrier had finally been conquered; now for the first time in a generation life in the West was relatively safe. The fitting climax of Dale Van Every's moving story is the coming of the pioneers—to the upper Ohio Valley where their cabins transformed Fort Pitt into the bustling village of Pittsburgh, to the river bottoms of eastern Tennessee, to the Blue Grass country of Kentucky where Daniel Boone and James Harrod and a host of frontiersmen laid out their "stations" in 1775. The story ends happily, but there are grim overtones for the future. The Men of the Western Waters were to feel the whiplash of Indian resentment again as the Revolutionary War plunged the frontiers into new conflict. But that is a tale to be told, it may be hoped, in a subsequent volume.

There are heroes in Dale Van Every's epic, but their names will have a strange ring to the average American. George Washington is there, of course, and Thomas Gage and Lord Jeffrey Amherst. But their roles were minor (in the case of Gage and Washington) or disastrous (as with Amherst). Those who spearheaded the drive westward were less-heralded heroes: Henry Bouquet, a Swiss mercenary who grasped the principles of Indian warfare as did few better-known generals; William Johnson, Indian diplomat par excellence whose adroit manipulations kept the peace or shaped the course of war as circumstances dictated; George Croghan, an unlettered fur trader who rivaled Johnson in diplomatic skills; John Stuart, whose hold over the southern tribes prevented the spilling of blood time and time again; even the Zane brothers—Ebenezer, Silas, Jonathan, and Andrew—whose palisaded farm, built on the site of Wheeling in

1769, held the furthermost frontier until less adventurous pioneers caught up with them. These are the men who won the West, and they are given their fair due by Dale Van Every.

Of heroes there are many in these pages, but of villains there are few. For this Dale Van Every's remarkable ability to understand the Indian is responsible. The Pontiac, Cornstalk and Attakullaculla he portrays were not savages ruthlessly slaying for the pleasure of the kill; they were disciples of a way of life that must be defended, even to the death. The reader can stand with the red man on the yonder side of the Appalachians and see the white invader as he saw him: an unclean, cowardly, greedy, untrustworthy intruder on hunting grounds that the Giver of Life had created for the Indian alone. He can share with the Indian his love of the land, and his belief that this divine gift should be used by all creatures, not just by one avaricious farmer. He can sense the love of freedom that was the red man's richest possession, and appreciate why this must be preserved at all cost. This viewpoint is a healthy antidote to that found in most books on the frontier, and makes easier an understanding of the wars that marked the course of Anglo-American settlement westward.

This is Dale Van Every's story, and he tells it superbly. He is unexcelled in distilling the essence from history—in cutting down the underbrush to reveal the broad sweep of human progress. With a lusty phraseology reminiscent of Francis Parkman, with an appreciation of the significance of the frontier borrowed from Frederick Jackson Turner, he reveals in the pages that follow something of the majesty of the westward movement of the American people as they grappled to win and hold the first great West beyond the Appalachians.

Northwestern University

RAY ALLEN BILLINGTON

Contents

[xi]

PART THREE

The Gates Unhinged

MAPS

Part One

❦

The Land Beyond

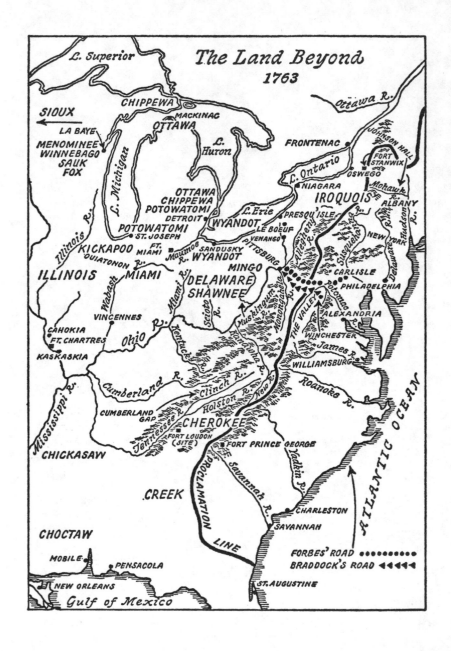

I

✢

The Worst Possible News

THE FAINT CHORUS of the forest's ordinary night noises, the furtive twittering and rustling, the thump of a rabbit's foot, the swish of an owl's wing, the squeak of a wood mouse, was suddenly stilled. Upon the waiting silence burst an alien sound, the unmistakable thud of hoofbeats. The unnatural hammering persisted, swelled. Sparks flew from the flinty and rutted path. The dozing Indian pickets leaped up too late. The shadowy horseman swept past, an apparition out of the night which as soon merged again with the night.

History does not record the name of the rider. This is a pity for not many couriers celebrated by history have carried a message of greater moment. Surely none has been subjected to a more prolonged hazard. He had even elected to multiply his perils. Instead of creeping stealthily through the forest's cover he was proceeding at this breakneck pace along the only road that traversed it. And the dangers he was rushing among were only beginning. Between Fort Pitt at the Forks of the Ohio, from which he had come, and the white settlements along the Susquehanna, which he must reach, stretched two hundred miles of mountain-ridged wilderness through which a score of Indian war parties were racing toward the same goal as he.

Very many lives beside his own hung upon the message he was bringing. Though he could not know it, there also hung on it the size and shape of the future United States. This was a consequence likewise veiled from his fellow Americans upon whom his news was about to burst. To them what he was to report was simply and baldly and horribly the worst news in the world.

What was to make it so bad was not just the warning that another Indian war was breaking out. There was nothing new about Indian wars. Americans long since had had to get used to them. They had been recurring ever since Englishmen had first stepped ashore to begin taking what had until then been Indian land. And his news was not quite new. People had already sensed trouble was brewing. What was to make the express rider's news so stupefying was not even his revelation that this was certain to be the greatest of all Indian wars. It was the brutal timing of the disclosure that was to make it so nearly intolerable. In the just concluded seven-year-long agony of the French and Indian War American Englishmen had fought beside British Englishmen at an unstinted cost of blood and treasure. That had been a desperate and memorable conflict, marked by heartbreaking disasters, then by heart-stirring conquests, and finally by overwhelming triumph. France, the great patron, friend, and ally of the Indians, had been driven altogether from the mainland of North America. For England it had been a world-wide war of imperial expansion but for Americans it had been a most domestic war on their own doorstep. For them it had been primarily a war to end Indian wars. In this it had ostensibly succeeded. English garrisons had replaced French in the main centers of Indian power on the St. Lawrence, the Great Lakes, and the Ohio. To be obliged now to realize, with the ink on the victorious peace treaty scarcely dry and wounds still open and graves still fresh, that the most general and formidable Indian war yet known had suddenly blazed up, that every Indian nation north of the Ohio had taken to the field with a unanimity which they had never exhibited when urged on by the French, that their armies were making simultaneous, organized attacks upon every outpost of English dominion from the Straits of Mackinac to the gorges of the Alleghenies, and that the recent scattered raids along the Pennsylvania frontier were only the first ripples of an onrushing wave of Indian invasion—all this was literally too much.

The bearer of these unwelcome tidings kept on. If himself without a name in history he was following a road with a most historic name. Forbes Road, later to be called The Pennsylvania Road, or, more popularly, The Pittsburgh Pike, had been torn from the wilderness five years before by the sickly and indomitable English general, John Forbes, on his way to wrest the Ohio from the French. Never more than a wagon track it was already being reclaimed by the forest and the weather. Nevertheless, the rider kept to it for it was the most direct route eastward. His sweating horse scrambled up Chestnut Ridge. At dawn he slid down the eastern slope to little Fort Ligonier, 56 miles east of Fort Pitt and one of the only two stations the English army, reduced by postwar economy, still maintained to guard the road. An Indian war party was already in the woods about the fort, hooting threats at the defenders and winging fire arrows at the walls. By a miracle he got into the fort, changed horses, rested a few hours, and by a greater miracle got out again.

He rode on eastward, over higher ridges and through wilder forests. The dying Forbes, grunting with pain as he swung in his horse litter, had with the understatement of an immense exasperation characterized this region between the Susquehanna and the Ohio through which he was building his road as "overgrown with trees and brushwood, so that nowhere can one see twenty yards." To every Europe-trained soldier who saw service in America no feature of the American scene was so disturbing as the so prevalent lack of visibility. It was like campaigning in a sack. But Forbes had ripped one gapping hole in the sack with his road. He had struggled on month after month against illness, weather, and Indians, and lived to drive the French and their Indian allies from the Forks of the Ohio. The landmarks along his route, Sideling Hill, Alliquippa Gap, Allegheny Ridge, Stony Creek, Laurel Hill, Shawnee Cabins,

Edmonds Swamp, Loyalhanna Creek, Callender's Meadow, were so far familiar only to Indians, soldiers, hunters, and traders. Of all the people about to be staggered by the express rider's message not the most farsighted could have dreamed how soon these same landmarks were to become equally familiar to families of homeseekers toiling westward over the mountains in the first trickle of a tide that was to sweep on all the way to the Pacific.

With the instinct of a woodsman for taking cover he paused occasionally to breathe himself and his horse. The third day he dropped down to Fort Bedford, where nerveless Captain Lewis Ourry imperturbably guarded the Juniata defile. Here, too, the forerunners of Indian invasion had preceded him. A number of peculiarly hardy settlers had taken the peace prospects seriously enough to have penetrated this far into the mountains to take up land in the narrow Juniata bottom. Warned in time by their wary hunters they had fled for refuge to the fort to become a welcome reinforcement to the dour captain's garrison of three corporals and nine privates. There were thus enough fighting men at Fort Bedford to sally out to cover the express rider's coming and going.

At last, after as precarious a journey as could have been made even in those tumultuous days, he reached the hamlet of Shippensburg, the first white man's town on Forbes Road and the westernmost settlement in Pennsylvania. Shippensburg was crowded with frantic refugees from outlying farms along the eastern foot of the mountains. Many were dazed by the memory of having witnessed members of their families struck down, others were themselves wounded, several had been scalped and left for dead yet had regained the despairing strength to stumble on in, all had lost all they owned, and the news brought by the courier meant that their torment was only beginning.

Such periodic Indian inroads provided spectacular personal misfortunes which all Americans then had of necessity to accept as among the inevitable facts of life. In that early summer of 1763, 154 years after Jamestown and only twelve years before the Revolution, the American colonies were still but a narrow thread along the Atlantic seaboard. Very many more people lived within a day's wagon haul of tidewater than lived farther than that from a sea-going ship's landing. The opposite limit of habitation was not so much farther the other way. The westernmost settlements were 70 miles west of Albany, 75 miles west of Philadelphia, 55 miles west of Savannah. The region beyond, extending endlessly westward to a distance no man yet knew, was the wild country, a land as different and as mysterious as the face of another planet. The nearness of that wilderness was a dominating circumstance even the most secure and preoccupied coastal townsman could not ignore. It increased his taxes, restricted his commerce, obstructed the growth of his province, and yet remained a circumstance so foreign to anything he had himself experienced as to confound his imagination. But to the settler who lived at the edge of it the wilderness was a dreadful daily reality. In that vast oppressive shadow crouched indescribable terror waiting to spring upon him and his family.

At Carlisle the news reached the one Pennsylvanian most able to evaluate it. George Croghan, veteran trader, knew the farther reaches of that western wilderness as other men might know the shores of the Chesapeake or the Hudson. For twenty years he had boated his cargoes of trade goods up and down the Ohio, the Muskingum, the Scioto, the Miami. He had lived in Indian towns, learned their languages, bargained, hunted, feasted, and gossiped with their men, slept with their women. To him their chiefs were not posturing, demoniac clowns to be distinguished from one another only by their outlandish names but old acquaintances with differentiated traits of character as recognizable as those of any English colonel or Philadelphia banker.

His trading operations had been disrupted by the French and Indian War. He had served during the war with most of the outstanding English commanders, Washington, Braddock, Johnson, Webb, Forbes, and Bouquet and when the tide had turned had been of indispensable assistance to victorious English commanders in establishing workable Indian relations in the territory they were taking over from the French. He had seen how unhappy the Indians were with their new situation. In his official reports he had repeatedly advised the English high command of this growing

Indian dissatisfaction. But his warnings had dealt with future difficulties which English policy was inviting. He knew how much Indians respected military prowess and he had seen how much they had been impressed by the extent of the English triumph. As recently as five weeks before he had been conferring with a group of Ohio chiefs at Fort Pitt. Nothing he had learned even as lately as that about Indian intentions from these representative Indian spokesmen had prepared him for what he was now hearing. He had always known, as had anybody who had had the slightest contact with Indians, that the strongest of Indian impulses was the impulse to repel the white mans' advance. Since white intruders had first begun to enlarge their foothold on the American shore a united Indian effort to drive them back into the sea had been a perpetual Indian dream. But no semblance of such united action had ever developed. The inherent qualities of the Indian nature, capricious, irresponsible, jealous, supremely individualistic, had compromised every hope to unite. But now, without the slightest warning, this entire image of Indian behavior had been transfigured.

Croghan concluded a leader capable of firing Indian imagination must have suddenly and finally risen. The miraculous revelation of such a messiahlike leader had always been an essential part of the Indian dream. There was no other way to account for every one of the strongest and most warlike nations beyond the Ohio having begun suddenly to move together in the waging of a combined campaign along a thousand-mile front. Soon Croghan was to hear the name of that leader. It was on every Indian's lips. It was a name about to echo out of the forest, and among the flames that consumed captives, and through the smoke of burning cabins, and above the tramp of marching armies, and in the wind that winged ships across the sea, and, most sharply of all, about the council table of England's ministers of state. That name was Pontiac.

At Philadelphia the courier's formal dispatch, penned by Captain Simeon Ecuyer, commander at Fort Pitt, reached the destination for which it had been intended, the eyes of Colonel Henry Bouquet, senior field commander of English forces in the middle colonies. The colonel might not know as much about Indians as George

Croghan but he knew something about fighting them. He had been with Forbes. "I see," Ecuyer had written, "that the affair is general. I expect to be attacked tomorrow morning. I am passably well prepared. Everybody is at work, and I do not sleep; but I tremble lest my messengers should be cut off."

Bouquet's first and continuing reaction was anger. He had had his fill of wilderness campaigning. But he was an old and most professional soldier and knew what he had to do. He also knew what the doing of it was going to be like: No glory, no honor even in victory, no room for the proper exercise of a soldiers' talent; just months of dragging supply wagons over mountains and through bogs, of sleeping in the rain and living on quarter rations, of stumbling through forests so thick a man could see little better by day than by night, of coping with a totally irrational enemy who might remain invisible for weeks on end or at any second spring screeching at his throat. As he considered the miserable prospect his aversion to Indians rose to a pitch of venom only a border settler might match. Still, he had to get on with it. In thirteen lonely army posts in the western wilderness soldiers of his command were beleagured by howling savages. They must be relieved and the Indians must this time be so worked over as to cure them for all time of presuming ever again to raise a hand against any man in the King's uniform. Within the hour he began grimly to make his preparations. He also got off an express to New York to Sir Jeffrey Amherst, England's commander-in-chief in North America, advising him that the late signs of growing unrest among the Indians had suddenly taken on the spectral proportions of a general war.

The bad news, still traveling fast, reached Amherst at his Headquarters in the Abraham Mortier house on Richmond Hill in the pleasantly green and rolling countryside south of Greenwich Village. It had been 137 years since a forward-looking Dutchman had purchased Manhattan from the Indians and nearly a hundred since an equally forward-looking Englishman had taken possession of it, but the general, looking from the porch over the masts of ships swinging at anchor in the Hudson, could see the wooded hills of northern New Jersey in which Indians still prowled. His rage and disgust could only have been exceeded had it been given him to realize that in another thirteen years an American commander-in-chief would be making this same house his headquarters while directing the defense of New York against the assault of an English army.

Private anxieties augmented his fury. Under the smoothest of circumstances a strong-willed and arrogant man, for the past many months his every personal inclination had been crossed. He conceived that his services in bringing the late war to a triumphant conclusion had not been sufficiently appreciated. He was desperately anxious to return to England to attend to his long-neglected personal affairs. His ancestral estate was going to ruin and his wife from whom his North American service had kept him so long separated had been committed to a madhouse. The new delay in his already long-delayed return that must result from this unexpected new war was the last straw. He began thrusting upon Bouquet such military directions as "I wish to hear of *no prisoners*" and "could it not be contrived to send the *small pox* among these disaffected tribes of Indians?"

Amherst lost no moment in getting off a series of indignant messages to the Mohawk frontier barony of Sir William Johnson, who, as Superintendent of Indian Affairs, had for twenty years borne the principal responsibility for England's relations with the Indians. This most recent example of Indian perfidy, wrote Amherst, "Surely Calls Aloud for the Severest Punishment that may be in our power to Inflict." He demanded that Johnson devise speedy methods "most likely to Succeed in Engaging them to Fall upon One Another."

Johnson had enjoyed an amazing career in which he had contrived to force each successive crisis to raise him to new heights but still the news of this newest crisis could not have come at a more awkward moment. He was in the process of crowning his many achievements by the establishment of what amounted to his own empire in the wilderness. His imposing new official residence, Johnson Hall, was in the last stages of completion. Half frontier stronghold, half palace, it had been designed by Samuel Fuller, Abercrombie's onetime chief engineer, as a baronial seat in keeping with Sir William's baronial station in life.

Unlike Bouquet and Amherst, he could not afford the luxury of relieving his feelings by the simple device of screaming imprecations upon all Indians. Every success of his unique career had sprung from his capacity to make and hold friends among Indians. The intimacy of his personal association with the Iroquois, most powerful and influential of Indian nations, had long presented the aspect of a family relationship. No other white man, before or since, has ever approached his talent for winning Indian trust and affection. As a trader he represented a class Indians accepted as at best a necessary evil. As a colonial and royal official he represented an alien authority Indians were bound to suspect or resist. As a landowner he represented a physical encroachment which Indians abhorred as the most pernicious of all calamities. Yet they had taken him to their bosoms. Iroquois regard for him had led to trade advantages and land grants which had gained him wealth. Iroquois readiness to march under his command had won him military renown. Iroquois conformance to England's wishes had earned him English title and rank. It was not Johnson the man, or Johnson the soldier, or Johnson the administrator who was regarded by his contemporaries as the most distinguished living American. It was Johnson the friend of the Iroquois. He could not very well turn on them now. Least of all now when he needed them more than ever.

"I herewith Enclose you Copies of what I have received from Colonel Bouquet," Amherst had written. "The Last part of the Intelligence seems to be greatly Exaggerated, as I Cannot Entertain a thought that they have been able to Cutt off any of the Posts where Officers were stationed." Johnson had been as surprised as Croghan by the spontaneity of the Indian outbreak but he had by now learned from his own Indian sources how far from exaggerated was Bouquet's estimate. He was depressingly aware that the situation was infinitely more threatening than Amherst yet suspected.

But there was one point on which he could not have agreed more wholeheartedly with the irate commander-in-chief. The imperative above all other imperatives was somehow to restrain the Iroquois impulse to support Pontiac's cause. The Iroquois had always regarded themselves as a people superior to other Indians. But they still were

Indians and they could not but be highly excited by the thrilling stories of these unprecedented Indian successes in the west. Were Iroquois prestige, power, and political sagacity thrown into the balance alongside the wild ferocity of Pontiac's Western hordes the eventual consequences were literally unforeseeable. It was too late to restrain the Seneca. That westernmost and most numerous of the Iroquois nations had already joined Pontiac. There might still be barely time, however, to persuade the other five of the Six Nations that their one sensible course was to remain deaf to the appeals of their far western brothers and to hold to their ancient English alliance. Johnson threw all of the mastery of Indian psychology that he had proved at a hundred former Iroquois councils into this desperately earnest effort.

The news was a little longer reaching Captain John Stuart, recently appointed Superintendent for Indian Affairs in the Southern District. Getting word from New York to Charleston took more than a month if sent by land, and by sea the time depended entirely upon how favorable the wind. Stuart knew enough about Indians to realize its full import. He had made many friends among them. Due to their personal regard for him he had been the only white officer to survive the fall of Fort Loudon in the desperate Cherokee War, the echoes of which were still reverberating through the Carolina mountains. He had little need to be told how essential was his duty to do his utmost to make sure the Southern Indians stayed out of this new war.

Last of all, the news reached the members of His Majesty's government in London. The Seven Years' War had raised England to the summit of imperial power and bestowed on her such remarkable territorial acquisitions as Canada, the whole eastern Mississippi Valley, the two Floridas, and much of India. But, as always, the immediate aftermath of war, however victorious, had found the English people turning abruptly back to their everyday affairs. The great Pitt had been succeeded by lesser men who were absorbed in the peculiarly intricate pattern of contemporary party politics and were agreed even among themselves only on the pressing desirability of governmental economy. This last, perhaps, was understandable. The war had left England burdened with a funded debt of £140,000,000.

The one deep-seated difference of opinion among politicians who on other issues were happy to compromise was with regard to England's new empire. A numerous and stubborn faction maintained that it had been a fatal mistake to claim these prizes of victory and that England's true interests might be better served were they all given back to the French, the Spanish, the natives, or whoever. The violence of this disagreement over what to do about installing in these new overseas dominions some sort of English civil government had resulted so far in nothing being done. Cabinet decisions relative to North America, for example, had been limited to informing the indignantly protesting Amherst that his army of occupation had to be cut to twenty battalions and to the study of tax schemes by which the American colonies might be required to pay a reasonable proportion of the costs of the late war by which they had so much benefited.

The stunning news of the new American war roused the lethargic cabinet. Obviously some definite and tangible policy must promptly be hit upon. But there was still no meeting of official minds and action hung fire. The news from America grew steadily worse, making it increasingly apparent that something had to be done. Even the least informed minister was able to grasp the basic factor in the American problem. That was the unhappy juxtaposition of the narrow strip of coastal land occupied by civilized white inhabitants and the vast expanse of wilderness occupied by wild beasts and wild Indians. From this general conception there emerged by a process as natural as the law of gravity a definitive government policy which all factions in the cabinet could support. It had the immense virtue of simplicity. It appeared to supply a sensible answer to every difficulty. The Board of Trade's recommendation was approved by the cabinet and passed up to the King. On October 7, 1763, he signed the proclamation incorporating its terms and the statement of imperial policy took on the force of a royal edict. By it the three recently acquired inhabited territories, Canada and East and West Florida, the one formerly French and the other two Spanish, were pronounced crown colonies under English common law in the same sense that the original thirteen were colonies. The status of the remainder of English North America, the western wilderness, was defined with the same precision. A north-south line was designated, running from Canada to Florida, dividing English America into two parts, an eastern and a western. The line was clearly, even exactly, located. It ran along the crest of the mountains, threading its way between the headwaters of the streams emptying into the Atlantic and those running the other way, northwestward, westward, and southwestward, into the St. Lawrence, the Great Lakes, the Mississippi, and the Gulf of Mexico. The claims of any of the original thirteen colonies to jurisdiction west of this line were annulled. Title to land west of the line, whether by Indian grant or by sanction of any colonial authority, could not henceforth be obtained by any private person. Any intrusion whatever west of the line, whether by land seeker, traveler, or trader, was to be only by the King's express permission. For the sake of the future maintenance of peace and order that portion of the King's dominions constituting the wilderness west of the mountains was henceforth to be reserved for the undisturbed occupancy of the Indians. Thus, the framers of the Proclamation confidently hoped, by one inspired stroke, the threat of future Indian wars was permanently averted and the white inhabitants permanently restrained within an area where they might be less trouble to govern.

II

The Line

NOT MANY OF MAN'S DESIGNS have absorbed more of his attention than his predilection for drawing lines upon the earth. A disposition to warn off trespassers has seemed a human impulse almost as basic as that of the cell to reject foreign proteins. The most simple and primitive societies have been obsessed by it. Later and more elaborate examples have ranged from the frontier of Rome to the Great Wall of China to the Iron Curtain of our own time.

Experience has indicated that if such a man-made line is to endure for long, other than as a breeder of wars, certain attributes are invaluable. Most helpful of these assets are that the line should so conform to natural geographical features as to be readily recognizable, that it should separate areas and peoples sufficiently different for the separation to make at least some sense, and, unless the people on one side are so much more powerful than the other that there is no need for a line, that the peoples on either side should be reasonably reconciled to its existence.

All three of these bolsters were possessed by the Proclamation Line of 1763 in overwhelming measure. No one could entertain a moment's doubt, real or pretended, as to its physical location. It loomed

against the sky, since by official definition it coincided with the crestline of the Appalachian Mountain chain. From either side that vast
forested height was visible from afar. Meeting the second test, it
marked a natural dividing line between two regions and two peoples as dissimilar as this world could afford. On the one side was a
civilized, politically and economically advanced community of in-
dustrious white men counseled by leaders of an intellectual capacity capable of identifying the lightning or composing a Declaration
of Independence and on the other was a trackless, primordial wilderness infested by scattered tribes of irresponsibly belligerent savages.
The contrast was between a time not so far from our own and the
Stone Age. Finally, establishment of the line was opposed by nobody.
It was welcomed and approved by every organized interest, racial,
diplomatic, political, economic, whose aspirations were in any way
involved.

The Proclamation Line was a mark drawn on a map by men who
were none too certain about what they were accomplishing. What
gave it some significance was that they were ministers of a nation
just victorious in a world war. But what gave the mark much more
significance was that it had represented something that had always
been there. The mountain barrier with which it coincided had so
long as there had been a continent been a rampart between the seaboard and the great interior valley. This had been a boundary so
natural that even the buffalo which had succeeded in spreading to
the farthest reaches and corners of the continent's middle had crossed
it only in trickles. The prehistoric mound-building Indians had left
those monumental demonstrations of their communal energy from
end to end of the Mississippi and along every one of the Mississippi's
eastern tributaries, but not one relic of their enterprise east of the
mountains. To the early English settler the line of cloud-wreathed,
blue heights looming against the western sky represented at once
the edge of the unknown and the limit ordained by nature to his
own advance.

Formal history has tended to minimize the significance of the
Proclamation Line because it did not endure. As a matter of fact it
endured for the next thirty-one years. When the forces that had

originally sanctioned it were challenged by new forces it continued to endure. The principle established by the Line was to be bitterly contested through years of international negotiations at the highest level. It was a principle that died slowly and very hard. Twenty of those thirty-one years were years of war with armies in the field fighting to hold or breach the Line. But we are not yet concerned with the circumstances accompanying the Line's ultimate overthrow. Let us first examine the circumstances accompanying its conception in 1763.

Among the great powers there was unanimity. The other two with interests in the Mississippi Valley, France and Spain, could only applaud England's declaration. They recognized the real purpose behind the move and the foreseeable long-range effects had for them the same appeal that they had for England's imperial-minded Board of Trade. The significance of that same real purpose began speedily to dawn on the least informed English minister who had so hastily concurred in the decision. Avoiding the expense of recurrent Indian wars was only a stopgap purpose. No one could imagine that the wilderness was to remain for all time a wilderness. Occupation and development by white men, possibly accompanied by civilization of the Indians, sooner or later was bound to come. The advantage of taking care that that development be one over which England could continue to exercise an appropriate imperial control was, so soon as it was contemplated, self-evident. The real and not so hidden purpose of the Proclamation was thus to nip in the bud any incipient migration of turbulent American frontiersmen into the great central valley. With this purpose France and Spain could not have more heartily agreed.

France had under duress divested herself of her immense North American dominions. She had ceded the territory east of the Mississippi to England and that west of the river, plus New Orleans, to Spain. But she was in no way reconciled to the loss. She still retained the residual advantages of her immemorial influence over the Indians and of a French population on the St. Lawrence, at the mouth of the Mississippi, and in wilderness villages scattered through the interior. She was resolved upon the recovery of her empire at the first shadow of an opportunity. The more favorable fortunes of the next world war might open the way. The one event certain to close the way forever was an intrusion of American settlers into the central valley. This France was determined to resist and meanwhile to encourage the English, the Spanish, and the Indians to resist. At the peace table following the Revolution her resistance was to be all but successful.

Spain's American empire began at the Mississippi and extended south and west in an unbroken sweep across two continents to immeasurably distant Cape Horn. This was an unconscionable area to defend. She was peculiarly susceptible to any threat, however remote, to her central treasure house in Mexico. The appearance of a few Russian fur traders in the northwest Pacific was presently to cause her hastily to extend a line of missions and presidios hundreds of miles northward into previously ignored California. Any movement of American settlers across the Appalachian Mountains would represent a threat à thousand times more ominous. Spain could not have regarded the Proclamation Line more highly unless she were in a position to hold it herself. Sixteen years later she was to move fleets and armies in a vigorous attempt to do just that.

Along with the attitudes of the several great powers the attitude of Americans, in view of their proximity, was an international consideration. Americans were not yet independent but they were very independent minded. Their elected assemblies exercised a measure of self-government which had necessarily to be taken into account by the parent English government. Paris and Madrid were as much relieved as London to note that neither then nor for years to come was there appreciable American opposition to the Line. On a clear day the average American, even though he lived in the tidewater centers of population, could see the mountains. Their blue crests suggested the existence of a physical screen between him and the dangers of the wild region beyond them. So far the screen had not proved too substantial. During the French and Indian War his own home had for a time seemed as threatened as any settler's. Always the Indians had been able to cross the mountains at will. It had been passage the other way that had proved enormously difficult. In 1755 an English army had marched over them to destruction. In 1758 a second army three times as strong had succeeded only after months of agonizing effort. Another must presently make the supremely critical attempt. It followed that the average American was moved to trust and pray that this newly proclaimed Line might somehow be finally and firmly established as a perma nent boundary. The possibility of future settlement west of the mountains appeared a prospect too distant to be seriously considered. Of much greater concern was the possibility of forestalling Indian wars in the present. Every colonial assembly, including notably the New York, Pennsylvania, Virginia, and South Carolina assemblies most involved in the Indian problem, gave the establishment of the Line their unreserved approval. This American political acceptance of the underlying principle persisted. Eighteen years later, toward the end of the Revolution, the Continental Congress by a vote of nine states to two was to instruct its peace commissioners to satisfy the demands of those great and good wartime allies, France and Spain, by accepting, if they continued to insist, the crest of the Appalachians as the permanent western boundary of the United States about to be.

Last among the international and political pressures at work, but the most effective for years to come, was that applied by the Indians. The Indian nations were as politically independent as communities can be. Much of their freedom of action from the earliest time of which they had memory had been directed to disputes with each other. In this respect they rivaled the ingrained contentiousness of the nations of Europe. Some of them on the other hand were gathered into more or less loosely knit regional confederations. But all were in constant touch with each other and all were united in their fierce opposition to any further advance of the white frontier. All realized that their very existence depended on the Line being held.

A line does not become a boundary merely by being drawn upon a map in a government office. More also is required than the affirmation, however ardent, of distant chancelleries or nearer legislatures and tribal councils. To invest a boundary with reality there must be the presence of physical force, or, at least, the imminent threat of force. Two such physical forces existed and they were equally committed to the maintenance of the Proclamation Line. The one organized military force in the area was the English regular army. Its garrisons were established at every more strategic point in the west. During the French War it had learned wilderness mobility the hard way. Under the direction of the English commander-in-chief in North America its primary duty was to enforce the formally announced will of the king. The other physical force in being and so situated as to make itself instantly effective was the Indian warrior class. Indian military power was handicapped by divided counsels and much innate heedlessness. Yet it remained a terrifying force, capable of a forever baffling swiftness of movement and peculiarly adapted to the unparalleled complexities of war in the forest. Even were the English army withdrawn a perpetual guardianship of the Line was vested in the long-continued Indian capacity to exact fearful penalties for every violation.

International, political, and military pressures were not, of course, the only influence bearing upon the stability of the Line. There was public opinion and in the colonies public opinion was becoming each year more violently articulate. But no important segment of that opinion regarded the King's Proclamation in any other light than as an eminently rational provision for public peace and safety. Little was to be lost and much was to be gained, it was generally agreed, if Indians and whites were to be kept to their own sides of the mountains. Church leaders earnestly advocated peace with the Indians, moved by the hope that this might lead to their eventual conversion. Commercial circles were eager to avoid the tax burden of new Indian wars. Most bankers, merchants, shippers, and shipbuilders were faced toward the sea and the trade with the West Indies and Europe. Large landowners deplored the westward drift of their tenants and indentured servants. An exceptionally vocal school of American thought which was to persist for generations to come was opposed in principle to westward expansion. According to this strongly advocated theory the area east of the mountains provided ample room for a population of untold millions and the public welfare was to be far better served by a homogeneous development of this area than by a reckless westward dispersal of the community's energies. No American of 1763 foresaw a United States and still less a United States inheriting a relentless and unlimited westward extension of its dominion. Manifest destiny was a conception that followed events, not one that produced them.

Two towering economic interests, the fur trade and the great land companies, were specially concerned with the west. Both were endowed with enormous political and economic influence, in London as well as in the colonies. Both supported the establishment of the Line, the one actively and the other passively. The fur trade, which represented a substantial share of North America's total commerce, by the very nature of its operations was very nearly as opposed to the westward extension of white settlement as were the Indians themselves. The land companies had been formed in the decade preceding the French War and their activities had had much to do with precipitating it. Their common design was the acquisition of immense land grants beyond the mountains upon which they could ultimately profit by eventual sale to carefully shepherded colonies of actual settlers. After the rout of the French the prospects opening to them appeared more glittering than ever. Nevertheless they accepted the Line as a preliminary necessity. They much preferred to await an orderly and discreet negotiation with the crown than to see their prospective tracts prematurely overrun by an unmanageable rush of land-grabbing frontiersmen.

It was these land-grabbing frontiersmen whose individual inclination was to prove finally decisive. But that decision was not yet in sight. What was in sight was the mountains. They appeared an insurmountable barrier. The generations of their forebears who during the last century and a half had edged the frontier slowly westward from the seacoast had been confronted by no such obstacle. The landless man who ventured to carve a place for himself out of the forest had had only to go into it a little way. Even though living on the outer fringe of settlement he was not totally isolated. He could feel just behind him the support of his increasingly numerous neighbors. Next year there would be neighbors in front of him. Year by year,

a cabin at a time and a mile at a time, the frontier had inched westward. Like water trickling through grass it was a process difficult to
stem. The Indians had periodically eased the tension by withdrawing. They required wide hunting grounds which in turn required
their keeping a distance from the frontier. Finally, most of the
Shawnee and Delaware, the principal nations on the middle border,
had moved to the freer hunting grounds on the Ohio on the other
side of the mountains. Within another ten years, however, the slow
and apparently inexorable advance of the frontier had come to a halt
at the foot of the mountains. The former cabin-by-cabin and mile-
by-mile advance was no longer possible. Ahead among the forested
heights were only rocky and isolated creek bottoms in which a first
settler would be defenselessly exposed. For the generation before
1763 the frontier instead of moving westward had skirted the mountains and pushed southward down the Valley of Virginia. But by
now this slack had been taken up. There was no more wild free
land to be had for the taking. There were only the mountains. And
beyond them the vengefully waiting Indians. The fierce Indian inroads of the French War and now of Pontiac's War had demonstrated how fearful was this Indian danger. The frontiersman who
might not hesitate to clear a corn patch and build a cabin a mile in
advance of his neighbors had to think hard before deciding to subject
his family to this two-hundred-mile jump into the fire. The King's
Proclamation meant no more to him than had the many former
attempts of provincial governments to set a limit to his land seeking.
What gave him pause were the physical facts with which he had
immediately and personally to deal. The mountains and the Indians
and the distance were brutal facts.

The foregoing were among the forces, physical and psychological,
that suggested in the fall of 1763 that the Line was a fixture likely to
remain as long as any man living could foresee. Still, as in most
human crises, much depended on the resolution of the leaders upon
whom fell responsibility for directing the play of these forces. Such
leaders were at hand and seldom has sudden demand been met by
a set of men more resolute. The Indian chiefs, military commanders,
royal commissioners, and master traders who bestrode the Line were

men accustomed to decision and to action. They commanded the physical power to sustain their will. They were on the ground and in positions to make their presence count. They were the lords of the marches. They were dedicated to their task by every precept of loyalty, duty, and personal interest. All had been tested and prepared by long wilderness experience. All were extraordinary men, natural leaders, bold, aggressive, violent, colorful. They were the men responsible for holding the Line were it to be held. They were The Gatekeepers. In the crisis of 1763, the first great test of the preservation of the Line, five stood out above all others: George Croghan, Colonel Henry Bouquet, Sir William Johnson, John Stuart, and Pontiac. We shall notice, presently, how each met the challenge.

These were the men who strove to keep the peace between two worlds so different that only by the maintenance of an impassable border between them could peace remain possible. Their striving was supported by every force then visible on any horizon. That they nevertheless failed was due to the sudden intrusion of a new force, a force whose imminent rise could not have been foreseen in 1763 because its first faint stirrings were not yet apparent. Then, within the brief lapse of three years, there came the transition. The great change was brought about by the mysterious and unheralded materialization on the border scene of men and women of a sort hitherto unknown, The Frontier People. These newcomers—their coming had been a movement no more extended than a straightening and turning from the ashes of their homesteads—were governed by needs and impulses that differed in almost as many respects from those of their white neighbors behind them as from those of their Indian enemies before them. The moment that they became fully conscious of this difference they took command. We shall also notice how this extraordinary event came to pass.

III

ꝋ

The New Country

E VERY ENGLISHMAN had a right to be proud that early spring of 1763. His ancient enemies France and Spain had been humbled. His tight little island had suddenly become the axis of an empire. Signature of the formal treaty on February 10th had made it official. However insular his former disposition he could not but be deeply stirred. He knew little about these newly won distant lands and he was seized by a natural desire to know more. Among all the prodigious acquisitions he was the most intrigued by what had been gained in the interior of North America. The train of tragic, romantic, and heroic events marking the long conflict with the French and Indians in the vast American wilderness had fired English imagination. Such unlikely names as Duquesne, Ticonderoga, Oswego, Frontenac, Toronto, Niagara, Detroit, and Mackinac had become household words. The relative military prowess of Braddock, Dieskau, Johnson, Forbes, Amherst, Wolfe, and Montcalm had been endlessly discussed in coffeehouses with all the attention usually reserved for racing odds or court gossip. Now with victory interest shifted to the fruits of victory. Everybody could see the general size and shape of the prize package but nobody could yet do more than speculate upon just what was in it. Within five months the Pontiac eruption was to demonstrate one of the things that was in it.

That people were able to envisage even this general size and shape was largely due to the Mitchell Map, one of the more famous maps in cartological history. John Mitchell had assembled the data for his celebrated map under a commission from the Board of Trade. After five years of strenuous labor it had been published in 1755. That timing had been more than fortuitous. It had been heaven-sent. Within months Braddock was in flight, Indians from far and near were ravaging the frontier, the border quarrel over the Forks of the Ohio was mushrooming into a world war, and England was grimly preparing to march army after army into wild regions of which the war office knew little more than could be surmised by peering at this map.

Mitchell had been a Virginia botanist and physician for the most of his career. As a botanist he was the discoverer of many species and a valued correspondent of Linnaeus. As a doctor his treatise on yellow fever was so well established an authority that it was still relied upon by Dr. Benjamin Rush in the Philadelphia outbreak of 1793. But, though this was his only map, it is as a great mapmaker that Mitchell will always be remembered. He had consulted and compared all former maps and charts, French and Spanish as well as English, had taken into account the geographical opinions of traders and Indians, and, when in doubt, had based his conclusions on a scientist's grasp of the laws of probability. His 1755 masterpiece presented a fair approximation of the courses of the St. Lawrence, the Ohio, and the Mississippi, of the shore lines of the Great Lakes and the Floridas, and of relative areas and distances in the tremendous reaches of the continent's interior. Also, to butter up the Board of Trade, it included some extravagant political claims, showing every colony south of Maryland extending to the Mississippi, in the case of Virginia into the far northwest, represented every most temporary English trader's post in the west as an "English settlement" or an "English factory," and based England's fanciful prewar claims to the Great Lakes region on the brief flurry of 17th Century conquests by England's Indian ally, the Iroquois. Nevertheless, the map's approach to reality made it every English staff officer's mainstay during every campaign of the war and kept it still a principal reference authority for the peace commissioners framing the treaty which ended the Revolution.

There were two concrete bits of semiofficial English evidence beside the memorable English map. Three years before they dispatched the young George Washington to warn the French to stand aside, the great land companies had sent out explorers to sniff out the land west of the mountains. Dr. Thomas Walker, retained by the Loyal Land Company, had struck west from southwest Virginia. The one lasting effect of his journey was his attachment to gap, river, and mountains of the inappropriate name of that "martial boy," the Duke of Cumberland. He then made a laborious circuit through the rugged, laurel-thicketed mountains of what is now eastern Kentucky and West Virginia and returned to his employers with the sad report that he had found no land worth having. Christopher Gist, commissioned by the rival Ohio Company and his visit tolerated by the Indians because he was vouched for by Croghan, had inspected the Indian centers of population along the Muskingum, Scioto, and Miami north of the Ohio, had caught one distant glimpse from a high knob of the more fertile part of Kentucky, and had then for a month floundered eastward through the same nearly impassable mountains that had so depressed Walker. Gist reported that he had seen some fine land and left it to the company to consider what to do about the Indians who were living on it.

But neither the map nor the land-company reports went far toward satisfying anybody's interest in what the new country might be really like. Traders who had been down the Ohio before the war had little to add. They were not eager to broadcast information for the benefit of potential competitors and in any event their narrowly commercial talk was concerned with the length of hauls, the depths of streams and locations of portages, the price of beaver, and the special art of getting an Indian drunk enough to bargain freely and yet not so drunk he came at him with a hatchet. Few soldiers had yet returned but all who had were agreed that wherever they had been, fighting Frenchmen and Indians through mountains and woods and swamps, always in clouds of gnats and mosquitoes and in the worst of weather, it was without doubt the most miserable country in the world.

The most rewarding recourse for the truth seeker, whether he was thinking of investing in the fur trade or a land company or merely entertained a patriotic interest in England's so suddenly accelerated growth, was to turn to the French. They had been there long enough to know the country well. There had been Frenchmen back and forth across the Great Lakes and up and down the Mississippi before the first Englishman had set foot in Pennsylvania. Those early Frenchmen, seeing with their own eyes, had taken as avid an interest in what they were seeing as could the most inquisitive or acquisitive Englishmen be taking now. Happily for the record they had included a succession of literate and perceptive observers who had written some of the greatest classics in all travel literature. Many of these had long since been translated into English and were available to any Oxford don, Fleet Street scribbler, Cabinet member, or City capitalist. Those early Frenchmen, the first white men to view the continent's mysterious interior, had pictured a rich and inviting land with many of the attributes of man's most nostalgic racial memories of a Golden Age, an Arcady, an Isle of the Blest, with, superimposed upon this Eden, the added attraction of an incredible primeval fecundity. Turning the pages the eager English reader was certain to be struck by passage after passage as vivid as a scene when lightning illuminates a landscape. Such as:

Marquette: "I never saw a more beautiful country. The prairies are covered with buffalo, stags, goats and the rivers and lakes with swans, ducks, geese, parrots and beavers. . . . The whole country watered by the Ohio is extremely fertile, consisting of vast meadows which feed thousands of buffaloes. . . . As to the forests, which almost entirely cover this immense country, there is perhaps nothing in nature to compare to them, whether we consider the size and height of the trees or their variety."

Gravier: "We saw so great a quantity of wild pigeons that the air was darkened."

Du Pratz: "I observed every day with new pleasure the more we advanced the more beautiful and fertile the country was, abounding in game of every kind."

Hennepin: "I am persuaded that the soil would produce all manner of Corn, Fruits, etc., even more plentifully than in any part of Europe. The Air is very temperate, clear and open, and the Country watered with Lakes, Brooks and Rivers. . . . There are abundance of Trees bearing good Fruit and of wild Vines which produce Bunches of Grapes a foot and a half long. . . . There are Mines of Coal, Slate, and Iron, and several Pieces of fine, red Copper, which I have found now and then upon the surface of the Earth, make me believe that there are Mines of it. . . . There are vast Meadows, which need not be grubbed up, but are ready for the Plow and Seed; and certainly the Soil must be very fruitful since Beans grow naturally. They are as big as one's Arm and climb up the highest trees, just as Ivy does. The Peach-Trees are like ours, and so fruitful that they would break if they were not supported. Their Forests are full of Mulberry-Trees and Chestnut-Trees and Plum-trees, whose Fruit is bemusked. They have also plenty of Pomegranate-Trees and Chestnut-Trees: And 'tis observable that all these Trees are covered with Vines, whose Grapes are very big and sweet."

Lahontan: "The River of the Illinois is entitled to Riches by vertue of the benign Climate and of the great quantities of Deer, Roebucks, and Turkeys that feed upon its Brinks. . . . The Banks are replenished with an infinity of Fruit Trees and among these Fruit Trees there are many Vines which bear the most beautiful Clusters of very large Grapes."

Charlevoix: "All the Country that is watered by the Oubache and the Ohio is very fruitful. It consists of vast Meadows, well watered, where the wild Buffaloes feed by Thousands. . . . The Meadows here extend beyond Sight, with little Clusters of Trees here and there, which seem to have been planted by Hand; the Grass grows so high in them that one might lose oneself amongst it."

These were the reports of Frenchmen who had had nearly a century to become acquainted with the immense sweep of country between the Lakes and the Gulf and who had fought with such understandable desperation to hang on to it. They were reports to

make any Englishman's heart beat faster. But of all Englishmen
who were interested in the new country that early spring of 1763
the one who was the most interested was the Englishman (or
Irishman or German or Scotchman) who already lived on its eastern
border. To the frontiersman the new wild land to the west beckoned
with an irresistible fascination. He knew nothing about government
maps or French travel books but he had talked with traders and
friendly Indians and neighbors who had served with Forbes or
Johnson or Rogers. What he had heard had dazzled him with an
impression of an astounding country where the trees were bigger
and the rivers wider, where the buffalo, which had long since disappeared east of the mountains, roved in herds, where flights of
wild fowl darkened the sun, where all game was incredibly plentiful.
He burned with an ever-increasing desire to see for himself if the
trees were half as big or the hunting was half as good as he had
been told. If he had a family the safety of his wife and children
while he was away was a concern that might give him pause. But if
he was footloose and unattached he had only to think of the greater
Indian risk in the western wilderness to his own person and this,
except at times of general war, was the sort of sporting risk that
but added to the fascination. Once he had yielded to the temptation
he had not far to go nor great preparations to make. He had only
to pick up rifle, bullet pouch, powder horn, knife, and hatchet and
step from the edge of his corn patch into the edge of the woods.
From there on he was already in the wilderness and on his own.
He could live off the country indefinitely. If he kept alert enough,
moved fast enough, and changed his camp often enough there was
a good chance his wanderings might escape Indian attention. A few
such hunters went over the mountains before the French and Indian
War. A few more went the moment the fighting stopped. Many
more were waiting now only for Pontiac's conflagration to die
down. Such hunters went alone, or in pairs, or, more rarely, for
they were a solitary breed, in groups of three or four. Each time they
ventured a little farther, driven by the impulse to see more of this
new country, perpetually led on by the discovery that the half had
not been told them about the size of the trees and rivers and cane,

the number of buffalo and elk and bear. Each time they went farther it took them longer. They began staying in the wilderness six months, then a year, then two years. They had come to be known as "long hunters." Whenever they came back they told marvelous stories of what they had seen.

So far we have been reflecting upon what people then had read, or been told, or been led to imagine, about the so little known new country over the mountains. What they imagined meant much more than what they knew. The man who waits to know before he leaps ordinarily does not leap. He takes a step. The long hunter went over the mountains because he could not stand sitting at home imagining what there might be to see. We, now, in attempting to visualize what there was for him to see are likewise driven to depend mainly on our imagination. What that same country is like now is no guide to our wondering.

We can, of course, contemplate the principal physical facts. Of primary concern to everyone that spring of 1763, whether governor, soldier, trader, settler, hunter, or Indian, were the three gateways in the great mountain barrier. If the Line was ever to begin to give way the breach would almost certainly come at one or the other of these three natural ways westward. Two had already been used by English armies during the war. One of these, leading westward from tidewater on the Hudson, was the Mohawk-Oswego route to Lake Ontario which there afforded water transportation via the Niagara portage to the western Great Lakes. The second was fed by the two military roads over the mountains, Braddock's and Forbes', which converged upon the Forks of the Ohio, connecting the settled portions of Virginia and Pennsylvania, respectively, with that great river gate to the west. The third, farther south, reported by Walker in 1750 but not to be used by white men until Daniel Boone's time, was the much more arduous Cumberland Gap-Wilderness route extending from extreme southwest Virginia into middle Kentucky and Tennessee.

Of next consequence after the location of the gateways and the great waterways upon which two of them opened was the location of the Indian nations. There had in earlier times been countless Indian migrations, some in search of more attractive hunting grounds, some fleeing from more powerful neighbors, some seeking trade advantages, some yielding to the pressure of white settlement. The Shawnee, for example, had in the short time since white men had appeared on the continent, moved from the Savannah River to the Cumberland, to the Susquehanna, to the Ohio; and the Wyandot from the eastern shores of Lake Huron to Green Bay, to the Mississippi, to Lake Superior, to Mackinac, to the south shore of Lake Erie. But every important Indian nation between the mountains and the Mississippi had by now occupied an area which it was determined thereafter to hold. The location of each in 1763 was to prove one for which it was to continue to fight for the next thirty years. The most commanding of these bastions of Indian defense was that held by the Iroquois.

Not many geographical situations in history and certainly none in our history have possessed more genuine strategic significance than that occupied by the homeland of this most famous and powerful of Indian nations. Their towns, termed "castles" because they were the fortified strongholds of a war-loving people, were ranged from the headwaters of the Delaware across the lake country of what is now western New York to Niagara. Often called the Six Nations, the largely independent member nations of the confederation were, from east to west, the Mohawk, the Oneida, the Tuscarora, the Onondaga, the Cayuga, and the Seneca. The inherent geographical importance of the region they occupied was later to be demonstrated by the Erie Canal, by the unparalleled development of the state and city of New York, and more recently by the St. Lawrence Seaway. But the Iroquois had long since demonstrated it. For more than a century they had been able to deny the French access to the Ohio while at the same time grasping with a unique display of brute force at a claimed monopoly of the western fur trade.

Their wars with the French had begun in Champlain's time, the year Hudson was discovering and naming his river and only two years after the English had landed at Jamestown, and had continued for generations during which they repeatedly threatened Quebec and Montreal. Their unrelenting hostility had enormously delayed

French penetration of the west. In order to reach the Mississippi the French had long been forced to circle painfully and laboriously by way of the Ottawa, Lake Huron, the Straits of Mackinac, Lake Michigan, and the Wisconsin or the Illinois. No other event can have had so enduring an influence upon the course of American history. Had the French at the outset achieved the same friendly relations with the Iroquois as with the other Indian nations of the interior, they might well have been established on the Hudson before the Dutch and on the Susquehanna before there was an Englishman on the Potomac or the Delaware. They would most certainly have been so long and firmly established at the Forks of the Ohio that there could have been no sensible occasion for the dispatch of a Washington or a Braddock to challenge their presence there. The English colonies' consequent continuing need for English protection against the French leads to limitless speculation. But there need be no speculation on what actually did happen. It was 145 years after Champlain's first encounter with the Iroquois and 81 years after Marquette reached the Mississippi before the first French post was established on the Ohio.

While maintaining their barrier to French expansion the Iroquois had been able to maintain an equivalent barrier to the westward advance of Dutch and English settlements. They had not needed to go frequently to war to manage this. Their control of so large a portion of the fur trade and their usefulness as occasional military allies in the long succession of England's wars with France had led English governors and commanders to accept and even to encourage the barrier. Thus this great northern gateway presented the one area along the frontier where there was a center of Indian population on the very threshold of white settlement. This proximity of a white population had not so seriously interfered with Iroquois hunting as in the case of other Indians. To the south and southwest they exercised control over extensive hunting grounds across the wild watersheds of the Delaware, the Susquehanna, the Allegheny, the Monongahela, and the upper Ohio.

Having traversed the northern gateway by Iroquois permission, the traveler of 1763 would have discovered a wide gap in Indian occupation, for the Iroquois kept their Indian neighbors at a respectful distance. The nearest Indian community to the westward along the south shore of Lake Erie was the Wyandot (or Huron) near Sandusky. Beyond, scattered about the shores of the Great Lakes were the towns of the Ottawa, the Chippewa (or Ojibway), the Potawatomi, the Menominee, the Winnebago, the Sauk (or Sac), the Fox (or Outgami), and the Kickapoo. These nations were historically important because from the beginnings of their contact with white men they had known only the French and because their territory was the principal source of supply for the fur trade.

Also scattered about the shores of the Great Lakes and along the Wabash, the Illinois, and the upper Mississippi were a dozen French communities: Detroit, Mackinac, Sault Ste. Marie, La Baye, St. Joseph, Vincennes, Fort Chartres, Prairie du Rocher, Kaskaskia, Cahokia, and Ste. Genevieve. All were very small. Each had developed around an original core of mission, fort, and trading post and each was surrounded by a far more numerous Indian population. Most of these wilderness French were soldiers or traders though there were a few who had turned farmer. Some of these had been joined by their wives and were able to enjoy, except for their extreme isolation, a comfortably normal family life. Many more of these self-exiled Frenchmen, whether soldier, trader, or farmer, had married the daughters of their Indian neighbors. A common custom, later adopted by many English and American traders, was the maintenance of an Indian family in the wilderness and a white one at Montreal or Quebec. These French communities in the west were inconsequential in themselves and too widely dispersed to contribute materially to their common defense. But influence over the Indians with whom they were so intimately associated gave them a strategic importance which they were to retain for many years to come.

The middle gateway, in complete contrast to the northern, was notable for the fact that the Indians had withdrawn their permanent towns to a distance. This was a mixed blessing for the withdrawal had made them less susceptible to English influence or military retaliation. Also, the gate was flanked by Iroquois hunting grounds. These friends of England whose whims had been so constantly pampered claimed dominion over the whole western watershed of the mountains, an assertion that the Seneca were presently to emphasize by joining Pontiac and destroying English garrisons in the area. The nearest Indian communities directly to the westward were across the Ohio three hundred miles from the white frontier in Pennsylvania. There in the pleasant valleys of the Muskingum, the Scioto, the Miami, and the Maumee were the fortified towns of the most difficult and obstreperous of all Indian nations, the Delaware, the Shawnee, and the Miami. The Shawnee and Delaware had formerly lived east of the mountains, knew white men well, and knew by painful experience the penalties inevitably to follow if the advance of white settlers resumed. They, together with the Miami and the Wyandot, were to prove the implacable enemies of the future Kentucky frontier.

In the south the rugged mountain valleys west of the Carolinas were held by the Cherokee, a talented and stubborn people who had but three years before fought a violent war with English regulars and were resolved to fight again as often as their homeland was threatened. Across the Gulf Plains below the Cherokee were ranged the towns of the Creek Republic, the most numerous of all Indian peoples. They were not to be dispossessed until Andrew Jackson's time. West of the Creek were the Choctaw and of the Cherokee, the Chickasaw. The latter represented a remarkable deviation from the political thinking of other western Indians. Active and warlike, they were always hostile to the French and persistently fought with their Indian neighbors but were invariably friendly first to the distant English and next to the intruding Americans. This curious policy totally failed to save them from the fate of their more orthodox brethren.

This brief sketch of the location of the principal Indian nations highlights one startling circumstance. Of more strategic significance in the years immediately to come than these locations of the centers of Indian power was the location of the area from which Indian power had removed. Between the southernmost towns of the Iroquois or the Shawnee and the northernmost towns of the Cherokee or the Chickasaw there were no Indian inhabitants. This singular situation had developed out of the age-old Indian proclivity for waging war on each other. The most persistent of these innumerable intraracial conflicts had been the traditional state of war between the Northern and Southern Indians. Year after year, since the early 17th Century, war parties from either region had made the long journey to commit depredations in the territory of the other. For mutual protection outlying Indian towns had gradually withdrawn closer to each nation's center. The intervening country became known as the Middle Ground or the Neutral Ground. Modern terminology might make it No Man's Land. This Indian withdrawal from some of the most pleasant terrain on the continent had already opened the way for swift white settlement of the Valley of Virginia between the Blue Ridge and the main mountain chain. West of the mountains Indian failure to reoccupy Kentucky and middle Tennessee was eventually to prove the fatal gap in the whole Indian defense line.

However, the Proclamation Line, the designs of the great powers, the mountain barrier, the gateways, the centers of Indian resistance, the wide rivers, the immense lakes, the great forests, the herds of game, all these were but the stage setting for the play that was about to be presented. Dramatic as was the setting, far more dramatic were the stresses to which the human actors were to be subjected. These were stresses which could not have been more cruel, more terrible, more final. They were laid upon two peoples who differed so radically that accommodation was inconceivable. It was a conflict from which even surrender could bring no release. The drama's climax was to come as both victor and vanquished were to realize too late what both were losing.

We already know how the play comes out. We know how inevitable was that outcome. The Stone Age must yield to the Industrial Age. The greatest good to the greatest number is an undeniable criterion. There is justice in the earth being inherited by those able to make the most practical use of it. Man must progress. All this we know. But the play is still worth watching. In what was being lost some of mankind's deepest and least expressible longings were entangled.

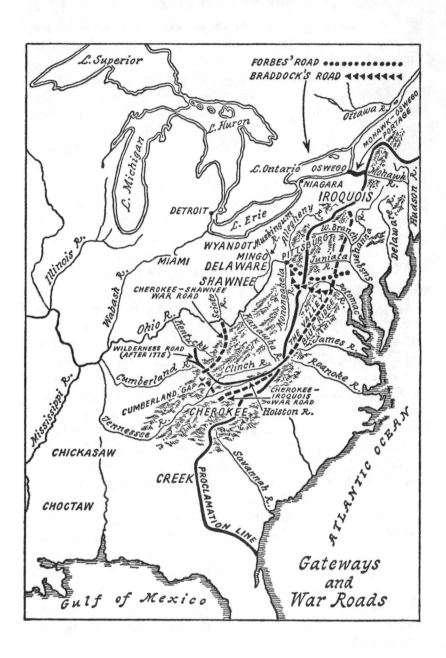

Gateways
and
War Roads

Possibly we can gain a clearer perspective if we attempt to survey what was passing from the world scene from the Indian's point of view. We can gather easily enough what that was. He was highly articulate and a born orator. At innumerable official conferences with his white adversaries or allies, arguments with his pseudo friends, the traders, and meetings with his worst enemies, the frontiersmen, he dilated at great length upon what he felt, how he felt, and why he felt that way.

Seagoing white traders had been visiting the Atlantic coast long before a De Soto or a Cartier had first pushed inland and the Indian had by now had nearly three hundred years to size up the white man. His considered conclusion was that he himself was a distinctly superior human being and that his way of life was infinitely superior. Judging the white man by every standard by which he judged himself, in every respect the white man fell short. In neither war nor peace did the white man exhibit or even appear to value what the Indian regarded as true courage, pride, dignity, or honor.

He had noted with incredulous disdain that in war the white man always marched shoulder to shoulder in the midst of a great company of his fellows dressed exactly like him to show that there was nothing about him that was different from them and that he never sought battle unless he had with him an overwhelming weight of numbers and guns. This anxiety to win at the least risk was typical of the white man's bent. To him war was never the supreme and heart-stirring test of a man's essential manhood. It was a laborious task always undertaken reluctantly and then only for some material advantage.

In peace the white man was to the Indian an even sorrier object. His life was not shaped by any concern whatever for his personal dignity as a man. His one ruling passion was to get money. To get it he would go to any length. He would lie, cheat, steal, risk his life, or, revealing even more sharply his inherent ignobility, hire himself out to serve another man. When he was his own man on his own land he made himself more than ever the slave, sweating dismally year in year out to raise a hundredfold more than he needed to feed himself and his family. That this love of money had bred a slavish industriousness that in some mysterious fashion had made him capable of manufacturing such useful articles as guns only made him more the fool. Only a fool would sell his worst enemy a gun with which his enemy could then shoot him.

As a person the white man was to the Indian the most revolting of all. His color was unhealthy. He lived in filth with no regard for those ritualistic purifications which alone kept a man pure in body and spirit. He trailed with him wherever he appeared a hideous miasma of drunkenness and disease and death. He was a weakling who was never ashamed to complain of fatigue and hunger and cold. He was a coward who screamed like a woman when burned. And, betraying the full depth of his degradation, he never kept his word. Of all the treaties he had made he had not kept one.

To the Indian, contemplating this strange and repulsive race which had suddenly materialized out of another world to undertake his dispossession, it was an incomprehensible injustice that the white man had so far so often prevailed against him. No Greek set upon by Scythians, or Roman by Huns, or Castilian by Moors, could have felt a deeper sense of outrage that his sacred soil was being thus defiled by a lower order of people. The Indian's world was threatened not by change but by total obliteration. Before his very eyes it was becoming an unrecognizably different world. Being a confirmed individualist he abhorred the idea of death but even more abhorrent was the prospect that this white man who was so bent on his dispossession and extermination would thereafter inherit it.

With the Indian's devotion to his world we may now find it difficult entirely to sympathize. But it was not an attachment so difficult for us to understand. His way of life was dedicated to the simple and all-inclusive principle that complete personal freedom is the first requisite to becoming a whole man. From dawn to dusk, from childhood to old age, he adhered to this cult of freedom. Whether he built a canoe, carved a pipe, hunted a buffalo, sought a woman, joined a war party, or stretched to doze away the day in the sun, whatever he did was at a moment of his own choosing. His lot was not always an easy one. He often starved, froze, fell ill, or suffered from every sort of misadventure, but never did he suffer what was in his estimation the genuine ignominy of being required to do what another man told him to do.

His earliest memories were of his individuality being encouraged. He was spoiled as a child. His every tantrum was applauded. If in a fit of temper he struck his mother or even his father the whole family laughed approvingly at this promising display of budding masculine aggressiveness. He grew up in a community which restricted his behavior no more than did his family. All members of it did as they pleased, their most eccentric deviations discouraged only slightly by a most tolerant public opinion.

Nothing about his existence ever became monotonous or habitual. Routine was unknown. The most unpremeditated projects needed no more than mention to be undertaken. On the spur of the moment his family set off on long trips, to try new hunting grounds or pay distant visits. A Chippewa of Lake Superior thought nothing of calling on his French friends at Detroit or Montreal or a Winnebago of Green Bay of visiting the long houses of the Iroquois. His town itself was periodically moved to a new site as the corn land around the old became less fertile.

As he grew older his destiny became increasingly apparent. If he was to become a man in the Indian sense of the term he must become more and more of an individualist. He must reject all discipline imposed by others while at suitable intervals he must most rigorously discipline himself in order to develop his skill, hardihood, and courage as hunter and warrior. Even his vices, including drunkenness, his saddest, were but further expressions of his innate freedom of choice. If in a prolonged debauch he wasted his substance and knifed his spouse the disasters but accentuated the basic principle by which he lived. Being a man he needed to subscribe to no rule but his own impulses and the more heedless these were the more proven was his manhood.

Any wish to accumulate wealth was not among these impulses. Thrift and avarice were to him equally contemptible. A surplus of food he cheerfully divided with neighbors or guests. Loot that he had won by the greatest effort and hazard in a raid on the distant white settlements he was likely to give or gamble away the day of his return. Acquisitions upon which he did set a value were articles with which he might decorate his person so as to improve his status as a figure of fashion and articles with which he might arm himself to improve his status as hunter and warrior. His lifelong twin ambitions were to prove himself a man of distinction at home and a desperado abroad. For all his scorn of manual labor he occasionally drove himself through a long hard winter collecting beaver to gain a gun, a silver brooch, and a brass kettle to support his favorite roles of fighting man, dandy, and host.

Among all the ways in which his values differed from the white man's it was between their respective attitudes toward land that there yawned the widest abyss. To the Indian the earth was a divine gift bestowed upon all men for their common good. That any one man should presume to claim personal ownership of any part of it was unthinkable. The narrow cultivated areas around an Indian town were apportioned among the community's families according to a rule of thumb by which each family used as much as it felt like taking the trouble to plant. The family gathered the harvest but nobody claimed ownership of the land or raised more than each needed for the coming winter. In the adjacent expanse of wilderness the nation asserted the right to hunt and sometimes fought with neighboring nations for the right but it was a right to use that was being disputed, not a title of possession. In practice the Indian hunter usually ranged as widely as he pleased. When an Indian nation went through the form, necessarily under duress, of selling tribal land to a white buyer it was the Indian hunting right in the area that was being relinquished and each such successive transaction engineered by the white man but confirmed in the Indian's mind his immemorial right to use the land that still remained to him.

No aspect of the creeping advance of the white frontier, therefore, so profoundly disturbed the Indian as the preposterous assumption of private land ownership. The newcomers' insanity in tearing down the forest and killing off the game was an infuriating spectacle. But that they should then fence off areas of the land itself as parcels of private property struck at the heart of the Indian's conception of man's ordained place on earth. His abhorrence of the whole idea of land ownership lent an added zest to the perpetration of those inhuman atrocities which characterized his every attack on the settlements.

These were among the elements that accounted for what and how the Indian felt and why he felt as he did. In spite of hardships and privations and seasons in which survival itself was doubtful his existence was one filled with satisfactions and fulfillments, which moved him to cling to it with all his might. To him the supreme reward that exceeded every difficulty was the priceless gift of personal freedom. His very difficulties were a part of that freedom. They were either of his own making or ones with which he could attempt directly to cope. Until the pressure of the white frontier bore down on him they were never difficulties imposed by forces beyond his reach. If he was hungry it was his aim that brought down the stag. If he was cold it was his fire that warmed him. If he was in danger it was his quickness that protected him.

In his view he was a natural man living in a natural environment that suited him. His world as he had known it was a vast and marvelous land of lakes and rivers, forests and prairies, alive with game. All this, in his deeply religious estimation, represented a higher power's gift to him for his sustenance and enjoyment. Through it he might roam as he pleased. The arch of the sky above him, the gathering of a storm, the splash of a salmon at dawn, the mating whistle of an elk, the lift of his canoe in a rapid, the glow of sunset over a lake, the start of a buck from a thicket, the hiss of raindrops in the dust, the scent of pines in the sun, all were miraculous parts of his world, as he was a part. It was a world at which he could continue to marvel because it remained perpetually novel to him. Each morning he was able to awake speculating upon what that day he might do—or not do. None of his occupations was one to which he was driven by any other compulsion than his own will. All were self-indulgences. His principal occupation, hunting and fishing to get food, was more of a sport than a task. His other more common undertakings were likewise diverting. He enjoyed the revelation of his eloquence in council, his endurance as a dancer, his calm while gambling, his prowess as a ball player, his taste in the decoration of his person, his singularity in having remarkable dreams. His greatest sport of all was going to war, in the days when the wars were with others of his own kind which could be started and stopped at will. All in all he found it a wonderfully good way of life. The last thing he wanted was to see it changed.

Certain as we are that our world now offers infinitely more rewarding satisfactions and fulfillments, that our civilization represents an immense step forward toward the state to which man was intended to aspire, we must sometimes be haunted by a stray, half-suppressed doubt. The most conventional modern man, leaning back from his desk to reflect upon a recent vacation, may for a moment be startled by the sudden piquancy of such a doubt. He may remember in that unguarded moment before he puts the thought from him that never does he know so deep a sense of well being, never does he feel so completely at peace with himself, as when he is on a trout stream, in a duck blind, on a mountain top, in the woods, by a campfire. For a little while he has escaped the clutch of clock and job. He has caught a momentary glimpse of what the Indian meant by freedom.

Debatable as this proposition may be to most of us the Indian's white contemporaries offer supporting testimony that is not at all debatable. To most of them who had had opportunity to experience it the Indian's way of life was irresistibly appealing. Frenchmen took to it from the first. Hundreds and then thousands were soon spending months of every year and then years at a stretch among the Indians. They not only lived among Indians but like Indians, they took Indian wives, they soon were scarcely to be distinguished from Indians.

The early Englishmen on the Atlantic seaboard were denied the Frenchmen's opportunity to wander familiarly among the Indians. From almost the beginning the English urge to acquire land involved them in Indian wars. But this for some led to an opportunity to become as intimately acquainted with Indian life as had the French. During the generations of border warfare the Indians carried off thousands of white captives to their most distant towns. Many were burned to adorn the climax of the Indian victory celebration. But many more of the younger and stronger, after suitable purification ceremonies, were adopted into the tribe. In the family which had accepted them they became sons, daughters, brothers, sisters, wives. They dressed, ate, and lived like Indians. They became, literally, members of the Indian community. Their sad plight had a poignant appeal for the bereaved relatives from whose midst they had been torn. The next white commander who had had any sort of military success made it his first demand that the defeated Indians return their captives. Sometimes, if sufficiently hard pressed, the Indians were compelled grudgingly to obey. On occasion hundreds of captives were delivered at a time. Many were glad to be redeemed. But a very great many after a half-hearted attempt to readjust to their former civilized environment ran back to the wilderness and to the Indians. They had tasted a special kind of freedom and they much preferred it.

The clinching evidence of the white man's instinctive inclination toward the Indian's way of life is presented by the Indian's bitterest enemy, the frontiersman. The long hunter, spending months and years wandering in the wilderness, was living altogether like an Indian and finding the same satisfactions in each new day's new freedom. The first settlers to make the great break over the mountains and on into the wilderness were to be distinguished from the long hunter only by the circumstances that they had brought a family along, that they built a log cabin instead of a half-faced camp, and that they planted a corn patch. They were not making so tremendous an effort and running so desperate a risk in order to improve their material condition. Had that been their purpose they would have remained a little longer in their former ordered world east of the mountains from which they had so irretrievably separated themselves. Certainly they would not have been moved to be among the first to take the fearful plunge into the far wilderness. Their real impulse was so strong as to verge on the irrational. They yearned to get to that wilderness while it was still totally wild. They were striving to escape the ordered world behind them and its clutter of such frustrations as quitrents, taxes, debts, wages, laws. The ideal of freedom they sought they themselves termed "elbow room." They were reaching for precisely what the Indians were struggling to save—escape from routine, those peculiar satisfactions known only to the confirmed hunter, the comfort of intimacy with nature, the assurance of self-dependence, license to roam. Those first comers were not truly settlers. They had not come to build up the country. Few ever settled down. They were always moving on. For them the border coined the word "mover." As the early transmountain settlements developed they kept on moving, always to the outermost fringe of the frontier. That this continued to be always the most dangerous of all possible situations where they were certain always to be the first attacked in every recurrence of border fighting did not deter them. They knew what they wanted and they were not to be denied it by whatever hardship or peril. They were still on that outer fringe when the kind of frontier that they had known came to an end hundreds of miles to the westward where the forest itself ended at the edge of the Great Plains.

They had succeeded, meanwhile, in dispossessing their bitter adversary, the Indian. But they had also been themselves dispossessed. The mirage of freedom which they had so ardently pursued had faded for them as swiftly as for the Indians.

Part Two

The Gatekeepers

IV

༄

Croghan

THE WILDERNESS WORLD OF 1763 was too diverse and too confused to permit the easy application of any such rule of law as the Royal Proclamation. The Indian who lived in it, the frontiersman who lived at the edge of it, or the soldier who was attempting to keep the peace between them, understood the clash of irreconcilable forces of which each of the three was a part but little more clearly than did the most distant and uninformed observer. They were antagonists striking blows while blindfolded. Neither could see where the blows were falling. There was one man, however, who had had a sufficiently wide personal acquaintance with both the Indian and the white worlds to enable him fully to appreciate all of the interrelated consequences of this random violence. George Croghan was able to encounter an Indian chief at his council fire on the Wabash, a trader with his pack train on the Tuscarawas, a settler rebuilding his burned cabin on the Susquehanna, a banker in his counting house on the Delaware, a governor in his mansion on the James, a general in his headquarters on the Hudson, or a cabinet minister in a palace on the Thames, and meet each on his own ground. He himself was trader, settler, merchant, soldier, magistrate,

Indian councilor and imperial administrator. The great tragedy of his life was that he still was never able to prevail upon his country to pay more than passing attention to his counsel.

Nothing could more eloquently suggest the scope and detail of his solid firsthand knowledge of both worlds than the most cursory review of his travels. He was the greatest traveler of his time and one of the most indefatigable of all time. He lived in an age when movement from place to place in the most civilized parts of the globe was a task but his journeys were over ranges of wooded mountains, up and down wild rivers, through the endless forests, and across the immense distances of the western wilderness. Long before the construction of Braddock's or Forbes' roads he was crossing the Alleghenies two and three times a year. He was the first English-speaking white man to become equally familiar with the shores of the Muskingum, the Cuyahoga, the Sandusky, the Maumee, the Scioto, and the Miami. His travels became more urgent when he became England's principal envoy commissioned to conciliate the western Indians during the closing years of the French War. Between October 1760 and October 1761 he traveled from Pittsburgh to Detroit by way of Lake Erie, back to Pittsburgh overland in midwinter, over the mountains to New York, back over the mountains to Pittsburgh, to Detroit again, and back to Pittsburgh. This was a tremendous journey, considering the ordinary difficulties and hardships of every kind of movement in the wilderness and the extraordinary circumstance that the Indians among whom he moved, as Pontiac was about to demonstrate, were still so far from pacified. But it was dwarfed by his next. Between September of 1763 and December of 1767 he traveled, almost without pause, overland from Bedford to Johnstown to New York to Carlisle to Philadelphia, by sea to London (he was shipwrecked on the coast of France en route), back to Philadelphia, over the mountains to Pittsburgh, down the Ohio and up the Wabash to Vincennes (he survived a Kickapoo tomahawking en route), overland to Detroit, by Lake Erie to Niagara, by Lake Ontario to Oswego, down the Mohawk and the Hudson to New York, on to Philadelphia, over the mountains again to Pittsburgh, down the Ohio to Fort Chartres, down the

Mississippi to New Orleans, by sea to New York, then to Philadelphia and over the mountains to Pittsburgh, through the wilderness to Detroit, back again through the forests to Pittsburgh, and finally back to Philadelphia from which he had sailed just four years before. Here was obviously a man who, when he spoke of distant places and peoples, spoke with authority. He had been there.

His exceptional knowledge of the wilderness and its inhabitants sprang from his early years as a trader. To his personal initiative was largely due the sudden capture by Pennsylvania traders, in the late 1740's, of the Ohio Indian market. He had pushed his trading activities steadily westward until his pack trains and batteaux were carrying goods from Philadelphia's wharves to western Indian customers within sight of the outraged French in Detroit and Vincennes. The Ohio Indians flocked to his posts in such numbers that his far-flung operation took on many of the aspects of a private empire. The French, becoming belatedly aware of how completely he was alienating their former clients and allies, were stirred to set a price on his head and to proceed against him by diplomatic and military means ordinarily employed only against a rival power. Before the first shot of the French and Indian War had been fired his trading empire had been overthrown. But his knowledge of the wilderness remained and served to lift him to different heights.

The pressure of events which had ruined his private enterprise now forced upon him the greater distinction of public service. Governors and generals were compelled to seek his advice since no one else knew so well the mysterious region beyond the mountains in which the storm of war was gathering. He entered upon the second phase of his career by becoming the great negotiator. Just as Johnson spoke for England to the Iroquois it fell to Croghan to speak for England to the Ohio Indians. During and after both the French War and Pontiac's War he presided over or took a principal part in 26 major Indian conferences, not to mention innumerable lesser negotiations.

In all his activities his influence was strengthened by a network of personal relationships. Ties of blood and marriage had made him the central figure in what amounted to a kind of Royal Family of the frontier. Sir William Johnson was a distant relative. His half brother, Captain Edward Ward, built the original Virginia fort at the Forks of the Ohio and thereafter took a prominent part in the history of this most strategic of all frontier regions. William Powell and Thomas Smallman, leading merchants of early Pittsburgh, and Daniel Clark, the famous New Orleans merchant, were his cousins. His nephew, Dr. John Connolly, played a principal role in Virginia's attempt to split the upper Ohio area away from Pennsylvania and then, during and after the Revolution, in England's hope to split the whole Ohio away from the United States. His daughter, Susannah, his only white child, married Lieutenant Augustine Prevost, son of the English major general who was to capture Charleston and Savannah. His second wife was the daughter of Niches, the Mohawk chieftain. His Indian daughter, Catherine, married Brant, the most renowned of all Indians, whose sister, Molly, was Johnson's consort.

In spite of these notable relationships and the fact that his name was probably more widely known among his fellow Americans before the Revolution than that of any other American except Johnson, Washington, and Franklin, we know literally nothing of his early personal life. We do not know the date or place of his birth. There is no record even of the name of his white wife, though his white daughter, Susannah, was born in 1750 when he was already wealthy and famous. All we do know of his background is that he had come from Dublin when he arrived in Philadelphia in 1741.

There was, of course, little about his having cut loose from his European origin to single him out among other men of his time. For very many others the American dream was in each of those 18th Century years becoming the American adventure. During the past generation Englishmen, Irishmen, Scotsmen, and Germans had been flocking to the new world by the hundreds of thousands. All were made soon to realize the harsh demands of their bold leap into the unknown. Overcrowded and underfed in the cranky little merchant ships of the time, their Atlantic passage was not much more endurable than in the slave ships which during those same years were transporting other hundreds of thousands of African natives into

American slavery. Many of the white immigrants themselves became virtual slaves upon arrival. Having been unable to pay their passage in advance, their services were sold to the highest bidder by the ship's captain who had brought them over. Most of these contracts ran for seven years, a distressing postponement of the larger opportunity the adventurer had come to seek. These contract workers were variously known as "redemptioners" or "indentured men" or "bond girls." They formed a considerable part of the colonial population. Most worked out their terms and merged with the ordinary citizenry. Others, rebelling against harsh masters, escaped to the fringes of the frontier where the willful inhabitants sheltered them from recapture. There were occasional instances of the great adventure progressing at so brisk a rate that in the short space of his first year in the new world the adventurer passed from the hardships of the ocean passage to the rigors of contract bondage, to the excitements of escape from it, to the perils of frontier life, to the ultimate vicissitudes of Indian captivity. There were enough ex-redemptioners to add a strong tinge of intransigence to the American character, particularly the frontier character. As a class they were resentful of every form of legal or social authority and predisposed to any form of rebellion.

Croghan apparently possessed the resources to pay his own passage, for his success was not delayed by the need to work for anybody but himself. For him the opportunity he had come to seek was not hard to find. He was new to the country but the country was itself so new that opportunity seemed everywhere. Men still lived who could remember the day the first Englishman had stepped on this Delaware shore where now hundreds of ships docked each year. Already the province was outstripping its so much older rivals, Virginia, Massachusetts, and New York. As Croghan walked the streets of Philadelphia, looking about him with the avid interest of the newcomer who had come to stay, he was surveying the largest, richest, and most important city in the colonies. The amazing rapidity of Pennsylvania's growth had been due in part to the care with which the Penn family, the nominal proprietors under the royal charter, had negotiated land purchases from the Indians. This had spared the province the Indian wars which had so retarded the early development of most other colonies. Indian readiness to sell the land had been due to another special circumstance. The arrogant Iroquois were absentee landlords who claimed the lower valleys of the Delaware and the Susquehanna on the basis of ancient conquests. They were glad to profit by the sale of land which they did not themselves occupy. The actual occupants, the Delaware and Shawnee, overawed by superior Iroquois power, could only give way and had presently withdrawn over the mountains to the Ohio, leaving white Pennsylvania to continue its rapid and peaceful development.

It was not, however, among the 40,000 inhabitants of bustling Philadelphia that Croghan found the sort of opportunity for which he was looking. As soon as he had got his bearings it was the frontier that attracted his interest and he promptly set out on the first of his innumerable journeys into the interior. New impressions literally beat upon him. Each hour as he rode westward the scene changed. The neighborhood of Philadelphia was occupied by the English, a majority of them Quakers, who had been the first to come and who still maintained political and commercial control of the province. These first few miles presented most of the civilized aspects of a European countryside. But a few miles beyond to the north and west there began to appear the heterogeneities of a rawer and newer country. First there was the wide belt settled by the Germans who had come next after the English. They were thrifty, hardworking, and eminently successful farmers, satisfied with their lot and clinging tenaciously to their own language and manners. Beyond the Germans were the Scotch-Irish, the last to arrive. They were unthrifty, restless, belligerent, supremely dissatisfied with their lot, and pre-eminently equipped by disposition to deal with the uncertainties of existence on a frontier. Their frontier was not distant from the peace and calm of Philadelphia. In 1741 it roughly followed the northeast-southwest line of the Blue Ridge. The present Easton and Harrisburg were on the fringes of the white country. The present Wilkes-Barre, Sunbury, and Altoona were deep in the wilderness.

He crossed the mile-wide Susquehanna at Harris' Ferry and was now upon land purchased so recently from the Indians that the price had not yet been paid. Here, five miles west of the site which 44 years later was to become Harrisburg, he erected his first house in America within sight of a minor gap in the mountain barrier which soon came to be known as Croghan's Gap. His instinct in locating here was prophetic. This was to become the first great gateway to the west. Forbes' Road was to begin here. Through this gap were to pass the pack trains of traders, then the long supply trains of armies, and finally the longer wagon trains of settlers. Here began the main avenue to the transmountain west.

Gaps, paths, and watercourses were already important to him for already he had recognized his opportunity. To the man without capital who was bold enough to take great risks the Indian trade offered the best possible hope swiftly to gain a fortune. It was a unique commercial institution in that it operated almost entirely upon credit. Manufacturers and merchants in England shipped goods on credit to merchants and factors in Philadelphia who in turn furnished them on credit to the individual traders who packed them to distant Indian towns to exchange for skins and furs. In most areas competition was active, making it necessary to extend this credit system even to the Indian customer. He was advanced goods in the fall for which he was expected to pay in the spring by the delivery of furs he had taken during the winter. In seasons when all went well there were handsome returns to everybody concerned. The profits to the trader were sometimes enormous. But the risks were always enormous. The risk to his goods in transit by storms, forest fires, robbery, and such miscellaneous accidents as an overturned canoe was constant. Any sudden contraction in the inflated credit system, due to a threat of war or a shift in Indian alliances, meant his instant ruin. Beyond every property risk was the perpetual risk to his life. By the very nature of his undertaking he must venture deep into the Indian country where he was completely at the mercy of his Indian customers. Ordinarily Indians were hospitable to traders, for they realized that regular visits by many traders meant more competition and cheaper prices. But international rivalries often interfered with this self-serving tolerance. Both English and French traders were forever inciting their Indian friends to pillage or murder their rivals.

This international trading rivalry was already beginning to shape the future of the whole continent. The year Croghan first crossed the mountains there were other Englishmen trading west from South Carolina and southwest from Hudson Bay, Frenchmen trading so widely across the interior that they had posts on the Missouri and Lake Winnipeg and had sighted the Rocky Mountains, Spaniards trading north from Pensacola and Santa Fe, and Russians trading on the shores of Alaska. The fierce competition between English and French traders was to bring on the French and Indian War which was in turn to open the door to American independence. After the Revolution competition between American and English traders was to run ahead of American westward expansion down the Ohio and across the Mississippi, the Great Plains, and the Rockies to the Pacific. A hundred years after Croghan's first pack train crossed the Appalachians American settlers on the Columbia were disputing with English traders title to the present states of Oregon and Washington.

In later years Croghan was to write letters and keep journals which shed much light not only on his own history but on the history of his times. But of this first of his countless ventures into the far wilderness he left no word. Very likely he was too preoccupied with his own first impressions to write about them. He had already made an extraordinary journey in leaving the land of his birth to cross the Atlantic and then to keep on westward to build his home on the outermost edge of the white frontier. Now while the commonest American scenes were still new to him he was embarked on one yet more extraordinary over the mountains which marked the rim of the white world into regions few white men had ever seen and from which no English-speaking white man had yet brought back the sketchiest written account. His path was an Indian trail that followed the trace made at an earlier time by buffalo, the first and greatest of all wilderness trail breakers. It kept to high ground as it angled across the successive ridges of the mountain barrier and tended to keep to the most direct route between the middle Susquehanna and the Forks of the Ohio. Though we have no accounting from him we can be confident of the contents of the packs with which his horses were laden. There is testimony to the range of items Indians most valued in the recorded list of goods turned over to the Iroquois in Pennsylvania's land purchase then being consummated:

"500 pounds of powder, 600 pounds of lead, 45 guns, 60 stroud match coats, 100 blankets, 60 kettles, 100 tobacco tongs, 100 scissors, 500 awl blades, 120 combs, 100 duffil coats, 200 yards of half-thick, 100 shirts, 40 hats, 40 pair stockings, 100 hatchets, 500 knives, 100 hoes, 2000 needles, 1000 flints, 24 looking glasses, 2 pounds vermilion, 10 tinpots, 1000 tobacco pipes, 24 dozen of gartering, 200 pounds tobacco, 25 gallons rum."

Having crossed the mountains by the trail later to become as familiar to him as the Dublin streets of his boyhood, he came to Queen Aliquippa's Town at the Forks of the Ohio where for the first time he saw the great river which was from then on to take so prominent a place in his career and soon to take one so notable in American history. His cargo made him welcome. He was undoubtedly greeted by salutes of pistol fire and musketry, as was the Indian custom in expressing their appreciation of a trader's arrival with a fresh selection of the goods they coveted. An Englishman was not a stranger to these upper Ohio Indians. Most of them had within the past few years migrated westward over the mountains from Pennsylvania or southwestward down the Allegheny from New York in the hope of keeping a more comfortable distance between their homes and the white frontier. Aliquippa ruled a town inhabited by Iroquois (Iroquois who had moved to the Ohio were already beginning to be known as Mingo) and Delaware, which was periodically increased by numbers of visiting Shawnee. The redoubtable old Iroquois chieftainess was termed a Seneca by Conrad Weiser, who for years had been Pennsylvania's most trusted contact with the Indians, but she was considered a Mohawk by Canachquasy, her best known son.* Throughout her long life she gave the English her unwavering support and as a consequence was driven out by the French when they took over the Ohio. Celeron, arriving in 1749 to proclaim French dominion over the region west of the mountains, called her town "the written rock village." This was in apparent reference to nearby McKee's Rocks on which passing traders had scrawled their names and various messages, much as a hundred years later and 1400 miles farther westward the covered-wagon people were to leave their inscriptions on Independence Rock. On the aged Indian queen Celeron reported sourly: "She regards herself as a sovereign and is entirely devoted to the English." On the situation of her town he reported enthusiastically: "This place is one of the most beautiful I have seen on La Belle Riviere."

Every other early viewer, including Croghan, was delighted by the noble prospect where the Monongahela and the Allegheny united to form The Beautiful River. But he was immediately struck as well by the geographical significance of the location. Behind him stretched the direct route by which he had just come from the white country on the seaboard. To the southeast ran the ancient Indian thoroughfare to the Potomac and Virginia, presently to become known as Nemacolin's Path. To the north, up the Allegheny, ran a third main Indian route of waterways, portages, and trails leading to the Iroquois country, to Niagara, and to western Lake Erie. To the northwest ran another Indian path, so well used that it was known as The Great Trail, to Sandusky and Detroit. Straight west ran a fifth Indian trail to the Delaware towns on the Muskingum, the Shawnee towns on the Scioto, and the Miami towns on the great Miami. The great river itself rolled away to the southwest, giving access by a score of tributary rivers to those fair and fertile regions upon which the states of Ohio, Indiana, Illinois, Kentucky, and Tennessee were

* In recognition of his faithful service to the English cause during the French and Indian War honorary names which he highly valued were bestowed upon Canachquasy by English leaders with whose operations he was associated. Washington dubbed him "Colonel Fairfax," after his own Virginia patron, and Governor Morris of Pennsylvania named him "Captain Newcastle," after the current English prime minister.

to be erected. It was this network of wilderness communications that was to make the Forks of the Ohio a primary base in all the wars in the west of the next half century and the principal gateway for the westward expansion of American settlement.

But when Croghan arrived the appearance of soldier or settler in this vast loneliness was undreamed of and to him the chief meaning of the web of trails and waterways was that the head of the Ohio presented an ideal location for his central trade depot. Here he built storehouses and living quarters and gained Indian permission to clear land to raise food for his men and grain for his pack horses. From it he carried his goods by boat and pack train to more distant Indian towns. His establishment was burned in the French War and again in Pontiac's War but each time he rebuilt it on a larger scale than before. In time it came to be known as Croghan Hall in recognition of the fact that it had become a not too modest rival of Johnson Hall.

Pennsylvania traders had originally crossed the mountains to follow their Iroquois, Delaware, and Shawnee customers with whom they had formerly dealt east of the mountains. But Croghan soon extended his operations deeper into the interior to trade also with the Miami, Wyandot, Piankashaw, and other more distant nations whose only former white contacts had been with the French. His phenomenal success was due to several factors, the foremost of which was his own tremendous energy. Most of his opposite numbers heading other Pennsylvania trading firms were more conventional merchants who remained comfortably in Philadelphia, delegating to employees all physical operations connected with getting their goods into the wilderness and into the hands of their Indian customers. Many of these haphazardly recruited traders for hire were lazy, dishonest, drunken, and irresponsible. Accounts of the time are filled with references to the generally low character of the average trader. Croghan on the other hand went himself into the wilderness and literally paddled his own canoe. He took the trouble to learn Indian languages. He respected Indian customs. He kept his word as carefully in the most distant Indian town as in Philadelphia. Hundreds of influential Indians became his personal friends. Naturally his business flourished. His success was accelerated by King George's War. Between 1744 and 1748 English naval supremacy in the Atlantic so sharply shut off the supply of French trade goods that the French fell behind in the competition for the favor of the Ohio Indians. English goods had always been better and now they were also more plentiful and very much cheaper. Croghan with his widespread system of supply lines and trading posts was in a position to take full advantage of this opportunity.

But from the peak of success he was plunged to disaster. The reopening of the sea lanes to Canada at the close of King George's War had replenished the French supply of trade goods while French concern over English trade gains among the Ohio Indians had steeled French resolve to recover their lost position. The English traders were soon overmatched. They could only meet the challenge with such commercial weapons as easier credit, cheaper prices, and appeals to their customers to remember past favors. Their competitors were more formidably armed. While the English trader was separated by many hundreds of wilderness miles from the protection even of his provincial government, which in any event recognized no responsibility for him, at the French trader's elbow were instructed representatives of the King of France. As a first gesture in this reaffirmation of French sovereignty Captain Celeron de Bienville was dispatched in 1749 with 200 soldiers, Canadian militiamen, and loyal Indians to show the flag in the upper Ohio area which formerly France had avoided in order to placate the Iroquois. Crossing from Lake Erie by the Le Boeuf portage, Celeron made a formal descent of the great river, attended by loud beating of drums, resounding salutes of musketry, and the planting of lead plates proclaiming the Ohio still as French as in the French view it had always been. The astonished Indians along the river were sternly admonished to cease trading with the English. From then on any Indian who persisted in the practice was denounced as a "rebel" and his more amenable Indian neighbors were incited to attack him.

French determination to implement this policy culminated in 1752 in their destruction of the principal Miami town, Pickawillany, near the present Piqua, Ohio. By cordial invitation of its chief the

English traders had fortified their storehouses here and made the place their main depot in the Ohio country. As a result of this commercial activity the town had increased notably in population and importance and its enterprising chief had been lifted, briefly, from his former wilderness obscurity into a glare of international attention. The French called him La Demoiselle for just what reason does not appear, but he was known to the English as Old Britain, in tribute to his sturdy good will. The sturdiness of his support had, however, made his downfall a French imperative. For two years they had tried without success to overcome the reluctance of adjacent Indian nations to attack a neighbor as powerful as the Miami. They at length solved the problem by bringing Indians from so far away that they need have no fear of Miami retaliation. Two hundred and forty hard-bitten Ottawa from Mackinac, under the leadership of Charles Langlade, whom we shall meet again under equally violent circumstances, took the town by surprise. The fort was burned and £3000 worth of English trade goods carried off by the victors. La Demoiselle was boiled and eaten. Only eight English traders chanced to be present on the day of the attack. One was killed, two escaped, and the other five were made captive. After much initial mistreatment the English prisoners were sent first to Quebec and then to France to be interrogated. Eventually four of them found their way back to Philadelphia where, destitute, they appeared before the assembly to petition for relief. The assembly congratulated them on their fortitude and voted them £16 each as a reward for their services to their country.

The fall of Pickawillany signaled the doom of the English Ohio trade. After La Demoiselle's demise there was no Indian too slow witted to perceive which appeared the stronger side. Except for a few near the mountains who had had long associations with New York and Pennsylvania, most hastened to renew their allegiance to the French. Throughout the area English trading posts were pillaged and English traders hunted down. Those not killed or captured were forced to flee for their lives. Croghan had spent the previous winter among his western posts but fortunately for his personal safety was at his Pine Creek headquarters among the still friendly

Indians about the Forks of the Ohio when the news of Pickawillany reached him. The magnitude of his operations had made his losses the greater. In building up his enterprise so rapidly he had extended his credit to the limit. His fall was therefore as precipitous as had been his rise. The year before he had been considered one of the colonies' richer men. Almost overnight he had become a bankrupt. He was even obliged to move his eastern home from Croghan's Gap to Aughwick on the Juniata, outside Pennsylvania's civil jurisdiction, in order to remain beyond the legal reach of the swarm of process servers which his creditors had set upon him.

Nevertheless, he endeavored with undiminished energy to save what could be saved, for his country as well as himself. The nearer Indians about the Forks of the Ohio, most of them Mingo, Delaware, and Shawnee, such as the inhabitants of Queen Aliquippa's Town, had not yet gone over to the French. To the English they were strategically the most important of all Indians. They professed eagerness to remain England's allies but after the example of Pickawillany they naturally feared French aggression. They begged the support of an English fort at the Forks. Croghan rushed back and forth over the mountains, alternately pleading with the Indians to wait and with the Pennsylvania authorities to build the fort. The assembly remained cold to any scheme so fantastic as the expenditure of public funds on a project so remote. The mountains, it was pointed out, represented Pennsylvania's western boundary. What transpired beyond them was completely outside the area of Pennsylvania's interests. Johnson's warning that the French were planning to seize and fortify the Forks of the Ohio caused no stir in Philadelphia. Even if they did, Pennsylvania's legislators comfortably noted, they then would still be a full two hundred miles from Pennsylvania's borders.

At this very moment when English traders from Pennsylvania were being deprived of their market in the west other Englishmen from Virginia were making the first move by English-speaking white men to possess themselves of the land itself on the western side of the mountains. This being likewise the moment the French were advancing to seize the key to the region, the Forks of the Ohio, there was provided one of those momentous coincidences which make an event a turning point in history. The expulsion of the traders might of itself have resulted in no sharper crisis than a desultory exchange of protests between the chancelleries of France and England. But the collision of the land-seeking Virginians with the empire-building French precipitated a world war from which flowed incalculable consequences.

That this first impulse to cross the mountains stemmed from Virginia may be ascribed to factors as fundamental as Virginia's geography. Unlike Pennsylvania, New York, and New England, the principal rivers of Virginia ran from west to east. Ships could sail well into the interior. It was not required of every early settler that he plod to his new home with what he could carry on his back, that he begin by hacking a tiny clearing from the forest, and that he next somehow contrive to stave off starvation while awaiting his first crop. The early comers in Virginia could step from shipboard to homesite and bring with them cargoes of supplies. Some of them, encouraged by royal grants, were able soon to take up vast tracts of land along the easily accessible banks of the rivers. In the midst of a population the majority of which remained small farmers, sharecroppers, redemptioners, or slaves, there had developed a veritable dynasty of landed families each of which owned vast plantations or groups of plantations. Possession of large areas of land imposes upon the proprietor an obligation to direct the affairs of tenants and dependents. Among these landed Virginians this invitation to dominate developed in time into a remarkable capacity for leadership which persisted for generations. The commander-in-chief of our Revolutionary armies was to be a Virginian. Four of our first five presidents were to be Virginians. But of all the extraordinary services rendered their country by these extraordinary Virginians far from the least was their initiation of this first attempt to cross the mountains. Coming at the critical moment it did their undertaking set in motion a train of events which in inevitable and unbroken sequence led during the liftime of these same men to revolution, independence, and a westward movement that was never to be halted. The first stage of so vital a process invites a second glance.

Having bred leadership, Virginia geography at the same time had produced a special kind of enterprise. In other colonies most men who became rich achieved their aim by devotion to shipping, manufacturing, banking, or commerce. In Virginia the sole source of wealth was land. For the rich man's proverbial compulsion to acquire more wealth the one recourse was to acquire more land. Much of the land in Virginia east of the mountains was still undeveloped but by the middle 1740's title to all of it had been taken by somebody. For whoever wanted more there was no place to look nearer than beyond the mountains. The time was yet distant when the individual border settler could so much as dream of venturing alone into the wild region on the other side. But the resources of a great landowner permitted him to contemplate the most difficult projects, however delayed the prospective returns.

A friend of the Washingtons, the indomitable Marylander, Thomas Cresap, who in the course of one pugnacious lifetime had moved progressively westward until he had established himself far up the Potomac on the westernmost edge of the frontier in the eastern shadow of the main Allegheny Ridge, provided the spark to kindle the ensuing conflagration. From hunting excursions and conversations with trader and Indian acquaintances he had begun to gather some idea of the kind of country that lay beyond the mountains. Cresap's Ohio talk excited the interest of his Virginia friends. They were resolute men accustomed to dealing with large affairs and making large decisions. A number of them joined forces to form a partnership called the Ohio Company for the declared purpose of engaging in trade and land development on the upper Ohio. Among the original partners were Lees, Washingtons, Fairfaxes, Carters, and Masons—the authentic first families of Virginia. Several influential London merchants were invited to participate with a view to accelerating imperial sanction for the project. This was speedily forthcoming from a receptive Board of Trade. On the one hand long experience with the East India Company and the Hudson's Bay Company suggested the possible scale of returns from such remote ventures and on the other any maneuver that might disconcert the French was welcomed. In effect, the English government elected to make use of Virginia as a cat's-paw to counter French activities on the Ohio. By order of the King, Governor Gooch of Virginia was authorized on July 13, 1749, to grant to the Ohio Company 200,000 acres of land in a location somewhat loosely described as west of the mountains on "the branches of the Mississippi." It was this same summer that Celeron was planting his plates advertising French sovereignty in this same area.

The Company was now in business. But so far no one connected with it had ever seen this land beyond the mountains that had been granted by the King of England beyond the sea. Few other white men ever had. The first hired woodsmen dispatched by the Company to look for and at their land were chased off by the Indian occupants whose suspicions had been aroused by Pennsylvania traders jealous of potential Virginia competition. The mountain barrier began to appear somewhat more perplexing than had at first been assumed. But these Virginians were not men who were easily discouraged. The next year the Company made a more considered attempt to examine their new possession by employing the North Carolinian, Christopher Gist, a veteran frontiersman and experienced surveyor. Gist circled to the north and approached the Forks by the Pennsylvania traders' route. He, too, however, had great difficulty with the Indians until he was befriended by Croghan, who in the light of Pennsylvania disinterest was already beginning to suspect the possible need of Virginia support against the French. Croghan's sponsorship enabled Gist to make a grand circuit through the farther Ohio country, a part of Kentucky, and back by a more southerly route over the mountains to Virginia. He had not, however, in spite of the range of his notable journey, yet caught so much as a glimpse of the Company's land on the upper Ohio and the next year, 1751, the Company sent him out again.

This time he kept on target. He identified and explored the Company's grant along the east bank of the Ohio between the Monongahela and the Kanawha. With the aid of Cresap and Cresap's Indian friend, Nemacolin the Delaware, a direct route over the mountains was blazed between the Potomac and the Forks which was to become Washington's Road, then Braddock's Road, and finally the National Road. A Company storehouse was established at Will's Creek, near Cresap's station. Gist selected land for his own station on the crest of Chestnut Mountain, the westernmost ridge of the mountain barrier, and persuaded eleven frontier families to join him there. Preliminary negotiations to secure Indian approval of Company projects were instituted at Logstown with some help from Croghan. All was going well enough when Johnson's warning that the French were advancing in force upon the Ohio was expressed on to Williamsburg by Governor Hamilton of Pennsylvania.

Most fortunately, as it was eventually to prove after very many intervening misfortunes, Robert Dinwiddie, the recently arrived new governor of Virginia, was a stubborn and impulsive man. His instructions from his home government had been explicit. He was to forward the interests of the Ohio Company but, it was trusted, not with a vigor which might bring on a war. If the French trespassed in the area along the Ohio vaguely claimed by England they were to be warned to withdraw and given time to react to the warning. Armed opposition was to be a last resort only after overt attack. Casting about for an emissary sufficiently venturesome to carry the warning over the mountains and through the Indian country in the dead of winter, Dinwiddie hit upon an inspired choice. The twenty-one year old George Washington, as he stated in the first sentence of his Journal recording his great adventure, "set out on the intended Journey the Same Day."

It was altogether fitting that the future Father of His Country should thus become the first officially commissioned representative of his country to cross the mountains. On this terrible winter journey through the wilderness he narrowly escaped death again and again. This, moreover, was but the beginning. During the wilderness campaigns of the next five years his hairbreadth brushes with death were literally innumerable. Perhaps nothing could have more clearly forecast that he was a man marked by destiny for later and greater achievements. On this first of these perpetually perilous ventures he was guided over Nemacolin's Path by Gist and was able with a surveyor's eye to familiarize himself with the geography of the wild region through which three other times he was to fight his way with the resistance of human enemies added to that of the elements and the wilderness. At the Forks of the Ohio he selected the site for the projected English fort. He could have had no way of knowing that cold blustery day that during only the last five years of his life would he be finally freed of the need to consider the movements of armies marching to attack or defend the spot upon which he was standing. His wary parleys with the Indians here and at Logstown left him still uncertain of how long even those who protested friendship could be trusted. He kept on toward Lake Erie to the portage posts where the advancing French forces had paused to winter and at Le Boeuf confronted the French commander. The French reply was urbane but as firm as might have been expected. In the French view the region west of the mountains incontrovertibly belonged to France and France's friends and allies, the Indians. On December 16th of that abnormally rigorous winter of 1753 he started back. Blizzards he ignored. Indian efforts to waylay him he eluded. His horses broke down and had to be abandoned. When his raft was overturned he swam powerfully through the icy waters of the Allegheny to an island. He scaled the snow-covered mountains and on January 16th reached Williamsburg with the French reply.

Without waiting for further instructions from London the aroused Dinwiddie determined the time had already come for the resort to arms against which he had been cautioned. Appeals for support were sent off to the other colonies. The House of Burgesses was persuaded after long ill-tempered argument to authorize a modest muster of militia. The Company undertook to build the fort at the Forks of the Ohio. Virginia enlistments were slow and support from other colonies slower. In April Washington was sent into the wilderness with two companies of Virginia recruits who had been enticed into the service by promises of land on the Ohio. He began to build a road over the mountains and to consider what action to take if and when confronted by the French. The day after he reached Will's Creek he learned that they had resumed their advance in the spring, had taken the half-built Company fort at the Forks, and were there undertaking the construction of the far stronger fortress which was soon to become known as Fort Duquesne.

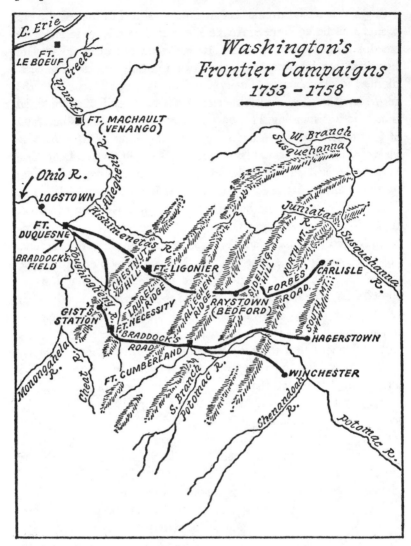

In his winter journey of 1753, Washington crossed the mountains to the Forks of the Ohio by the route later taken by Braddock's Road, then kept on overland to Fort Le Boeuf by way of Logstown and Fort Machault. In his campaign of 1754 he opened Braddock's Road as far as Gist's Station.

Croghan, meanwhile, had been continuing to rush back and forth over the mountains, trying to save as much of his property as he could before the arrival of the French, trying to hold his Indian friends to the English cause, trying to persuade Pennsylvania authorities to do something. During the previous winter he had fed at Aughwick upwards of 200 still friendly Indians who had fled from the French. Convinced at last that nothing was to be expected of Pennsylvania's pacifistic assembly he offered his services to Virginia. He contracted with the Company to supply its fort at the Forks and with Dinwiddie to furnish Washington with pack horses, food, and friendly Indian aid. The French took the fort before he could be of much help there and none of the support destined for Washington arrived in either a time or a quantity to satisfy that impetuous young commander, who was just beginning to discover the stupendous supply problems inseparably attached to any campaign in the wilderness.

Washington hacked his road over Laurel Mountain, across Great Meadows, and on to Gist's new little settlement on Chestnut Mountain.* His superior officer, Colonel Joshua Fry, was on his way to take over but was delayed at Will's Creek by a suddenly fatal illness. Command as a result remained with Washington. It was perhaps as well he was so young and eager for any more experienced commander must have been appalled by his situation. He was receiving dribbles of reinforcement but the French force toward which he was advancing was being built up so much more rapidly that soon it would outnumber him four to one. However, Pierre de Contrecoeur, the French commander, made no immediate move. Neither government had professed to want a war. The governors of both Canada and Virginia had been instructed to avoid any overt act that might lead to armed conflict. But with forces in the field

---

* Much map-reading confusion in connection with Washington's campaign has arisen from the tendency of contemporary Virginians to refer to the extension south of the Youghiogheny River of the westernmost ridge of the Appalachians as Laurel Mountain instead of Chestnut Mountain. Great Meadows and the site of Fort Necessity were in the hilly area between the two ridges, near the present Farmington, Fayette County, Pennsylvania, and well to the west of the range of heights that in all later years has been known as Laurel Mountain.

already on the verge of contact some overt act was inevitable unless one or the other drew back. There ensued the affair of the French "ambassador." Contrecoeur dispatched Ensign Villiers de Jumonville with a party of 34 partisans and Indians in Washington's general direction. The French afterwards maintained, and made much ado about it in every court in Europe, that Jumonville advanced upon Washington in the character of an emissary with instructions to do no more than to call formally upon the Virginians to cease this armed intrusion upon French territory in time of peace. Jumonville, however, instead of openly approaching Washington's camp, made a circuitous march, keeping in hiding and conducting his movements as though they were those of either a reconnoitering or raiding party.

Warned of Jumonville's maneuvers by his Indian allies, among whom were Queen Aliquippa herself and her son, "Colonel Fairfax," Washington led forty Virginians and Indians on a night march over rocky heights through storm and darkness to take the French camp by surprise. In that rainy dawn of May 28, 1754, there rang out the first shots of the war for the west which was to continue through endless campaigns, countless battles, with never more than the briefest lulls until forty years, two months, and twenty-three days later Mad Anthony Wayne, at the end of another spectacular advance ordered by Washington, won a finally decisive victory at Fallen Timbers. In this first engagement of that war one Virginian was killed and one wounded. Every Frenchman except one was killed or captured. Young Jumonville was among the dead.

Washington received another trickle of reinforcements, including a royal South Carolina company under a regular captain who insisted that his King's commission gave him higher rank than could be held by any Virginia officer of whatever rank. Lieutenant Colonel Washington wrote long letters of furious protest to Dinwiddie but in the field made the best of the rank dispute which was one that continued to torment all provincial officers to the end of the war. The road building was resumed and he entertained briefly the hope that he might yet take Fort Duquesne. But the indignant French had rushed down from Canada other reinforcements under the command of Coulon de Villiers, the brother of Jumonville. Made aware by the reports of his Indians how much he was outnumbered, Washington retreated to Great Meadows where he paused to rest his starved and exhausted army in an entrenched camp presently to be called Fort Necessity. The vengeful Villiers closed in on him. Washington's men had for so many days had so little to eat that their prebattle issue of rum made half of them rolling drunk. Nevertheless, a stubborn defense was kept up throughout that long rainy day and until one out of five of the defenders had been killed or wounded. But by nightfall Washington was forced to face the hard fact that there was no alternative to surrender. It was an inglorious end to his first campaign. His reputation further suffered in the eyes of most of the contemporary world through a peculiar collateral circumstance. Misled by the stupidity of his interpreter he unwittingly signed articles of capitulation which described the death of Jumonville as an "assassination." In other respects the French terms were lenient. Since no state of war existed the Virginians were somewhat contemptuously permitted to go home. The next morning Washington set out through the still pouring rain with his bedraggled little army on the dreary way back over the mountains. It was a desolating experience for a twenty-two-year-old commander. The date, the Fourth of July, 1754, remained for him a bitter memory over which he brooded through all the years until the anniversary took on both for him and for his countrymen another and greater significance.

This first defeat, moreover, was not to be his last. During the desperate war years immediately to come he was to be repeatedly thwarted and mortified, to be set upon by every form of discouragement and frustration, and to be involved in other and more disheartening defeats. In our early history there again and again were turns of fortune so favorable that they inevitably suggest the direct intervention of providence. Few of these could have been more providential than this series of wilderness tests to which Washington was subjected in his formative early twenties at the very outset of his career. It was a harsh schooling indeed, calculated to break any but the strongest spirit. In him it happily served only to strengthen that iron-souled resolution which enabled him to endure the greater trials of the Revolution with so much patience and fortitude.

When word of Washington's campaign reached Europe the French set up a great outcry that the peace had been breached. English reaction was mixed. No one felt very strongly about the conflicting claims to a far-off expanse of empty wilderness. It was true that in capturing the Company post on the Ohio the French had seized English property and affronted English dignity but the Virginians had unquestionably fired the first shot. The trials of the long War of Austrian Succession and the alarms of Bonnie Prince Charlie's uprising were of too recent memory for many Englishmen to welcome a new war. Nevertheless, traditional English hostility to everything French stirred deep English impulses to strike back. There were also in London mercantile circles close to the government influential men interested in the American fur trade and in American land schemes. After much confused discussion the cabinet, under Newcastle's muddled leadership, devised a program which presumed to shift responsibility for the consequences from England to France. To take military action against the French encroachment without going to war was something of a problem but one which members conceived they had solved. The principal border area disputed by France and England had long been claimed by the Iroquois on the basis of century-old victories over other Indian nations. By the terms of the Treaty of Utrecht between France and England in 1713 the Iroquois, without their knowledge or consent, had been described as "English subjects." Following this labored theory to its conclusion any English attempt to gain control of the upper Ohio was not, therefore, an aggression against the French but instead was merely a justified effort to restore order within the natural bounds of his Majesty's dominions. The theory worked within certain limits. The French resisted with extreme violence but neither power declared war until nearly two years later.

Newcastle's policy determination led to action that was both prompt and direct. Parliament voted a generous appropriation for the King's military establishment and adjourned. The King's second son, the Duke of Cumberland, the veteran of Fontenoy and Dettingen and the hero of Culloden, was, as Captain-General, in a position to take control of events from then on. He selected Major General Edward Braddock as the indicated man of the hour and sent him with two regiments of regulars to restore the situation in America.

Much has been made in our history of Braddock's mistakes. The judgment with which he measured his most unusual difficulties was, however, probably as intelligent as could have been expected of any commander all of whose military experience had been European. The major strategic decision which had already been made, by Cumberland, had already inflicted upon him almost impossible handicaps. The assigned purpose of Braddock's expedition was to drive the French from the upper Ohio. The most direct approach to that objective would have been to attack their line of communications at Niagara. In an advance upon Niagara Braddock's artillery and stores could have been entirely water-borne except for the relatively short portage from the Mohawk to Oswego. The Indians of the area, the Iroquois, were either friendly or neutral. Niagara must promptly have fallen before an army as strong as Braddock's and its fall have left French military power throughout the west stranded and helpless. Instead, he was sent to Virginia and directed to take the long, harsh route taken by Washington. Every conceivable disadvantage accompanied this basic decision. In Virginia the principal crop was tobacco and there was little surplus food to feed an army. Virginia with her rivers had few roads and fewer wagons while the distance he must travel to get at the French was far longer here than at any other point on the seaboard. His base camp at Will's Creek was itself a hundred miles beyond the farthest Virginia frontier and even there the mountain barrier still reared between him and the French. At the time there were many unkind allusions to the probability that Cumberland's decision must have been influenced by Ohio Company interests. It is more likely that it was a routine determination made by an imperial headquarters staff largely ignorant of American geography.

Braddock's difficulties proliferated from the moment he disembarked at Alexandria. It had been presumed that he might count on support from the several American provinces. Very little was forth-coming, even from Virginia whose immediate border he had come to protect. The French threat on the Ohio seemed oddly less real in America than it had in London. Though the French wolf which formerly had terrorized only the northern borders of New England and New York was now also at the back doors of Pennsylvania and Virginia most people were even yet slow to take alarm. To the aver-age seaboard citizen of the middle colonies the mountains seemed very far to the westward and the French and Indians on the farther side of them as far away as the moon. There was, moreover, a general feeling that the French threat was being calculatingly inflated on the one hand to serve the private interests of land companies and traders and on the other to enable royal authorities to put pressure on pro-vincial legislators. The assemblies of Virginia, Pennsylvania, and New York successively refused to vote more than perfunctory de-fense funds. Only New England, stirred by her ancient antipathy to the French in Canada and by her pride in her own recent martial success at Louisburg, began, under the leadership of William Shirley, the vigorous old governor of Massachusetts, to prepare for war.

Bitterly denouncing American apathy, Braddock worked his army painfully westward to Will's Creek where he built a fort to which he gave the name Cumberland in honor of the man who had placed him in so dismal a predicament. Lack of transport was by now forc-ing him to conclude that the campaign must be abandoned. But two rays of light brightened his gloom. He had the rare sense to make Washington his aide and to give frequent ear to the young Vir-ginian's advice. Then Benjamin Franklin came forward with the offer of 150 wagons. The Pennsylvania assembly had continued to refuse official support to the expedition but Franklin, with that clarity of vision that always informed his judgment, had perceived the reality of the French menace. He rounded up the wagons among Pennsylvania's prosperous farmers, got them delivered in time, and Braddock was able to start west.

Croghan had been with Washington the year before through all the last days of his travail, furnishing him the few supplies he re-ceived, helping him with his Indians, giving him counsel based on his long experience in the wilderness. After the Fort Necessity debacle he had again spent the winter at Aughwick still trying to foster the latent English sympathies of his colony of dispossessed Delaware and Mingo. The Pennsylvania assembly continued to object to aiding him meet the expense of their upkeep, professing to attach little importance to the drift of Indian opinion. Croghan, even more clearly than Franklin, appreciated the deadliness of the French threat. Seeing in Braddock the one last hope for the future safety of the frontier, he joined him with 50 pack horses and a restless band of his more loyal Indian protégés.

Braddock needed the horses more than he needed as many regiments and he also took a lively interest in the Indians. From the day on his way to Will's Creek that the shrouding forest had first begun to close in around him he had felt like a man in a tunnel. Nobody could see fifty yards in any direction. There were no local inhabitants to question. So far as any man could tell there might at any time be swarms of French and Indians within half a musket shot. He was much relieved, therefore, by the arrival of this encampment of friendly Indians. Their value as an addition to his fighting force did not impress him but he did realize their possible usefulness as spies to report to him on the activities of the French and enemy Indians. He visited the camp of his new allies, gave them presents, paid his earnest respects to their chiefs, and in general made much of them. These were the first genuine wild Indians his command had ever seen. For the Indians it was likewise their first sight of regular soldiers with their flags, tents, uniforms, and cannon. Both parties were fascinated. The army entertained the Indians with cannon salutes and massed fife and drum concerts while the Indians entertained in their turn with long and excessively exuberant war dances. Braddock valued Croghan's Indians the more highly in that he had been denied the promised help of the Southern Indians. After being attacked by Virginia frontiersmen while en route to join him those bands of Catawba and Cherokee had returned to their towns in angry disgust. Nevertheless, he was disturbed by the scandalous attentions paid by his officers to the women in the Indian camp so near his own. When he ordered the Indians to send their women home most of the Indian men, who may have been equally disturbed, went with them. Only eight Mingo who were personally devoted to Croghan remained to serve Braddock as scouts and messengers. They were enough to fulfill their mission. Throughout his march they kept him constantly informed of French dispositions and particularly of the failure of the French at Fort Duquesne to receive reinforcements. As evidence of how closely they watched, one of them just two days before the battle brought Braddock the scalp of a French officer that he had taken within a half mile of the French fort.

The prodigious task of building a road through the endless forest and up and down the craggy slopes slowed the army's westward advance to a mile or two a day. Washington's road had been little more than a pack trail. It had now to be widened and leveled for Braddock's heavier guns and wagons. The road and the sweating army which was making it inched onward over ridge after ridge, past the blackened ruins of Fort Necessity and Gist's Station. One circumstance lightened the backbreaking labor. In contrast to the deluges of the year before which had added so much to Washington's difficulties there this year was a welcome drought which kept the ground firm and the rivers easy to ford. Informed that Fort Duquesne's garrison had still not been strengthened, Braddock at Washington's suggestion left half of his army with his more cumbersome impedimenta behind under Colonel Thomas Dunbar while he himself on June 19th pushed on ahead with a flying column of 1200 picked men.

Meanwhile the excessively hot dry weather which had so much eased Braddock's progress had apparently doomed any hope to which Contrecoeur might formerly have clung. Toward the close of Washington's campaign the French army on the Ohio had swelled to a total of 2000, approximately equal to the force Braddock was bringing against it this year. But due to the extreme difficulty of supplying so isolated a post Contrecoeur had been left at Fort Duquesne with a winter garrison of but 80 regulars and 220 militiamen. These were still all he had even though the new campaign season was well under way. Stream levels had fallen so low that the portage route by which reinforcement could reach him from Canada had become impassable even to bark canoes. His small garrison could not possibly be expected to hold out for long against Braddock's powerful army and heavy artillery. The Ohio Indians who had been hanging about waiting to note which side might seem more likely to prevail were drifting away. Even the 500 more faithful western and Canadian Indians camped about the fort were becoming more and more uneasy. The inexorable English advance continued, each day bringing nearer the moment Contrecoeur must make the hard choice Washington had made at Fort Necessity.

Contrecoeur's second in command, however, was Captain Daniel Hyacinth de Beaujeu, scion of a military family distinguished since the 11th Century for its services to France and among whose forebears was a Grand Constable of France and a Grand Master of the Templars. Here in this far-distant wilderness among wild men on the bank of this wild river he was about to prove worthy of his illustrious name. Unwilling to submit to the apparently inevitable capitulation in prospect without first striking at least one blow, he asked permission to lead out a mixed force of volunteers, soldiers, militiamen, and Indians, to attempt an ambush of the English as they forded the Monongahela. Contrecoeur dubiously approved but the Indians upon whose numbers the project depended declined to lend themselves to so heedless an enterprise. For weeks they had been observing the English army during its steady advance over the mountains. They had noted its numbers, the unprecedented size of its cannon, and most of all the businesslike assurance that marked its every move. They were convinced that to risk an attack upon this so obviously superior force was merely to invite senseless loss. Beaujeu pressed his appeal through a day and a night without effect. At last he declared that if they would not go with him then he would go alone. The implied reflection upon their personal valor as warriors posed a challenge any Indian was constrained to accept. Whooping with sudden angry resolution they leaped up to accompany him. With soldiers, militiamen, and Indians streaming behind him in a wildly disordered throng Beaujeu started off at a run down the forest path leading to the Monongahela ford eight miles away.

But the hours lost in arguing with the Indians had made him too late. The English were already across the Monongahela and almost within sight of Duquesne. In order to avoid the deep ravine of Turtle Creek, which it was feared might offer the French and Indians an ambush opportunity, Braddock had ordered the river crossed above the creek's mouth and then again below it. Croghan and his Indian scouts determined the fords were unguarded and the army made its double crossing without incident. Duquesne was now so near that there was every expectation of reaching it before nightfall. The defenders' weakness was well known. So manifest was English superiority that it was taken for granted the fortress must yield upon demand. Today then was to be the day to reward all their immense exertions in traversing the mountains. So notable an event was one which Washington, as he had written his brother, "would not miss for five hundred pounds." He crawled from the wagon in which he had been bedridden with a fever for the last two weeks, and mounted his horse, with a pillow in the saddle to support him, to ride beside Braddock. Just beyond the ford was the cabin of John Fraser, the trader, in which he had taken refuge on his winter journey to deliver to the French the warning that had seemed then so hollow. Now he was back with a conquering army to justify that warning. The long, closely ordered column, preceded by Croghan and his watchful Indians,* by axmen to widen the way, and then by the vanguard of picked regulars and Virginians under Lieutenant Colonel Thomas Gage, resumed this short last lap of its long march on Duquesne. The trail, like all Indian paths, kept to high ground. On either side were brush-filled ravines. It was along this same path at this same moment that Beaujeu had started to run toward the river at the head of his motley pack of volunteers.

When the two forces met it was not Braddock but the French and Indians who were surprised. It was the English who first sighted their enemy and who were first to open fire. Gage's grenadiers got off a volley, the vanguard's two cannon were wheeled into action, and a charge was launched to clear the trail. Beaujeu, yelling and waving his hat, endeavored to urge on his followers. But most of the French militia had been so taken aback by this sudden and un-

---

* There were only seven of them now. The week before one had been shot in the back by an overly nervous English sentry.

expected sighting of the head of the English column that they fled to the refuge of the fort. The Indians dove into the cover of the forest on either side. Beaujeu was killed. The remaining French officers conceived the day to have been already hopelessly lost. But the Indians, comfortably aware that they could wriggle away safely through the forest whenever they chose, lingered in the tangled brush of the ravines to snipe at the English column in the open trail above.

It was then that the Indians made their fateful discovery. This great English army whose apparently irresistible march they had for weeks past watched with so much awe had of a sudden proved actually to be composed of incredibly foolish men who were ridiculously easy to kill. The essence of the Indian discovery was that every element of strength which made an 18th Century regular army formidable in the field, its iron discipline, its close-ordered formations, the controlled fire power of its volleys of musketry and batteries of artillery, became automatically transposed into so many elements of weakness when battle was joined in the forest. The Indian warrior scoffed at discipline and listened to his leaders only when he so elected but instinctively he was a skilled and adaptable fighting man. It took the Indians only a matter of minutes that day on the Monongahela to realize the full virtue of the tactic upon which they had stumbled. They could crouch, invisible, in their thicket and fire at will into the solid column of red-coated infantry standing before them in the open. The English soldiers could not get at their hidden enemy without plunging into the forest which they could not do without breaking formation which from the day of their enlistment they had been rigidly schooled never to do.

Innumerable English volleys of musket balls and rounds of cannon fire crashed into the woods. Not more than a score of the French and Indians chanced ever to be hit. But of the 73 English officers 48 were killed or wounded, of the 137 noncommissioned officers 91 fell. The army's total loss was 853, a casualty rate for that portion of the expedition present on the field of over 75 per cent. The slaughter lasted for three hours while the English continued to endure as helplessly as cattle being butchered in an enclosure. Finally Braddock, himself mortally wounded, ordered a retreat. The retirement became at once a rout. The Indians, fortunately for the survivors, did not pursue beyond the ford. They became preoccupied instead with collecting the loot of the battlefield and with tormenting those wounded who had been left behind. The dead remained unburied on that haunted field until their skeletons weathered away. After having fed on the slain the bears of the region were said to have become fiercer than other bears and from then on unafraid of man.

The dying Braddock was attended during his army's headlong flight by Washington and Croghan. His stern courage did not fail him even while the wagon in which they had placed him was jolting the life out of him. Almost his last words were: "We shall know better how to deal with them another time." He was buried in the center of the road in order to conceal the place from the enemy. His grave was within view of the ruins of Fort Necessity, making of the twin sites a stark joint reminder of the failure of the first two efforts to force the mountain barrier.

The terror of the survivors fleeing from the Monongahela was transmitted in redoubled measure to the other half of the army at the base camp. Though no man pursued, Dunbar, too, took flight. He spiked his cannon, burned his stores, dumped the groaning wounded into wagons, and scrambled frantically back over the mountains. He did not pause even after he had regained the Virginia frontier. Though his was the only organized military force in the middle colonies he rejected all appeals that he consider himself in any way responsible for the unprotected border. He continued his precipitate retreat to Philadelphia and then at a slower pace on to New York, so timing his movements as to keep his army completely out of action the remainder of that fearful year.

Thoughtful men such as Washington, Franklin, and Croghan had foreseen the potential danger inherent in the French lodgment on the Ohio. The French were there in a position to make their fort a rallying point for their Indian allies from which war parties, moving with their characteristic speed and secrecy, could in the next war cross the mountains at will. But no foreboding could have foreseen how terrible were to be the immediate consequences of Braddock's defeat and Dunbar's flight. Johnson still managed to hold most of the Iroquois to their traditional neutrality but every other Indian nation north of the Ohio lent itself to the French purpose. This was so utterly to terrorize the English frontier that any idea of its further westward extension must be forever abandoned. Those former fair-weather friends of the English, the Delaware and Shawnee, forgot their interest in English trade goods, remembered only their antipathy to English land seeking, and threw themselves into this enterprise with as much gusto as the wildest Huron or Ottawa from the farthest Lakes. In every Indian there was a burning consciousness that he was being steadily dispossessed of the land that had been his birthright. Whatever his outward professions of friendship, at heart he regarded the settler as his mortal enemy. In this sudden opportunity to punish that enemy there was for him a release of long pent-up emotions. It was an opportunity of which he took terrible advantage. That late summer and fall Indians filtered through the mountains in packs of twenty, fifty, or a hundred warriors. Wherever they emerged from the forest into the clearings they burned houses and barns, butchered livestock, men, women, and children with equal abandon, carried off captives by the hundred. A belt twenty to forty miles wide along the whole western border of Pennsylvania, Maryland, and Virginia was laid waste. The attacks ceased only with the first snowfall and were resumed with even greater ferocity the next year and the year after that.

The frontier upon which this appalling storm burst was unprepared to cope with the onslaught. The middle colonies had not known an Indian war for a generation. To the people on the border an attack by Indians was an entirely unfamiliar experience. Their first and overwhelming impulse was to flee, which they did in panic-stricken droves. The more resolute were engulfed in the general dismay. Upon provisional governments which had so recently declined to build in time the single fort on the Ohio which might have forestalled the French or to support Braddock with more than token appropriations, there now fell the crushing burden of building scores of forts and raising thousands of men. Virginia attempted hastily to expand her militia but a fighting force is not brought into existence merely by summoning men to answer a roll call. Virginia's commander-in-chief, Washington, spent the next three years in an agonizing effort to guard the province's northwestern border. Plagued by desertions, always short of men and supplies, it was a perpetually discouraging task. Indians continued to slip through his cordon of outlying forts to spread devastation far into the more settled regions. Pennsylvania's experience was even more painful. There many months passed before any governmental effort was made to defend her own borders. In the assembly there was a Quaker faction pacifistically disinclined to participate in any war and a political faction, led by Franklin himself, which was determined never to vote funds until the proprietors consented to being taxed like other citizens. While this dispute dragged stubbornly on, the people of the border were left to shift for themselves. They became so outraged by the failure of their own government to recognize responsibility for their fate that on one occasion they brought to Philadelphia a wagonload of their scorched and mutilated dead which they deposited in ghastly protest on the statehouse steps.

Croghan had suffered by intimate personal participation through three successive disasters in the west, first of his own private trading enterprise and then in his attempts to assist Washington's and Braddock's military efforts. But he now with undiminished resolution placed himself in the forefront of the frontier defense. He became a captain of border rangers, supervised the construction of frontier forts, and fortified and held for months his own house at Aughwick though it was situated forty miles west of the Susquehanna and was a special target of French and Indian attack. The Pennsylvania assembly became so conscious of the province's need for his services that it hastily passed an act shielding him from his creditors for a ten-year interval. Still, despite his great aid in the defense effort and the obvious fact that no one had suffered more from the French and therefore could have had greater reason to resent French success, he was widely suspected of working in the French interest. This suspicion was fed by the double supposition that being an Irishman he must be a Catholic and that being a trader he must be overfriendly to Indians. Both charges were baseless. Even had he been a Catholic there is no shred of evidence that American Catholics of the time were inclined in any way toward the Catholic French. Actually he was an Episcopalian, insofar as the circumstances of his life gave him opportunity to adhere to any faith. And, though he had many Indian friends, throughout his career he set white interests above Indian interests, frequently at cost to his own interests. But people behind the Pennsylvania-Virginia frontier had become hysterical and were repeating every sort of wild rumor. Even Washington was suspected, briefly, of French sympathies in that dreadful period after Braddock's defeat when settlers by the thousand were fleeing from hordes of savages, and there were lively fears for a while that a French-Indian army might sweep on to the gates of Philadelphia.

Disturbed by his fellow citizens' ingratitude, Croghan was glad to accept Johnson's invitation to consult with him in what might be done to salvage the wreck of England's Indian policy. Johnson had just been made a baronet and was the one authentic English hero the war had yet produced. On his recommendation Croghan was appointed Deputy Superintendent of Indian Affairs and given responsibility for the Indian problems of the Pennsylvania-Virginia frontier, where most of the Indians were hostile, while Johnson kept personal responsibility for the New York border, where most of the Indians were England's allies.

Johnson understood as did no other imperial official that to wean the nearer Indians from their French alliance had a place in the war effort as essential as the operations of fleets and armies. As long as the French capacity to furnish the Indians guns and gunpowder remained intact there was no way to halt their depredations. The deployment of fifty regiments along the border could not begin to guard all the points at which Indians could dart from the cover of the wilderness, spread pillage and murder for a day or two, and then withdraw ahead of any possible pursuit to disappear again into the wilderness. To contemplate the dispatch of armies against their towns hundreds of miles away beyond the mountains was to invite a multiplication of the difficulties that had destroyed Braddock. The one useful recourse was to strive to recapture Indian respect and regard.

Croghan embarked upon his share of this task with unremitting diligence and patience. The ensuing progressive defection of the Ohio Indians from their French attachment was largely his achievement. During Johnson's intermittent illnesses in 1757 and 1758 he assumed most of Johnson's duties as well, even to the extent of commanding Iroquois contingents in action. Iroquois regard for him was second only to their regard for Johnson. They had known him almost as long and as well. As early as 1746 they had made him an honorary member of their Supreme Council at Onondago.

Some notion of the range of his activities during this period may be gained by a glance at his movements in 1757 and 1758, the years in which England's fortunes in the war were making their slow turn from repetitive disaster to the first intimations of conceivable victory. In 1757 he was holding Indian conferences in three different provinces, in March at Harris' Ferry, Pa., in May at Winchester, Va., and Lancaster, Pa., in July and August at Easton, Pa., and in September at Johnson Hall, N. Y. From January to June of 1758 he commanded Iroquois detachments guarding the New York frontier, in July he commanded Iroquois forces in Amherst's Ticonderoga campaign, and, Johnson having recovered enough to take over, the same month was rushed to Forbes in Pennsylvania, then preparing his advance on Fort Duquesne. His indispensable service to Forbes was his management of the great Easton conference in October at which French influence over the western Indians was so much weakened. At Easton Indian attention was finally gripped by England's promise, approved and confirmed by the English ministry, that the territory west of the mountains would be thereafter accepted as reserved for Indian use and occupancy and that any former land claims held by any American province were by the same token annulled. In November, before the ashes of the French fort had more than cooled, he was a hundred miles west of the Ohio urging a truce upon Indians upon whose hands English blood was still wet.

His responsibilities increased with English victories and the capitulation of Canada. In 1760 he was at Detroit assuring Indians who had never before known Englishmen except as enemies that while they were now English subjects they were soon to be better off than they had ever been before. At the greater and more formal Detroit conference the next year he and Johnson renewed the effort to impress this message upon the Indians.

But it was a hopeless task. Their words rang hollowly because their assurances had already been contradicted by English official actions. The glaring features of England's postwar Indian policy were already too apparent. The Indians wanted trade resumed and otherwise to be let alone. The actual English response which neither Johnson nor Croghan could adequately disguise was bruskly to deny both desires. After having spent so much to defeat the French the English government wished least of all to spend more to placate the Indians. Instead, trade was discouraged to deny them ammunition and garrisons were introduced to keep them quiet. The rigid economy imposed on Amherst by the cabinet as soon as the French were beaten made his reaction even more severe than it might otherwise have been. His personal program for handling the Indian problem was to give them nothing and meanwhile to keep them in order by military force. Traders were ordered to deal with them only at army posts, forcing more distant Indians to make long journeys to market their furs. The bestowal of ceremonial presents to keep their chiefs in good humor, a practice Amherst termed bribery but nevertheless one to which Indians had been accustomed for generations, was abruptly halted. Every separate phase of England's new Indian policy served to disappoint and affront the Indians. Croghan was dismayed. He could see what was coming. But to his every warning Amherst replied with another reprimand. Croghan's expense accounts were questioned so sharply that he was writing Johnson, "I can say now I serve the King for nothing," and to Bouquet, "I don't chuse to be beging eternally for such necessarys as is wanted to carry on the service." He asked to resign but Amherst declined even to sanction that.

For all his presentiments and warnings of a new Indian war the news of the actual explosion took him as much by surprise as it did Bouquet or Amherst. While he had known it was coming he had not detected any indications that it would come so soon and he had not foreseen Pontiac's amazingly swift success in organizing the Indian effort. But now that it had come he realized all too well how much more was coming. Again there were to be the massacre and expulsion of the traders, again the swarms of marauding war parties descending upon the settlements, again the march of armies among the fearful hazards of war in the wilderness. All the intolerable miseries of the last ten years were soon to be repeated. Throughout those years he had striven with all the strength that was in him to bring about some kind of endurable balance between the white and Indian worlds. All he had tried to do had so soon come to nothing. He was discouraged. But not for long. He was not a man ever to be discouraged for long. Active as had been his life so far, still greater enterprises and services were yet ahead.

V

ℰ

Bouquet

BUT ONE MILITARY COMMANDER in history has had at once the capacity and the opportunity to become a master of the art of war as it was practiced at its uttermost extremes on the conventionalized checkerboard of 18th Century Europe's open fields and in the shadowed depths of 18th Century America's tangled forests. Only Henry Bouquet was still able, after having been thoroughly schooled in the one, fully to grasp the principle that the classic tactics there proved essential to success were the very ones certain to invite disaster in the other.

There were two quite dissimilar types of wilderness campaigns. The first was the convulsive and relatively impromptu reaction of a white border that had suffered beyond endurance from Indian inroads. A body of border militia or of informally assembled settlers made a sudden dash across the frontier to attack an Indian town and burn its storehouses. Surprise was always sought and the sole purpose was to punish a specific Indian community for recent outrages. Due to their perpetual need to hunt, the warriors of the threatened locality more often than not were widely scattered. By the time the defenders had reassembled, the intruders were dashing back to the shelter of the white side of the frontier. These hit-and-run raids, repeated year after year and generation after generation until sheer familiarity with the procedure gave it the standing of an established custom, had no more lasting effect than the similar and much more numerous Indian raids on the white settlements. The other type of campaign, of enormously greater risk and significance, was a prepared and calculated bid for a decision. This was the undertaking of an organized military expedition under a responsible commander to advance into strategically sensitive territory which Indians must defend, with the deliberate purpose not of achieving surprise or of avoiding battle but of forcing Indians to accept battle in order to break their will to continue the war.

In the 1754-94 span of Indian wars, before Indian military power had become so overmatched as to make the inter-racial conflict no contest, eleven such decision-seeking expeditions were launched, seven under English commanders and the last four under American. Bouquet led two, both of which were military successes. Of Grant's two, one was an agonizing disaster and the other a punitive operation conducted after his Cherokee antagonists ran out of ammunition. Braddock and Dalyell were routed and Montgomery repulsed. Of the four American commanders, who, of course, were not handicapped in advance by extensive European training, Harmar was outgeneraled and outfought, St. Clair suffered a defeat more disastrous than had been Braddock's, Sullivan won a battle but failed to gain his assigned objective, and only Wayne, after three years of patient preparation, pressed on to a permanent and decisive victory.*

It is in the light of these realities of the world in which he moved that we can observe how boldly Bouquet stood out among his contemporaries. Very many years were to pass before Indian power was to become so enfeebled that Indians must flee at the first sound of

---

* The hard fought Battle of Point Pleasant between Lewis' Virginia militia and the Shawnee might conceivably be added to this list of major engagements but if so it should be recognized that this was a somewhat special case. The Virginians were not a formally organized army and the engagement was forced on a single Indian nation which had previously been deprived of the support of its natural allies by Iroquois co-operation with white interests.

trumpets announcing the approach of regulars to the rescue. In Bouquet's time it was the regulars themselves who more often required rescue. His success sprang first from personal qualities which enabled him to hold, at times of mortal stress, the trust of his men and the confidence of his officers and, after that, from a store of native intelligence which enabled him precisely to appreciate how different was war in the woods from war by the book.

His background was that of a professional soldier in the truest sense of the term in an age when the mercenary who sold his sword to a foreign power was commonly regarded as a more honorable figure than the native-born officer who was expected to buy preferment. His military schooling began early and continued through a dozen campaigns on two continents under circumstances that varied as much as did the shores of the Mediterranean, the Rhine, and the Ohio. In each he served with a distinction that earned him repeated promotion.

Bouquet was born in 1719 in the placid atmosphere, so much in contrast to the violence marking the most of his later life, of the village of Rolle, overlooking Switzerland's Lake Geneva. Adopting the career so often chosen by his young countrymen through the centuries before they found opening to them the more profitable callings of banker, chocolate maker, and hotelkeeper, at the age of seventeen he enlisted in the Dutch Republic's Regiment of Constant. His first advancement came quickly. Two years later he was commissioned ensign in the Sardinian army by that shrewd judge of military promise, Emmanuel III. The ensuing War of Austrian Succession, during which for eight years the armies of Austria, England, Russia, Holland, Saxony, and Sardinia marched, countermarched, and engaged in battle with the opposing armies of France, Prussia, Spain, and Bavaria, provided the young soldier with ample opportunity to learn his trade. When the war had ended he returned to the service of Holland as a lieutenant colonel of Swiss Guards.

In 1756 the English government, beginning uneasily to anticipate the demands of the war in America, determined to raise in the provinces a regiment of regulars to be known as the Royal Americans. A large proportion of the sort of recruits considered most amenable to discipline was to be found in the communities of recent German immigrants. Since few of them spoke English, a need for German-speaking officers was indicated. Bouquet accepted one of these commissions, becoming lieutenant colonel of the new regiment. Its nominal colonel, the Duke of Cumberland, who was campaigning on the continent, never saw his regiment. Bouquet, then 37, became its senior officer in America and field commander of one of its four battalions.

Arriving in Philadelphia in the fall of 1756 he entered upon a scene darkened by three successive years of English frustration and defeat. The war that was never to become a real war upon which the Newcastle ministry had so blithely embarked had developed into a most bitterly real conflict which by now had been formally recognized by the declarations of both nations. Shirley had been superseded as commander-in-chief in America by Colonel Daniel Webb, then by General James Abercrombie, and then by Lord Loudon, but these hasty shifts of responsibility had not served to instill new vitality into the English war effort. Montcalm, the new French commander in Canada, had, on the other hand, already begun to demonstrate a military talent that marked him as a great captain. The English designs upon Crown Point, Niagara, and Duquesne formerly contemplated by Braddock and Shirley had come to nothing and instead it was the French who had taken the offensive. Growing Iroquois doubt of English military prowess, already aroused by Braddock's defeat, had been strengthened by the French seizure of Fort Bull, guarding the all-important Mohawk-Ontario portage, followed by the stupefying blow to New York's frontier defense of Montcalm's capture of Oswego, the English fortress and naval base on Lake Ontario. New York's catastrophic fear that the calculating Iroquois might be preparing to follow the Ohio Indians into the French camp had been lent a final grim urgency by the support given Montcalm's attack on Oswego by some hundreds of Seneca.

The past year had meanwhile seen the desperate defenders of the Virginia-Pennsylvania border so hard pressed that hundreds of Southern Indians had been imported as mercenaries in the hope that their native woodcraft and mobility and their firsthand acquaintance with Indian tactics might make them more successful in resisting the inroads of the French Indians than had been the provincial militia. The unabated distress of the province's own inhabitants had still failed to stir the Pennsylvania assembly to take more than the most narrowly defensive view of the situation. Pennsylvania's refusal to support the general war effort had made the province so doubtful an operations base that no new stroke against Duquesne had been considered and after Dunbar's flight but a single battalion of regular troops was allocated to all of Pennsylvania and Virginia.

The prolonged horror inflicted upon the middle border had terrified the southern provinces where people feared they might be the next to suffer French and Indian attack. The ministry took a sufficiently serious view of these southern fears to hasten forces to the rescue. In early 1757 Lieutenant Colonel Archibald Montgomery with 1000 Royal Highlanders sailed directly from England to Charleston and Bouquet was moved south with his battalion of Royal Americans plus 200 Virginia militia. As it developed there was no need for the troops which could have been much more usefully employed in more critical theaters. The Cherokee had already backed their protestations of friendship by asking for the establishment of an English fort on the western side of the mountains to protect them from French aggression. This appeal received a readier response than had the similar request of the Ohio Indians in 1753. Fort Loudon was built and garrisoned at a site on the Little Tennessee roughly comparable in geographical and strategic importance in the south to the Forks of the Ohio in the north.

By the spring of 1758, however, the great Pitt's return to power had begun to excite that astounding world-wide explosion of English energy that has made his administration forever memorable. The dismal record of English arms in America had drawn his particular attention. He was resolved, above all else, upon establishing English supremacy there. His two principal American projects for 1758 were to be an attack on the French seagate to Canada at Louisburg and a drive northward from the Hudson by way of Lake George and Lake Champlain against the French center on the St.

Lawrence. Yet at the same time the endless torment of the middle border demanded relief. The Pennsylvania assembly had at last been convinced of the necessity of coming to grips with the war and was ready to vote supplies and troops on a scale to make the province available as a base of operations. Virginia had agreed to raise Washington's regiment to full strength and to add another. It had long been obvious that the one adequate defense against the ubiquitous Indian raiding parties was to extirpate the French supply center at Fort Duquesne from which they sprang. This meant a third attempt to force the fateful mountain barrier which had confounded Washington and Braddock. With the same unerring perception with which he had selected Wolfe and Amherst, Pitt assigned command of this formidable undertaking to the young Scotch brigadier, John Forbes, an ex-medical student who, as he was shortly to demonstrate, was also a most apt student of the science of war.

In early April he arrived in Philadelphia armed with nothing but the copy of his directive in his pocket. The army with which he was to carry it out was still about as widely scattered as it was possible for one to be at the opening of a campaign season. Later in April Bouquet disembarked in New York and marched his battalion to Lancaster. But it was not until June 7th that Montgomery's Highlanders who were to provide the backbone of regulars for the army arrived from South Carolina and not until June 14th that Forbes' stores and artillery arrived from England. It was the middle of July before Washington and his Virginia regiment reached Fort Cumberland on the Potomac, while the Pennsylvanians, with their lesser military experience, were involved in even longer delays. Bouquet had meanwhile pushed westward to Raystown over the road laid out by Croghan in the spring of 1755 and there had established Fort Bedford as a first advance base. Forbes' army when at last assembled was to number more than 6000 men, with Bouquet commanding the First Division and Washington the Second. It was a force so strong that it must surely crush French resistance once it had reached the Ohio. But it was also so large an army that to get it over the mountains, and keep it supplied during the operation, presented a nearly superhuman task.

From the outset it was this attack on the mountain barrier, far more than any eventual attack on the French, that necessarily absorbed Forbes' attention. Since the mountains must somewhere be crossed the great question was where. Should the army drop south forty miles from Fort Bedford to Fort Cumberland and there take the road formerly built by Washington and Braddock? Or should a new more direct road be cut straight westward over the ridges along the old Indian route used by the Pennsylvania traders? Consequences infinitely more important than the outcome of his campaign hung upon Forbes' decision, for it was to provide the first great impulse to the westward movement. It was a difficult choice at best and provincial prejudice made it more difficult. Pennsylvania was at last beginning to sense the advantage of inheriting at the end of the war a fine military road leading to the west while Virginia was incensed by the proposal that the existing Virginia road which was so completely a product of Virginia's original initiative should now be given a rival under the guise of serving the war effort. The argument was embittered by charges that regard for Ohio Company interests underlay Virginia's insistence and countercharges that new road advocates were catering to Philadelphia merchants.

Forbes, still back at Philadelphia occupied with army organization, relied heavily on the advice of Bouquet at the advance base. As a professional soldier Bouquet favored the shorter more direct route if the cutting of a new road could be proved feasible. The reports of his reconnoitering parties inclined him each day more firmly to feel that it might be. Washington was the vigorous and outspoken advocate of the Virginia point of view. He proclaimed it positive idiocy to waste months building a new road when there already existed a road which had already been proved usable by an army. Bouquet argued that the shorter road offered military advantages worth almost any effort and that Braddock's Road swung back and forth across rivers that unseasonable storms could make impassable. Washington replied that building a new road would so delay the army's advance that it would find itself still many miles from Fort Duquesne when autumn rains made all roads impassable.

The seriousness of the subject and the earnestness of the debate heated tempers. Forbes was writing to Bouquet that Washingtons' "Behavior about the roads was in no ways like a soldier." And Washington was writing Governor Fauquier of Virginia, "the Pennsylvanians, whose present as well as future interest it was to have the expedition conducted through their government, because it secures their frontiers at present and their trade hereafter . . . had prejudiced the General absolutely against the old road." There is nothing, however, in the complete record of the Forbes-Bouquet correspondence to suggest that either was actuated by any other than purely military considerations. And Washington, after losing the argument, proved his unselfishness by serving under Forbes' command to the end of the campaign with the most dedicated loyalty and devotion.

While this road dispute was boiling Forbes was prostrated by an attack of dysentery from which he was never to recover and which prevented him from making a personal inspection of the forward situation. Accepting Bouquet's views, in late July he made his final decision and issued from his sickbed the order to undertake the new road. On August 1, 1758, Bouquet began cutting a wagon road up the forested, rockbound face of the main Allegheny Ridge and on over the even more forbidding heights of Laurel Mountain beyond. This was one of the great dates in American history. Only an army under the pressures of wartime could have underwritten the stupendous cost and labor of constucting such a road. Not in the foreseeable future could it have been undertaken by private initiative or the resources of a single province. There was to be no need to wait for a distant future to make the overwhelming significance of the new road apparent. It was just ten years later that the existence of two roads over the mountains, one from Virginia and the other from Pennsylvania, was to provide those twin routes which permitted the sudden competitive rush of settlers from both provinces that assured American possession of the upper Ohio during the Revolution. Braddock's Road and Forbes' Road were made avenues of empire by the rolling wheels not of gun carriages but of movers' wagons.

With all the materials, numbers, and discipline at the command
of an army the task of constructing the new road over the mountains proved as prolonged a task as Washington had prophesied. It
was early September, with the campaign season already nearing an
end, before Laurel Hill was surmounted and, in the narrow valley
beyond, a new forward base established which the English then
called Loyalhannon and afterward Fort Ligonier. During August
Washington had continued to clear Braddock's Road and to make
demonstrations in that area in order to persuade the French that
that was still the projected route of advance for the English army
but now he joined Bouquet at Loyalhannon and took charge of the
road building west from there. There were only the gentler slopes
of Chestnut Ridge remaining to be crossed before the final approach
to Duquesne. The French had been so taken in by Washington's
August maneuvers that they still regarded the new road building
as a feint and were still concentrating their defensive dispositions
along the old road. But the time was at hand when they must become aware of actual English intentions and then this army must
be subjected to that same violence of French-Indian reaction that
had ruined Washington and Braddock. When the blow fell it
proved every bit as terrifying and very nearly as ruinous.

Forbes was still confined to his sickbed and had not yet reached
Bedford. Bouquet was therefore in field command of the active portion of the army centered at Loyalhannon. Major James Grant, commanding an advance force of 800 Highlanders and Virginians
covering the detachment cutting the road on west from Loyalhannon, sent back word that there was no visible enemy between him
and the fort. He requested permission to try a night approach on
the chance that a sudden thrust at dawn might take the French so
much by surprise that the fort itself might be seized. Reluctant to
deprive a fellow officer of his bid for glory, Bouquet assented.
Grant, after making confident and complicated dispositions, was
set upon so suddenly and violently by French-led Indians at daybreak that his troops were thrown into immediate confusion and
then driven in headlong panic all the way back over Chestnut
Mountain to the refuge of the fortified base camp. Of his 800 men

nearly 300 were killed or taken. Both Grant and his second in command, Major Andrew Lewis, a Virginia officer later to achieve equally striking successes, were among the captured.

The blow that had fallen upon Grant fell almost as heavily upon the whole army's morale. Again in a first establishment of actual armed contact with the enemy the French and Indians had proved their military superiority in the wilderness. Grant had been no more able to cope with them than had Braddock. There had even been a repetition of the disorderly flight of panic-stricken survivors to the base camp. But Bouquet was not a Dunbar. There was no further flight. The fortifications of Loyalhannon were strengthened, a screen of reconnoitering parties kept on patrol in the forest, and the road building doggedly resumed behind breastworks to shield the working parties. The French, aware now of the main axis of English advance, took the initiative. A strong force under Charles Aubry, Governor of the Illinois, made determined attacks on the road builders and on the outworks of Loyalhannon. The attackers succeeded in killing, wounding or taking another 60 Englishmen and claimed another victory. But it was the onset of torrential autumn rains more than the French attacks that put an end to the road building. There was little use cutting new miles of road when every mile already opened was hub deep in mud.

Forbes, swinging painfully in his horse litter, reached Loyalhannon on November 3rd to hold a finally decisive council of war. During the late summer he had not been too perturbed by the delays in his army's westward progress. He had sound reasons for concluding that every postponement of the ultimate battle for Duquesne embarrassed the French defense more than the English offense. His slowly lengthening road with the intermediate forts and magazines established along it furnished him that adequate supply required by an army while the French were distracted by a precarious supply line which furthermore had in late August been completely interrupted by Colonel John Bradstreet's naval raid on their intermediate base at Frontenac. During these same weeks of delay intricate Indian negotiations being conducted by Croghan and Christian Post, the heroic Moravian missionary, culminating in the great Easton conference, were loosening the French hold on the Ohio Indians. All this combined to give Forbes confidence that time was working more for him than for the French. What he had not contemplated, however, was the loss of so much time that there could be no battle at all. It was this specter of total failure that confronted him at Loyalhannon. The rains continued, transport was bogged down with half the army still at Bedford, and there could be no other conclusion than that the campaign season was over. Washington's warning that the delays inseparably connected with building a new road would inevitably preclude an approach to Duquesne that year had been completely justified. Upon the afflicted general was forced the grim decision to go into winter quarters and wait for another year. His one basic accomplishment had been the establishment of a strong base on the French side of the mountain barrier. To point up the importance of this achievement he wrote Pitt that he had named the new English position on the Loyalhanna "Pittsborough."

Forbes had no way yet of guessing that depressing as was the English situation that of the French was still more critical. During the summer the defenders of Duquesne had numbered more than 3000. But after the defeat of Grant many of their Indians had conceived the English to have been as totally defeated as had been Braddock and they had scattered to their distant towns to flaunt their trophies and celebrate their victory. Others, particularly among the nearer Shawnee and Delaware, had been intrigued by the solemn English assurance in the Treaty of Easton that England would consider the country west of the mountains forever Indian and therefore saw less point than before in fighting for the French and against the English. But of more vital concern to the French even than these Indian defections had been the lack of food. Duquesne had always been difficult to keep stocked with supplies over the long portage route stretching across the lakes to Canada and after feeding so many Indians during the months of waiting for Forbes' slow advance there was not enough left to maintain more than a token garrison through the winter. Convinced that the rains had permanently halted the English advance most of the French forces

were withdrawn to more easily supplied posts on the lakes, leaving
to hold Duquesne only 200 men under Captain François de Ligneris,
the redoubtable, one-eyed hero of innumerable wilderness raids and
forays.

At this last moment chance took a hand to save the English and
ruin the French. Late on the rainy afternoon of November 12th a
French forest patrol engaged in reconnoitering the English camp
was jumped by two English patrols. In the ensuing brief skirmish
a number of French prisoners were taken. But, confused in the
dusk, the English patrols also fired upon each other. Washington
was caught in the cross fire. Of all his narrow escapes from death
during these wilderness years he himself always described this as
his narrowest. The prize gained, however, was worth even a risk
of such historic proportions. Among the French prisoners was an
Englishman captured years before by Indians. He revealed to his
countrymen the extreme weakness of the garrison left to hold Duquesne.

The pall of depression hanging over the English army was dispelled by a new burst of enthusiasm. The rains ceased and more
troops could be brought over the mountains from Bedford. Washington with 2500 picked men advanced rapidly on Duquesne, clearing the trail but not pausing to make a road. The army, following,
left its heavy transport behind. On the night of November 24th
Washington camped on Turtle Creek almost within sight of those
dreadful thickets from which three years before he had carried the
dying Braddock. During the night there began to echo through the
forest the rumble of explosions from the direction of the French
fort. Unable, with his tiny garrison, to resist the onset of the English army, Ligneris was burning and abandoning Fort Duquesne.

The next morning the English marched in. In taking unopposed
possession of the smoking embers of the French fort they were taking possession of the key to the west for their country and for the
new country soon to be. The skeletons over which they stepped in
crossing Braddock's field had offered macabre testimony to the
nature of the wild forces over which they had prevailed and there
was more such testimony as they passed through the abandoned

Indian encampments about the site of the French fort. There they were unable to avert their eyes from the terrible array of stakes, each grotesquely swathed with kilts and topped by the head of one of Grant's Highlanders. On the next day the army held a thanksgiving service. On the day after that Forbes wrote a second and better remembered letter to Pitt, notifying the great minister that he had taken the liberty of giving this newest outpost of empire the name "Pittsbourgh."

The commanders who had supported each other so well in achieving this success were soon separated. Bouquet remained to assume command west of the mountains and to begin the construction of Fort Pitt. Washington, after his five desperate years of devotion to border defense, returned to Virginia to marry Martha Custis and to retire from soldiering for the next seventeen years. Forbes, failing rapidly, was borne eastward in his litter, racked by constant pain from which he was intermittently relieved by periods of coma. In early March he died in Philadelphia. He had been welcomed there as a public hero. People imagined that his campaign had forever ended the danger of Indian attack upon their border. Of this they were soon to be most brutally disillusioned and the proposal to build him a monument was even sooner forgotten. But his greater monument was his road. For years to come other armies were to use it until the last one, Wayne's, marched over it to win the final victory in the war for the west.

Bouquet, like so many others before and after him, was deeply stirred by his first view of the Forks of the Ohio. On the very day of the army's arrival, November 25, 1758, he was writing Anne Willing, the Philadelphia Quaker girl to whom he was affianced, attempting to give her "a more particular account of what may deserve your curiosity, chiefly about the beauty of this situation which appears to me beyond my description." It was as well he appreciated the splendor of his wild surroundings for here he was to suffer many trials, tribulations, and heart burnings. Not the least of these was the demand presently made on him by his "dearest Anne." She harbored ethical objections to war and made his withdrawal from the army a necessary preliminary to their marriage. His profession had been too long a part of him for him to consider such a break and he felt obliged most regretfully to refuse. He was often uncomfortable in the English service and several times thought of resigning from it but to have done so would merely have meant his returning to some other nation's service in Europe. He was a professional soldier, first and last, who could have been satisfied in no other career.

At Fort Pitt he proceeded, with Croghan's help, with the negotiated pacification of the Ohio Indians and with the occupation of the former French posts at Venango, Le Boeuf, and Presqu'Isle. And it was here that he entered upon his duties as a principal gatekeeper, charged with the responsibility for keeping the peace along the line of demarcation between white men and red that existed as definitely then as after its official definition by the king's Proclamation five years later. By the Treaty of Easton, eagerly negotiated by the English while Forbes' army was marching over the mountains, all land west of the mountains was barred to settlers and reserved for Indians. The hope that this promise might deprive the French of at least some of their Indian allies had been fulfilled. At later Indian conferences at Fort Pitt the English promise was repeated and reaffirmed. It had become established doctrine, approved by the commander-in-chief, that enforcement of the treaty was an army responsibility. The army, officers and men alike, also approved and with ample reason. The appearance of settlers always stirred up the Indians and when the Indians were stirred up it was the army that had to fight them. A most sensible first step, therefore, was to keep the settlers out.

At the time few ordinary settlers were disposed to risk crossing the mountains to look for land in the Indian country. The savage excesses of the recent war were still too fresh a recollection. A number of families were permitted by special arrangement with the army to settle about Fort Ligonier and Fort Pitt to raise food for the garrisons in the shadow of the posts where they could be sure of protection. Aside from these miniature colonies the so recently ravaged white frontier was still two hundred wilderness miles to the east. But even in these first years after the planting of the English flag on the Ohio, while the French War was not yet formally ended and Indian peace remained most uncertain, there came the first stirrings revealing the birth on that frontier of a new spirit, the first faint portents of what was to come. There was beginning here and there to appear another kind of settler who was far from ordinary. There were not many of them yet. But to these hardy and aggressive few the risks west of the mountains were less dismaying than inviting. They began trickling over the mountains from Virginia and westward along the wooded banks of the Monongahela. Bouquet ordered them out. They kept coming back. They maintained that they were only hunters but they blazed trees to mark land claims, cleared patches for corn, and some of them even built log huts. The Indians, indignant that the treaties had so soon been breached, protested to Bouquet. He protested to Governor Fauquier about the trespasses of these "vagabonds" as he called them. Still they kept coming back. In October of 1761 Bouquet declared in a formal proclamation "this is therefore to forbid any of His Majesty's subjects to settle or hunt west of the Allegheny Mountains on any pretense whatever." He sent soldiers to drive them off. The Virginia intruders were as woods-wise as Indians and as hard to run down but some of their horses were taken and all of their log huts burned.

To such tedious tasks as dragooning illegal settlers, regulating irresponsible traders, and conferring endlessly with increasingly dissatisfied Indians Bouquet devoted the next five years. Discouraged by the continuing lack of military opportunity and depressed by the news of Anne's sudden marriage, he for a time contemplated withdrawing from the service. In the spring of 1763 he went to New York to confer with Amherst who managed to persuade him at least to postpone his resignation. He was in Philadelphia, where he had landed in the new world just seven years before, still pondering the bleakness of his personal and professional situation, when he received the stunning news of the outbreak of Pontiac's War. In comparison to the demands now awaiting him he had so far served only his apprenticeship in wilderness warfare. The great test to determine whether the apprentice had become a master was now upon him.

VI

༂

Johnson

WILLIAM JOHNSON'S ADVENTURES were so varied, his achievements so unusual, and his personality so striking that we may wonder that he has not been more vividly remembered. It could be that the very plainness of his name has contributed to his having seemed a less dramatic figure than many of his lesser contemporaries who have remained schoolbook heroes. The name William Johnson has after all a rather more prosaic sound than Israel Putnam, Ethan Allen, Molly Pitcher, or Daniel Boone. Actually his family name had originally been McShane. The story of his remarkable exploits might quite probably have been much more often told and retold had they been the feats of Bill McShane.

Moreover, his was the kind of story for which we have a particular weakness. The success story has always held a unique place in American regard, possibly in part because uncommon success has marked our career as a people. Among all success stories the circumstantial recital of a poor boy's rise to riches has been the most durable favorite. Scarcely less absorbing has been every account of a country boy's success in circumventing the designs of a more sophisticated competitor. Probably next in appeal has been the saga so often repeated that the protagonist has become a folk hero, describing the feats of the young man who takes to the wilderness, whether forest, river, plains, or mountains, and there proves by his innate skill and resolution his capacity to rise to the most unfamiliar and fearful demands. Finally, like all people, we hunger to be told about the successes of our military heroes, though these stories have only won our truly rapt attention when the victor is an amateur commander whose advantage has been gained at the expense of professional rivals, whether allies or enemies. All these favorite American success stories have one element in common. We pay our sincerest tribute to the nonconforming individualist whose success has been achieved while disregarding accepted conventions and precedents.

Johnson's career fulfilled within the compass of a single man's accomplishments every most meticulous demand of all four of these success stories. He arrived a penniless immigrant youth and in a few short years had made himself the richest man in the colonies. While still a backwoods farmer who traded with Indians on the side he was proving himself able to outwit and outmaneuver city merchants, royal governors, and French agents. Coming directly from a European background that had provided him no slightest preparation for the frontier's peculiar demands, he took to the wilderness so successfully that he was presently able to make himself uncrowned king of the most powerful of all Indian nations. Entirely without formal military training, he electrified his countrymen by winning battles while his fellow commanders, England's foremost generals, were continuing to encounter frustration and defeat. Perhaps even more remarkable, these major successes were not interspersed with minor failures. His desires and aspirations were varied and headlong but each he satisfied in turn and in full measure. Whatever it occurred to him to want, whether great or small, public or private, from a major general's commission to a new concubine, he got. In the course of achieving all this he profoundly affected the whole future of his adopted country. His is a success story to cap all success stories.

The impetuous young Irishman, just turning twenty-three, arrived in New York in 1738. The city then was relatively even younger than he, with a population of but 8945 whites and 1719 blacks. Later opportunities he was to make for himself but his first in the new world was waiting for him. His mother's brother, Commodore Peter Warren, soon to be knighted and made an admiral for his services at Louisburg, had married Susannah DeLancey, sister of New York's chief justice. Along with this American interest Warren had acquired an interest in American land. Warrensbush, as his grant was currently known, was a 14,000-acre tract of undeveloped frontier land in the Schoharie Valley 28 miles west of Albany. He offered his nephew employment as land agent with instructions to realize upon the estate's potential value by a program of alternate sale and settlement. Johnson happily accepted the offer and set out for the Mohawk Valley, the stage upon which in the years to come he was to play every conceivable sort of part except a small one.

A young man as bold and imaginatively ambitious as he could only have been intensely excited by that first journey up the magnificent Hudson. The fabulous American wilderness of which he had heard as long as he could remember was immediately before him. And he was approaching it at the very point where its dangers were the most threatening, its challenges the most dramatic. Over the New York frontier hung the implacable shadow of French dominion in Canada. France, England's immemorial enemy, was resolved to bar English advance on the upper Hudson. There were French forts as near as Crown Point on Lake Champlain and Niagara on Lake Ontario and in them Frenchmen waited for the opportunity that returned with each of the recurring wars between the two nations to unleash their savage allies upon the English settlements. The suspense generated by this perpetual French threat subjected the New York frontier to a strain such as was known by no other. Unlike the New England border, which also suffered cruelly from periodic French-Indian attack, it was not backed by the solid mass of a near and numerous population to underwrite its defense. The entire province of New York was little more than a precariously narrow beachhead of English lodgment thrust north-

ward along the still thickly wooded Hudson. By the census of the
year before Johnson's arrival its total non-Indian population
amounted to but 60,437 of which 8941 were Negroes. Albany, the
only established community on the upper river, had had white inhabitants for 125 years but they still numbered fewer than three
thousand.

An attribute of the New York frontier even more dramatic than
the proximity of the French was the proximity of the Iroquois. It is
difficult now to appreciate how profoundly impressed were the white
men of Johnson's time by the Iroquois. Innumerable legends and
stories clustered about the exploits of these redoubtable savages. The
first explicit accounts of their nature and habits had reached the
outer world a century before in the Jesuit Relations. That report on
the martyred missionaries who had essayed Iroquois conversion had
been a chronicle of horror and terror. Every later report had added
to Iroquois reputation for violence, cruelty, cunning, and sagacity.
The confederation was held together by a fascinatingly elaborate
fabric of clan relationships and political conventions that gave their
councils an atmosphere of ceremonial mystery. In international
negotiations they considered themselves, and with some reason, the
diplomatic equals of France and England. They represented a local
balance of power between the two rival world powers, realized that
they did, and took every advantage of the circumstance. Their favor
was well worth seeking for in 1738 they had enjoyed a century of
unparalleled military triumph. They had carried their trade war
conquests of competing Indian nations to the distance of the mountains of Carolina, the prairies of the Illinois, and the shores of Lake
Superior and they had ravaged the French settlements in Canada so
ferociously that in 1653 the French were at the point of abandoning
even Quebec. Their sudden peace offer to the despairing French
that year had been a matter of calculated policy. Rather than to
drive the French altogether from the St. Lawrence they had chosen
to keep them there as a counterweight to the other islands of white
power then represented by the Dutch on the Hudson, the English
on Massachusetts Bay, and the Swedes on the Delaware. This balance of power advantage they had since maintained and exploited.

They had kept every other Indian nation within a thousand miles of their New York strongholds trembling at their every frown while at the same time keeping France and England anxiously deferential to their every whim. In his first contacts with these Iroquois neighbors, therefore, the young Johnson was not encountering a tribe of simple and naïve natives but a nation of haughty warriors and domineering diplomats who were regarded by the white world of the time as the veritable Romans of the Indian world.

The white side of the New York frontier was not without a special character of its own. In its settlements were mingled a hodgepodge of Dutch, English, Germans, transplanted New Englanders, and semicivilized Indians who were in most respects as much on guard against each other as they were against the French. Along the Hudson were the immense holdings of the Dutch patroon class. New settlers seeking new land had been required to go beyond these huge grants to the edge of the Iroquois country in the lower Mohawk Valley. The Mohawk, the easternmost of the Six Nations, had occasionally been willing to sell land for a sufficient price. Iroquois dominion extended so far to the west and southwest that for a while these few narrow strips near the Hudson seemed to them of little consequence. They had as early as 1712 even allowed the planting of one German colony at German Flats, thirty miles west of the general white settlement line.

In this mingling of racial stocks along the New York frontier the Mohawk themselves provided the most picturesque element. Their intermittent readiness to sell land had inched the white frontier westward until the lower Mohawk castle, commonly called Fort Hunter after having been fortified for their benefit by white engineers, was well east of the white settlement line and their other two castles not far west of it. The Mohawk had formerly been the most aggressively warlike of all Iroquois when in the 17th Century they had been the terror of New France and the scourge of New England, but continued losses in war and from the diseases that had attended their long association with whites had much reduced their numbers. In 1738 they could field something less than 200 warriors. Contact with whites and the proceeds from land sales had also much adulterated their original way of life. Most dressed in white man's clothing, many spoke English, and some had been ostensibly converted to the English church, but they were still Indian enough to spend months of every year hunting as deep in the wilderness as the banks of the Ohio, to leap at every excuse to make war, and on all ceremonial occasions to intrigue their white neighbors by painting their faces and donning all of their most barbaric accouterments.

Johnson struck this remarkable and exotically hybrid frontier with something of the natural vigor of a cyclone. Fresh from Ireland and a stranger to all he was experiencing, he made himself immediately a part of it and soon thereafter its master. He attended to his uncle's business with such dispatch that within four years he had sold off or otherwise realized upon two thirds of the Warrensbush acreage and with capital contributed by his uncle had branched out into the Indian trade. But during these same four years he had so astutely invested his share of the proceeds that he was able to embark upon independent enterprises of his own. Despite his uncle's pained remonstrances he left Warrensbush and crossed the Mohawk to occupy land he had bought for himself. Here he built his first home, Mount Johnson, which was before long to be succeeded by the progressively more impressive establishments of Fort Johnson and then Johnson Hall. Though he continued to grasp at land until his holdings became a principality, he had recognized with his first look at the frontier, as had Croghan in Pennsylvania, his greater opportunity. Land was good and bound in time to become immensely valuable but in the meantime there was more immediate money to be made in the Indian trade. He threw himself into it with the vigor which marked his every undertaking. Other traders waited in Albany for the Indians to come to them. He took his goods to the Indians. His post at Oghwaga on the upper Susquehanna prospered and the year he moved to his own house he established another under the walls of the English fort at Oswego on Lake Ontario. Not only did he rapidly outdistance his Albany competitors but his profits soon enabled him to undertake the importation of Scotch-Irish families to become tenants on his Mount Johnson lands. Already he was beginning to flourish like the proverbial green bay tree.

For all the vigor and diligence with which he pursued material advantage his was not a temperament that could become completely absorbed in business. He was a whole and natural man with a nearly primeval lust for living and he was equally vigorous and diligent in the satisfaction of his every personal need and inclination. Toward the end of his first year on the Mohawk he bought a sixteen-year-old German bond girl, Catherine Weissenberg, from then on better known as Catty. She was his helpmate in the cottage at Warrensbush and then in the more pretentious stone house at Mount Johnson. By her he had three children, two daughters and the son who was to become Sir John Johnson. He was devoted to Catty when at home and married her on her deathbed in 1745 but his activities in the Indian country kept him often away from home. The same year Catty's first child was born a Mohawk girl whose name is not recorded bore him the first of his Indian sons. There ensued a very long succession of Indian offspring. It was commonly said on the frontier in his later years that the number had by then exceeded a hundred. Most of them were the products of passing relationships and the children remained members of their Indian mothers' families. But nine of them, resulting from more enduring attachments, were named in his will and to each of these he left money, farms, livestock, and other property.

Johnson's courting of Indian belles was but a lighter phase of the assiduity with which he courted the favor of the entire Iroquois nation. At his every encounter with Indians, whether it was a trading transaction, a social occasion, or a chance meeting, he sought to make them his friends. There was in him none of the average white man's aloof and supercilious assumption of racial superiority. Indians instantly sensed this and responded with equal good will. Before he had been at Warrensbush a full year or had had time to pick up more than a smattering of the Iroquois tongue, his Mohawk neighbors elected him war chief and gave him the wondrously sonorous name of Warraghiyagey. He had more difficulty with the more distant Iroquois and most of all with the westernmost, the Seneca, who were much influenced by their French neighbors at Niagara, but he persisted until he had eventually succeeded also with them. His native geniality, robust temperament, and earthy sense of humor made his way easier. His was the kind of outgiving nature Indians could understand. But he worked at it, too. He wrapped himself in their fantastic regalia, stamped through their dances, squatted by their fires, laughed at their jokes, humored their prejudices, sat with respectful patience through the interminable tedium of their councils, joined cheerfully in their even more tedious carouses, kept his house always open to them, showered them with presents. When Catty died he chose Iroquois women to take her place, first Caroline, niece of Hendrik, the great Mohawk sachem, and then the beauteous and soon famous Molly Brant. These two Indian semiprincesses he in turn publicly recognized as his official consort. Caroline's residence in his feudal household was comparatively brief but Molly, often called "the brown Lady Johnson," was his wife in all but name for 21 years, bore him eight children, and was the honored hostess presiding at a table at which the guests often included governors, generals, and peers of the realm.

The success with which he had developed his trading and social contacts with the Iroquois, which had already made his private fortune, was now about to make his public fortune. When in 1745 the War of Austrian Succession spread to America, where it was known to the English colonists as King George's War, the eyes of New York were immediately upon him. With the outbreak of war the French in the north had suddenly become an active menace threatening the survival of the Mohawk frontier. All depended upon the inclination of the Iroquois whose former hostility to the French had been diluted by their growing suspicion of the advancing English settlements. Were the Iroquois to side with the French the whole upper Hudson must inevitably be lost. It was in this crisis that Johnson strengthened his standing with the Mohawk by taking Caroline as his Iroquois wife, Catty having died the year before. The emergency speedily brought him to the attention of Admiral George Clinton, the irascibly strenuous new royal governor of New York. It did not take Clinton long to appreciate Johnson's value when he realized that it was Johnson who was able to report on French activities in the mysterious depths of the wilderness, Johnson who knew what was transpiring at the great Iroquois council fire at Onondaga, Johnson who could bring his fellow Mohawk chiefs to Albany to reaffirm their English alliance, Johnson who could spur Mohawk war parties into action in defense of the English frontier. He hastily appointed Johnson Commissary for Indian Affairs, then Colonel of the Six Nation Forces, and next gave him command of the Albany County militia.

The French-English competition for Iroquois favor during King George's War was touch and go for some time. Johnson had swept his Mohawks into the English camp but the other five nations of the confederation reserved decision or leaned toward the French. His great rival for Indian influence was Philipe de Joncaire, French agent to the Iroquois. Each offered a reward for the other's head and each dispatched trusted Indian retainers to undertake the other's capture or assassination. Johnson had known Indians but five years while Joncaire had lived among them since he was ten and had been preceded in the French Indian service by his father. The Seneca, the least friendly to the English of all Iroquois, were neighbors of the French at Niagara upon whom they much depended for trade. Joncaire, with the wisdom of his long experience, deluged the Seneca with presents, food, attention, and promises. Again and again they were reported on the verge of taking arms in the French cause. But in the end the only Iroquois to take sides were the Mohawk who had become active English partisans. The others remained neutral throughout the war and as a result the French hesitated to attack Oswego as did the English to attack Niagara, each fearing its aggressiveness might anger the Iroquois. This local stalemate was heartily welcomed by the local settlers.

Johnson's success in denying the French Iroquois aid was not gained without many difficulties and irritations. Early in the war the New York assembly, as was standard practice in every colony in those rigorous days, voted a bounty to be paid for the scalps of Frenchmen and enemy Indians. Johnson's Mohawk war parties came back with a number. The emergency having eased, the assembly refused to pay. It even refused to reimburse him for his personal expenditures in the course of his sustained effort to influence the

Iroquois. This was but another example of that obstinate parsimony so often exhibited by every colonial assembly. It was an attitude that for the next thirty supremely critical years infuriated English governors and generals and poisoned relations between mother country and colonies. In Johnson's case, however, the check, like most of his difficulties, worked to his actual advantage. In his indignation at this lack of appreciation of his services he resigned his post as Indian agent but in the meantime his quarrel with provincial authority had attracted much approving attention from imperial authority. He was appointed to the New York crown council and higher appointments were thereafter waiting for him.

Though he had turned back to his private affairs he continued to keep his finger on the wilderness pulse and in the process to become ever better prepared for the greater role he was to play in the far greater crisis that was developing. Soon he was repeatedly warning English authorities of the enormity of this impending crisis. He was the first to see that the French were preparing to occupy the Ohio and thus to set up a barrier to whatever future expansion west of the mountains the English might ever contemplate. In 1750 he was writing Governor Hamilton of Pennsylvania, warning him that the French were planning an expedition to develop the portages between Lake Erie and the Allegheny. In 1751 he was writing Hamilton again that the French were planning to attack the Pennsylvania traders' depot at Pickawillany on the Miami. In 1753 he was once more warning Hamilton that the French were now preparing actually to seize and fortify the Forks of the Ohio. Hamilton hastily got off an express to Virginia with this momentous news and Virginia thereupon dispatched the young Washington to demand French withdrawal. The Iroquois were excited by these portents of expanding conflict between their white neighbors and impressed by the vigor with which the French had made their reach for the Ohio. Johnson was forced to make ever greater exertions to persuade them to hold aloof.

These years which were made increasingly ominous by the gathering threat in the west offered Johnson one romantic interlude. Caroline was no longer in his house. Whether she had died, had been divorced by an Indian ceremony as simple as had been their Indian marriage, or had merely of her own volition returned to the lesser demands of her forest home, is not recorded. She had in the meantime given him a son, William of Canajoharie, whom he always regarded with affection and for whose education and endowment he made generous arrangements. Johnson was not a man, however, who could be content for long with the life of a bachelor. In 1753 he met the sixteen-year-old Molly Brant, daughter of a distinguished Mohawk family and older sister of Joseph Brant who was in the time to come to be tried by tests more harsh than any to which Johnson was ever subjected. According to the pleasant story current at the time, Johnson first saw Molly when she galloped past him on a spirited horse, her long black hair flying in the wind, and was at once so impressed by her charms that he carried her off that very day to Mount Johnson. In any event there can be no question that they lived most happily together to the day of his death.

The surrender of Washington at Fort Necessity in July of 1754 explosively revealed the proportions of the new danger on the Ohio. In this emergency the English cabinet, for all its bumbling ministers' ignorance of American realities, had grasped one fact. Now that the French-English frontier had been so much extended, were the nearer Indians to side with the French immeasurable calamities must ensue. Each province, as in the past, was still attempting to deal with the Indians on its borders without regard for any but its own immediate interests. This multiplicity of white representations had long bewildered and exasperated the Indians. The cabinet decided that continuation of a practice so perverse was intolerable in the present crisis. The colonies therefore were instructed to appoint commissioners to work out a form of unified control over Indian affairs.

The resulting Congress of Albany in 1754 represented one of the outstanding might-have-beens in all our history. Franklin, who dominated the political aspects of the congress, proposed a simple and feasible plan for united action among the colonies, not only with regard to Indians but in many other matters of common interest. The plan came to nothing, being regarded in England as granting too much power to the colonies and in the colonies as vesting too much power in the crown. Had Franklin's "unite or die" advice been followed the ensuing course of events leading inexorably to the Revolution must certainly have been vastly altered.

With respect to the primary purpose for which the congress had been called, the more sensible organization of Indian relations, another great opportunity was ignored. Johnson, who on account of his influence with the powerful Iroquois dominated the proceedings in this field, thought first of the Iroquois and the Iroquois as always thought only of themselves. They elected to pursue their cynical policy of selling land claimed by them on the basis of ancient conquest but which was actually used by other Indians. Just as they had formerly sold the original Delaware homeland east of the Susquehanna they now sold the whole expanse of wilderness between the Susquehanna and the Ohio. This was not only Shawnee and Delaware hunting grounds but included the area about the Forks of the Ohio in which the French were now firmly established and from which point of vantage they were now earnestly wooing the Ohio Indians. Shawnee and Delaware indignation at the Albany sale made it inevitable that they would yield to this French pressure and sooner or later take up arms against the English. Rectification of this Albany blunder was negotiated at the Treaty of Easton in 1758 and the redress of Ohio Indian grievances underlined by the King's Proclamation in 1763 but the damage had already been done. Thousands of settlers had meanwhile been killed and fires of hatred between settler and Indian had been kindled which were never to be extinguished.

The Newcastle cabinet, having clapped its uncertain hands to the American plow, now went on to run a furrow much less intelligible than the calling of the Albany congress. Determined to repel the French encroachment they proposed to undertake four simultaneous expeditions to eject the trespassers. One was to drive the French from the Ohio, two others to expel them from Niagara and Crown Point, and the fourth to clear them from the borders of Acadia. Braddock was dispatched to America to supervise these operations. The watching French, taking note of Braddock's embarkation, promptly assembled and got off to Canada six battalions drawn from some of France's oldest and most famous regiments. Formal war was still well in the future but meanwhile some remarkably bitter and deadly fighting was to take place. In our day we have coined the term "brush wars" for such impromptu conflicts. The one in 1755 was in terrible truth a brush war, as thousands of European soldiers struggling and dying in the depths of the American wilderness were most painfully to discover. Then, too, as we so actively fear may be the case today, the local and limited collison rapidly developed into a world war with fighting spread across four continents.

Braddock, arriving in Alexandria, dealt with his most nagging problem by appointing Johnson Superintendent of Indian Affairs with full authority and responsibility for all Indian relations in the principal theater of war on the borders of New England, New York, and Pennsylvania. He also announced the necessary orders for the four expeditions which the ministry had directed. He himself with his regulars would advance upon the Forks of the Ohio; Shirley, designated as his second in command in America, was to undertake the capture of Niagara; Lieutenant Colonel Robert Monckton was to deal with Acadia; and Johnson was given command of the attempt against Crown Point. Of the first three commanders even Shirley had had some military experience while Johnson had had none but it was felt that the probability of his being able to bring with him a contingent of fierce Iroquois warriors more than made up for this disadvantage.

The first three expeditions came to varying degrees of misfortune. Braddock suffered a defeat so devastating as to have become a military legend. Shirley, shackled by supply and transport difficulties, was unable to advance his expedition beyond his base camp at Oswego. Monckton, after ejecting the French at Beausejour as directed, became involved in that deportation of the Acadians celebrated in American tradition by Longfellow's poem, which, however rationalized by reference to local conditions, proved then no more than now an episode about which Englishmen could bravely cheer. Only Johnson provided pleasanter news in that dismal year. He got no nearer Crown Point than had Shirley to Niagara but, most happily for him and for England's current morale, he won a battle. This brief tumult of confusion and butchery on the forested shores of Lake George was not an important engagement except for its one great consequence. The sudden prestige Johnson gained that day was to establish him as the major single factor in every frontier development for the next twenty years.

His influence over the Iroquois had so far stood the strain. He had managed to restrain them from joining the headlong assaults of the western Indians upon the white frontier after Braddock's defeat. But in assuming command of an army he was meeting an array of demands as novel to him as he could have encountered when as a newly arrived young immigrant he had first peered into the depths of the Mohawk forest. In his recent rank as Colonel of New York militia his experience had been largely limited to scanning muster rolls or persuading Mohawk war parties to undertake scalp-hunting raids on the French. This was, moreover, not an army easy for anyone to command, composed as it was of some 300 totally undisciplined Mohawk and Oneida warriors and some 3000 scarcely more disciplined provincial militiamen, most of them New Englanders.

There was no serious friction at first. He signalized receipt of his temporary major general's commission by painting his face and participating in a war dance with his Indian companions-at-arms. His was a personality so colorfully unorthodox and so totally unfamiliar that for a time the New Englanders were almost as ready to accept him. In any event they were too preoccupied with disputes involving precedence among themselves to take vigorous issue with their commander. It was a most articulate army, its members endlessly writing long letters home enlarging upon their views on the campaign and particularly upon the lesser understanding of the situation being manifested by everyone in authority from corporal to general. It was also a most God-fearing army, devoting much of its time to earnest religious services. Some chaplains insisted upon assembling their puzzled Indian comrades to listen to long sermons which gave the hard-pressed interpreters exceptional difficulty. Transport and supply depended on arrangements made by five different provincial assemblies resulting in nerve-racking delay and confusion. Johnson was two months getting a portion of his army as far toward his objective as a temporary camp on the southern tip of the Lac du St. Sacrement which he hastily renamed Lake George. Realizing he had struck a happy note, he next named his two camps for King George's grandsons, Edward and William Henry.

Meanwhile the French, forewarned in detail of all English plans by the capture of Braddock's official papers, were heavily reinforcing Crown Point under the personal supervision of Baron Dieskau, commander-in-chief of the expeditionary force recently arrived from France. Dieskau, a veteran of many European campaigns and close friend of Marshall Saxe, was not impressed by what he had been able to learn of Johnson's army. A rabble of farmers and storekeepers led by an Indian trader did not seem to him to suggest very serious opposition and he determined himself to take the offensive. With a picked force of some 200 regulars and 1400 about evenly mixed Canadian militiamen and Indians he made a surprise descent of Lake Champlain by batteaux and canoes and crossed through the rock-studded forest to plant himself astride the road between Johnson's Lake George camp and his base camp on the Hudson. The Indians of Dieskau's forward screen became so absorbed in looting a passing supply train that some of the drivers escaped to report to Johnson the presence of what they described as a large war party on the road. Johnson ordered a mixed detachment of 500 militiamen and his own Indians to attack the enemy raiders before they had had a chance to withdraw. The more developed military instincts of Hendrick, the old Mohawk war chief, led him to protest the insufficiency of this force with the celebrated words which have made his comment one of the more pithy of all tactical maxims: "If they are to fight they are too few; if they are to die they are too many." Johnson insisted. The detachment was enveloped by the superior French force, 200 were killed, including the farsighted Hendrick, and the survivors driven in wild rout back upon Johnson's camp.

Had the pursuers followed the fugitives all the way into camp a catastrophe to rival Braddock's must have ensued. Dieskau's soldierly principles, however, got the better of him. He recalled his men and delayed the attack until their ranks could be reformed. The interval gave the unnerved defenders time to recover their wits. A low breastwork of logs and overturned carts and boats was improvised. The militiamen crouched behind it had been accustomed from childhood to the handling of the fowling pieces, muskets, and rifles with which they were armed. They were far from soldiers but they were men for whom it was second nature to take aim before pulling a trigger. The French assault was struck by a storm of bullets each one of which was directed toward some particular French officer or soldier. The Battle of Lake George presented an early example of that deadliness of aimed small-arms fire which was later to be so much more memorably signalized at Bunker Hill and New Orleans. Most of the white-uniformed French regulars were soon down. The French militia and Indians lost heart. The repulse became a retreat and when the English sprang in pursuit a panic-stricken flight. To add a final dramatic note to the triumph the twice-wounded Dieskau was captured. Johnson had great difficulty protecting him from the vengeful Mohawk who were determined to boil and eat him in retaliation for the death of Hendrick. In a noteworthy memoir on his campaign Dieskau later dwelt in much pungent detail on the bizarre variety of his personal experiences in the fantastic American wilderness that desperate day.

Johnson was shot through the thigh early in the action and much of the responsibility during the later phases of the battle fell upon his second in command, the Connecticut lawyer, Phineas Lyman. After the victory, Johnson, handicapped by his wound and by an eye inflammation, exhibited, aside from his failing to mention Lyman in his official report, little of his usual penchant for grasping at opportunity. The shattered French forces were not pursued beyond the first few miles and though the elated northern provinces rushed him reinforcements he made no move to resume his advance upon Crown Point. His unschooled military judgment may have been sounder than critics of the time were ready to admit for during the next three years far stronger English armies than his were to recoil in bloody confusion from the French Champlain defenses. It is more likely, however, that with the intuition with which he seemed always to recognize genuine opportunity he preferred to keep the luster of the success he had already won untarnished by any shadow of later failure.

When the campaign season had ended he visited New York, still hobbling from his wound, where he was received with wild popular acclaim. As in every war people were inordinately excited by a first victory. This impulse was even more apparent when the news reached England. After what had happened to Braddock there was some consolation in the defeat and capture of the French commander-in-chief. The government made all that could be made of the event, in part to confound the opposition. Johnson was knighted by the king and voted £5000 by parliament. At the early age of forty he had won fame. And it had come to him not in recognition of his proven talents for trading, developing frontier land, and managing Indians, but of his still unproven talent for commanding an army.

Fortune continued to favor him. Continuing twinges from his wound and recurrent bouts of ill health kept him largely inactive for the next three years. These were years of frustration and defeat in which Braddock's successors, Shirley, Webb, Abercrombie, and Loudon, were repeatedly outgeneraled and outfought by Dieskau's successor, the brilliant Montcalm. Johnson's health had relieved him from any considerable part in this dreary spectacle. When in the spring of 1759 he was able again to take the field his victory at Lake George was still the only land battle of the war so far won by the English. And there was now awaiting him the opportunity to demonstrate that Lake George had been no flash in the pan by winning a greater and far more decisive victory at Niagara.

The operation against Niagara in 1759 was a strategic imperative. Its capture would cut the French life line at its most critical point, divide the French in Canada from the French in the west, and demoralize French preparations to recapture Pittsburgh. Amherst, the iron-willed new commander-in-chief, selected Brigadier General John Prideaux to command the expedition, assigning to him two regiments of English regulars, a battalion of Royal Americans, and a considerable corps of provincials. Johnson was relied upon to attract Iroquois support and the importance of this duty was accentuated by his designation as second in command. For the last three years he had succeeded in keeping the Mohawk attached to the English and the rest of the Iroquois officially neutral. But more than neutrality was now required. The French defenders of Niagara could summon hordes of western Indians to their aid. The advance against Niagara could only proceed if it were reinforced by enough English Indians to counter the French Indians. The extreme vulnerability of regular troops when set upon by Indians in the depths of the wilderness had by now been indelibly impressed upon English commanders.

Johnson well realized how much was required of him. The Iroquois neutrality policy was dedicated to the maintenance of the balance of power. They had everything to lose if either France or England completely dominated the other. Upon Johnson fell responsibility for persuading them to violate this time-tested principle. It was a nearly impossible task but the emergency left him no choice. His twenty-year-long courtship of the Iroquois must now, if ever, reach the climax of marriage. At his great Canajoharie conference that spring Indian delegates listened to his endlessly repeated argument that their one sensible course was to join the English since the English, despite their many setbacks, were certain eventually to win the war. Between bouts of eating and drinking most of the delegates appeared, with varying degrees of reluctance, to agree. But unless Iroquois performance matched Iroquois promises the expedition must still be abandoned. The French and their Indian champions at Niagara redoubled their efforts to impress the Iroquois with the folly of taking the side of England against the rest of the Indian world.

When Prideaux' army of 2200 regulars and 3500 New York and Rhode Island provincials marched from his Schenectady camp early in May the issue was still in doubt. It was put to the ultimate test as the expedition began laboring over the portages between the Mohawk and the ashes of Oswego. Each day began then to bring new evidence that Johnson had succeeded. Pack after pack of Oneida and Onondaga and Cayuga were emerging from the forest to join his Mohawk. By the time the expedition embarked at Oswego to make its run along the Ontario shore his Indian contingent numbered 700.

When it had arrived before Niagara the Indian total had risen above 900, including some hundreds of the formerly pro-French Seneca. The long struggle for Iroquois allegiance had at last been won, as had Johnson's desperate personal duel with Joncaire.

The English army, its forest flanks guarded by Johnson's Indians, dug trenches, planted batteries, and invested the French fortress with formal siege lines. Then there came to Johnson another of those opportunities for which he seemed always to be ready. On the ninth day of the siege Prideaux was killed by a shell fragment from one of his own mortars. To Johnson's immediate assumption of command there was no objection from any of the regular officers present. This was an unprecedented expression of confidence. In the later years of the war the English regular establishment's scorn of provincial officers had become notorious.* The lowliest English subaltern was considered more fit to command than the highest ranking provincial. Washington himself had at last been so disgusted by the prejudice against American officers that he had resigned from the service and was spending this climactic summer of the war honeymooning at Mount Vernon. Some of Johnson's acceptance by these English colonels at Niagara may have been due to an appreciation of his control over the indispensable Iroquois but most of it was apparently due to a professional recognition of his capacity for leadership.

Captain François Pouchot, French commandant at Niagara, had been surprised by the swiftness of the English approach. He knew that his garrison of less than 500 could not hold out for long against the combined weight of English artillery and numbers. But he also knew succor was at hand. At Venango and Presqu'Isle Aubry had assembled a force of western Frenchmen and western Indians to undertake the recapture of Fort Pitt. His army already totaled a thousand Frenchmen and a thousand Indians and every new day new fleets of canoes from the west were adding to its strength. His

* As one example of this, Wolfe, in a letter to Lord George Sackville, wrote: "The Americans are in general the dirtiest, most contemptible cowardly dogs that you can conceive. There is no depending on them in action. They fall down dead in their own dirt and desert by battalions, officers and all. Such rascals as those are rather an encumbrance than any real strength to an army."

second in command was Ligneris, most famed of all French wilderness fighters, and with them was nearly every partisan leader who had led French and Indian attacks upon the English during this war and the last. These Frenchmen and Indians alike had come from the farthest reaches of the western wilderness in which they had been born and bred. Those who were white were scarcely to be distinguished from those who were red. They had grown up in Indian communities, lived by hunting, trapping, and trading, knew the wild forests, prairies, lakes, and rivers as other white men might know their native streets and fields. Many had Indian wives, others had had Indian mothers. They accepted Indians as their friends and brothers. To western Frenchmen and western Indians the immense western wilderness was their homeland. Had they known its future was about to be decided by their prowess in battle they would have welcomed the challenge. They would have entertained no slightest doubt of the outcome. They considered themselves invincible in their native forests. They had known the distant English, whether soldiers or settlers, only as the enemy and as the enemy over which they had always prevailed. Aside from their major triumps over Braddock and Grant they had been invariably the victors in any number of lesser engagements. Year after year they had made their descents upon the English settlements, spreading consternation wherever they appeared, killing or taking captives as they chose. When informed of Niagara's danger they immediately set off at all speed to the rescue, supremely confident that this new English army which had so rashly ventured so deep into the wilderness must fall as certain a prey as had its predecessors.

On the third day after he had assumed command Johnson was informed by his Iroquois scouts of Aubry's approach. The fate of Niagara was to depend not on a siege but on a battle. It was a crisis to test the most experienced commander. But observers saw in him now no signs of uncertainty. He made none of the mistakes he had made at Lake George. His dispositions were calm, calculated, and sufficient. Dividing his siege army, he left a covering force in the trenches and stationed a screen of regulars flanked by provincials behind a low breastwork across the portage road along which Aubry was advancing. So necessarily short a defense line could be swiftly and fatally enveloped by the French attack and to guard against this he placed his Iroquois in the woods flanking the road.

So confident were the French that they pressed on impetuously along the road and straight into Johnson's waiting trap. No blunders ever made by the English in forest warfare could have matched those made that day by these French and Indian veterans of many forest battles. To their left was the Niagara gorge but to their right was the forest and they made no effort to extend a covering force into it to guard their flank nor did they swing the weight of their main attack through the forest in order to come at the English under circumstances in which their own superior skill in bush fighting might have been expected to give them an advantage. Not only were they aware that numbers of Iroquois were in those woods on their right but in the last moments before battle was joined they had had a brief parley with them. But they remained convinced that the Iroquois had accompanied the English to Niagara only to eat English beef and drink English rum. They took it for granted that at the final moment when the Iroquois could no longer conceal their real intentions they would stand aside and gloat over the spectacle of Frenchmen and Englishmen further elevating Iroquois importance by endeavoring to exterminate each other.

The French frontal assault upon the breastwork had scarcely commenced, however, before it was made apparent that it was their trust in the Iroquois, not Johnson's, that was misplaced. The sudden realities of battle, the sound of shots, the smell of smoke, the sight of blood, generated an excitement Iroquois affinity for violence could not contain. That exposed French flank presented too great a temptation. They surged from the woods to begin striking down Frenchmen and western Indians with equal abandon. The French column, strung out helplessly along the portage road, its vanguard recoiling before the volleys from the English breastwork and its middle assailed by the Iroquois, was thrown into hopeless confusion. Aubry and his veteran captains had inexplicably embraced every disadvantage for which on so many other fields they had exultantly penalized the English. Ligneris was mortally wounded. Aubry and a dozen of his most noted captains hastily surrendered to the English to save themselves from the Iroquois. The whole French and Indian force dissolved into wild flight. Within minutes it had ceased to be a battle and had become a hunt. Two hundred or more were killed before the howling Iroquois had tired of the chase. The fugitives who had escaped did not pause when they had regained their beached canoes above the falls. They paddled desolately westward until they had reached the sanctuary of their native wigwams and cabins at Detroit, Mackinac, Vincennes, and Kaskaskia.

Pouchot could not at first be made to believe the extent of Aubry's defeat. It was not until his messenger was conducted to the English camp under a flag of truce to behold with his own eyes the array of captured captains that he was forced to realize how completely his last hope had been extinguished. That same night he surrendered. He was surrendering more than a fort. He was surrendering an era. Half a continent had changed hands during that fearful half hour on the Niagara portage road.

The French had built Fort Niagara, on the east bank of the junction of the Niagara River with Lake Ontario, by permission of the Iroquois in 1726. This softening in the century-old Iroquois policy of hostility to the French had been another gambit in the perpetually dangerous Indian game of playing off one great power against another. They had imagined that the French settlement there would require the English to place an even higher value on Iroquois friendship and that thereafter the Iroquois might expect greater benefits from both powers. What they had sacrificed, however, was something more than a pawn. Fort Niagara, below the Falls, Fort Little Niagara, above the Falls, and the portage road that ran between the two forts comprised the indispensable link that connected the Atlantic, whether by way of the St. Lawrence or by the Hudson and Oswego, with the immense trade empire of the Great Lakes region. That fourteen miles of cart path along the cliffs of the Niagara gorge was the geographical, military, and economic key to the northwest. Its capture in 1759 had consequences that rivaled the significance of Wolf's capture of Quebec the same year for it had opened the way to England's quick advance upon the other French posts on the Great Lakes.

Had it not been for those already established English garrisons in the west the peace negotiations must have taken a quite different turn. Phenomenal as had been England's eventual successes in the Seven Years' War it was realized that France could not be required to give up all of her North American possessions, those on the mainland as well as those in the West Indies. The victors were obliged to choose which of the two forfeits to demand. A formidable faction in parliament favored claiming the West Indies. Had France come to the peace table still in physical possession of Niagara and her western posts, the already conquered and proven riches of the West Indies must certainly have been preferred. As it was the debate was long and bitter. Feeling ran so high that charges of treason were freely exchanged. Pitt put the full gravity of the question to the House in his memorable statement: "Some are for keeping Canada; some Guadelupe; who will tell me which I shall be hanged for not keeping?" He was not hanged for choosing Canada. But he lived long enough to realize just thirteen years later how momentous had been that choice. Freed of the French menace on their borders Americans were free to rebel. The choice had amounted to England's exchange of her own colonies in America for the French colony in Canada.

For Johnson personally his Niagara victory was a culminating success crowning a twenty-year span of literally uninterrupted lesser successes. Every goal toward which he had driven had been reached and new vistas which even his vaulting ambition had not foreseen were opening. There was no longer any question of Iroquois allegiance. He now held that ancient center of Indian power in the palm of his hand. His influence over them was swiftly extending to the wilder and ruder nations to the west. Delegations of them came to visit him. Molly's housekeeping responsibilities were enlarged by the need to feed and entertain hundreds of Indian guests, many of whom lingered for weeks. Some had come to angle for a share of the favors formerly shown only the Iroquois, others just to gape at the great man. In Indian eyes Johnson had become a figure of towering stature. England's military might had been overwhelmingly demonstrated by the overthrow of France and in all matters with which Indians were concerned Johnson spoke for England. The Indian country for which he was responsible had suddenly expanded from the Mohawk to the Wabash and the Wisconsin. His last great Indian conference in the spring of 1759 had had to be assembled in the safety of Canajoharie at the edge of the white frontier. His next in 1761 was at Detroit, 600 miles to the westward, where Ottawa and Chippewa and Huron and Potawatomi who had always been England's traditional enemies gathered about him with respectful acclaim.

This era of postwar good feeling turned out to be brief. None of the benefits of peace which the Indians had anticipated proved forthcoming. A victorious England was no longer so impressed by the need for Indian friendship, even that of their allies, the Iroquois. The regime of rigid economy that succeeded the outpouring of treasure during the war denied Johnson's Indian service necessary funds to conduct Indian diplomacy in the manner Indians had been taught to expect. In insisting so categorically upon these restrictions Amherst was complying with the firmly expressed wishes of the ministry but he himself thoroughly approved of the new policy, at any rate insofar as it affected the Indian Department. He saw the Indians as a conquered people who had now no recourse other than to become submissive subjects. His directives were couched in peremptory phrases which soon were to return to haunt him: "The more Indians get the more they will expect . . . whatever idle notions they may entertain can be of very little consequence . . . when men of what race so ever behave ill they must be punished not bribed . . . I do not see why the Crown should be put to that expense . . . when Indians find they can get it on Asking for, they will grow remiss in their hunting, which should industriously be avoided; for so long as their minds are Intent on Business they will not have leisure to hatch mischief."

Johnson was sufficiently aware of how instantly and deeply the Indians resented this sudden English about face. In the place of being ardently wooed with presents and promises they were now coldly repulsed with regulations and admonitions. But, knowing the Indian tendency to procrastinate, he was confident that this Indian resentment would not for some time develop into any sort of a crisis. His anxieties were not for the present but the future. Meanwhile, he was glad of the opportunity once more to concentrate his attention on his personal affairs.

These were both interesting and substantial. His land holdings were no longer measured in hundreds of acres but in tens of thousands. His Highlander tenantry now numbered over a hundred families. They were bold and hardy retainers, accustomed to bearing arms. Personally loyal to him, they constituted a kind of private army. Aside from indentured servants and Indian employees he owned seventy Negro slaves. He had imported herds of horses, cattle, and sheep. He sold his flour in the West Indies by the shipload. His second and larger house at Mount Johnson, known as Fort Johnson after its fortification during the war, seemed to him no longer an establishment adequate to serve as the capitol of so considerable a realm and he embarked upon the construction of a more pretentious residence, Johnson Hall. About it he was laying out the streets of Johnstown which was to have an Established Church, a potash works, a gristmill, a carding mill, a tavern, a free school, shops for a tanner, a wagonmaker and a blacksmith, public stocks, and a whipping post.

That fateful spring of 1763 he was particuarly engaged in reordering his family arrangements. The spring before he had married his older daughter, Nancy, to Daniel Claus, his administrative assistant. This spring he celebrated the marriage of his other daughter, Polly, to Guy Johnson, his young nephew whom he was grooming to become his deputy in handling Indian affairs. Guy spent his honeymoon shepherding an indignant delegation of Iroquois on a pilgrimage to Connecticut to protest the recent invasion of Iroquois lands in the Wyoming Valley of northeastern Pennsylvania by Connecticut settlers. Meanwhile, there was a shuffling of residences within the family to engage Johnson's attention. He and Molly moved into the not quite finished Johnson Hall. His son John and John's pretty young housekeeper, Clara Putnam, were moved with their two daughters into Fort Johnson. The original Mount Johnson house was assigned to Nancy and Claus. A new house, Guy Park, was under construction for the newlyweds, Guy and Polly.

This pleasant preoccupation with domestic concerns was devastatingly disrupted by the news from the west. Johnson was taken as much by surprise as had been Amherst. He had repeatedly warned both Amherst and the Board of Trade of growing Indian unrest. But he had gathered no idea that the dangers he had forecast were in any way imminent. The difficulties which had always before stood in the way of every Indian impulse to unite had appeared still to stand. He was especially chagrined by the recollection that as recently as April he had had a long conference with the Seneca without getting the slightest inkling that they had already determined upon war. He realized immediately how acute was the threat. Everything that he had achieved, either for his country or himself, was in jeopardy. Grimly he set himself to defend it.

VII

༆

Stuart

L IKE CROGHAN AND JOHNSON, John Stuart was attracted to the new
world by the appeal of its wider opportunities to a restlessly
active nature. But he was no wide-eyed immigrant youth with his
every achievement still before him. Though only thirty when he
arrived, in 1748, he was already a man of the world, informed by a
most cosmopolitan experience which had made him as acquainted
with the coasts of Africa, South America, China, and the Indies as
he was presently to become with the cloud-wreathed mountains of
Carolina or the steaming Gulf plains of Alabama. The high point
of his earlier career had been his service aboard Anson's flagship on
that indomitable captain's famous freebooting voyage around the
world which had culminated in the capture of the treasure-laden
Manila galleon. Stuart's share of the prize money comprised the
major portion of the fortune he brought with him to Charleston to
invest in new enterprises. This fortune he shortly lost. He soon ac-
cumulated another and then lost that one, too, during the nearly continuous alarms, emergencies, and wars which turned out to be the
principal opportunities he found awaiting him in America.

His adopted homeland, South Carolina, had had a past as varied, as violent, and as colorful as his. From the moment of the colony's initiation in 1670 it had been closely encircled by a ring of the most numerous and powerful Indian nations on the continent. Its first two generations of settlers had been tested and retested by some of the most desperate wars ever fought between the two races. At times the relatively few white inhabitants had been all but driven into the sea. That they had finally prevailed had been chiefly due to the Indian propensity in moments of greatest crisis to fall to fighting among themselves. The dangers of these Indian wars had been made the more threatening by the nearby presence of the Spanish in Florida and soon by the establishment of French posts on the Gulf and the Mississippi. Both rival powers encouraged and supplied the Indian attackers and during those periods when England was at war with one or the other or both there was the added prospect of foreign invasion of this most exposed of England's American colonies. Through these same feverish years there had been the hazard of Caribbean buccaneer descents upon the Carolina coasts. These pirate incursions had at times become so frequent and so menacing that the necessary defense measures amounted to a sustained state of war. To all of these threats from without had been added a more fearful threat from within. The rapidly increasing importation of slaves from Africa kept every white family living outside Charleston constantly apprehensive of an insurrection of black men which could be expected to spawn horrors even more dreadful than the excesses inflicted by red men. Like the salamander, South Carolina had had to learn to live in the midst of flames.

In 1748 the province's population approximated 70,000, a large proportion of the number being recently imported and still primitive African slaves. The fears of a black uprising were well enough founded. In the early slave-trade shipments the overwhelming majority were males. Condemned to a laborious and unnatural existence in which they were deprived of women as well as freedom the newcomers were murderously dissatisfied. Resort to slave labor had, however, been a necessity. The first seventy years of the colony's development had centered about large plantations along the banks of the tidal rivers where, after 1700, rice became the staple crop. Meanwhile, even though the tidewater and piedmont Indians had been cowed, expelled, or exterminated, the westernmost line of settlement had at few points been pushed more than sixty miles from the seacoast, roughly a third of the way toward the mountain barrier which in the western Carolinas reared to higher and more rugged heights than at any other point in the Appalachian range.

A noteworthy preoccupation of many of these outlying settlers, one which they shared with their fellow frontiersmen of North Carolina and Virginia, was their quick adaptation to a special type of cattle raising. Herds numbering hundreds, sometimes thousands, were turned loose to run wild in the woods and marshes. At calving time they were rounded up by neighborhood groups of mounted herdsmen and driven into large wooden pens where the calves were branded with their owner's mark and the cows, bulls, and steers were sorted, counted, and an indicated proportion selected for market. Though the enclosures were called pens instead of corrals and no references to roping are recorded, the way of life of these mounted herders of semiwild cattle in the far eastern forests is a recognizable forerunner of that of their more famous successors, the 19th Century range cattle people of the far western plains. Certainly the so much earlier prototype tended to develop the same unruly and obstreperous self-reliance. According to the disapproving comment of one visiting English observer: "The Cowpen Men are hardy people, are almost continually on Horseback, being obliged to know the Haunts of their Cattle. You see, Sir, what a wild set of Creatures our English Men grow into, when they lose Society." This comment was more perceptive than its maker could have realized. These people, forced swiftly to adapt themselves to the strange pressures of frontier conditions, were forgetting many former values. But the new ones that they were discovering in the process were to have a decisive effect upon the whole course of our history.

Of greater immediate significance, however, than the ways of the cowpen people were the extraordinary ventures of the South Carolina Indian traders. South Carolinians traded earlier, more extensively, and more successfully than did Englishmen from any other colony. Among the Southern Indians, frequently at war with each

other and forever at war with the Northern Indians, there was an
avid demand for guns and gunpowder. Though they soon learned
also to crave axes, kettles, hoes, blankets, rum, and manufactured
clothing and ornaments, weapons and ammunition remained a necessity. Well before the end of the 17th Century Charleston traders
had penetrated as far into the Indian country as the Mississippi.
There were in the south no Iroquois to bar the way and, at first, no
Frenchmen to compete. It was the one area in the continent's interior where early Englishmen preceded early Frenchmen. The first
Frenchman to see the Mississippi, Marquette in 1673, also saw Indians along it in possession of guns, knives, hatchets, cloth garments,
and glass gunpowder flasks. With each outbreak of South Carolina's
Indian wars many traders were killed before they could escape from
the interior but with each return to peace the survivors and new
recruits flocked back into the Indian country. In 1748 they had,
throughout the thirty years the French had by then been established
on the lower Mississippi, been exasperating the French by continuing to trade almost as freely with the Chickasaw and Choctaw deep
in French territory as with the Creek and Cherokee on the edges of
English territory. On occasions they had even crossed the Mississippi
to trade with the wilder Indian nations beyond it.

Among the Southern Indians there was little beaver, the great
trade staple in the north, to offer the trader in exchange for his goods.
In the early years of Carolina wilderness enterprise the chief trade
was in Indian slaves. Some of these were prisoners taken by white
forces in wartime but the most were prisoners taken by Indian nations in wars upon each other, wars often undertaken for the express
purpose of obtaining captives to supply traders' demands. As an
illustration of these several trends, in 1708 the population of South
Carolina consisted of 6680 whites, 2900 Negro slaves, and 1400 Indian slaves. The employment of Indian slaves on Carolina plantations, however, soon proved uneconomic. They brooded and pined,
were most unindustrious, and were too often successful in escaping
back into their native wilderness. Thereafter most Indian slaves were
transported for sale to the West Indies or to Pennsylvania and New
England. When demand there also faltered the Indian slave trade

died out for want of profit. The principal Southern Indian exchange commodity thereupon became deerskins which were available in apparently inexhaustible quantity among the immense herds ranging the valleys and canebrakes in the interior. Year after year the Carolina export of deerskins exceeded the total value of all other exports with the single exception of rice.

Most of these Carolina traders were as irresponsible as their counterparts in the north but there were also among them men of integrity and vision. There was, for one example, James Adair, who left in his notable book a vivid and detailed account of the Indian world of his time, and, for another, Ludovic Grant, of a noble Scotch family, who during his long life in the wilderness continued earnestly to sympathize with Indian aspirations without ceasing as earnestly to sympathize with white. South Carolina's Indian trade began so early and lasted so long that there had been time for the development of a pattern of interracial relationship comparable, within certain limits, to the French-Indian experience and in complete contrast to the racial prejudice prevailing elsewhere on the English frontier. Responsible traders were welcomed and accepted in the proudest Indian households. Prominent traders so frequently married the daughters of prominent Indian families that the time was to come when the greatest Indian chiefs bore such names as Watts, Ross, Ridge, or McGillivray.

France and Spain had by the end of the 17th Century begun to recognize the danger developing in South Carolina. Indian rejection of English trade and resistance to English settlement were from then on vigorously encouraged by the Spanish at St. Augustine and Pensacola and, soon thereafter, by the French at Mobile and Fort Toulouse, near the present Montgomery, Alabama. South Carolina's defense against the intermittently hostile Creek confederation, ranged across the lowlands to the southwest, was aided by the defensible line of the broad Savannah River and, after 1733, by the establishment of the new English colony of Georgia. But their other powerful Indian neighbor, the Cherokee, occupied the high mountains directly to the west that literally looked down upon the province's border. Ten years before 1748 the Cherokee had been reduced by half by smallpox but they could still field 5000 warriors and their military power was accentuated by their situation in a mountain fastness from which they could sortie at will and into which they could retire when pressed. Their towns, numbering nearly a hundred, were clustered in three groups, then commonly called, from east to west, the Lower Towns, the Middle or Upper Towns, and the Overhill Towns. The first of these occupied the eastern mountain valleys which opened into the Carolina lowlands, the second were in the higher valleys of the central ranges, and the third were in the valley of the Tennessee River on the western side of the mountain barrier.

The Cherokee represented among eastern Indians the single instance of an Indian occupation of a mountain area. As has so often been the case with mountain people the world over their character reflected the invigorating influence of their environment. They were energetic, willful, independent, belligerent, and fiercely devoted to their mountain homeland. It is not too difficult to sympathize with their attachment to so favored a region. The great naturalist, William Bartram, visiting the Cherokee country before it had been scarred by white occupation, was almost ecstatically impressed by what he saw. In reporting his observations he painted some unforgettable vignettes: "In these cool, sequestered, rocky vales, we behold the celebrated beauties of the hills, blushing Rhododendron, sky-robed Dephinium, fiery Azalea, flaming on the ascending hills . . . Keowe lies in a fertile vale, at this season enamelled with the incarnate, fragrant strawberries and blooming plants, through which the beautiful river meanders, environed by high hills and mountains, whilst others more lofty, misty and blue, majestically mount far above . . . The ample Occonne vale, encircled by a wreath of uniform hills, their swelling bases clad in cheerful verdure, over which, issuing from between the mountains, plays along a glittering river . . . Between the stately columns of the superb forest trees, rushing from rocky precipices under the shade of the pensile hills, the unparalleled cascade of Falling Creek, rolling and leaping off the rocks . . . The fruitful vale of Cowe in which the river is incredibly increased in size by the continual accession of brooks flowing in from the hills on each side, dividing their green turfy beds, forming them into parterres and vistas, profusely productive of flowers and fragrant strawberries, their rich juices dying my horse's feet and ancles, exhibits one of the most charming natural mountaneous landscapes perhaps anywhere to be seen: ridges of hills rising grandly one above and beyond another, some boldly and majestically advancing into the verdant plain, their feet bathed with the silver flood of the Tanase, whilst others far distant, veiled in blue mists, sublimely mounting aloft with yet greater majesty, lift up their pompous crests and overlook vast regions ... From the summit we enjoyed a most enchanting view: a vast expanse of green meadows and strawberry fields; a meandering river gliding through, saluting in its various turnings the swelling, green, turfy knolls; flocks of turkies strolling about them; herds of deer prancing in the meads or bounding over the hills; companies of young, innocent Cherokee virgins, some busy gathering the rich fruit, others, having already filled their baskets, lying reclined under the shade of fragrant Magnolia or Jessamine, disclosing their beauties to the fluttering breeze, and bathing their limbs in the cool fleeting streams." It was to this mountain paradise that the Cherokee were to cling so tenaciously that their grasp upon it was not to be finally broken for another ninety years.

In 1748 the basic Cherokee difficulty was that, secure in their mountain citadel, they had for generations past yielded even more often than most Indian nations to the general Indian impulse to make war. This had intensified their need for trade goods, particularly weapons, which in turn had increased their dependence on either French or English supply sources. But they had no choice for they were intermittently at war with their neighbors, the Chickasaw, the Choctaw, the Creek, and the Tuscarora, and perpetually embroiled with the distant Iroquois. Each year parties of eager young Cherokee warriors sought the repute to be won by taking Iroquois horses, scalps, or captives while similar Iroquois parties were making the six-hundred-mile-long journey south to return the attention. The route followed in this traditional exchange of hostilities had been used so long and so regularly that it had become known as the Great War Road. But by 1748 the most bitter Cherokee hostility was directed toward Ohio and Illinois Indians who were intimately associated with the French. It was this involvement that most embarrassed French efforts to bring the Cherokee under French influence and most inclined the Cherokee instead to turn to English traders to satisfy their trade needs. There remained in the critical period about to open a strong faction in Cherokee councils deeply suspicious of English land seeking but to the majority the English frontier seemed still distant and Cherokee supremacy in their mountains unthreatened.

For years before and after 1748 the most persuasive pro-English influence among the Cherokee was the vigorous personality of Attakullaculla, the nation's paramount civil chief. In his youth Attakullaculla, more usually known to the whites as the Little Carpenter, had been a member of the Cherokee embassy conducted to England by the flamboyant Sir Alexander Cuming. There he had been received at dinner by King George II, shown all the sights of London, entertained by every novelty from puppet shows to the Horse Guards, and become a favorite subject for English artists, poets, and journalists. He had returned, loaded with presents and honors, so impressed by all things English that for the rest of his very long life, despite the bitterest of disappointments and disillusionments, he never ceased to be a firm friend of the English.

Upon his arrival in 1748 Stuart associated himself and his capital with a Charleston mercantile partnership. The business did not do well but he was so strongly attracted to this new country that three years later he returned with his wife, Sarah, and his infant daughter, Sarah Christiana, to make South Carolina his home. His business still failed to prosper but he was a hearty, convivial, and gregarious man and was fast becoming one of the colony's most widely known and popular figures. In 1755 a conjunction of quite disassociated events became the great turning point in his career. In Charleston his mercantile business finally failed, obliging him to seek employment to support his family, and in the Monongahela forests Braddock suffered his great defeat, obliging South Carolina, in common with every other province, to give immediate attention to the defense of its frontier. Stuart accepted a captain's commission to command one of the province's newly raised companies of militia. He was thereafter to continue in the public service, as soldier, magistrate, and administrator, for the remaining twenty-four years of his life. The vigor and warmth of his personality, his easy ability to make and hold friends, and his unswerving devotion to duty were to prove him better fitted for this new career than for any of his earlier ventures.

Braddock's defeat brought the Cherokee, as well, to a turning point. They were situated squarely on the borderline between the two conflicting world powers. Both were exerting every persuasion and every pressure to secure their alliance. The Cherokee would have much preferred to avoid the choice and their councils were agitated by intense internal dissension. Apprehension of English land-grabbing proclivities inclined them toward the French. Their hostility to the French Indians across the Ohio inclined them toward the English. Virginia was bombarding them with petitions for aid against the invasion of Virginia by the same Ohio Indians who had so long been Cherokee enemies. Meaning only to temporize, the Cherokee took the position that they could not afford to support the English unless the English built forts to guard them against the inevitable French retaliation. To their astonishment South Carolina promptly built Fort Prince George on the eastern slopes of the mountains among the Lower Towns and shortly afterward dispatched an expedition under Captain Raymond Demere over the mountains, transporting his disassembled cannon on pack mules, to build a fort among the Overhill Towns on the Tennessee. Stuart and his company were with the expedition. The fort, as was the case with other forts built that critical year in other provinces, was named Fort Loudon in honor of the newly appointed English commander-in-chief, the totally inept Lord Loudon. The Cherokee had already repented of their invitation but it was now too late to be easily rid of the camel in their tent.

Fort Loudon was the first English lodgment west of the mountain barrier anywhere along the colonies' long western frontier stretching from the Mohawk to Florida. But its establishment had not been a consequence of any sudden forward lunge in the white man's slow westward advance. It was founded by Indian consent and separated from the nearest English settlement by 250 miles of Indian country, the most of it forested mountains. The little garrison of some two hundred provincial militiamen was almost as isolated as any ship-wrecked crew on a South Seas island. The social atmosphere of their situation was soon presenting other South Seas parallels. Their In-dian neighbors were a simple and primitive people of another race with ways that were strange and mysterious. They were as curious about the soldiers as the soldiers were about them. On both sides there was a readiness to be friends that was at first guarded and then, for a brief period, cordial. Fraternization developed rapidly. The only white visitors the Indians had previously known had been traders and they welcomed the chance to learn more about these carefree young white men who had nothing to sell. To the eager soldiers it was an unprecedented opportunity to wander freely through towns of genuine wild Indians.

Most members of the garrison were increasingly delighted by so many novel sights, experiences, and sensations. They were fascinated by so much of what they saw: the theatrically striking Cherokee costumes dominated by swans' wings painted red or black and by high white crowns surmounted by circlets of eagle feathers, the pageantry of their Green Corn Dance and Eagle Tail Dance, the feverish excitement with which they were so often absorbed in their games of ball, chungke, or marbles, the spectacle of their purification rituals in which whole communities marched in procession to bathe in the river. But most of all were they fascinated by the Cherokee women. This was an interest which the women returned and were free to return. In the Cherokee nation women enjoyed the freedom born of a largely matriarchal society. Women owned the home, had control over the children, and had a full voice in council. The station and authority of women of rank were recognized by such formal titles as Beloved Woman, Beautiful Woman, or War Woman. Along with these uncommon privileges was the absence among the Chero-kee of any law against, or punishment for, adultery. These free women were intrigued by the uniformed, white strangers who were so obviously starved for female companionship. Numerous romantic associations developed. Some were mere sensual liaisons.

Others were more abiding attachments. Many an Englishman in the desperate days ahead was to owe his life to the faithful devotion of his Cherokee wife or mistress.

No one among the Englishmen marooned at lonely Fort Loudon embraced the opportunity to know Indians with an enthusiasm to match Stuart's. There was in his irrepressible nature an instinctive sympathy for the heedless improvidences of the Indian temperament. Their scorn of every personal restraint entranced him. He feasted with them, drank with them, sang with them, danced with them, succeeded in making himself in every respect accepted as one of them. His love affair with the Cherokee people was no passing whim. It was an affection that never faltered, a feeling more real, more sincere, and more faithful than any entertained by Croghan or Johnson for their Indian friends. His impulse to make himself a part of the Cherokee world led him within a few weeks of his arrival at Fort Loudon to take the most personal of all steps. Undeterred by thought of his family in Charleston, he married, by Indian ceremony, Susannah Emory, the three-quarter white granddaughter of Ludovic Grant. By her he had a son called Oonodota by the Cherokee, in reference to the glowing red hair he had inherited from his father, but by the English, with their extraordinary talent for misinterpreting the most mellifluous Indian names, Bushyhead. But by far the most significant of Stuart's experiences at Fort Loudon was the friendship he contracted with Attakullaculla. It was a friendship that was profoundly to affect their personal lives and the affairs of their respective nations and to endure undiminished until their deaths at almost the same moment during the new and more extreme trials of the Revolution.

The English alliance to which they had been maneuvered into giving so dubious an assent led the Cherokee along a most rocky and sterile road beset by all manner of pitfalls. It was the first large-scale attempt by English authorities to gain from an important segment of Indian power the sort of military co-operation the French had so regularly enjoyed. Success could have eased England's Indian relations for years to come. But no semblance of success attended the undertaking. During the next three years that Cherokee war parties were traveling northward to assist in the defense of the Virginia and Pennsylvania frontiers English response to the effort ranged, in Cherokee estimation, from persistent ingratitude to outright betrayal.

In 1756 Washington, straining to hold the Virginia border, dispatched a flanking expedition by a roundabout route through the mountains of eastern Kentucky to counterattack the principal Shawnee town on the Ohio. The little army of 263 Virginia frontiersmen under the command of Major Andrew Lewis was joined by 130 Cherokee, pleased to be able to strike so shrewd a blow at their Shawnee enemies. But the midwinter march was delayed by inexpert planning and the expedition so insufficiently supplied that starvation set in long before it had plowed through the snow to the Ohio. After the horses had been eaten the force disintegrated during a disorderly retreat which became a case of every man for himself with the least heed of all paid to the fate of their Indian companions. This first campaign with their new English allies, thereafter sardonically termed in frontier reminiscence even by whites as the "Sandy Creek Voyage," got the process of Cherokee disillusionment off to a flying start.

The next year some 400 Cherokee journeyed north to serve with the hard-pressed frontier defense forces. They operated in the wilderness well west of the Pennsylvania-Virginia cordon of border forts and in a number of instances succeeded in destroying French and Indian raiding parties before they had even approached the settlements. For this service they were to have been compensated, in lieu of ordinary soldier's pay, by presents and scalp bounties. The presents were delayed by administrative disputes among the various provincial and imperial officials charged with the matter and proved scanty when at length received. The scalp bounties offered by Virginia and Pennsylvania were to be collected only by formal application and were usually withheld on one pretext or another. There is an instance of Washington's having attempted to help his Cherokee allies with their bounty claims. In a note to Governor Dinwiddie accompanying a parcel of scalps among which was one that had been taken from a French officer, he wrote: "I hope, though one is not an Indian's, they will meet with adequate reward, as the

Monsieur's is of much more consequence." The Cherokee, moreover, were often made to feel that they were not wanted by the
people they had come to help. There was considerable objection,
on moral grounds among townspeople and professional among officers, to this reliance upon savage allies. On this score Washington's
opinion was definite. He reported to Dinwiddie that in his estimation: "They are more serviceable than twice their number of
white men. Their cunning and craft cannot be equalled. Indians are
the only match for Indians."

The third year of their effort to serve the English cause, 1758, 600
Cherokee went north to join Forbes, this time attracted by £6000
worth of presents which they were more confident of receiving
since Croghan himself was managing the distribution. But, disgusted by the interminable delays in Forbes' advance, which they
attributed to cowardice, and becoming aware that the main French
force had withdrawn from Duquesne, most of them had gone home
before the end of the campaign. Forbes, who had attached no great
value to their presence but was angered by their absence without
leave, ordered the apprehension and arrest of Attakullaculla. Evi-
dently his military police failed to overtake the southbound Indians
for there is no record of the warrant ever having been served.

But among all the misunderstandings and disappointments accompanying the three-year-long effort of the Cherokee to co-operate
with the English war effort, overwhelmingly the greatest difficulty
was the attitude of the white frontier people they had been summoned to help defend. To reach the northern battlefront the Cherokee war parties were obliged to travel up the Valley of Virginia
along the outlying fringe of Virginia's westernmost settlements. To
the average frontiersman there was little distinction worth making
among Indians. All were his enemies. To him an Indian was an Indian and a Cherokee scalp delivered in Williamsburg was worth
the same bounty as a Shawnee's. The north and south passages of
Cherokee contingents were attended by repeated brawls, exchanges
of insults, mutual accusations of horse stealing, and all too often by
armed encounters. Many more Cherokee lives were lost in these
skirmishes en route with their Virginia friends than in battle with

their French enemies. And as each returning war party brought new accounts of indignities and worse suffered at the hands of the Virginians Cherokee resentment ceased to smolder and began to blaze.

In 1759 the capture of Niagara and Quebec made certain the downfall of New France. The innate heedlessness of Indian political and diplomatic judgment has seldom been more clearly illustrated than by the impulse of the Cherokee to select this precise moment to get themselves into a war with the English. After having supported the English during years when English fortunes were at their lowest ebb, they elected to change sides this year when it had become apparent that French ability to furnish them with sufficient ammunition to supply their war needs was obviously on the wane and at the same time that powerful English regular forces were being made available for Carolina service by the progressive success of the main English campaign in the north. Nevertheless, the Cherokee had at last been convinced by the afflictions that they had suffered along the Virginia frontier that it was the English and not the French who were their natural and essential enemies. A last straw was provided when Lieutenant Richard Coytmore, commander at Fort Prince George, and a group of drunken companions raped several Keowee women whose men were away fighting for the English. The war faction among the Cherokee, egged on by Creek and French agents, sought to commit the nation to war by launching a series of raids on the Carolina border. The peace faction, led by Attakullaculla, regained control of Cherokee affairs long enough to send a delegation, headed by Oconostota, their paramount war chief, to Charleston to negotiate a new understanding. But it was already too late to turn back. The pressure of past wrongs and present suspicions led on inexorably to two years of horrors and tragedies which gained none of the peoples involved any advantage whatever.

Governor William Henry Lyttleton of South Carolina, outraged by the killings of settlers which had already totaled 23, jailed the peace delegates on the charge that their representations were not sincere and marched into the Cherokee country with a hastily assembled army of provincial militia. Pausing at Fort Prince George, he ceased seeking battle and resumed negotiations. The burden of his

demands was that the Cherokee were to hand over for English punishment a number of warriors to equal the number of settlers killed
in the recent raids. Until they did so he proposed to continue to
hold the ambassadors as hostages, though he did release Oconostota
on the somewhat curious theory that the indignant war chief
might persuade his people to deliver up for hanging more than a
score of their warriors. Without awaiting further developments
Lyttleton as hastily retreated across the frontier and disbanded his
army. He had failed to impress the Cherokee with South Carolina
military power while at the same time infuriating them beyond endurance by his imprisonment, in violation of all recognized diplomatic conventions, of their ambassadors. The lighted train had now
burned all the way to the powder keg.

In February, after more vain appeals for the release of the hostages,
Oconostota arranged an ambush in which the hated Coytmore was
mortally wounded and undertook the siege of Fort Prince George.
The garrison, instead of being intimidated by their commander's
death, thereupon murdered the hostages, each of whom was a prominent Cherokee chief. This united the nation. All factions were now
equally resolved. Fort Loudon was also invested, English traders
killed, general raids on the frontier instituted, and Creek and French
support urgently solicited. The South Carolina assembly declared
a state of war, voted to raise 1000 more men, increased the scalp
bounty to £35, and got off an appeal for help to Amherst in
New York. Amherst's response was prompt. Six years of foreign
war had schooled the English army and navy in mobility. In April
Montgomery paid a return visit to South Carolina with 1200 Highlanders.

There were delays in getting his campaign under way. Not expecting him so soon South Carolina had failed to have the promised
provincial forces ready. The South Carolinians also asserted, possibly with some reason, that most of their militia was needed at
home to guard against the danger of a slave insurrection. In late
May Montgomery marched into the eastern edges of the Cherokee
country, burning several of their Lower Towns as he advanced,
killed and captured some 80 Cherokee, many of them women and

children, and on June 4th relieved Fort Prince George. Here he
paused for three weeks. His men were already exhausted by the
rigors of campaigning in these mountains and he clung to some
hope that the damage that he had so far inflicted among the Lower
Towns might persuade the Cherokee to sue for peace. But it had not.

Montgomery was not well and relied heavily upon the advice and
energy of his second in command, Major James Grant, who had
been recently exchanged after his capture by the French Indians at
Duquesne. Grant had had bitter firsthand experience with the difficulties of dealing with Indians in their native wilderness and he
could see by merely looking around that these rugged mountains
might present even graver problems than the Allegheny forests.
He argued that it was clearly impossible to get a regular army over
them in the face of the Cherokee resistance that must be expected.
Montgomery, however, could not forget that a principal purpose of
his campaign must be to save the 200 Englishmen beleaguered at
Fort Loudon and he ordered the attempt made.

So far the Cherokee had avoided battle to husband their dwin-
dling supply of ammunition. Montgomery's army had toiled over
the divide and reached the headwaters of the Little Tennessee before the Cherokee found the moment to attack. If they had too little
gunpowder they made what they had count. The Highlanders
strung out along the trail in the depths of the narrow gap were
easy targets to the fire of the Indians hidden on the wooded mountain sides. Montgomery, taking a loss of a hundred killed and
wounded, stubbornly pushed on six miles to the next Cherokee
town, Echoee, which he burned. Here he paused two days while
giving new thought to his situation. The result of his reflection was
that he became as convinced as Grant that there was no alternative
to leaving Fort Loudon to its fate. Abandoning his baggage in order
to provide transport for his wounded, he retreated rapidly to Prince
George and then on to Charleston where he reembarked for New
York, proclaiming that in punishing the Indians by burning so
many of their towns he had fulfilled his assigned mission.

The jubilant Cherokee conceived that they had won a great victory. South Carolina agreed with that view. People were filled with

consternation and indignation by Montgomery's hasty withdrawal. The frantic assembly increased the scalp bounty to £100 and failed by the narrow margin of a tie vote to take the unheard of step of authorizing, as a last resort, the raising of a regiment of slaves to aid in the Province's defense.

Fort Loudon was now doomed. The Cherokee had made no assault, knowing the garrison must presently starve. They needed only to wait. Many of the Cherokee wives and mistresses of the soldiers braved the wrath of Cherokee warriors by smuggling in packages of corn and game but they were unable to furnish enough food to make a material difference. On August 7th Captain Paul Demere, who had succeeded his brother Raymond when the latter fell ill, capitulated on terms permitting him to march his garrison back over the mountains. At the end of the first day's march the Cherokee attacked the English camp, killing 23 and taking the rest captive. They claimed that they had taken care to halt the massacre at this number because it exactly matched the number of hostages slaughtered at Fort Prince George. But evidence of the passions of hatred the war had by now aroused was presented by the manner of Demere's death. He was scalped alive, his arms and legs cut off, and his mouth stuffed with earth, with the words: "You want land, we give it to you." Many of the prisoners not killed in the first attack were later tormented to death in the various towns among which they were distributed while others were treated so well that at the end of the war they declined to be repatriated.

Of the officers of Fort Loudon the only one to survive the massacre was Stuart. His Cherokee friends saved his life but endeavored to persuade him to show them how to use the Fort Loudon cannon against Fort Prince George. When he refused and was being once more threatened, Attakullaculla gave another proof of his devotion by personally arranging his escape and then conducting him northward through the wilderness to the sanctuary of Major Andrew Lewis' camp guarding the Virginia frontier.

Though flushed with victory the Cherokee paused to take stock of their situation. They had not received the promised aid from their Creek neighbors. They were more fully aware by now of how completely the French had lost their war in the north and how little support therefore could henceforth be expected from them. They were on the whole satisfied with the eye for an eye retribution that they had imposed for the murder of their ambassadors. Instead of making the expected attacks on the South Carolina forts at Prince George and Ninety-six, they indicated that they were willing to discuss peace terms. So were the South Carolinians who took advantage of the preliminaries by ransoming 113 of the Fort Loudon survivors. But Amherst in New York was not. "I must own I am ashamed," he wrote Governor William Bull, Lyttleton's successor, "for I believe it is the first instance of His Majesty's troops having yielded to the Indians." Presumably he ascribed Braddock's and Grant's yieldings at Duquesne entirely to French prowess and he could have had as yet no faintest premonition of how many stunning instances of sadder yieldings to Indians were soon to burst upon him. In any event, he was beginning to become aware of one uncomfortable consequence of his great victory over the French. England had suddenly been confronted with the necessity of adopting an official attitude toward an array of more than forty Indian nations, occupying a wilderness area stretching from the arctic slopes of Labrador to the Everglades of Florida, each one of which was in a position to affect vital English interests and no one of which had yet recognized English sovereignty. The same victory over the French had made available to him a surplus of battle-hardened regulars most of whom were soon to be recalled to England. It seemed to him therefore certain to save trouble in the long run were he to seize this opportunity so drastically to punish the Cherokee that all these other Indians would be lastingly impressed by English might. He singled out Grant, now a lieutenant colonel, sure that Grant having failed twice with Indians might therefore this time be doubly anxious to succeed, and sent him to South Carolina with two regiments of Highlanders.

Grant realized upon arrival that continued prosecution of the war had become unnecessary but his orders were explicit and, as Amherst had foreseen, he was resolved to erase the memory of his two former failures. In May of 1761 he led into the Cherokee country as adequately organized and equipped an army as has ever proceeded against Indians. He had, besides his regulars, a South Carolina regiment officered by such natural leaders as Francis Marion, Henry Laurens, and William Moultrie, Robert Rogers at the head of a company of his noted Rangers, and a corps of Mohawk, Catawba, and Chickasaw Indian scouts. Making Fort Prince George his base, he marched deliberately deeper into the mountains, methodically burning the Lower Towns as he advanced, until he reached Echoee Pass where Montgomery had been so painfully mauled. Here the Cherokee again were waiting. But Grant's column was preceded by Marion's and Rogers' rangers and flanked by screens of his Indian scouts. The Cherokee could not reserve their first fire for their favorite target, the regulars, their attack was necessarily premature, and for want of ammunition it could not be sustained. Grant gave the grim order to ignore the Indian fire and to keep on marching ahead along the narrow winding trail in the depths of the gorge. The English column, accepting some seventy casualties, doggedly obeyed. Presently the fire began to die away. The mortified Cherokee on the wooded mountainsides above could only lean on their empty guns and watch. It was Adair's opinion that "twice the number of Grant's men" could not have got through the pass if the Cherokee had had ammunition. Grant himself reported: "Never was an army in so dangerous a position. This part of the country is impenetrable if defended by fifty men." He could not have known how heedlessly during their winter hunting the Cherokee had wasted the powder they had taken the previous summer at Fort Loudon or that the French replacement shipment being rushed to them had foundered en route up the Tennessee. When he ordered his column to keep marching it could only have been the fury of a determination born of his former failures that steeled him to subject his army to a risk so fearful.

Having destroyed the Lower Towns he kept on and as rigorously laid waste the Middle Towns in those upper valleys which had never before known the foot of an invader. But, unmistakable as has been his demonstration of military superiority, he did not feel himself strong enough to attempt to complete his passage of the mountain barrier and thus to crown his success by re-establishing English power at Fort Loudon, the capture of which his campaign had been intended to avenge. Instead, he withdrew his army to Fort Prince George and waited for the Cherokee to sue for peace.

Stuart had not been with Grant, having through the spring and early summer been representing South Carolina in behind the scenes discussions with the Cherokee. He now brought Attakullaculla to Grant at Prince George, to Governor Bull at Charleston, and then to a general conference at Ashley Ferry where peace was readily arranged on the same status quo terms that might have been had the year before or, for that matter, the year before that when the ambassadors had been seized. The war, as was so often the case when the principal effort was a punitive one designed merely to impress the Indians with white military superiority, had achieved little. The Cherokee had not been much impressed. They had not lost a battle to which they had committed their full forces. Few of their warriors had fallen. Their simply constructed towns could soon be rebuilt and their ravaged cornfields replanted. They could still feel almost as secure as before in their mountain citadel. It had not been taken and, indeed, had only been threatened because they lacked powder, and even then only by the introduction of a great army from beyond the seas. They felt as well able to withstand the Carolinians and the Virginians as they had before. What the war had achieved was to teach them a more savage hatred of white men. Marion feelingly forecast this consequence in his reference to the return of Indian children to the ashes of their ruined towns: " 'Who did this?' they will ask their mothers, and the reply will be, 'The white people did it.' " This hatred was to be the Cherokee War's one enduring legacy. The Cherokee mountain stronghold was on the immediate flank of the main overland route to Kentucky of the future. Only a few tens of Highlanders died in Echoee Pass. In the years to come many more hundreds of American settlers were to die before the passions there aroused were quelled.

The one result of the war that was to prove useful to both races was the elevation of Stuart to a post where he might attempt to arbitrate differences between them. During the peace negotiations the Cherokee urged that he be made the King's Superintendent for Southern Indians. South Carolina heartily approved, as did Amherst, and the English cabinet accepted the recommendation. When the appointment came his first great task was to persuade the suspicious Creek and Choctaw that the coming English occupation of the former Spanish and French posts in the south meant no hostile English intentions.

The geographical group of Southern Indians represented a solid bloc of Indian power which if once ever it were to be exerted in combination could constitute a menace of gigantic proportions. Factions among the Cherokee, Creek, and Choctaw formerly under French or Spanish influence were agitating for immediate united action before the English grip became unbreakable. The startling news of Pontiac's War in the north was the signal to these anti-English factions that, regardless of the long antipathy between Northern and Southern Indians, now was the time for all to strike. To Stuart, the new Superintendent, the news was an ominous warning of how enormous was the responsibility that had descended upon him.

VIII

❦

Pontiac

GOVERNMENTAL AND HISTORICAL ARCHIVES contain thousands of pages of documents, reports, and letters, dealing with Pontiac the great rebel, the Indian Hannibal, the champion of his people. His meteoric career blazed against the western sky, casting a lurid glow over the whole vast wilderness, inflaming the tumult of more than twenty sieges and battles, and scorching the white frontier from end to end. For the little while that he dominated half a continent we can watch whatever he did. We can listen to what he said in council. We can examine his exercise of command. We can trace every terrible consequence of his decisions. But of Pontiac, the man, before he had stepped into that fierce glare of responsibility, we know next to nothing. All that we can certainly know is that he emerged from the forest to become immediately a colossus bestriding his world.

Prior to that spring of 1763 he had attracted scant attention. There had been little, even in the view of other Indians, to set him apart from a hundred other tribal chieftains. French officials with whom he had dealt and French commanders with whom he had served had taken no marked notice of him. The first certain official mention of him was not French but English and not until 1763. In the dispatch from Major Henry Gladwin, commander at Detroit, reporting that his post was being besieged by a thousand Indians, he remarked, almost in passing, that their leader was an Ottawa chief whose name was Pontiac.* Upon the obscurity of his career before it had reached that climactic moment faint light is shed by the legends, reminiscences, and secondhand accounts which gained currency only after his renown had been established.

The date and place of his birth is not even a legend. He was thought to be about fifty by Englishmen who saw him at Detroit. In physical appearance he was vigorous and imposing and his manner was as imperiously self-confident as though he had been from birth accustomed to command. Indians, who were connoisseurs of oratory, considered him a compelling public speaker. His most dubious hearers, including his most envious fellow chiefs, were again and again carried away by his eloquence in council. This was an indispensable talent in one who sought to move Indians to concerted action. They had always first to be persuaded. His influence may have been augmented by his post as titular head of the *Metai,* a semireligious secret society having ramifications among the Potawatomi and the Chippewa as well as his own Ottawa. Perhaps of greatest assistance in the swiftness of his rise was his very lack of former importance. Indians had long been waiting for the miraculous appearance of a Messiah.

As one of the war chiefs of the Ottawa, he had had some military experience. Of all the Lake nations, the Ottawa were the most rabidly belligerent. The warriors of no other had so often made the

---

*Major Robert Rogers, in his book, *A Concise Account of North America,* detailed a dramatic encounter with Pontiac on the rain-swept shores of Lake Erie in 1760 when Rogers was on his way with his Rangers to occupy Detroit after the surrender of Canada. But the book was published in 1765 after the name Pontiac had already become famous in every corner of the civilized world. Rogers' *Journal* of the 1760 expedition, kept at the time and published before the *Concise Account,* made no mention of ever having met Pontiac either en route or at Detroit. George Croghan accompanied Rogers and at Detroit held a great Indian conference in 1760. The next year Sir William Johnson and Croghan held a greater one at Detroit. These conferences were widely attended by influential Indians. In their reports Johnson and Croghan list the names of very many chiefs, including two Ottawa chiefs, but neither mentioned Pontiac.

long journey across lakes, up rivers, through forests, and over mountains to attack the distant white settlements. During the last generation they had lost half of their fighting men in such enterprises. Pontiac was said to have been at Braddock's defeat and with Montcalm's Champlain campaigns. This is possible since he appeared to have gained at some earlier time a good working acquaintance with the white man's methods in waging war.

Our estimate now of Pontiac's actual capacities can best fall back on their measurement by his recorded deeds. And these in turn need to be measured by the unparalleled difficulties with which he coped. To attempt to organize and control the combined operations of hordes of irresponsible savages of a score of separate nations, in each of which no man accepted the authority even of his own tribal chiefs, was a stupendous undertaking. It was a task only to be exceeded by that of a military commander each of whose soldiers was a predisposed mutineer.

That he had the rare personality of a natural leader is abundantly indicated. There remains the greater question of his intellectual endowment to comprehend the immensely broader problems that demanded his appraisal. He had grown up in the forest as had any other Indian with few opportunities to acquaint himself with the complexities of that outer world which was beginning to bear so harshly upon his Indian world. For three years, he had brooded in his lake shore wigwam upon the sudden new threats which were looming on every Indian horizon. Before challenging the military might of the British empire, he had need to be certain that he had fully grasped the realities of the Indian situation. Again our conclusion must rest on the testimony of his actions. Never in his most passionate speeches in council did he reveal his innermost thoughts. He concealed the full scope of his intentions from his most trusted associates, going even to the length of using different aides to handle his incoming and outgoing messages. But the course he elected to pursue is clearer evidence than any he could have proclaimed. It demonstrated with what painful thoroughness he had considered the areas of relative strength and weakness in the Indian position and had weighed the risks and opportunities with which the Indian cause was confronted.

The fundamental weakness in the Indian position was sheer lack of numbers. During the nearly three hundred years since their first contact with white men they had suffered terribly from exposure to the white man's diseases. There were probably fewer Indians then than there are now. The white population along the seaboard in 1763 outnumbered all Indians living east of the Mississippi by more than ten to one. Were Pontiac to be joined by every warrior of the nations upon which he could most certainly rely, the Lake, Ohio, and Illinois Indians, plus the Seneca, his maximum force would still fall short of 7000 men. Were the eastern Iroquois, their adjacent vassals, and the Indians of Canada drawn into the war, another 2500 warriors at most would become available. The Southern Indians could furnish another 10,000 if they, too, could be brought in though he did not consider this a serious possibility since they were still at war with the Northern Indians. All of these were merely total numbers of adult men. The intermittent need to hunt, individual Indian irresponsibility, and the number of younger warriors who did not yet possess a gun, reduced by more than half the effective Indian military strength that could at any given moment be brought to bear. The whites, were they to make a genuinely determined effort, could put overwhelmingly larger and better armed armies into the field. They could, moreover, be reinforced at will by additional regular troops from England. Pontiac's necessary hope was that they would not make so sustained an effort and that such effort as they did make would be confounded by the excessive difficulties of war in the wilderness.

The next greatest Indian weakness was the universal Indian need for trade goods. However distinctly the white man was recognized as the Indian's mortal enemy, he had also to be recognized as the sole producer of those manufactured implements upon which the Indian had learned to depend. This dependence upon the enemy was a fearful weakness but not since the first white trader had anchored off the Atlantic coast had there been any hope of complete escape from it. No Indian could ever close his eyes to the usefulness of what the white man was offering to trade for skins and furs. A steel ax was unmistakably more serviceable than one of stone. Stewing venison in an iron kettle was a far more sensible process than putting it into a wicker basket with heated stones. Above all, guns and gunpowder were such a manifest improvement upon bows and arrows as to become a decisive advantage to a man who lived by hunting and an absolute necessity when he went to war. This supreme importance of firearms had early been ground into the Indian consciousness. Possession of these weapons had enabled the first weak white settlements to lord it over their Indian neighbors. Guns furnished by the French had enabled the relatively weak Algonquin to drive the warlike Iroquois from the St. Lawrence. When the Iroquois in turn had been supplied by the Dutch on the Hudson, they had been able to spread their conquests from the shores of Lake Superior to the mountains of the Carolinas.

The Indian's practical resort to a few selected articles of white manufacture had not yet so much altered the outer forms of his way of life. The new implements had merely taken the place of the cruder implements he had formerly been using for the same purposes. He continued to plant, cook, hunt, fish, and make war, to shape his house, his sled, and his canoe, as he had before, with these new, more efficient tools. The effort to acquire them, however, had undermined his former sense of values and trade contacts had visited the plagues of disease and drunkenness upon the whole Indian world. In Pontiac's lifetime these trade goods so necessarily esteemed by Indians had come from the English on Hudson Bay, from the French on the St. Lawrence, from the English at Albany by way of the grasping Iroquois middleman, from the English packing over the mountains from Pennsylvania and South Carolina, from the Spanish on the Gulf coast, and from the French coming up the Mississippi from New Orleans.

A principal strength of the Indian position on the other hand was that the multiplicity of these sources of supply, together with their geographical range, had allowed the Indian to play one white competitor against another to maintain a partially free market and his own relative independence. This invitation to take advantage of white rivalries still existed in spite of the French disaster in the recent war. The English had occupied the former French posts on the St. Lawrence and the Great Lakes under the terms of the capitulation imposed upon the defeated French commanders. But permanent title had not yet been settled at the peace table and the French still held the Illinois, the lower Wabash, the length of the Mississippi, and New Orleans, while the Spanish were still established in the two Floridas. The Indians were thus still in a position to bargain almost as effectively as before with competing traders seeking their custom. And they could still expect to continue to be favored and courted, as they had always been before, by each of the great powers as each sought to win Indian military support against the other.

The most apparent danger to the Indian position had been flagrantly emphasized by the attitude of the newly arrived English who had thrust their armed forces so many hundreds of miles beyond the white settlement line. Though their coming had been under the terms of the capitulation and had not been resisted, once they were ensconced they had begun to pose not as friends but as conquerors. They had swiftly established army posts throughout the Indian country, garrisoned by regulars and commanded by officers who regarded Indians with contempt. Always before the English had wooed Indian favor as ardently as had the French and Spanish. Even during the late war, when most Indians had been killing and scalping Englishmen, English governors and commanders had invited them to conferences, lavished upon them wagonloads of presents, promised them undying friendship. But these new Englishmen had forgotten all that. They were cold and arrogant and supercilious. No longer was a white man's outpost in the wilderness the center of sociability, conviviality, and pleasant barter to which Indians from the earliest times had been accustomed. It was a police post in which any Indian visitor was treated with disdain. If this new kind of Englishman had truly come to stay, then the French defeat had been as great an Indian as a French disaster.

Balanced against this growing English danger, in Pontiac's necessary calculations, was the great Indian opportunity. Never had all

Indians been so restless, so uneasy, so disturbed, so excited. Two
years before the Seneca had created a sensation by sending secret
war belts among the western Indian nations proposing an immediate
combined attack upon the English. The suggestion was directed
primarily to the Shawnee and Delaware, former vassals of the Iroquois and of all Indians the most hostile to the English. The western Indians had not then been ready for so bold a step. But the
Seneca overture had made a profound impression. As Iroquois, they
had long been intimate with the English. Knowing them so well, it
was felt that they must have penetrated English intentions and have
already begun to realize the full enormity of the English threat.
Another stimulant of Indian unrest had been the preaching of the
Delaware Prophet. He was a weeper and a shouter and at most
times not too coherent. With tears streaming from his eyes and his
voice shaking with emotion, he addressed whoever would listen.
Many came from great distances to listen. Presumably he was a little
mad but Indians ascribed a special clairvoyance to madness. The
burden of his doctrine was that Indians were suffering divine punishment for their sins. Their one hope of salvation was to return
to the original state of purity that they had known before the white
man's appearance, when they had been so much more numerous,
healthy, and happy. As a first step toward regaining that purity,
the Prophet implored them to cast away everything that they owned
that had ever been defiled by a white man's touch. Not even fire
was pure when ignited by white man's flint and steel. Many of his
hearers threw away trade blankets, trinkets, and utensils. Guns,
however, presented an insoluble problem. An Indian might hunt
without a gun but how could he resist the white man without one?
Nevertheless, the Prophet's admonitions appealed to very deep
springs in the Indian nature. In every Indian who had heard him
or heard of him, resentment of the white man's intrusion upon his
world was kindled to new fury. More worldly fuel was at the same
time being added to the fires of Indian discontent by his time-tested
white friends, the French inhabitants of Detroit, Mackinac, Vincennes, and Kaskaskia. Their stories varied from day to day but all
were provacative. They said that the English occupation was only

temporary since Canada would be returned to France when the final treaty was signed. They reminded their eager listeners that once before the English had taken Quebec and then, too, it had been promptly restored to France. They said the English knew all this and therefore were planning to kill all Indians before they withdrew in order to deny the French their future services as allies. This last story was made the more credible by the now obvious English hesitation to supply the Indians with guns and ammunition. All in all it had not been a quiet winter. Around every campfire west of Niagara and Pittsburgh, there had been endless and feverish talk.

Pontiac continued to ponder the possibilities. Then in January, there came the thunderbolt that decided him. News reached Detroit of the preliminary peace terms agreed upon in Paris in November by Spain, France, and England. It was stunning news, incredibly worse than the gloomiest forecast. The English were not only to stay on the St. Lawrence and the Great Lakes but were to have as well the whole country east of the Mississippi including even the Floridas. No longer would Indians have room to maneuver, to play off one white power against another. They were doomed to be helplessly dependent upon one and that one the England that they had the most reason to hate and fear. The ability to shut off all trade at will gave England a stranglehold upon their throats. If ever they were to resist, it would seem surely to be now, while the French supply route up the Mississippi was still open.

Pontiac became de facto commander-in-chief of this Indian resistance by the simple device of announcing his readiness to assume the responsibility. Most of his fellow Indians were convinced by the treaty terms of the need to strike at the chains of English control before they became unbreakable. He told them where to strike and when. They needed a leader as they never had before and he was already striding on ahead, waving their standard.

Indians had no written language but by means of elaborate belts upon which colored beads were arranged in various conventionalized designs, they were able to transmit by messenger the most detailed communications. In response to Pontiac's belts, representative chiefs and warriors of every western nation assembled in late April at the River Ecorces, eight miles south of Detroit. He opened the council with an impassioned address in which he dilated upon the many grievances they had suffered from the English and returned again and again to his principal theme: "We must exterminate from our land this nation whose only object is our death . . . We must destroy them without delay. There is nothing to prevent us . . . Why should we not attack them? Are we not men? . . . What do you fear? The time has arrived . . . Let us strike. There is no longer any time to lose."

The Indian temper had so hardened during the winter that Pontiac's call to arms was almost unanimously approved. The few voices expressing qualms or doubts were silenced by the scornful hoots of the majority. The council proceeded to a discussion of ways and means. Every area of strength and weakness in the Indian and white positions was canvassed, every strategic and tactical problem examined. This time Indians would fight a war of their own instead of allowing themselves, as so often before, to become embroiled in wars among the whites. For once they would strike together and according to plan. There was good reason to hope that as soon as the western nations' commitment to war became unmistakable, the Seneca might be able to bring in the other five nations of the Iroquois. There could then be little doubt of the English being driven from the St. Lawrence, the Mohawk, and the Susquehanna or of the advance of the white frontier being permanently discouraged. The increasingly enthusiastic council, inspired by Pontiac's eloquence and confidence, envisaged a supreme effort to make the Indian world safe for Indians.

All of the women, as well as those sociable Frenchmen who always liked to hang around to share in the excitement of Indian assemblies, had earlier been removed to a distance from the meeting place so that there might be less chance of loose talk betraying any hint of the council's momentous decisions. When the council adjourned, early in May, each delegate returned to his nation fully prepared and exactly instructed to undertake the regional objective assigned to him. Pontiac himself took responsibility for the most difficult and important objective of all, the reduction of Detroit.

Detroit was in all respects the metropolis of the wilderness world. Its location made it a focus of supply routes, whether trading or military. Its French population was the most numerous in the west. Its Indian population, residing in their nearby towns, was likewise the largest. Its English garrison was the strongest west of Pittsburgh or Niagara. Founded 62 years before by Cadillac, who had had to circle by way of the Ottawa and Lake Huron to get around the Iroquois barrier, it had increased in importance ever since.

The present fort at Detroit, which the English had inherited from the French, was a considerable structure. The stockade of 20-foot poles enclosed an area of 1200 yards in circumference occupied by 80 houses and a church in addition to barracks and storehouses. Its walls extended to the riverbank with a water gate to facilitate the unloading of trade and military supplies. The fort's major weakness was that it was built on a slope rising from the shore. Indians across the river were able to see most of the interior.

The number of French inhabitants was not easy to estimate at any given time since trading involved so much seasonal coming and going. In addition to the traders, there was an agricultural colony, long since planted by the French for the sake of supplying food for their western posts. The permanent residents, generally considered to number around 1200, lived in large family groups in whitewashed, picket-fenced farmhouses along the river above and below the fort and raised produce for sale, formerly to traders and now also to the garrison. Though situated so deep in the wilderness, they had not in the memory of the oldest inhabitant had trouble with Indians. Their pleasant, lazy, peaceful existence presented a remarkable contrast to the harsh experience of the contemporary English settler east of the mountains. Much of their interest and energy was devoted to dancing, card playing, lacrosse, canoe racing, and similar diversions. During his 1761 visit the irrepressible Johnson had thrown light on the social atmosphere of Detroit by such entries in his journal as: "I opened the ball with Mlle. Curie—a fine girl. We danced until five next morning"; and again: "Danced the whole night until 7 o'clock in the morning, when all parted very much pleased and happy." Grimmer events were about to engage Detroit's attention.

The English garrison was composed of two companies of Royal Americans and one company of Queen's Rangers, numbering probably no more than 125 men since there had been several detachments to man lesser posts. Cannon were mounted in the corner blockhouses. Two small armed schooners were anchored off the water gate. The commander, Major Henry Gladwin, was a sensible soldier. Unlike most English regular officers he did not regard Indians as invariably contemptible antagonists. He had reason to know that at times they could be excessively difficult. He had been with Braddock.

Against the small English garrison in its overlarge fort, Pontiac was able to bring an attacking force far superior in number. It was a number, however, that frequently fluctuated as Indian enthusiasm for the war waxed and waned after each successive advantage or disappointment. The hard core upon which he could generally rely was a fairly cohesive corps of some 900 warriors of the nearer Lakes nations, Ottawa, Chippewa, and Potawatomi. Some 60 to 70 Wyandot were at times most aggressive in battle and at other times almost as aggressive in council. When all was going well, which was usually the case during most of the summer, he often had available upwards of 1600 fighting men.

The third, and involuntary, party to the conflict, the French, was in some respects the most important of all. In spite of their traditional friendship for the Indians and hostility to the English, the majority made a persistent attempt to remain neutral. A few, mostly traders who conceived they might in the future find more need for English approval than for Indian, embraced the English cause. They stayed in the fort and assisted in its defense at the side of Gladwin's other armed auxiliaries, the English traders. A few other Frenchmen, taking an opposite view of the future, became open partisans of the Indians. But most of the French squatted stubbornly on their farms and waited for the hurricane to pass. Their hoarded stores of pork, corn, and beans represented literally the balance of power in the struggle. Pontiac strove the first half of the summer to prevent this food supply reaching the garrison and the second half yielded to the necessity of confiscating it to feed his own forces.

Pontiac's plan for the capture of Detroit had been discussed in detail at the Ecorces council. Had he had artillery to breach the walls Gladwin would have had to surrender on demand. Even without a breach a determined, simultaneous assault from several quarters must surely have succeeded, in view of the length of the walls and the limited number of defenders. But such an assault had no place in Pontiac's planning. He knew the Indian military temperament was not inclined toward mass attacks across the open against gunfire coming from loopholed walls. The individual warrior was capable of bursts of the most extraordinary personal daring. He had not, however, the discipline to lend himself to a formal operation in company with his fellows in which it could be known in advance that a certain proportion of them must fall. He regarded making war as a sport in which the highest score was to be made by demoralizing and humiliating a foe and in which the game was irretrievably lost by any player who lost his life. Pontiac, moreover, concerned with the war as a whole as well as with the siege of Detroit, had no wish to have Indian resolution diminished by heavy losses at the very outset of the first campaign. In any event, he foresaw no need to storm the place. If not taken by surprise or stratagem, before Gladwin had begun to realize his danger, then it must certainly soon be starved out. The garrison was already short of food and anxiously awaiting the spring supply fleet from Niagara.

Pontiac's hope to gain possession by trickery was promptly disappointed. He had sent word to Gladwin of an Indian wish to stage a calumet dance in front of his headquarters to pledge English-Indian friendship. The gates were opened to Pontiac and 60 of his subchiefs. Under their blankets they had concealed sawed-off guns. At a signal from Pontiac, Gladwin and his staff were to be shot down and the gates thrown open to the hundreds of warriors waiting outside. But Pontiac did not give the signal. He could see the moment he had entered that Gladwin had not been hoodwinked.

The entire garrison was assembled, waiting, armed, watchful. Gladwin, too aware of his own weakness to wish to precipitate a war, permitted the chagrined Pontiac to withdraw.

There are any number of legends to account for Gladwin's justified suspicions of Indian intentions that May morning. One story is that he was warned by a young Chippewa girl, Catherine, who had been accustomed to visit his quarters during the long winter. Another is that the enchanting Mlle. Curie, who had so captivated Johnson and had in turn been so deeply impressed by her distinguished beau, had had the quickness of mind to attach significance to the number of Indians who were suddenly eager to borrow the files they needed to shorten their gun barrels. A third, less romantic, maintains that an old squaw who had developed a taste for rum traded her information for a bottle. The simplest explanation may have been that Gladwin was so experienced a soldier that he required no warning. In any event from the hour of the abortive calumet dance, the walls and gates were always manned and the garrison always vigilant. Pontiac saw that he was committed to a formal siege.

His warriors thronged from the forest to encircle the fort. They danced and capered, shouted threats, beat drums, shook rattles, and perpetually howled their eerie war whoops. They crept nearer under cover of nearby barns, farmhouses, stumps, and orchards, deluging the wooden walls with gunfire. Pontiac wanted Gladwin to see the multitude and appreciate the ferocity of the attackers. To give ruthless point to the demonstration, the Indians murdered every member of the only two English households living outside the fort. Then Pontiac made the offer Indians traditionally made when investing a place with overwhelming superior numbers. If Gladwin surrendered, thus sparing the Indians the losses of an assault which must surely succeed, the defenders' lives would be spared. But if the Indians were required to storm the place everybody in it was doomed. Those defenders who died in combat would be fortunate. Those who remained would die by torment. Their commander would be the first to burn.

Gladwin declined to surrender. But he was sufficiently aware of his peril to permit his seccond in command, Captain Donald Campbell, and an aide, Lieutenant George McDougal, to approach the Indian lines under a flag of truce to reason with Pontiac. In defiance of the rules even of wilderness warfare, Pontiac seized the two emissaries and held them as hostages. He was determined to convince not only Gladwin but his own followers that the war now starting was to be one from which there could be no turning back.

The first Englishman to fall in the conflict had been a bystander, though a noted one whose macabre fate aroused so much indignation when the news reached England that it helped for a while to gain Amherst ministerial support for the vigor of his projected countermeasures. For the moment, however, it also gave Pontiac further opportunity to impress Gladwin with the dreadful reality of the threats he had been making. Sir Robert Davers was an early example of the globe-trotting English traveler, half sight-seer, half scientist. With a companion, Lieutenant Charles Robertson, he had been making a canoe tour of the Great Lakes, enjoying the hunting and fishing, inspecting the scenery and observing the natives. They had wintered at Mackinac to study Indian languages. As they neared Detroit on their return, they were set upon by a pack of Pontiac's warriors, murdered, boiled, and eaten. Articles fashioned from their dressed skin were shown in Detroit. This was only the first of the Indian excesses that marked the siege. Most prisoners were put to death by inhuman torment. This was no departure from long-established Indian custom but at Detroit the practice was the more revolting in that it was made a calculated feature of the war of nerves upon the garrison.

In the fort all hopes were centered upon the arrival of the spring supply convoy from Niagara with the food and ammunition so much needed if resistance were to be long continued. To hurry it up and to carry a report on his situation to Amherst, Gladwin got one of his two schooners, *Michigan,* off for Niagara. Thanks to an opportune wind, *Michigan* succeeded in running the gauntlet of attacking Indian canoes and, to the immense relief of the garrison, in breaking free into Lake Erie. But when, a few days later, the supply flotilla appeared in the river, the spectacle was one to stir the defenders not to jubilation but to despair. The white men rowing the barges, many of whom were known to the agonized watchers in the fort, were naked and bleeding prisoners being kicked and beaten by their savage captors.

Lieutenant Abraham Cuyler, commanding the expedition, had set out from Niagara with 96 men in ten oared barges loaded with supplies for the western posts. Having missed sighting Gladwin's eastbound schooner and knowing nothing of the new war, he had taken only routine precautions. Skirting the north shore of Lake Erie, he disembarked for the last overnight encampment of his journey near the mouth of the Detroit River. Wyandot, waiting and watching for the convoy which they had known was due, pounced on the encampment just before midnight. The awakening English broke and fled for their beached boats. Cuyler, with some thirty of his men, managed to escape in two of the boats and to get back to Niagara to report the calamity. The others who had not been butchered in the first heat of action were taken by their captors to the Detroit camps of the besiegers. Enough rum had been found among the supply cargoes to get the Indians drunk by the hundred. At the conclusion of the wild victory celebration to which the defenders had had to listen for endless hours, the burned and mutilated bodies of the prisoners were allowed to drift down the river past the fort for the closer inspection of the garrison.

Pontiac could now feel that his confidence that Detroit might be speedily starved into submission was justified. His master plan for the prosecution of the general war was meeting elsewhere even more striking success. Each fresh report that came in made it more evident that the English grip on the whole west was being broken. Fort after fort was falling. Again and again the main Indian army at Detroit received new batches of haggard prisoners over which to exult and about which to taunt the heart-stricken garrison. The uninterrupted succession of Indian victories had indeed been remarkable.

Fort Sandusky, scene of the first of these widespread Indian triumphs, stood on the estuary of the Sandusky River. The English army post in the wilderness had been established at sites which served either to control important communication routes or to control an adjacent center of Indian population. Sandusky fulfilled both objectives. One of the two principal Wyandot towns was nearby and the fort straddled the main route from Detroit to the Delaware country on the Muskingum to the southeast and to the Shawnee country on the Scioto to the south. During the two years that Sandusky and its companion posts had existed, their garrisons had suffered few tribulations more onerous than bad food, mosquitoes, and unutterable boredom. For months on end they had known no society other than their own and that of their Indian neighbors. The more they had seen of Indians, the lower in their estimation Indians had sunk. Indians of standing tended to hold themselves aloof. The kind of Indians who did frequently visit the forts came ordinarily to beg or to grasp at other disreputable benefits. They wanted rum, or a gun repaired, or a boil lanced, or acceptance of the temporary services of a wife or daughter. There was nothing about a garrison's daily contact with such riffraff to keep soldiers convinced of the deadly danger that might at the most unforeseen moment swoop upon them out of the forest. On May 16th seven Wyandot came to the gate asking to see Ensign Christopher Paully, the Sandusky commander. Paully had no way of knowing that morning that the siege of Detroit had already begun or that upon every other English post in the wilderness was settling the same shadow that was darkening his. He had known the seven Indians for nearly two years and had no reason to imagine that this visit was to be in any way different from the many others each of the seven had made. No sooner were they admitted than they seized him. Other Indians burst through the open gate before the inattentive guard could get it closed. The confused garrison, many of those off duty still in their beds, was cut down. The fort was set on fire, the watching Wyandot howling with glee over this obliteration of one of the symbols of English domination. Paully, the sole survivor of his command, was taken to Detroit so that his burning might have a more considerable audience to appreciate Wyandot prowess. Dismal as must have been his forebodings, he was soon to learn that the fortunes of an Indian captive were as unpredictable as was nearly everything else about Indians.

He was being subjected to that beating, prodding, and lacerating by women and children which was the usual accompaniment of a captive's progress toward the stake when the proceedings were brought to a sudden halt. An Ottawa woman inspected the naked and bleeding young Englishman and demanded the right to adopt him in the place of her recently fallen husband. The right of adoption was a traditional one that Indians did not often deny. Paully was bathed in the river to cleanse him of his white impurity, his head was shaved to a scalp lock, his face was painted, and he was accepted as an Ottawà warrior. Presently he was able to smuggle a letter by way of a Frenchman to Gladwin, reporting the circumstances of the loss of Sandusky. A short time later he managed to escape his savage spouse and to join the defenders of Detroit.

The next English post to fall was Fort St. Joseph's, near the present Niles, Michigan, on May 25th. It had originally been a Jesuit mission, then a trading post, and eventually a small French settlement. The location was important in that it guarded the portage between Lake Michigan and the Illinois River as well as the main overland route from Detroit to the Illinois. There was a large Potawatomi town just across the river. To control this center of wilderness activity, the English had recently established a fort garrisoned by fourteen men under Ensign Francis Schlosser. The inadequate force was overcome even more easily than had been Sandusky's. A delegation of Detroit Potawatomi arrived to visit their St. Joseph's relatives. Schlosser knew no more than had Paully that the war had begun. The visitors from Detroit were admitted to the fort. There were already a number of French traders inside. They do not appear to have been parties to the plot but they were very much in the way when the shooting started. Other Indians rushed through the gates and eleven of the garrison were killed before Schlosser could organize any semblance of defense. Schlosser and the three surviving soldiers were taken to Detroit to exchange for some Potawatomi prisoners Gladwin had been holding.

Next on the roll of disaster was Fort Miami on May 27th. This location, that of the present Fort Wayne, Indiana, was of extreme importance since it guarded the portage between the Maumee and the Wabash on the greatest of all wilderness travel routes from the St. Lawrence, Lake Ontario and Lake Erie to the lower Ohio and the Mississippi. The Fort's Indian neighbors were the Miami (sometimes termed Twigtwee by English traders before the French and Indian War). They were a restless and intransigent lot who had often troubled the French, who were to become a scourge to the future Kentucky frontier, and who were to provide the great Indian commander, Little Turtle, in the American wars to come. Ensign Robert Holmes, commanding at Fort Miami, was the only one of the English wilderness commanders perceptive enough to sense the change in the Indian temper that spring. He had sent a message to Gladwin warning his superior that a general outbreak was impending and had himself taken every precaution to keep his garrison on the alert. In spite of all this prudent forethought, a young Indian girl whom he had taken as mistress and to whom he was warmly attached proved his undoing. She begged him to come with her to treat her mother who had suddenly fallen ill. Holmes trustfully accompanied the savage Delilah to her mother's wigwam nearby. Scarcely was he out of sight of the fort when shots rang out. His sergeant ran out to investigate. He, too, was shot down. Holmes' head was thrown over the wall. A French trader, acting as interpreter, called out to the remaining defenders that immediate surrender offered the one hope of preserving their lives. The terrified and leaderless garrison opened the gates. All were butchered except six who were reserved for burning at later appropriate occasions. Only one man, who had the fortune to be adopted, eventually survived to tell the story of that May morning.

Fort Ouiatonon, at the western end of the Maumee-Wabash portage and the southern end of the St. Joseph's-Wabash trail, near the present Lafayette, Indiana, was the next to fall, on June 1st. This post marked the western limit of English occupation under the terms of the capitulation of Canada. All territory beyond was still held by the French, at Vincennes, Kaskaskia, Cahokia, and at their great stone stronghold, Fort Chartres, on the Mississippi. This proximity of French establishments indirectly eased the peril of the garrison. The French Lieutenant Governor at Fort Chartres, Neyon de Villiers, was suffering all the pangs possible to indecision. Pontiac had appealed to him for aid against their common English enemy. Until he was officially notified of the formal conclusion of the final treaty of peace, Neyon was still technically at war with the English and therefore morally justified in assisting Pontiac's attacks upon them. Though that notification did not reach him until September 24th, he still found reason to hesitate. The English, he took it for granted as a soldier, were bound eventually to overthrow Pontiac if they chose to make a sufficient effort. He did not want their wrath then turned on the weak French settlements in the Illinois. This atmosphere of French indecision influenced the investment of Fort Ouiatonon. The Indians involved, the Wea, were themselves half-hearted in their support of Pontiac's War. Lieutenant Edward Jenkins, the commander, was fully aware that his was the most isolated of all English posts. He could not conceivably hope for relief, even though he held out for months. French traders intervened, for once sincerely. A surrender was negotiated. The fort was burned but the life of every member of the command was spared.

The taking of Mackinac, providing one of the classic episodes of all frontier warfare, came next on June 4th. Mackinac had already had a long history. Founded in 1670, it was the oldest white settlement west of Montreal. Its situation at the juncture of the three western Great Lakes made it the center of the richest fur-producing region on the continent. The French installation, which they had termed Michlimackinac, consisting of the mission, trade depot, and army post characteristic of most of their wilderness establishments, had through the years from time to time been moved back and forth from the north shore to the island to the south shore, each move accompanied by the small white population and the much larger number of Indians who hoped to profit by living alongside their French patrons. The fort taken over by the English in 1761 was on the south shore near the present entrance to the great bridge which now spans the storied strait. Some months even before that, a number of enterprising English traders had appeared, to suffer at the hands of the sullen Indians alarms and indignities nicely balanced between Indian aversion to all Englishmen and Indian desire that trade be resumed. Major George Etherington commanded a garrison which in his official report he indicated to be no more than 35 men but which other evidence indicated was nearer 95. His Indian antagonist, Minavavana, the Chippewa chieftain called by the French Le Grand Sauteur, sufficiently expressed his attitude toward the English intrusion in his recorded address: "Englishman, although you have conquered the French, you have not conquered us. We are not your slaves. These lakes, these woods and mountains, were left us by our ancestors. They are our inheritance." Etherington had been warned by French and English traders that the Chippewa were planning to seize the fort. He not only scoffed at the idea that they could accomplish anything against a garrison as strong as his, but announced that any man who continued to disturb the community by the circulation of such tales would be shipped to Detroit in irons. June 4th was the King's birthday. The Indians, no doubt inadvertently, had scheduled that day an apparently important game of lacrosse between the local Chippewa and a visiting team of Sauk from Green Bay. The Indian players and onlookers gathered at the field in front of the fort's gate where the game got under way. Indians customarily took such competitive sports very seriously and laid large wagers on the outcome. Etherington, his two subalterns, and some of his soldiers not on duty, gathered outside the fort to watch the game and lay a few bets of their own. At a given moment the ball was hit toward the open gate. The players of both teams rushed in pursuit of it. Squaws, standing among the spectators, handed the players weapons that had been concealed under their blankets.

For what next took place, we have the detailed testimony of an eyewitness, Alexander Henry, an English trader who survived, after many desperate months during which again and again he escaped death literally by inches, to write a famous book about his experience. The sweating ballplayers, now armed, sprang upon the garrison with the same zest with which they had been throwing the ball in their interrupted game. Boiling through the gate, they continued to strike down English soldiers and traders while carefully sparing the French residents. Henry bolted into his house. Imme-

diately realizing the insufficiency of this refuge, he ran out the back
door, vaulted the fence and begged sanctuary of his neighbor,
Charles Langlade, a French trader and formerly one of the most
noted of all their partisan leaders. Langlade was a half-breed but
of distinguished family on both the side of his French father and
his Indian mother. He frankly said there was nothing he could do
to save Henry with the Indians in their present frenzy. A Pawnee
slave girl in the household surreptitiously beckoned to Henry and
hid him in the Langlade garret.* Through a crack Henry could
see Indians in the street below quaffing the blood of their fallen
foes in their cupped hands. He crawled into a corner behind a pile
of birchbark vessels used in sugar making but could still hear the
howls and screams as the Indians hunted their victims from house
to house. Presently they searched the Langlade house, including the
garret, but in their impatience failed to discover Henry. Eventually
the tumult died down. Of the garrison only Major Etherington,
Lieutenant William Leslie, and some twenty soldiers were still alive.
They had been stripped naked and tied to trees and posts while
their captors became involved in an increasingly drunken debate
over what should be done with them.

Langlade, becoming aware of Henry's presence in his house, felt
compelled for the sake of protecting his family to turn the fugitive
over to the Indians. The captive passed into the possession of one
Indian after another, each of whom evidenced every intention of
killing him but each of whom was diverted at the last moment by
some minor accident. At long last, Wawatam, a subchief of the
Chippewa, appeared. He had taken no part in the massacre. A year
before he had had a dream in which he had been instructed to adopt
an Englishman and had selected Henry to be that friend and brother.
After painful days of argument, Wawatam's claim was recognized
and Henry passed into his protective custody.

Meanwhile, the debate over the disposition of Etherington and his

* Even in the midst of so much excitement, this is an interesting sidelight. The
Pawnee country was 800 miles away. However, Indians of the forest were frequently
at war with Indians of the plains and as a result of a kind of Indian slave traffic
Plains Indian captives were not uncommon as far east as the towns of the Iroquois
and the Cherokee.

surviving men had taken an astounding twist. A numerous body of
Ottawa from their town twenty miles away at L'Arbre Croche, the
present Cross Village, Michigan, appeared to demand a voice in it.
The Ottawa were outraged that the Chippewa had taken Mackinac
without asking their assistance or even informing their neighbors
and allies of their intentions. They insisted upon a share of the loot
and captives. The argument developed into a prolonged intertribal
drinking bout which increased, if that were possible, the alarm of
the English prisoners waiting to learn their fate. But the boisterous
debauch led to no new outbreak of violence. Instead, there developed
from it a Chippewa-Ottawa reconciliation with maudlin protestations of amity which endured into the cold gray dawn of sobriety.
Etherington, Leslie, and eleven enlisted men were turned over to
the Ottawa who took them home to L'Arbre Croche. Here their
continued safety was largely due to the earnest intercession of Father
Junois, a French priest whose personal qualities and services had
won the respect of the Ottawa. Etherington was even permitted to
send a letter by Junois to Gladwin and another to the commander
of the still-existing English post on Green Bay.

At Fort La Baye, near the present town of Green Bay, Wisconsin,
Lieutenant James Gorell and his garrison of seventeen had been
living in a day-to-day suspense which was intensified by Etherington's dispatch reporting the Mackinac massacre. The local French
population was hostile and the small fort surrounded by overpower-
ing numbers of Sauk, Fox, Winnebago, and Menominee. Gorell
could not hope to hold out for long if he was attacked. The suspense
continued. To add a last turn to the strain he was invited to address
the Indian council debating his fate. As the discussion neared its
climax, a delegation of Sioux appeared to announce the belligerently
definite views of that powerful nation which then occupied the
forests of what are now western Wisconsin and eastern Minnesota.
They demanded that the Englishmen be spared, not because they
loved the English but because they so bitterly hated the Chippewa.
Sioux and Chippewa had been inveterate enemies for more than a
hundred years, since the time the Chippewa, having been first to
get firearms through their earlier trading contact with the French,

had driven the Sioux from the shores of Lake Superior. Whether
or not it was the Sioux intervention that was decisive, the council
finally decided to let the Englishmen go. With a Menominee escort,
Gorell and his command paddled across Lake Michigan to L'Arbre
Croche. After another protracted debate, the Ottawa there turned
over Etherington and their other Mackinac prisoners. The refugee
expedition ran the Chippewa gauntlet in the Straits of Mackinac,
crossed Lake Huron, and reached Montreal safely by the old French
Ottawa River route.

Gorell had abandoned Green Bay June 21st. Three days earlier
Fort Presqu'Isle, five hundred miles nearer the English frontier, had
fallen. The loss had been a severer blow to English military prestige
than had been any of the former disasters. The earlier Indian successes had been by surprise and stratagem over garrisons which had
been subjected to the disadvantages of an unfriendly local French
population and of a trading post atmosphere in which groups of
visiting or loitering Indians were everyday occurrences. But this was
a different case. Presqu'Isle was primarily a fortress; there was no
local French or Indian population and the commander had known
for days that he could expect attack. The capture was in every respect a military operation, the outcome of which was as exhilarating
to the Indians as it was dismaying to the English. Fort Presqu'Isle
at what has become Erie, Pennsylvania, had been founded by the
French in 1753 as the first step in their move into the Ohio Valley,
taken over by the English in 1759 and maintained since by them to
guard their communications within the Niagara-Pittsburgh-Detroit
triangle. The usual stockade enclosing storehouses and quarters had
been strengthened under the supervision of Bouquet himself by the
construction at one corner of an exceptionally strong blockhouse
dominating the walls and approaches. Ensign John Christie, commanding a garrison of 21, had been warned of the outbreak of the
new war by Lieutenant Cuyler returning from his debacle at the
mouth of the Detroit River. Six of Cuyler's men were left at
Presqu'Isle to raise the garrison to 27 which was considered ample
to hold the blockhouse against any attack not supported by artillery.
Christie had twelve days after Cuyler's warning in which to brace

himself. He made diligent use of the interval, laying sod on the roof of the blockhouse as a protection against fire arrows, adding heavy plank to make the principal fire-fighting stations more nearly bulletproof, and arranging bark gutters to distribute water to the points where the gravest threat might be expected.

At dawn of the 15th, the Indians appeared. They were an elite corps, composed of 200 selected warriors dispatched by Pontiac from Detroit who had been joined by a number of war-wise Seneca and a few ardent Delaware. Wasting no time on preliminaries, the attackers got at once to work in a most confident and businesslike manner. They seized positions under the riverbank so near they could toss contemptuous handfuls of pebbles at the blockhouse. They erected a breastwork of logs from which they kept a murderous fire at the loopholes. Discovering the garrison had been concentrated in the blockhouse, they broke into the stockade, occupied buildings there, and denied the defenders the use of the well. The loss of the well was a terrifying handicap to the defense. The principal Indian threat, as always in their assaults upon wilderness fortifications which were necessarily constructed of wood, was their repeated efforts to set fire to the blockhouse. The defenders began desperately to dig a tunnel to the well. The Indians constructed a movable breastwork of planks which they pushed forward until they could toss fireballs against the base of the blockhouse walls. With water from their remaining barrels, the garrison managed to extinguish each new fire. The second day of the siege there was a lull. The Indians, too, were digging. Shortly after noon the officers' quarters immediately adjacent to the blockhouse were fired. But by then the defenders' tunnel had reached the well and they had a fresh supply of water to fight the flames. Evening found the blockhouse scorched and blackened but still intact.

Christie, however, impressed by the extreme exhaustion of his men and convinced that the Indians had been able to dig beneath the walls of the blockhouse to a point where they were certain to succeed in setting it on fire, opened negotiations. The intermediary was a former English soldier who during the years that he had been a captive had become so attached to his Indian associations that he was happy to fight with his captors against his former countrymen. Christie was given until the next morning to make up his mind. When the time limit expired, he surrendered. The surviving members of his garrison, including one woman, a sergeant's wife, passed into the hands of the Indians. Two of the prisoners, taking advantage of the Indians' preoccupation with looting the blockhouse, jerked away, plunged into the woods and found their way to Fort Pitt. The others were taken to Detroit with the now familiar Indian intention of using them to entertain the besiegers and horrify the garrison. Christie himself was eventually exchanged and survived to face a court martial for what was considered not only by his superiors, Bouquet and Amherst, but by some of his own men, a premature surrender.

Fort LeBoeuf, at what is now Waterford, Pennsylvania, took its place on the dismal list of English reverses on the day after Christie surrendered. It had been built by the French in 1753 in time to become the scene of Washington's confrontation of the French commander at the end of his winter journey. The post guarded the portage from Lake Erie to French Creek and the Allegheny but had fallen into disrepair and was held by a garrison of only thirteen men under Ensign George Price. A party of Indians appeared that day ostensibly to ask for a kettle in which to boil their meat. When they were denied entrance, they seized a position in the stone cellar of a nearby storehouse from which they began shooting fire arrows to the roof of the fort. By nightfall the garrison was unable longer to extinguish the flames and was in danger of being buried under the collapsing timbers of the blazing roof. They managed to cut a hole in the wall on the side opposite the Indians entrenched in the cellar and to crawl away in the darkness while the Indians were still shooting into the flaming fort in which they triumphantly supposed the defenders to be roasting. Price and eleven of his men succeeded in reaching Fort Pitt just before it in its turn was invested.

Fort Venango, at what is now Franklin, Pennsylvania, provided the last and most tragic English catastrophe in the swift and swelling tide of Indian victory. It was a new and strong fort commanded by Lieutenant Francis Gordon who exercised supervision, under the

Fort Pitt commander, over the communication line between Lake Erie and Pittsburgh. On the day after the fall of Presqu'Isle a body of Seneca appeared. Since they were Iroquois, Gordon presumed them friends and allies of England. No white man survived to relate what happened after he had opened the gates. The Seneca later boasted that they struck down the garrison but kept Gordon alive under torment after requiring him to write out a statement of Indian grievances against the English. They devoted so much skill and care to the project that the unhappy commander did not expire until late the next day. When Price and his men, fleeing first to Venango, burst out of the forest, they found instead of refuge the still smoking embers of the fort with which were mingled the charred bodies of the garrison.

The day after Gorell had abandoned Green Bay, the westernmost English post, Pittsburgh, only 200 miles from the white frontier, was invested. War parties were crossing the mountains to make their fearful descents upon the settlements. The news Ecuyer's express rider was bringing could not, indeed, have been much worse.

IX

༠

Bouquet II

LORD JEFFREY AMHERST had just won a great war and could not bring himself to believe that there could be any faintest possibility of his being destined to lose this so much lesser one. But even the first fragmentary reports of the Indian uprising in the distant west began at once to suggest how harassing his command problems were to become. Like Pontiac, his basic difficulty was lack of enough fighting men. The ample armies he had commanded during the French War had already been so much reduced by peacetime economies that he was compelled to allocate his forces not by regiments but by half-strength companies. He could see at once that the immediate military requirements of his situation were simple enough. Pontiac, of course, must be promptly subdued but even before that measures must be taken to discourage any impulse among the eastern Iroquois and the southern Indians to support the Indian cause.

For all his arrogance and bad temper Amherst was an intelligent and energetic commander. He had almost within hours decided upon a comprehensive plan that appeared to meet every most serious contingency. He sent his trusted aide, Captain James Dalyell, with reinforcements to Niagara, first to assure the security of that all-important post, next to make there a show of force to assist Johnson's effort to regain control of his Iroquois, and then to proceed on westward to run Pontiac to earth. He assigned Lieutenant Colonel Augustine Prevost to the occupation of the former French post at Mobile and Major Robert Farmar to that of the former Spanish post at Pensacola, the two of them to make another show of force in that region which might help Stuart keep the Southern Indians in line. Finally, and in some respects the most important of all, he ordered Bouquet to march over the mountains to Pittsburgh to put an immediate end to that resumption of Indian attacks on the Pennsylvania-Virginia frontier which were arousing so critical an outcry throughout the English world that the scandal must soon find an echo in the House of Commons.

But, aggravating as were these several most unexpected demands upon his military resources, his greater aggravation was the task of adjusting his thinking to the preposterous proposition that this might develop into anything more than a routine police action to be promptly and readily handled by his regular establishment. His five-year experience in America had bred in him contempt for Indians and disdain for Americans. Indians who had taken part in the French War on either side had appeared to him to have had nothing to contribute of military value. Provincial forces had been consistently so untrained and undisciplined as to prove to him to have had not much more. His only faith then and now was in the English regular soldier commanded by regular officers. In his estimation the surest way to keep Indians in order was a musket butt in the teeth. The early reports of the Indian upheaval had done nothing to modify these views. "The post of Fort Pitt, or any others commanded by officers," he was writing Bouquet early in June, "can never be in danger from such a wretched enemy."

In that June of 1763 when word of the new war had burst upon him, Bouquet was stationed with a skeleton headquarters at Philadelphia, occupied by routine duties which essentially were those of a desk-bound quartermaster. His regiment had been dispersed in garrison detachments among wilderness posts from Bedford to Mackinac. The disturbing news was made the more personally disturbing by his realization that it was his own men who were being attacked. He was under few illusions about the nature of the trials ahead. Though as a sensible old soldier he outwardly agreed with Amherst's scornful assumption that the Indians would scuttle back into the woods at the first show of English force, privately he knew better. He had himself for three years commanded at Fort Pitt and knew well the perpetual dangers against which every wilderness garrison must guard. Continually harassed by resentful Indians, illegal traders, and trespassing settlers, the commander was locked in a powder magazine toward which a train was always burning.

Bouquet was not kept long in doubt about what was to be required of him. Amherst was writing "I am determined to take every measure in my power not only for securing and keeping entire possession of the country, but for punishing those barbarians who have thus perfidiously massacred his Majesty's subjects." The commander-in-chief's directive instructed Bouquet to make an example of the Indians in the upper Ohio area and then to continue by way of Lake Erie to Detroit to join in the speedy subjugation of the Great Lakes region. Amherst was seething with impatience to see immediate results but as the reports from the west became more explicit the dimensions of the danger began finally to dawn on him. "All the troops from hence that could be collected are sent you," he wrote Bouquet, now already at Lancaster on his way westward, "so that should the whole race of Indians take arms against us, I could do no more."

Bouquet, too, for all his earlier forebodings, was beginning to realize how much more critical was his task than he had foreseen at Philadelphia. The mountains, now in sight, reared against the sky before him. To force a way over them Forbes had had an army of 7000. He had less than 500, a third of them sick. And whatever the dangers that might await him beyond the mountains they were rivaled by the frustrations that he was experiencing on this side. If he was to march at all he required horses, wagons, and oxen to haul the supplies consumed by an army advancing far from its base. These could only be obtained from civilian sources but he was encountering the greatest difficulty in assembling this necessary transport. A major purpose of his campaign was to parry the Indian threat to the borders of Pennsylvania, yet the people of Pennsylvania, including those most immediately threatened, offered him little support. This indifference to measures in their own defense he found "disgusting to the last degree." "I find myself utterly abandoned," he wrote Amherst from Carlisle, his staging point, "by the very people I am ordered to protect."

The Pennsylvania assembly, called into emergency session by Governor Hamilton, reluctantly voted on July 4th to raise 700 men but directed that they were not to be used to reinforce Bouquet, that under no circumstances were they to undertake any offensive moves against the Indians, and that they were to confine their services to guarding farmers attempting to gather their crops. The dogmatic pacifism and traditional sympathy for Indians of Philadelphia's Quaker majority was shared by many other citizens of the city. In the prevailing Philadelphia view it was the land-greedy settlers' own wrong-headed fault that they were being scalped by the long-suffering Indians. They had repeatedly been warned by provincial authorities, as well as by royal authorities, to stay off Indian lands. Having disobeyed their own government, they could scarcely expect that government to come flying to their rescue. Deeply seated racial and religious prejudices aggravated this attitude. The English population long established in and around Philadelphia had little in common with the more recently arrived Scotch-Irish Presbyterians and German Lutherans who had tended to collect in the newer settlements to the west. Though thousands of these fellow white men were now in panic-stricken flight the still unthreatened residents of Philadelphia remained unmoved, except for a few charitable gestures toward providing food and shelter.

The border people themselves appeared to have no thought beyond a general impulse to scramble toward the protection of Bouquet's muskets. The time was to come when their first thought was to be the fighting of their own battles. But that time was not yet. Disgusted as he was by their hysterical unreadiness even to furnish him with the volunteer company of woods-trained rangers that he needed, Bouquet was nevertheless affected by their miseries. "The list of people known to be killed increases every hour," he wrote Amherst. "The desolation of so many families, reduced to the last extremity of want and misery; the despair of those who have lost their parents, relations and friends, with the cries of distracted women and children who fill the streets—form a scene painful to humanity and impossible to describe." These were not isolated scenes Bouquet was viewing. Croghan, who probably knew the border better than anyone, estimated the number of settlers killed and taken during that twelvemonth to amount to 2000.

It may have been this spectacle of suffering inflicted by the marauding Indians, coupled with the infuriating delays in organizing his expedition, that accounted for Bouquet's stepping out of soldierly character long enough to reply to Amherst's smallpox suggestion: "I will try to inoculate the bastards with some blankets that may fall in their hands and take care not to get the disease myself." There is no evidence that Bouquet made any such attempt, though one of those smallpox epidemics to which Indians had periodically been subject since their first contact with whites did strike the Ohio Indians before the year's end. But he was all soldier again when, on July 3rd, he received the crushing news of the fall of Presqu'Isle, Le Boeuf, and Venango. He had himself built the Presqu'Isle blockhouse and had taken pride in making it strong. "Humanity makes me hope that Christie is dead," he wrote Amherst, "as his scandalous capitulation, for a post of that consequence and so impregnable to savages, deserves the most severe punishment."

Finally, on July 18th, having somehow gathered the necessary transport, Bouquet marched out from Carlisle. His was a pitiful little army. He had 214 men of the 42nd, the Highland regiment already known as the Black Watch, 133 men of the 77th, also a Scotch regiment, and 113 of his own Royal Americans. Drums beat, bagpipes skirled, and the Highlanders swung off bravely in kilts and tartans, but still the martial display could not have been one to strike terror into the heart of any enemy. Small as was his command, 60 men of the 77th were still so weak from tropical diseases with which they had been infected at the taking of Havana the year before that they had to be carried in the wagons.

The column of red-coated infantry, laden pack horses, herded beef cattle, and trundling ox wagons began its slow crawl over the succession of ridges that intervened between Carlisle and Pittsburgh. As always on such a march into the wilderness, the greatest of all dangers, as Bouquet had well learned during his seven years of frontier service, was the constant danger of surprise attack. At any moment on any day the apparently empty forest might spew forth hordes of savages, leaping from tree to tree and setting up so terrible a commotion of yelling and shooting as to throw the most disciplined troops into confusion. His Highlanders were in most respects the best soldiers in the world but they were baffled by the forest. "I cannot send a Highlander out of my sight without running the risk of losing the man," he wrote Amherst, "which exposes me to surprise from the skulking villains." At Bedford he managed to hire 30 backwoodsmen who, though too few to provide the guard he so much needed for his van, flanks, and rear, were able to give him some warning of any suddenly gathering danger.

But so far there had been no danger, not so much as a stray shot or any sign whatever of Indians. Their raiding parties were still devastating the settlements behind him but there appeared to be no Indian interest in his advance. Each day there was only the silent forest and then another ridge to climb. Actually the Indians were taking a sharp interest in him. They were watching his progress and waiting confidently for him to push on ever deeper into the wilderness. The main Indian force, except for the one conducting the siege of Detroit, was vigorously pressing the investment of Fort Pitt. The strength of the place had been greatly reduced by abnormal spring floods but its remaining brick-faced walls had so far resisted every attempt to set them afire. Until there was a breach, the attackers were thwarted. Captain Ecuyer, though wounded, remained calm and resolute. He was certain that his garrison could hold out until starved into submission. But Bouquet could not know that. He had heard no word from Pittsburgh in over a month. For all he knew the all-important fort might already have fallen.

His sweating army toiled over the main range of the Alleghenies and then Laurel Mountain and on August 3rd reached Fort Ligonier. The few Indians who had been harassing the post for the past two months scattered at the approach of the column. Ahead, now, loomed the last ridge. Beyond Chestnut Mountain the descending tier of lesser wooded hills rolled down to Fort Pitt at the Forks of the Ohio. Indian reaction to his approach could not be much longer postponed. He could be certain that somewhere on this last ridge or among those wooded hills beyond, they would be waiting for him.

It had been in that same grim expanse of forest between the Monongahela and the Allegheny that Braddock and then Grant, each nearing the end of just such a march as this one, had encountered disaster. With Grant had been a battalion of these same Highlanders now with this third English army to enter the ill-omened arena. Bouquet had particular occasion that night to ponder Grant's defeat. Everything about his surroundings reminded him of it and that he himself had been partially responsible for it. Five years before he had been encamped on this same spot. He could still see those red-coated fugitives streaming in panic toward him down the slopes of Chestnut Mountain and the heads of those others who had not been able to flee stuck on the pointed tops of that dreadful row of poles before Fort Duquesne. Tomorrow he was to advance over the same ground as had Grant, with an army half as strong and against an Indian enemy conceivably twice as numerous. These were somber reflections for a commander on the eve of battle.

He left his ox wagons at Fort Ligonier to free his movements of their slow pace. Taking only a small herd of beef cattle and what supplies he could carry on 350 pack horses, he crossed Chestnut Mountain. The Indians still had made no move to oppose his advance. The woods on the ridge remained as empty and as silent as on every other day of the march. Each hour the mounting suspense intensified the strain. Men could not be held indefinitely to so sharp an edge of expectancy. For the seventeenth time since leaving Carlisle the army cleared a space in the woods and bivouacked, its rest disturbed as on every former night by the thought that the worst was still to come. Tonight one thing more was known. Whatever was to come it must surely be tomorrow. Fort Pitt was now less than forty miles away. Somewhere along those few remaining miles of forest track the test must be met.

At dawn the march was resumed. The column swung along for another 17 miles. Fort Pitt now was but 20 miles away. Still the forest remained empty. With each mile the tension became more nearly unbearable. Then, when at last the attack came, it was with as much stunning abruptness as though it had not been so long expected. Just before the vanguard reached the little stream of Bushy Run it was fired upon. Two companies charged with fixed bayonets to clear the road. The Indians fell back before the charge but at the same time their fire from the forest's cover encircled the whole column and crashed most heavily of all upon the pack train at the rear. Bouquet was forced to pull back to save his convoy.

The Indians developed their attack with unprecedented resolution. Each warrior, forgetting his usual aversion to discipline, was fitting into his assigned place in the Indian plan of action. They were being skillfully led by two able commanders, Custaloga, the Delaware, and Guyasuta, the Seneca. Custaloga, head of the Delaware's Wolf clan, was a veteran of many former encounters with white men, both at the council table and in the field. In his younger days Guyasuta had been Washington's guide on the winter journey to Le Boeuf and was to live to burn Hannastown, five miles east of this same battlefield, in the last year of the Revolution.

The essence of the Indian style of attack upon regular soldiers in the wilderness, which had always before succeeded, was to remain hidden, except for intermittent leaps and capers to disconcert the already distracted soldiers. Crawling, slipping from tree to tree, taking as much advantage of the forest's cover as might so many wild animals, they kept pressing closer so that their continual aimed rifle fire became each moment more effective. The soldiers, refused permission to break ranks or, if they were given permission, too inexperienced to take equivalent cover, were committed to standing in the open where they remained targets for a fire which they were helpless adequately to return. If charged, the Indians melted away only to begin encircling the advancing detachment which had immediately to fall back again. The Indian's wild howling suggested the fate in store for the vanquished. Their near invisibility made them seem invulnerable. When an Indian was momentarily glimpsed, his naked form painted red and black, perhaps with grotesque white or green circles about his eyes and mouth, he appeared more akin to a demon from the nether regions than a human antagonist. This form of Indian attack in the dense thickets of the wilderness, by now horribly familiar, had been one with which a regular army had until now been quite unable to cope. It was inevitable that a premonition of doom began soon to settle over the frantic soldiers. Suffering punishment which could not be returned became a strain which they could not indefinitely endure. Sooner or later came the dread moment when one man and then his neighbor and then the next three or four and then a whole platoon yielded to the impulse to run, each imagining that in the confusion there might be some vague desperate chance that he might save himself.

The supreme tribute to any commander is his influence over his men at such a moment. Bouquet's did not waver. They looked only to him, waited for him to determine what to do, steadily did what he directed. Near the spot where the convoy had been attacked the road ran up over the shoulder of a low hill. He ordered the hill seized. The cattle and horses of the convoy were tethered to trees on the upper slopes. The wounded were collected in a slight depression near the top and further sheltered by a bulwark of grain bags. Those of his men still fit for action he arranged in a perimeter about the lower slopes of the hill, each facing outward from the circle toward the enemy. He was establishing the forerunner of the thin red line famous in England's later wars.

The Indians pressed their attack. They now had their prey driven to cover and completely surrounded and were more than ever confident of the outcome. Though the soldiers had been permitted to take cover in hollows or behind logs it was still an unequal contest. Soldiers were being killed, hour after hour, while the Indian losses were insignificant.

When darkness fell the Indians slackened fire, to conserve ammunition, but continued closely to invest the hill. The long night was made to seem longer by their howls, and taunts, and the shouted forecasts by one Indian who knew English of the fate the morrow must inevitably bring to every white man. Bouquet needed no Indian reminders of his peril. He had staved off destruction during the first day of battle but his situation remained one that could hardly have been less encouraging. His small army had already lost 60 killed and wounded. He could only assume that the next day, as his line grew weaker, his rate of loss was more likely to increase than diminish and his army steadily wither away. To attempt to hold this position was in any event impossible for there was no water on the hill. Yet to attempt to break out and fight his way through the forest back to Fort Ligonier was to admit defeat and invite catastrophe. It was difficult to imagine that on that long road back over Chestnut Mountain there might arise a better chance to beat them than he had had when they first attacked him. There remained, then, but the one recourse. Some way must be hit upon to beat them here. His men held their lines in the darkness and trusted that he would think of something. The wounded, listening through the night to the Indian clamor, could only wait and shudder. Their prospects for tomorrow were as dreadful as any men could contemplate. If the army marched they must be left behind. If it stood here until overwhelmed Indian torment must as surely be their lot. Indians occasionally made captives of the strong but took invariable delight in adding to the suffering of the helpless.

When morning brought enough new light to aim, the Indian fire recommenced. More confident every hour of the certainty of victory they pressed their attack with fresh ardor. The day was excessively hot and the lack of water on the hill became a major factor in the battle. The English, especially the wounded, were suffering agonies of thirst. The incessant Indian fire struck also among the animals. Wounded horses broke from their tethers and galloped, screaming terribly, up and down the wooded slopes. From time to time, to the Indians' great glee, they disordered the English line by trampling the recumbent soldiers.

Bouquet had been coolly waiting for the opportune moment to make his bid. Toward noon he made it. His maneuver was the simplest and most time-honored of all tactical stratagems—the feigned retreat. By taking a precisely calculated advantage of the terrain and the mood of his enemy he made of it a gem of generalship. At his direction, the men of the company holding the south face of the hill slope began to give way. Soon more and more of them were getting up and running. The overconfident Indians, already awaiting and expecting the first signs of English panic, rushed forward, yelling exultantly, to spur the flight into a rout. The company on the west slope, hidden from Indian view by the contour of the ground, advanced suddenly around the hill to take them in the flank. The Highlanders charged, for once enjoying the unprecedented satisfaction of getting at a mass of Indians with the bayonet. The astonished Indians recoiled. The company from the east slope, its sudden advance likewise concealed by a shoulder of the hill, now took them in the other flank. The Indians broke and were driven in headlong flight by the now jubilant Highlanders.

The counterattack had been so totally unexpected, its success so complete, and their losses so heavy, that the entire Indian force broke off the action. They had been convinced that Bouquet's men, far from having been dispirited, were more ready to keep on fighting than they had been the first day. It was a basic principle of Indian military thinking that an attack should be pushed only when there appeared a clear promise of demoralizing the defense. The victors, after burying their dead, resumed their advance, though not triumphantly. Having lost his horses, Bouquet was obliged to destroy most of his supplies. Slowed by the need to carry so many wounded in litters and by sporadic Indian sniping, he was three days making it the rest of the way to Fort Pitt. Ecuyer's welcome was made the more heartfelt by his recent misgivings. After the first day of the battle Indians had appeared outside the walls brandishing scalps and announcing the destruction of the English army.

At Bushy Run, the matching of red warrior against white soldier was more nearly even, longer in duration, and more gallantly and stubbornly fought than in any other battle in which they ever met. In every other the weakness of the loser early became apparent, the victor correspondingly encouraged, and the engagement soon degenerated into pursuit or debacle. But at Bushy Run for hour after hour, through two days and a night, the antagonists stood toe to toe, each accepting and inflicting punishment without flinching. The two forces were about equal. The English lost 115 killed and wounded, a quarter of their number. The Indians lost approximately as many. Though a minor battle if judged by the numbers engaged, it was as desperately waged an action as is often recorded in military annals.

Bouquet did not delude himself with the presumption that his victory had been in any sense decisive. When he had limped into Fort Pitt it was at once apparent that his losses in men and supplies had been too severe to permit the further offensive move into the Indian country that Amherst had directed. The immediate military effect of Bushy Run was therefore limited to raising the siege of Fort Pitt. All that actually had been achieved was a reinforcement of the garrison. The general course of the war had been but little influenced. Not even the nearest Indian positions along the upper Ohio had been threatened. After a few days' lull the Indian devastation of the Pennsylvania frontier was resumed with greater savagery than ever. But the consequences of a victory can often be more certainly appraised by considering the results had the battle been lost. Had Bouquet lost, Pittsburgh must soon have fallen, the war have been painfully prolonged, and settlement west of the mountains have been delayed for years. More immediately important, perhaps, was the effect on the Indian morale. They had lost some of their former assurance that in the forest they were the white soldier's certain master. Again, as so often before, they had attacked a white army on ground and at a moment of their own choosing. But this time for the first time they had been beaten off. The reverse bit deeply into Indian consciousness. When Bouquet next marched into the wilderness against them they were not so ready to throw themselves upon him.

X

ૐ

Pontiac II

REPORTS OF INDIAN SUCCESSES from the Wisconsin to the Susque-hanna continued to pour in upon Pontiac. Every event of that early summer of 1763 gave him new reason to be satisfied with the progress of his war. Already, but little more than a month since he had stalked through the Detroit gate with a sawed-off gun under his blanket, the only living Englishmen west of Pittsburgh and Niagara who were not captives were the handful almost as helpless as captives within the walls of Detroit. The whole vast wild territory so brazenly bequeathed to England by the Treaty of Paris had been snatched from England's grasp and restored to Indian custody. More successes seemed imminent. Pittsburgh could not hold out for long. The Southern Indians were stirring and certain soon to recognize their great opportunity. The Pennsylvania-Virginian frontier was experiencing a devastation to match the worst it had suffered during the worst of the French War. The New York frontier, under the overconfident Johnson's very nose, was gripped by fear. The English response to so many continuing threats and disasters had been revealingly slow and ineffectual. Their one noticeable effort so far

[185]

had been Bouquet's preparations to cross the mountains. With him was an army too small to cause any Indian concern.

Pontiac could feel certain by now that Detroit, suffering more each day for lack of food, must soon yield, releasing new hordes of Indian attackers to ravage the English settlements so mercilessly that England must beg for peace on Indian terms. The elated Indians pressed the siege with renewed vigor. Entrenchments were dug closer to the walls to keep the defenders under a more effective fire. Attempts were made to breach the walls by pushing against them carts loaded with burning logs. The haggard garrison was given no rest. No effort was spared to dispirit them with new evidences of Indian ferocity. When a nephew of the Chippewa chief, Wasson, was killed during a sortie, the hostage, Captain Campbell, Gladwin's predecessor as commander of Detroit, was barbarously put to death in retaliation.

But it was now, at the moment when Pontiac's hopes were brightest, that he was confronted by a threat which he could not have foreseen and which, when it sprang upon him, he must have begun to suspect might foreshadow his doom. Here in these deepest reaches of the wilderness, he was made to feel the impact of that English seapower which had confounded so many of England's enemies in so many other wars. Late in June, the schooner *Michigan,* which in early May had got away for Niagara with Gladwin's report of Detroit's peril, reappeared in the lake, waiting for a favorable wind to make an attempt to run up the river to the fort. Aboard was a cargo of provisions and ammunition and the survivors of Cuyler's force making this new effort to fulfill their original mission.

The Indians realized as well as did the frantically anxious garrison how much depended on the arrival of this relief. They built leaf-covered breastworks on Turkey Island and on the banks of the river at its narrowest point, and waited in ambush, as from time immemorial they had so often before crouched in hiding to surprise an approaching enemy. At length *Michigan* made her try. At a critical moment, the wind failed and she was forced to anchor in the river. Under cover of darkness, the exultant Indians that night attacked in fleets of canoes, sure of their prize. But what they won instead was their first harsh lesson in sea warfare. The silence of river and forest was disrupted by a most unfamiliar sound, the reverberating roar of broadsides from the guns of a warship. Grape ripped their frail bark canoes to shreds. Withdrawing precipitately to their breastworks on solid ground, they hammered the schooner with bullets from hundreds of rifles. *Michigan* pulled anchor and drifted down-river out of range. On June 30th the wind held. The schooner sailed briskly upriver, undeterred by rifle fire from the shore-bound Indians and, for good measure, in passing bombarded the Wyandot town on the east bank. Coming to anchor before the water gate, supplies and reinforcements were landed to sustain Detroit for weeks to come. The investment had become, in effect, a new siege.

Now that he had two ships, Gladwin could moreover afford risks that he had been reluctant to assume with only one. Possession of a fleet was an advantage that could be rubbed in. The first day offering a fair wind to maneuver, his two schooners set sail and, taking favorable positions at will, raked the besiegers' towns and camps with ball and grape. The Indians, unable to reply in kind, were forced to take shelter in the forest until the ships withdrew. Pontiac met this new challenge with spirit. Fire rafts were constructed to be carried by the current against the anchored schooners. But the English had had long experience with naval tactics. They contrived a boom of chains to fend off every threat.

The morning of July 29th brought a third and even more impressive manifestation of the effectiveness of sea power. The fog lifted to reveal a sight as unexpected by the garrison as by the Indians. A fleet of 22 oared barges filled with English soldiers was making for the Detroit water front. Favored by an unusually dark night and a morning fog, they had made the run up the river undetected by the Indians until too late. A last minute burst of rifle fire from the Potawatomi town on the shore just south of Detroit killed or wounded fifteen but every barge made the water gate. This, the first full-scale expedition to come to Detroit's relief, was a detachment of 260 men commanded by Captain Dalyell, aide-de-camp to Amherst, who had organized the project after his successful reinforcement of Niagara. With him were the even more distinguished Robert Rogers, who in the late war had so often proved himself as much at home in the wilderness as any Indian, and twenty of his famous Rangers.

Gladwin was happy to receive a reinforcement that more than tripled the strength of his hard-pressed garrison but troubled by the impetuous proposals Dalyell began at once to press upon him. The one way to handle Indians, Dalyell maintained, echoing the opinion of his commander-in-chief, was to shove the war down their throats. If boldly attacked, he insisted, they would always scatter. He implied that Gladwin's remaining on the defensive within the walls had unnecessarily prolonged the siege. In the place of this policy of caution, he advocated a daybreak assault upon Pontiac's Ottawa town. Gladwin differed guardedly, as did most of Dalyell's own officers, including Rogers. The Detroit commander was technically Dalyell's superior but he was undoubtedly impressed by the fact Dalyell was fresh from headquarters and was a favorite of Amherst. At any rate, he yielded.

Some hours before dawn on the 31st, Dalyell marched out with 287 men along the road which ran north from the fort along the shore of the river. Rogers and his Rangers, the only experienced Indian fighters with the command, whose presence in the vanguard might have been more than useful, were assigned a position back in the middle of the column. Pontiac and his watching Indians could scarcely credit their good fortune. The war afloat had not been going too well for them but here were Englishmen not only on land but in the night and in an area where Indians knew every stick and stone. By the hundreds they filtered swiftly and silently into positions in French houses and barns and behind fences and thickets. They held their fire until the head of the column had reached the center of the narrow wooden bridge over Parent's Creek, thereafter known as Bloody Bridge.

The appalling howl of Indian war whoops hit the men on the bridge with almost as stunning an impact as the first Indian volley. Within a minute, half the vanguard was down. The rest naturally recoiled. But Dalyell brought up his main force and led a charge across the bridge and up the brush-dotted slope beyond. No Indians were encountered. Yet, from all sides the fire of the invisible enemy continued. The willing but confused English soldiers, milling about in the open and peering helplessly into the darkness, could see only the innumerable flashes of gunfire stabbing at them. Then, adding enormously to their uneasiness, far behind them, about the column's rear guard, there erupted a new din of musketry and unearthly whooping.

It was rapidly becoming apparent, even to Dalyell, that there could be no question of a continued advance upon Pontiac's town. The graver question, more doubtful every minute, was to be his ability to get his men back to the shelter of the fort. Attempting to rally them he was twice wounded and then killed. His senior captain, Robert Gray, was mortally wounded. Captain James Grant and the other surviving officers, with that fortitude the English regular service traditionally exhibited when the going was at its worst, began attempting to organize an orderly retreat, always the most precarious maneuver in any battle. Dalyell's body was overlooked and left to the Indians who in their victory celebration next day made much sport with it. But few wounded were abandoned. Most were embarked in the two barges that had been coasting along the riverbank abreast of the advance. The soldiers, reassured by their officers' calm, steadied. It was the provincial, Rogers, the only nonregular officer present, who gained the retreat and the precious time that was imperative. He drove the Indians from one of the houses overlooking the road and then from another, continuing to cover the withdrawal by keeping hundreds of the Indians preoccupied with his sudden moves and stands, though it meant his little rear guard was bound to be cut off.

The coming of daylight saved the English from a far greater disaster than they had already suffered. The barges returned, bringing sea power again into play, and the gun crews of the three-pounders mounted in their prows were now able to see their targets. Naval cannon fire drove the Indians from their positions commanding the road. Even Rogers' rear guard was able to rejoin the main column in its escape into the fort. The protecting gates closed, putting an end to Dalyell's rash venture which had cost the English 61 killed and wounded.

The bloody repulse of Dalyell was accepted by Indians and English alike as a great Indian victory. Gladwin realized that he was even more committed than before to an indefinite defensive. He must remain shut up within the walls of his fort until Amherst proved able to mount a far stronger relief expedition than had been Cuyler's or Dalyell's. The Indians were correspondingly jubilant. As by the memorable routs of Braddock and Grant at Fort Duquesne, so now had the rout of Dalyell at Detroit once more demonstrated the personal superiority of the Indian warrior over the English soldier.

Nevertheless, Pontiac still had much to think about. He had Gladwin shut in, tighter than before, but much less than before dared he risk an assault on walls defended by the reinforced and now well-supplied garrison. In council other chiefs pointed out that they could afford to wait until the garrison again got hungry, a process likely to prove more rapid now that there were so many more mouths to feed. After Dalyell's failure, there was little likelihood that the English would prove able to organize another relief expedition for months to come. There was equally no occasion for Indian alarm over reports of Bouquet's laborious march over the Pennsylvania mountains. Before he reached Pittsburgh, he was certain to stumble into the same sort of trap as had Braddock, Grant, and Dalyell. Even if he did reach Pittsburgh, he would remain, in any military sense, no nearer Detroit than he had been at Philadelphia.

But Pontiac was not convinced. His military education had been immensely broadened by the events of the past thirty days. English sea power, as manifested by the arrival of *Michigan* and Dalyell's fleet and by the cannon of Gladwin's schooners firing upon his towns and of the barges covering the retreat from Bloody Bridge, represented a continuing threat against which Indian arms, however superior on land, had no effective defense. Detroit had to be taken, for so long as it was held it was a perpetual invitation to

English armies to come into the heart of the Indian country. The logic of the situation was inescapable. If it could not be taken by assault, then it could only be taken by shutting off its supplies which in turn could not be achieved as long as the English remained invulnerable when they came with them by water. The one section of Detroit's long supply route, stretching back to the English frontier, which was on land was the Niagara portage. Pontiac's attention was directed upon Niagara.

Amherst had in the spring been well enough aware of Niagara's decisive importance to make first of all the most urgent efforts to reinforce its garrison. Twice in earlier times the Seneca had eliminated posts which white men had established here but the stone walls of this one posed a military problem which they could not solve with the weapons at their command. After a few desultory attempts to annoy the garrison by rifle fire, they became more interested in attacking lesser posts and frontier settlements. More of the pressure was relieved by Johnson's partial success in out-talking the war faction among the eastern Iroquois. After a series of private and personal conferences he had at last, on September 7th, managed to assemble a general council of St. Lawrence and New York Indians at which he had been able to persuade the Iroquois, with the exception of the Seneca and a portion of the Cayuga, to remain neutral. It had not been an easy summer for Johnson, however. Again and again, the New York frontier had been on the verge of a mass evacuation. The attacks had not amounted to the cruel devastation visited upon the Pennsylvania frontier but had been severe enough to excite the most acute public alarm. At one time Johnson himself, after all the years of his acceptance as the great and good friend of the Iroquois, had been so uncertain of the course of events that he had requested and received a detachment of soldiers from Amherst to protect him at Johnson Hall. His uneasy peace conference was still in session when the storm burst over Niagara.

Arrival of the western warriors Pontiac had dispatched from Detroit had stimulated the Seneca to resume aggressive action. On September 13th one of the usual supply trains was proceeding along the portage road under a guard of 24 soldiers. The combined Indian attack struck the convoy just as it had reached that part of the cliffs which reared above the portion of the gorge aptly named Devil's Hole. The onslaught was so sudden and was pressed so hard that there were only three white survivors. John Stedman, contractor in charge of the train, spurred his horse to a desperate gallop and miraculously escaped the hail of bullets sent after him. The two others who lived were wounded who had been left for dead. Indian love of violence for once was satiated. They could listen to the screams of victims cast from the cliffs and drive horses and tip wagons into the boiling abyss below. Indians who had had the privilege of sharing in the exploit were much given so long as they lived to the fond recounting of stories of their experiences that day.

Hearing the firing, a detachment from Fort Schlosser, as the English had renamed the fort above the Falls, rushed to the rescue and rushed straight into the ambush of the Indians who had been counting on their intervention. From selected positions behind rocks and trees they shot the column to pieces while themselves suffering slight loss. When the action ended the English death toll at Devil's Hole had risen to 70.

Major John Wilkins, commanding at Fort Niagara, pushed vengefully out with a force of over 500 men. But he found only the English dead littering the portage road. The Indians, as they were able to do whenever they chose, had faded into the forest beyond his view or reach. This Indian capacity suddenly and unexpectedly to appear and then as suddenly and unexpectedly to disappear had confounded many more capable commanders than Wilkins and was to continue to confound them for thirty years to come.

Wilkins' primary responsibility, after making sure of the continued safety of the Niagara portage, was to mount a relief expedition of such strength as to make it absolutely certain that Detroit could be held against Pontiac. But none of his arrangements and preparations had escaped Indian attention. When, at length, he shoved off from Fort Schlosser for Detroit, the Indians were again waiting expectantly. From the rocky and wooded shores of the river, they poured a fire so intense that his force was thrown into confusion and he was compelled to turn back. After more adequate preparation he broke through into Lake Erie. Aboard his great fleet of barges was a Detroit reinforcement of 600 men and ample supplies to maintain so enlarged a garrison. Reliance on sea power at times exacts a price. This was one of those times. One of those sudden late autumn storms for which Lake Erie has always been notorious scattered and wrecked Wilkins' boats. Seventy men were drowned. Gladwin at Detroit was forced to face the winter unsupported.

Measuring what he had achieved by what he had set out to achieve, Pontiac in mid-September still had reason for grim satisfaction. The three major English posts, Detroit, Pittsburgh and Niagara, still held out against him. But, except within their walls, not even a single English trader remained anywhere in the Indian country. No Indian position anywhere west of the mountains was in danger. It was the white men east of the mountains who were in panic-stricken flight from their homes. His fierce followers had killed some 3000 English while losing less than a tenth as many of their own. Deprived of the profits of the fur trade which had led them originally to invade his country, they must surely soon realize the uselessness of continuing a war in which they now had so little to gain. While on the other hand the Illinois French, becoming aware of the new opportunity he had opened to them, must just as surely realize the reward to be gained by coming to his support. Meanwhile the Creek, the greatest Indian nation in the south, had at last begun to rouse and, under their English-hating war chief, The Mortar, were driving white men from their borders. Pontiac's War, according to his understanding of war, was all but won.

XI

ຽ

The Frontier People

THE CONFLICT had made the most extraordinary demands upon the soldiers engaged in it. The threats and fears springing from the unavoidable horrors of any war were in this one remorselessly exaggerated. For some it both began and ended in lonely wilderness outposts with the sudden strangling terror of an ordinary day's calm being transfigured during the passing of a single second into a pandemonium of butchery. Many languished through months of starvation that could be longer endured only because the sole alternative was the flames of the burning stake. Others toiled over mountains or rowed the length of storm-tossed inland seas to perish helplessly in thickets by the hand of an enemy never once glimpsed. For all who had survived the initial outbreak there was the shattering strain of anticipating death, not with a soldier's ordinary expectation during the swift short hours of a battle but continuously without a moment's intermission for days and weeks and months. It was not, however, in this bloodstained welter of marches, cruises, sieges, and battles nor by the achievements of commanders, governors, or lawmakers that the ultimate issue of the war was being decided.

That was being decided by the obduracy and perversity of people upon whom even crueler demands were being made, the white inhabitants of the border. To the settler the principal theater of war was his own clearing. He could never know when howling savages might not burst from the woods enclosing it to burn his home, ax his children, disembowel his wife. If he was near he fell beside them and his fears for them which so long had haunted him were over. If he was at a little distance he was confronted with the dreadful choice of returning to share their fate or seeking his own safety in flight alone. If for a time Indian attack passed him by to strike at his neighbors this but made his dread more harrowing for the postponement made it ever more likely that the next would not spare him. If then he chanced to be warned in time his one recourse was to bundle his family off to the refuge of the nearest fort or the reluctant charity of the nearest town, leaving all he owned behind him. In 1763 this perpetually hovering horror which darkened his existence was an agonizingly familiar recurrence, a renewed tearing at wounds still unhealed. Of the border's last eight years four had been dominated by it. In every Indian war the basic Indian hope had always been so severely to punish the border settlers as to discourage their creeping occupation of the land. In these last two so much greater wars this trial by violence of the Indian capacity to harass and the settlers' capacity to endure reached a pitch of fury only to be exceeded in the still mercifully veiled years to come.

The people upon whom this long torment was inflicted were to breed a race of conquerors whose conquests were to prove wider, more lasting, and more fruitful than any the world ever before had witnessed. Their sons were to add in the span of a single lifetime the span of a continent to the infant dominion of a new nation. These people now fleeing in terror from Pontiac's exultant warriors were the progenitors of the long hunter, the Kentucky frontiersman, the Ohio boatman, the Missouri trader, the transcontinental explorer, the mountain man, the Santa Fe trail driver, the covered-wagon pioneer, the gold seeker, the pony-express rider, the cowboy. It would be gratifying to detect in them this early many promising signs of this future greatness. But of these there were few and those most faint. Only their imperfections and weaknesses were clearly discernible at the time.

The mid-18th Century inhabitants of the Pennsylvania-Virginia frontier being subjected to this test were neither by character nor experience in any way prepared to withstand stresses so fearful. Due to the prudence of the proprietors' land purchase policy Pennsylvanians had never known an Indian war before Braddock's defeat swept the whirlwind of Indian invasion upon them. Virginia had in that colony's earlier years experienced some of the most violent on record but in the year the French built Fort Duquesne the oldest inhabitants could no longer remember Indian trouble graver than an occasional altercation. The sudden avalanche had therefore fallen upon victims who had yet to begin to learn how to defend themselves. The majority of them, moreover, lacked the kind of background or social attitude to help them quickly to adjust to the problems of resistance. Population on the middle border had increased rapidly during the peaceful first half of the 18th Century but little of this influx were people fitted for what was awaiting them. Most had come to the outer settlement line merely because there was more room for them there. Their former condition had been so unfavored that they could be attracted to the deprivations and hardships of frontier existence. Most lacked furniture, utensils, tools, livestock. They were animated by no more than a hope of proving able to win a bare subsistence from the raw new land. A large proportion of them were recently arrived European immigrants. Another considerable proportion were ex-redemptioners, ex-convicts, fugitives from justice, runaway bond servants, and nondescript drifting men whose only common quality was their having failed in every former undertaking. For these struggling occupants of the forest clearings on the western fringe of settlement their more substantial eastern neighbors had coined the derisive term "back-country people." They were popularly and most unsympathetically classified as peculiarly ignorant, improvident, and insensate else they would never have subjected themselves to the peculiar handicaps and hazards of the frontier. Unjustified as was this estimate eventually to prove there was as yet little evidence of this. The frontier population had yet to become a community. It was a society still unformed, inchoate, a chance assembling of individuals who trusted neither themselves nor each other. Imbedded in it were totally alien groups, such as the Pennsylvania Germans who even clung to their own language. In no single respect were these people of the frontier in 1755 or 1763 fitted to deal with the appalling ferocities of a general Indian invasion. Every other unfitness was underlined by the circumstance that many lacked even the first essential, a gun. They were too poor to own one and too unaccustomed to handling one to know what to do with it if one was furnished.

There were, of course, even in these early and most frantic years a few bold and resolute men on the border who stood out among their neighbors. Some were stable men of constructive vision and energy whose clearings had already become productive farms, often with the equally productive adjunct of a sawmill, gristmill, or ferry. Others, as outstanding in an opposite way, were men of a more restless cast who made their living by hunting and trapping, in the course of which they had become acquainted with the essentials of woodcraft. These two types of frontier success presented between them the dissimilar and complementary twin facets of the true frontiersman destined to dominate the era about to dawn. Such men were already the nuclei about which gathered scattered centers of resistance in 1755. Some of them were soon moved by the impulse to strike back. In 1756 two such attempts were made. The Sandy Creek Voyage was a fiasco that reflected on their leaders' military acumen but not on their resolution. The other was a more successful enterprise in which 300 volunteers, led by John Armstrong, a Cumberland settler, crossed the mountains, surprised and burned Kittanning, a Delaware town on the Allegheny, killed 30 or 40 Indians, rescued a number of white captives, and made a successful withdrawal back over the mountains. These two efforts, however, were the only instances of frontier initiative exhibited during the remainder of the French War. The forces attacking the frontier and those engaged in defending it had seemed thereafter too great for the settlers to feel responsible for their own fate. Either they had been driven in helpless flight by an overwhelming Indian invasion, as during the earlier years of the war, or they had been largely relieved of the Indian threat by victorious English armies, as during the war's later years. In either case they had not been forced to depend upon themselves.

Provincial authorities had belatedly labored to raise and organize militia to defend the border and especially to garrison the frontier defense forts then being desperately built. It was natural to expect that the men of the frontier, whose families and property were the most endangered, might become the backbone of this citizens' defense force. The majority of them, however, evaded service on the plea they needed to stay with their families and most of those who were enlisted proved to be indifferent soldiers. Most of their officers, to be sure, had not had military experience to prepare them for command but the men in the ranks were essentially unwilling to serve. Throughout the war English regular officers regarded provincial troops with unlimited contempt. The appraisal of informed American observers did not rate the American militia of the time much more highly. In 1756 Washington was writing from his command post on the Virginia frontier: "Militia, you will find, Sir, will never answer your expectation; no dependence is to be placed on them . . . Ordered to certain posts for the protection of the inhabitants, they will on a sudden resolve to leave them and the united vigilance of their officers cannot prevent them . . . Out of four hundred received at this place, 114 have deserted . . . I have a gallows near forty feet high erected."

In 1763 the inroads of Pontiac's warriors produced among the border people the same hopeless panic, the same general impulse to flee, the same disposition to wait for the regular army to come to their rescue. Yet when it came they continued to stand aside in stony indifference. Bouquet's little army marched on into the mountains to fight a battle which was essentially their battle without a single man of the border volunteering to accompany it. Even after all they had suffered there was still ingrained in their consciousness the ordinary civilian's feeling that this, after all, was a war and that any war was something the army was supposed to wage.

Dreadful as had been their familiarity with war they still clung to the assumption that conducting one was a responsibility reserved to their government. As citizens it was their inherent right to be defended.

However, though they were still as little disposed to support Bouquet in 1763 as they had been Braddock in 1755, the intervening years of suffering had had two great effects. Upon them had been made two indelible impressions which were from now on to shape their every impulse and action until their eventual westward surge had crossed the Mississippi. There had been implanted in them a consuming hatred for all Indians. And there had at the same time been implanted in them a lasting scorn for all manifestations of governmental authority. Considering all that they had endured from Indians the hatred was inevitable. The end result of their relations with their government had made the scorn almost as natural. Imperial armies had consistently arrived too late to save them and the measures reluctantly voted by their own assemblies had consistently been too little as well as too late. The opinion had become fixed that they had been abandoned by the more prosperous and protected majority of their fellow citizens.

In late 1763 there came the first premonitory stirs of response to these two impressions which demonstrated their growing conviction that Indians and easterners were enemies differing only in degree. These were unreasoning responses, as blindly instinctive as reactions to pain. They were unconsidered, fumbling, awkward, even brutish. But they were overwhelmingly significant as the first evidence that the frontiersman was about to take command not only of his own destiny but of his country's.

Bouquet had been permitted to march on past unaided and there was equally no thought on the border of launching any independent attack on the Indians beyond the mountains. So difficult and perilous an undertaking was still considered the province of the army. But in frontier estimation some of the continuing Indian raids were coming from several small mountain towns along the West Branch of the Susquehanna. These were inhabited by a mixed lot of wanderers and half-breeds, including a number of stray Delaware. Unquestionably some Indians from these towns, or Indians who had passed through these towns, had participated in raids on the settlements. In any event they were the nearest wild Indians and the only ones not too difficult to get at. Three volunteer expeditions of settlers successively made the attempt to get at them. One brisk engagement was fought in the intervening forest with an unexpectedly encountered war party from beyond the mountains in which the volunteers, to their somewhat surprised elation, better than held their own. A number of the West Branch villages were burned and community stores of corn destroyed.

This demonstration of the frontier's hatred of Indians was followed almost at once by an equally violent demonstration of their scorn for their government. Instead of applauding the West Branch exhibitions of settler initiative, Philadelphia denounced them as unwarranted and provocative. This latest evidence that the older section of Pennsylvania seemed consistently to feel more sympathy for Indians than settlers further inflamed border tempers and set off a train of events that brought Pontiac's War right into the peaceful streets of the Quaker city.

Small colonies of Christian Indians, Mohican and Delaware converts of the Moravian Brethren, had been established in the Lehigh Valley near the present Lehighton and in the Wyoming Valley near the present Wilkes-Barre. Their hopes to lead a pious and peaceful life had been dashed as rudely as has been so often the case with people who elect neutrality. Both distant belligerent Indians and nearby suspicious settlers persistently accused them of complicity with the other's designs. During the French War raiding Indians had killed eleven of the converts. In this war a party of border militia had killed four more and the settlers were threatening to destroy all of them. The missionaries assembled their congregations in Nazareth where the Christian Indians, 140 in number, prayed, sang hymns, and fingered the few arms they possessed. The embittered settlers still threatened them. The Pennsylvania assembly, taking pity on their helplessness, yet not wishing further to offend the settlers, voted in November to have them disarmed and moved to the safety of Philadelphia. The Moravian Indians, having no choice, turned over their weapons and plodded sadly to the city. Along the way they were reviled, stoned, and abused by white residents every step of these first fifty miles of what was to prove a prolonged and eventually tragic pilgrimage.

At Philadelphia they were welcomed by the Quakers but not by the soldiers who already occupied the barracks to which the Indians had been assigned for shelter. These were a company of Highlanders, recently returned from Fort Pitt, who, having been at Bushy Run, had no greater liking for Indians, whether they chanced to be wild or tame, than had the average settler. Denied entrance to the barracks by the cursing soldiers, the Moravians huddled in the street where a mob of Philadelphia's common people, less broadminded than the city's more respectable burghers, spat upon them and pelted them with vegetables. At length, shepherded by Quakers, they were moved to Province Island where they found shelter from the winter weather in some temporary shacks.

Another community of tame Indians was next to suffer and this one far more barbarously. In a wood near Lancaster were clustered the huts of the several Indian families, numbering a total of twenty people, who were all that remained of the once powerful Conestoga nation. They had chosen to stay here in the land of their forebears when most other Pennsylvania Indians had migrated over the mountains and had been making an ineffectual struggle to cross the abyss between the Indian and the white way of life. They lived inoffensively by hunting, fishing, and begging. Their rude hamlet was regarded by their immediate white neighbors much as they might have regarded a gypsy encampment. It was a nuisance.

Fifty miles away, near Harrisburg, was a community of another sort. The frontier settlement of Paxton had been cruelly ravaged during the French War and often threatened in this one. Literally every inhabitant had lost members of his family. Its young men had grown up possessed by an inbred aversion to all Indians. They, joined by other young frontiersmen of a like mind, were about to become known as the Paxton Boys, idolized by everybody on the border and abhorred by everybody on the seaboard, particularly by their fellow citizens in Philadelphia.

When winter brought its usual interruption to Indian attacks upon the frontier, Paxton's attention, which all summer had been devoted to fighting off raiders, turned to the Conestoga. Here were Indians still within reach. That they had presumably taken no part in the war was not considered significant. They were Indians. Before dawn of December 14th fifty shadowy horsemen rode to the door-steps of the Conestoga huts. They burned the cabins and killed three men, two women, and a child but the other fourteen Conestoga eluded them. John Penn, of the proprietor family, who had just taken over the governorship, issued a proclamation denouncing the act and calling upon the local authorities to apprehend the guilty. The sheriff of Lancaster, more sensitive to border public opinion than the governor, confined his official activities to rounding up the fourteen surviving Conestoga and lodging them in the Lancaster jail. Two days after Christmas the Paxton Boys returned to complete their project. This time there was no surreptitious approach by night. In broad daylight they rode into town, overawing citizens and sheriff at gunpoint. Breaking into the jail, they butchered the remaining fourteen. The Conestoga men, women, and children were disemboweled and dismembered in exact imitation of the fashion in which raiding Indians treated their white victims.

The governor issued another proclamation, offering a reward of £200 for information leading to the identification of the assailants. The reward went begging, though the name of every man was well known. The men themselves boasted publicly of their participation in the exploit. The whole border was united in approval of it. Matthew Smith, informal leader of the Paxton Boys, instead of quailing before the governor's blasts, boldly threatened next to march on Philadel-phia to exterminate the Moravian Indians sheltered there. The idea caught on. To the frontier, it appeared imperative to purge the capital of its perverted partiality to Indians.

Philadelphia was in a ferment of indignation and apprehension. Governor Penn appealed to General Gage in New York to send English regular troops to help defend the city. Rumors that the borderers were already on the march threw the townspeople into terrified confusion. Boats were supplied the Moravians so that in taking flight they might take with them the invitation to violence represented by their continued presence. The first rumors proved false but the problem remained so long as the Indians did. With some vague idea that they might be turned over to Sir William Johnson's keeping, they were hastily sent off northward under the guard of the Bushy Run Highlanders who had been ordered to rejoin their base in New York. These grim veterans had by now been won over by the Indians' Christian composure in the face of so many tribulations and guarded them against the insults showered upon them all the way across New Jersey. At Amboy word came from the governor of New York that the Indians would most positively not be permitted to enter his province. The New Jersey government insisted as peremptorily that they could not remain in New Jersey. The patient and weary Indians trudged back through the snow to Philadelphia, this time guarded by the regulars Gage was sending to defend the city.

Their arrival there on January 24th stirred new consternation. There could no longer be any question that the frontiersmen were coming. The word ran along the streets that Matthew Smith and some hundreds of his fellow barbarians were approaching the Schuylkill. Now that crisis was actually upon them the citizens' latent bellicosity was aroused. The townspeople flew to arms. Quakers, casting aside their nonviolence principles, shouldered muskets and fowling pieces. Cannon were set up to defend the barracks on the great central square where the Indians were now housed. Streets were barricaded. Citizens were formed into companies of foot, horse, and artillery. Benjamin Franklin was recognized as the leader in organizing the defense effort. There were alarms by night and by day and much clanging of church bells and rolling of drums.

The borderers made a surprise crossing of the Schuylkill but paused at Germantown. The Quakers, by now the most belligerent of all the city's defenders, were opposed to any parley with the seditious invaders but milder counsels prevailed. Franklin went out to reason with them. He found them more ready to listen than anyone had imagined. Since the start of their march they had heard of the city's martial preparations and of the arrival of the detachment of English regulars Gage had sent in response to Governor Penn's appeal for help. They agreed to withhold their attack and Franklin agreed to present to the assembly their written petitions reciting their wrongs and their demands for a more adequate frontier defense.

So no shot was fired in the near civil war. The frontiersmen, after thirty of them had ridden boldly but peacefully through the streets of Philadelphia, returned to their ravaged homes. The Quakers regretfully laid aside their arms. The assembly pigeonholed the petitions. The Christian Indians remained in Philadelphia to the end of the war, losing a third of their number to smallpox while they waited. They then established a new colony on the Susquehanna but their doom had merely been postponed. After a longer and more arduous pilgrimage they were at last destroyed by frontiersmen during the even fiercer border stresses of the Revolution.

However, these border disturbances of 1763 constituted merely a presage. The change in frontier temper was as yet merely in process. It was so far only a ferment. The winter belligerence some of them had exhibited in their extermination of the Conestoga and their march on Philadelphia had cooled when spring brought its resumption of Indian attacks. To appeals for frontier support of Bouquet's 1764 expedition aimed at the very towns where these continuing attacks were mounted there was as little response as the year before. Bouquet was not a man who concealed his opinions. On July 19th he was writing John Harris, a representative and influential border leader:

"After all the noise and bustle of your young men upon the frontiers everybody expected that they would have offered their services as Soldiers or Volunteers for the defense of their Country, as being the fittest men for an Expedition against Indians and as the best way to wipe off Reproaches cast upon them for the Violence committed and offered to defenceless Indians. Instead of such Honorable conduct I see by your letter that they go as Pack Horse Drivers and Waggoners, employs for which a coward is as fit as a brave man. Will not people say that they have found it easier to kill In-

dians in a gaol than to fight them fairly in the woods? . . . I make
no doubt when His Majesty is informed what little assistance I
have had from the Frontier inhabitants . . . that they will hereafter
be left to fight their own battles themselves . . . For my own part
I am so much disgusted at the Backwardness of the Frontier People
in assisting us in taking Revenge of the Savages who murder them
daily with impunity that I hope this will be the last time I shall
venture my Reputation and Life for their sake."

Generals and governors in 1764 might not yet be able to detect
any change. The border people appeared as unruly, as heedless, as
obstinate, and, unaccountably, as pusillanimous, as ever. But a
change was brewing. It was a change which when it came to a
head was to take on historic proportions. Bouquet had impugned
their courage. But it was not courage they lacked, as they had
abundantly demonstrated. Again and again during these last ten
bitter years they had been driven from their homes and as often
they had returned to the ashes. What they had so far lacked was
an identification of themselves as a people. And it was this, after
years of brooding and mourning, that they were now beginning to
gain. They were beginning to realize that they were a people set
apart. Their hatred of their Indian enemies and their mistrust of
their own governments were only the outward signs of this growing
awareness that they were separate. They were beginning to realize
that it was their suffering that distinguished them, that was drawing
them together, that was singling them out, that was cutting them off
from their unthreatened neighbors to the east who had been made
alien by their inability to understand what the frontier had endured.
Ten years of misery had taught frontier people that they were not
to be saved by waiting upon the efforts of those neighbors, or upon
the acts of their governments, or upon the occasional march of
armies. They were beginning to realize that if they were to be
saved they must save themselves. Bouquet had called them the
Frontier People. That, at last, they were about to become.

XII

෴

Bouquet III

To AMHERST in his New York headquarters the news at the close of the war's first campaign year was little better than it had been at the beginning. His every effort exerted with so much angry energy had failed to loosen Pontiac's grasp on the wilderness. His confident double-barreled offensive of 1763 had not re-established English dominion beyond the Niagara-Pittsburgh line. Bouquet was stranded at Fort Pitt, his forces so depleted that he was committed to all the labors of raising another army east of the mountains the next summer and beginning all over again. Wilkins' massive undertaking to relieve Detroit and crush Pontiac had been thrown back into Niagara, first by the Indians and then by the elements. Detroit and Pittsburgh still held but their mere survival seemed to the haughty commander-in-chief a pale tribute indeed to the might of English arms.

Impatiently he set to work on plans for a 1764 campaign to be prosecuted on a scale that must surely succeed. For it he needed more regular troops. He was still convinced that only upon regulars could full dependence be placed. But now that the first shock of horror had passed England was less concerned with the new American war. The cabinet remained cold to his pleas for reinforcements. Swallowing his pride, he circulated an urgent appeal to provincial governors to furnish larger contingents of militia. His vaunted regulars required help, even though the enemy was only Indian. For some time he had detected a certain stiffness in London dispatches. His premonition was justified. While still engrossed in his plans for the next year's campaign he was relieved of command and ordered home. On November 10th he sailed for England. He had had at the end of the French War a right to anticipate a return in triumph as the brilliant conqueror of New France. Instead this was a return in near disgrace, his earlier great victory over a rival world power shadowed by his more recent frustration by a savage.

His successor, Major General Thomas Gage, later to be confronted by even more vexing problems at Lexington, Concord, and Bunker Hill, inherited the thankless responsibility for directing the coming year's renewed attempt to subdue Pontiac. He had not had so distinguished a military career as Amherst but he was an experienced soldier and he possessed the advantage of having had some personal experience with war in the wilderness. Not only had he been with Braddock but he had been in command of the advance guard and had been badly wounded that bitter day on Turtle Creek.

Gage's appraisal of his task was clarified by his notification on December 1st of the King's Proclamation. By its provisions the entire wilderness theater of war came under his exclusive command. No longer could overlapping and conflicting provincial jurisdictions interfere with imperial jurisdiction. No longer need Indians be given unnecessary pretexts for going to war by the varying demands of the several provincial governments. Still, though the Proclamation gave promise of forestalling future Indian wars, there remained this one first to be won. The new Line dividing the two races in the name of peace could have no real significance until Pontiac and the wild nations he had marshaled could be brought also to acknowledge it.

Gage adopted and prepared to put into operation Amherst's comprehensive plan for the 1764 campaign. Converging attacks launched from New York, Pennsylvania, and Florida were to descend upon the centers of Indian power between the Ohio and the Lakes. Though the hastily improvised 1763 effort had been a dismal failure, there was reason for hope that these three simultaneous thrusts coming at Pontiac from as many quarters must surely accomplish his downfall. Colonel John Bradstreet was to command an expedition of regulars, supported by provincial troops from New York and New England, which was to move westward by way of Oswego, Niagara, and Lake Erie, drive the Indians away from Detroit, overthrow Pontiac and re-establish the lake posts. Bouquet was for a second time to cross the mountains with a stronger army of regulars, supported by Pennsylvania and Virginia provincial contingents, to make an end to the warmaking capacity of the Ohio Indians, who had been Pontiac's most aggressive followers and the most active in ravaging the white frontier. Major Arthur Loftus at Pensacola was to ascend the Mississippi with a sufficiently strong force of regulars to take over Fort Chartres from the French and to deny Pontiac the supplies he was drawing from the French traders in the Illinois.

Pontiac, for his part, had plans to make, too, though fewer resources upon which to base them and more difficulties with which to cope. In November he had reluctantly raised the siege of Detroit. Every late fall Indians were obliged to scatter into the woods to hunt to get food for the winter. He could expect most of them back with him in the spring but he had meanwhile received a blow far more severe than any the English had so far been able to deal him. Having finally been officially notified by his government in Paris of the signing of the treaty of peace, Neyon had written Pontiac from Fort Chartres that the last glimmer of hope of help from France had faded. He bluntly reminded him that he was waiting to turn over every French post to the English whenever they arrived and that from then on the English would have become the sole source of supply for Indian needs, including that absolute necessity, gunpowder.

As spring approached Pontiac was forced even more clearly to realize that his extraordinary successes of the year before had not left him in so strong a position as he had had some right to expect.

Most of his warriors had been scattered during the winter beyond the reach of his influence and, with long months in which to reflect, had lost some of the first flush of enthusiasm with which they had embarked upon the war. This cooling off was especially noticeable among the Lake Indians. So many of them had been slow to return in the spring that he was unable to resume the investment of Detroit. They inhabited the richest of all fur-bearing regions and had been accustomed for generations to the benefits of the fur trade. They were therefore the more perturbed by the war's interruption of trade. A growing peace party among them was beginning to argue the advisability of coming to terms with the English since if the French really were leaving, it would be only from the English that trade goods could ever be obtained. The Seneca, being the most exposed to English attack, were also beginning to have second thoughts. Aside from the constant attendance of four or five hundred young warriors who were personally devoted to him, Pontiac's most dependable adherents that second year of the war were still the Ohio Indians. They had been jolted at Bushy Run but they were still full of fight. Supplied with some powder during the winter, by French Illinois traders, they were harassing the Pennsylvania frontier again as soon as the snow was off.

Pontiac was well enough aware of the dangers before him. The spreading influence of the peace faction could be fatal. The supply problem represented a perpetual crisis. Enough powder to hunt and kill settlers was not enough to carry on a war. But the voice he raised in council was as confident and resolute as ever. To hearten his wavering supporters he busily circulated the story that the King of France was on his way with a great army. Accompanied by his large and tumultuous bodyguard he went in person to Fort Chartres to demand more adequate supplies. If the French acted only a little like men, he declared, they could still be saved from the English and he, Pontiac, would save them. All that he required was more guns and gunpowder. Neyon, commander of a fortress which had already been surrendered on paper to a conqueror who was still hundreds of miles away, was disgustedly waiting for the English to appear to relieve him of his barren responsibilities. When he remained necessarily deaf to Indian exhortations, Pontiac went over his head to appeal to D'Abbadie, the French governor at New Orleans. He took care that the embassy he sent down the Mississippi was composed of chiefs who were eager to continue the war. With them went an immense red and black war belt, said to have been the largest ever woven.

The size of the belt made a great impression on Indians along the river but a lesser one on the French at New Orleans. There Pontiac's last lingering hope of French support was dispelled. His embassy found D'Abbadie so sick with grief that he had had to take to his bed. He had just been informed by his government of the secret treaty of December 2, 1762, by which France, after having already lost everything east of the Mississippi to England, had ceded New Orleans and all the country west of the Mississippi to Spain. He was in no mood to be bothered by Indian concerns and even if he had been was in no position to do anything about it.

The other part of the embassy's mission was more fruitful. Loftus' attempt to ascend the Mississippi with his expeditionary force of 400 regulars was promptly fired upon by the aroused Indians of the lower river country. Loftus was sharply criticized for having turned back after having lost only five killed and four wounded. However, he had made another of the painful discoveries about war in the wilderness that so often before had given pause to other English commanders. An advance by river, he had been made to realize, could present problems if anything more difficult than an advance through the forest. The current in midriver was too strong for his heavily laden boats to make headway upstream. If on the other hand the boats took to the weaker current of the shallows near the banks they came under an Indian fire from the wooded shores which could not be returned. It was altogether a bad business and Loftus made the best of it by hastily returning to the seacoast.

The repulse of Loftus on the 20th of March 1764 relieved Pontiac's principal immediate anxiety. Now that they in their turn had been relieved of their fears of an imminent arrival of the English, French traders in the Illinois could furnish him at least the minimum he required to make a show of continued resistance. Accompanied by delegations of his more fiery followers, he toured the Indian country, haranguing local councils and attempting, with considerable success, to revive the resolution with which Indians had taken the field the year before.

The Loftus prong of the triple attack had proved a fiasco. But Bouquet and Bradstreet were energetically organizing their respective expeditions, a process in which each was delayed by the exasperating tardiness of the provincial authorities who had undertaken to support them with men and supplies. Meanwhile, Sir William Johnson had been achieving diplomatic successes more significant than were English military operations at any stage of the war. That insight amounting to genius which enabled him to understand and to manipulate the idiosyncrasies of the Indian temperament was never more clearly evidenced than in this crisis. During the most ominous days of the previous summer he had managed to restrain the eastern Iroquois impulse to follow the Seneca into Pontiac's coalition. During the winter he had deepened and hardened this cleavage within the political structure of the Six Nations by bribing parties of eastern Iroquois to attack the belligerent Indian towns on the upper Susquehanna. These were relatively unimportant but the news that the lordly Iroquois had actually taken up arms for the English and against fellow Indians had sent a shiver of foreboding through the whole Indian world, as Johnson had known it would. Now, in the spring, he sent discreet messages to the peace factions among the Lake Indians informing them that he was prepared to discuss a resumption of trade and a redress of their grievances. Hundreds of Indians, instead of rejoining Pontiac at Detroit, paddled to Johnson at Niagara to listen to what he might have to propose. They had not come to surrender or as yet to negotiate a final peace but they were eager to make a firsthand examination of the material rewards that might ensue were they to bargain seriously with the English. The Seneca, pressed between the disapproval of their eastern Iroquois brothers and this wave of western Indian pacifism, began to appreciate their predicament. They had, after all, had their sport at Presqu'Isle and Venango and Devil's Hole and they now grasped at the opportunity to return, unpunished, to the English fold. The signing of the formal Seneca peace treaty on July 18th was a striking demonstration of the progress Johnson was making in his effort to promote division and suspicion in Indian ranks.

Among the Lake delegations swarming to Niagara were the captors of Alexander Henry who brought him along to be handed over in return for an appropriate reward. His wartime adventures that had begun so sensationally at Mackinac and had continued through more than a year of captivity now took a new turn. Bradstreet, who had arrived at Niagara with his army on his way west, prevailed upon Henry to take command of an extemporaneously recruited corps of hired Indian auxiliaries. The night after the Indians had received their enlistment bounties all but eleven deserted but Henry nevertheless continued west with Bradstreet in the hope of recovering some of his lost property.

Bradstreet himself had been so struck by the Niagara spectacle of two thousand Indians of a dozen western nations milling about Johnson, all pretending to talk peace, that his resulting misconceptions undermined every purpose for which his expedition had been designed. Sailing west along the southern shore of Lake Erie he himself instituted peace talks with any Indian representatives he could lure out of the forest. Amazed, they accepted his rum and his presents and listened to his assertions that he had come not to fight but to make friends. All of them he soothed with assurances that all was forgotten and forgiven and with astonished delegates from the still very actively belligerent Shawnee and Delaware who had come to have a look at the size of his army, he concluded a formal written treaty of peace which they later were triumphantly to show Bouquet. He reached Detroit without firing a shot and with equal ease sent a detachment to re-establish the garrison at Mackinac, that traditional trading center which had this summer became a hotbed of Indian pacifism. To every Indian whose attention he could attract at Detroit he continued to promise peace and absolution.

Pontiac, having learned the year before the difficulties of coping with English sea power, had not attempted to oppose the advance of Bradstreet's fleet. Instead he had withdrawn up the Maumee with his loyal forces intact, hoping to draw the English army farther from its water-borne supply base and deeper into the wilderness. Bradstreet, possibly fortunately for him, made no effort to follow. In his estimation the time for fighting Indians had passed. He saw himself as the benevolent negotiator, the benign peacemaker. So persuaded was he of the universal Indian yearning for peace that he sent off a single young officer, Lieutenant Thomas Morris, to carry the English flag through Pontiac's camps and on to Fort Chartres to take over that key fortress from the French. In passing, Morris was to direct Pontiac to come to Detroit to surrender. With the lieutenant's embassy went a modest retinue of five Mohawk attendants, twelve friendly Indian boatmen, and Jacques Godefroy, a French trader about to be hanged at Detroit who was pardoned so that he might serve Morris as guide. The Mohawk promptly stole the envoy's ceremonial supply of rum and decamped. But the trader stuck loyally with him through dangers which kept the lonely and bewildered young ambassador at death's door hour after hour of day after day. Morris survived to write a fascinating book detailing his nightmarish adventures which ranged from a most argumentative public debate with Pontiac through his being furnished a copy of Shakespeare to read while Indians debated his fate to his being stripped and tied to a post in preparation for burning. Pontiac's nephew interceded to save his life and he was eventually permitted to return to Detroit so that he might inform the English that Pontiac and his genuine followers were no more ready to surrender than when the war had started.

Meanwhile Bradstreet was sailing homeward across Lake Erie, convinced that his had been a triumphant expedition triumphantly concluded. He was so certain of his own judgment that he disobeyed Gage's direct order forthwith to drive the Indians from Sandusky and to advance upon the rear of the Shawnee and Delaware confronting Bouquet. The blessings of peace, however, did not continue to attend him. Storms wrecked so many of his boats that 150 of his provincials had to be left behind to follow on foot along the lake shore as best they could. Many of his officers accused him of mismanagement and demanded an inquiry. For his premature and unauthorized peace treaties with the Indians he was denounced by his fellow commander, Bouquet, and by his superior, Gage. Behind him he had left the western Indians with the quite correct impression that England had little inclination to press the war to a military conclusion and a much greater inclination to angle for peace at almost any price.

While Bradstreet was making his aimless tour of Lake Erie Bouquet was suffering all the trials inevitably connected with the organization of an expedition in conjunction with Pennsylvania authorities and in attempted co-operation with the province's frontier population. These became so aggravating that he asked Gage's permission to resign. Gage refused. To any commander-in-chief Bouquet was as nearly indispensable as one man could be.

Bouquet's outrage at the lack of energy among the people in Pennsylvania's government and the lack of spirit among the people on Pennsylvania's border was compounded by the disgraceful behavior of many of his own regulars. It was a most unhappy development that threw new light for him on the eccentricities of the American temperament. His men had been under his command for years and yet the experience had failed to plant in them the disposition to respect authority which with the European soldier so soon became second nature. The seven-year enlistment periods of most of the Royal Americans had expired but Amherst and then Gage had insisted, in view of the emergency, on their being held in the service. Wearied with wilderness dangers and hardships and convinced that they were being treated unjustly, they were deciding the question for themselves. They were deserting in droves. Some companies were reduced by more than half. Despite Bouquet's stern countermeasures these wholesale desertions represented a nearly insoluble problem. The frontier people, with their instinctive aversion to all manifestations of official authority, invariably sheltered them. To a dedicated soldier with Bouquet's ironbound regard for discipline, desertion was a crime only slightly less repellent than cowardice in action. That the settlements should welcome and protect the rascals redoubled his ire.

Not until May 30th did the assembly vote the contingent of 1000 militiamen the province had agreed to furnish. The continuing two-year-long devastation of the frontier began finally, however, to kindle among Pennsylvania officials some sparks of war spirit. They were most un-Quakerish sparks. Governor Penn and the Provincial Commissioners for Indian Affairs on June 12th announced a schedule of rewards for the taking of Indians, dead or alive. The bounties ranged from 150 Spanish dollars for a male Indian prisoner to 134 pieces of eight for a male scalp and 50 pieces of eight for a female scalp. One of the first upshots of this bounty offer was the case of David Owens, once a trader, next a soldier, and then a deserter, who had lived among the Shawnee long enough to raise an Indian family. In a hunting camp in the woods he killed his wife and children in their sleep and brought their five scalps to Philadelphia. Governor Penn refused to reward him for the scalps but sent him to serve Bouquet as guide and interpreter.

Provincial authorities managed at last to round up the recruits promised Bouquet. They were so slow to assemble that he was unable to march from Carlisle until August 5th, a year to the day after Bushy Run. Before he reached Pittsburgh 700 of them had deserted. This loss was in part made up by Virginia. That province, preoccupied with the defense of its own long frontier, had declined to give him any official support whatever. But he was joined by 280 Virginia volunteers. They were experienced backwoodsmen and led by the veteran border commander, Andrew Lewis. This was the sort of backing Bouquet had hoped to get from the Pennsylvania frontier. It was a seemingly fortuitous development but it was the first clear sign of the change that was coming. Preoccupied with a soldier's indignation at the general spectacle of duties shirked and responsibilities evaded, he could not have guessed how great and how swift the change was to prove. This summer when frontier resolution appeared at its lowest ebb had also brought the moment when the tide had begun to turn. There was never to be another summer when the people of the frontier waited for others to defend them.

The many delays forced on him had cost Bouquet the chance to advance westward from Pittsburgh by the Ohio while seasonal high water made river transport simple. An unprecedented summer

drought had by now made dependence on the river altogether impossible. Resort to the far more difficult overland march through the
forests necessitated the assembly of land transport and more delay.
It was not until October 3rd that he could feel his preparations were
sufficiently complete to justify the risk of advancing into the center
of the Indian country. Among his last measures in getting ready to
march were to catch and shoot two deserters and to limit the number of camp followers accompanying the army to one woman to
each corps.

His army was still not a large one, numbering but three times as
many as he had had at Bushy Run. But it was an immeasurably
stronger army because it was secure against surprise attacks. About
the hard core of 500 regulars ranged hundreds of frontiersmen, some
of whom were by now as skilled in woods fighting as any Indian.
Cutting a road before it, the army marched at a deliberate pace of
not more than eight or nine miles a day. Bouquet was content that
the Indians should know that he was coming and have ample time
to think about it. For it was an inexorable advance and it was
straight at the principal towns and storehouses of the Shawnee, Delaware, and Mingo. They were facing the threat alone. They could
expect no help from Pontiac who was watching Bradstreet who did
not break camp at Sandusky until October 17th. They had also been
deprived by Johnson's Niagara treaty of the support of most of the
Seneca.

The Indians hovered about Bouquet's advance but kept their distances. They had too little gunpowder to see them through a long
battle. They could only wait for an opportunity that gave some
promise of a short one. None came. Whether on the march or in
camp, Bouquet presented a front as constantly secure as though his
army were within the walls of a fortress.

The relentless advance continued. He crossed the Muskingum.
He was now within miles of their principal towns. They must either
give battle or flee into the deeper wilderness, abandoning their homes
and their food stores on the eve of winter. Indians were confirmed
realists. The obviously wiser course was to negotiate. Custaloga and
Guyasuta, who had commanded at Bushy Run, headed the embassy

that came now to ask for terms. Bouquet's reply was crushing. His first demand, which he said must be met before peace could even be discussed, was that they return every white captive now in their possession. No exaction could have seemed to the Indians more harsh. At the end of the French War they had given up some hundreds of captives in return for ransoms, presents and other benefits but most of the whites still with them had long since been adopted and had become members of Indian families. To give them up was to give up their own. No greater blow could have been struck at Indian pride or, in many instances, at Indian affections. It had been a calculated blow, shrewdly designed to emphasize the abjectness of Indian submission. The envoys protested violently but Bouquet remained adamant. He gave them twelve days to produce the captives. Every white man, woman, or child among them, he insisted, whether captives or runaways or even French, must be handed over. During the twelve days, he slowly marched ever closer. It was now too late to think of fighting, even had it not been before. The Indians had no choice.

On the appointed day, they returned to Bouquet's fortified camp shepherding the straggling procession of captives, most of them in dress and deportment scarcely to be told from their Indian conductors. Of the 206 being delivered 81 were men and 125 were women and children, 116 of them from Pennsylvania and 90 from Virginia. The Indians admitted that nearly as many more were missing. They explained that the others had run off into the woods when they had learned they were about to be returned. It would take a while to track them down.

It was now well into November. Bouquet, realizing the risk to his army if the first winter storms caught him still deep in the wilderness, grudgingly accepted their excuses. He took hostages as a guarantee that the remaining captives would be delivered in the spring. Then for the first time he relented enough to shake hands with the Indian envoys. When in the spring they had produced the last captive, they could then appeal to Johnson for the return of their hostages and a final peace, he advised them.

Some of the captives delivered that day to the English camp on the Muskingum were overjoyed to be restored to the society of their own kind. Others had been so long among the Indians that they were merely bewildered by the uncertain prospects awaiting them in their former homeland. Yet others were as unwilling to come as the Indians had been to bring them. There were a few family groups which the Indians had allowed to remain intact. More common groups were those of a mother whose older children were white and her younger red. The red ones she was required to leave behind. The rolls upon which the names of the captives were painstakingly listed, together with the rude contemporary maps upon which Bouquet had depended in his advance into the Indian country, cast fugitive gleams of reality across the obscurity of that primitive world in which captors, captives, and rescuers were confronting one another. Listed among the places from which the captives had been brought were New Comer's Town, Salt Lick Town, Bull Head's Town, Grenadier's Town, Grenadier Squaw's Town, White Woman's Town, French Margaret's Town, Mohican John's Town, Hurricane Tom's Town. Most of the captives were listed on the rolls under such sound old English names as John Potts or Molly Metch. Others were entered as family groups, "Margaret Bard and five children" or "Nancy Raneck, her sister, and four brothers." A number had been taken so young that they had forgotten every former white association, including even their names. These were carried on the rolls as Soremouth, Crooked Legs, Betty Black Eyes, Sour Plumbs, Girl with Sore Knee, A Dutch Girl. Also recorded were the names of the first captives to escape and flee back to their Indian homes. They were two young women, Rhoda Boyd and Elizabeth Studebaker.

Bouquet returned to Pittsburgh on November 28th. He had not fought a battle but he had subjected himself to every risk of battle and had won a solid victory. He had been the first white commander, and for the next thirty years was to remain the only white commander, capable of completely outmaneuvering and outgeneraling Indians in the depths of the wilderness. He had so thoroughly cowed the Shawnee and Delaware that they had entirely halted their attacks on the Pennsylvania and Virginia frontiers. The assemblies of

BOUQUET III [219]

Pennsylvania and Virginia were voting him their heartfelt thanks. There were bonfires and bells ringing and sermons of praise throughout the colonies. On December 5th Governor Penn proclaimed the end of the war. On December 13th Gage was writing Lord Halifax: "I must flatter myself that the Country is restored to its former Tranquility and that a general, and, it is hoped, a lasting Peace is concluded with all the Indian Nations who have taken up arms against his Majesty."

But no more than he had the winter before did Bouquet at Fort Pitt harbor any illusions about the war having been won. Pontiac had not been beaten. No Indians had been beaten anywhere except on that single day at Bushy Run. Pontiac was still defiant and still commanded many hundreds of warriors. Other hundreds who had flocked to talk to Johnson at Niagara might next spring as unreasoningly flock back to him. Except around the Forks of the Ohio and two posts on the shores of the Lakes, the Indians were as much in control of the wilderness as they had been when Pontiac first had called them to arms.

Others who knew the wilderness better than did Governor Penn or Gage agreed with Bouquet's estimate. On December 26th Johnson was writing the Board of Trade: "This Pontiac is at the head of a great number of Indians privately supported by the French . . . The Western Indians, who it seems ridicule the whole expedition (Bradstreet's) will be influenced to such a pitch by the interested French on the one side and the influence of Pontiac on the other that we have great reason to apprehend a renewal of hostilities." In the opinion of Thomas Hutchins, the military engineer and geographer, driving Pontiac by force from his position blocking the English army's way to the Illinois would prove more difficult than "the taking of a dozen such places as the Havanna with its Moro Castles."

Whatever the difficulties, they loomed great enough in London to have deflated the cabinet's earlier determination to bring Pontiac to heel. Bouquet could tell by the tone of the dispatches reaching his outpost of empire that no further serious effort was to be made to finish the war. Personal irritations added that winter to his weariness with the service in which so much had been demanded of him these last nine years. With the frontier's fiercest enemies, the Shawnee, Delaware, and Mingo, quieted, at least for the moment, he could be sure that in the spring there would be another wave of white hunters and squatters. He was a soldier, not a policeman. He did not relish the prospect of spending the better part of his time and energy harrying the exasperating rascals back over the Proclamation Line. A more immediate and much more aggravating irritation was his quarrel with Virginia. Lewis' Virginia volunteers had been of vital service on the Muskingum campaign. But Virginia, now that her frontiers had been relieved of the Indian menace, had refused to pay them, forcing Bouquet, as commander, to assume the obligation. Presently Pennsylvania, for once rising to an occasion, relieved him of the threat to his purse by appropriating the necessary funds. But Virginia's ingratitude, from which later frontier commanders were likewise to suffer, added to his depression. After four wilderness campaigns and as many tours of frontier garrison duty he was still the same lieutenant colonel he had been when he entered the English service. Victories had won him no advancement. Under existing army regulations he, a foreigner, could expect none. He had had enough.

In January he left Captain William Murray in command at Fort Pitt, as Forbes once had left him, and went to Philadelphia. On March 3rd he became a naturalized English citizen. On March 4th he resigned his commission. Going to New York to confer with Gage, this time he made the resignation stick. Returning to Philadelphia, his only personal plan for the future was to pay a visit to Europe. Then, on April 17th, came the totally unexpected sunburst of Gage's letter that changed his whole outlook. He was notified that it had been his Majesty's pleasure to commission him brigadier general. General rank in the English army was an almost unprecedented preferment for a foreign-born officer. He was by profession a soldier and he was rejoiced to accept. With the rank went command of the Southern Department.

He had scarcely arrived at Pensacola to assume his new duties on August 23rd when he fell ill of a fever of which he died just nine days later on September 2nd. He was then only 47 and all his active life had enjoyed the most robust health. His untimely death came at a moment when belated regard for his past services was opening to his view a vista of future preferment in which the highest posts were possible. Some measure of his expectations is suggested by the later career of his friend and fellow Swiss, Frederick Haldiman, who entered the English service with him and succeeded him in the Pensacola command. Haldiman became Governor-General of Canada during the Revolution.

Bouquet was first and last a soldier. But he had a capacity uncommon among soldiers for adapting himself to new or strange conditions. For all of his perception, he could not possibly have guessed that his wilderness victories under England's flag were destined to prove of infinitely greater service to the United States of which nobody yet dreamed. Had he lived to continue to serve England the shoe might have been very much on the other foot. During the Revolution the royal cause suffered from nothing so much as from the ineptness of English generals. It is not too likely that the foreign-born Bouquet might have been given over-all command. But there is need only to imagine him in the place of St. Leger, for one example, or of Cornwallis, for another, to imagine how different the story might have been.

XIII

♉

Croghan II

Looking ahead that winter of 1764 toward the coming third year of Pontiac's War Gage could perceive awaiting him about as exasperating a problem as could confront a commander. The war against France had long since been won. Seven years had elapsed since Forbes had taken Fort Duquesne, six since Johnson had taken Niagara and Wolfe Quebec, five since Rogers had occupied Detroit, three since France had by the Treaty of Paris formally ceded the entire region east of the Mississippi to England, and still the great French stronghold on the Mississippi, Fort Chartres, was held by a French garrison.

For these last three years the bored and disgusted French commander had been ready and willing, not to say eager, to turn it over to the English army. But the English army had as yet hit upon no way to get to it. For Pontiac still stood in the way. He still commanded a formidable following made many times more formidable by the natural strength of his midcontinent situation. He had relinquished the shores of the Great Lakes to English sea power but in the recesses of the wilderness to which he had withdrawn his continued supremacy had not yet been threatened. On land his dominion in this third year of the war still extended from the Muskingum to the Mississippi. To attempt to force a passage through this dominion to Fort Chartres, either by way of the Ohio or the Mississippi, was to undertake a military venture which, considering the inadequacy of the forces available to Gage, invited unacceptable risk.

Gage's problem was made the more insoluble by the cabinet's waning interest in the war. Though the past two years of desperate campaigning had produced no English victories of a brilliance to match Pontiac's initial successes, English plodding operations had served to blunt the two chief threats he had originally posed. Bradstreet's Great Lakes cruise had, by reopening that rich region to trade, quieted the storm of protest formerly voiced in London commercial circles. Bouquet's march to the Muskingum, by putting an ending to Indian attacks on the frontier, had likewise quieted the outcries from the Pennsylvania-Virginia border. The cabinet, no longer badgered by appeals for action, was increasingly reluctant to authorize further expenditure of men and money. Gage's position remained, nevertheless, an ignominious one for any self-respecting commander-in-chief. He had no more won this war than had Amherst. Pontiac was still defiant and Fort Chartres still French. He therefore listened with the closest and most eager attention to the proposal made by Croghan upon his return from London.

Croghan had been out of the country during most of the war but his activities while away were to have more to do with its conclusion than those of anybody present who had been actively engaged in it. If he had been surprised in June of 1763 by the scope and timing of Pontiac's onset he had known well enough what next to expect. As at the outbreak of the French War the traders were bound to be the first to suffer. A good many had rushed west the moment French Canada had capitulated and were clustered in and about the forts Pontiac was attacking. A few of the more reckless who had ignored Amherst's regulations had gone directly to Indian towns. Disaster fell upon all except those who had managed to gain the refuge of Detroit, Pittsburgh, or Niagara. In Croghan's department between Lake Erie and the Tennessee 104 traders and their employees were killed or taken the first month of Pontiac's War. This time Croghan's own financial loss was limited to the destruction of his Pittsburgh property. He was still technically a bankrupt and his only income was his Deputy Superintendent's salary.

In this new emergency, as in the earlier one, he began at once to take an active part in the defense effort. He garrisoned Fort Lyttleton on the Pennsylvania frontier at his own expense, rushed a convoy of ammunition to Fort Bedford that enabled Captain Ourry to continue to hold that vital post, and assisted Bouquet in assembling transport for his march to Bushy Run and the relief of Pittsburgh.

But his eyes were on the wider picture. If there was some bleak satisfaction in realizing how fully events were justifying his many warnings there was no satisfaction whatever in realizing how gratuitous was the whole outrageous tumult. To him the answer seemed so plain that it was ludicrous that other men were unable to perceive it. Admittedly friction between red men and white could not be avoided. But senseless aggravation of that friction could most certainly be avoided. This war had been brought on by the ignorant mistakes of men in authority who did not realize what they were doing. Were uninformed men to continue in authority the mistakes would continue and Indian wars would continue. The obvious solution to the problem was to place in authority men who did realize. Before him loomed the great opportunity of his life and within him he found the reserves of courage and energy to grasp it. Leaving his departmental duties in the capable hands of his assistant, Alexander McKee, he went to Johnson with his project.

Johnson gave it his wholehearted approval. For months he had been deluged by London with ministerial inquiries requesting his informed views on just what should be done about those immensely provoking Indians but to his written replies little heed had been paid. He fully agreed with Croghan that one of them should go immediately to London. By making a personal appearance with a sufficiently forceful statement ministers might be compelled to listen. He himself could not go. He could not afford to quarrel with Amherst and he was in the midst of the supremely critical discussions and maneuvers by which he was endeavoring to suppress the Iroquois impulse to join Pontiac. He agreed, as Croghan had foreseen he must, that Croghan was therefore the man to go.

Sustained by that driving energy which had so often before carried him to the most difficult and distant destinations, Croghan set out. His first stop was New York to grasp the nettle of asking Amherst's consent to the London trip. As he had also foreseen, the commander-in-chief was infuriated by what amounted to an appeal over his head to the higher authority of the cabinet. "If his presence ever was of any consequence," Amherst acidly wrote Bouquet of Croghan's proposal to leave his post in the middle of a war, "it certainly is so at this present time." But Croghan had made up his mind. He resigned so that he might go without Amherst's permission. "I know many People will think I am wrong," he wrote Bouquet, "but had I continued I could be of no more Service than I have been this eighteen months past which was none at aul."

For the last ten years he had been a public official but at heart he was still a businessman. At Philadelphia he conferred with other principal traders who like him had suffered enormous losses in the French War and most of whom were now incurring new losses. They had sought reimbursement for the earlier ones by France, the defeated enemy, but this expectation had not been met in the peace treaty. They now sought compensation directly from England. According to their argument, in subjecting themselves to the extraordinary risks of the Indian trade they had served their country's interests. Hence they deserved restitution. These claims of the "suff'ring traders," as they came to be called, were to have an impact for years to come on frontier developments. Croghan's primary mission was to persuade the government to free the Indian Department from the interference of military commanders and provincial governors so that it might deal more effectively with Indian affairs. But his secondary objective was to do what he could for the traders, including himself.

Before he sailed from Philadelphia he had been informed of the King's Proclamation. This in his estimation was a long step in the right direction. Even more heartening, it suggested that the cabinet at last was beginning to do some thinking. Nearing the end of his stormy midwinter crossing his ship was wrecked on the rocky coast of Brittany. This cost him the loss of most of his papers and personal effects but he was used to taking ordinary disasters in stride. Finally reaching London, he devoted the time during which he was forced to wait for a hearing to an exchange of views with whoever of influence he could buttonhole. There were any number of influential people in London who had invested in the fur trade and therefore were very nearly as sympathetic to it as he. Nevertheless, it soon became apparent that for the "suff'ring traders" there was no immediate prospect of any cash settlement. Governmental economy continued to be the ruling watchword.

At last, on June 7th and 8th while Bradstreet was assembling his army at Albany and Bouquet his at Carlisle, and Loftus was retreating from the Mississippi, and Johnson conferring with the Seneca at Niagara and Stuart with the Seminole at St. Augustine, he got his hearing before the Board of Trade. In this meeting between imperial ministers of state and the rough-hewn colonial he carried all before him. He spoke with the authority of an expert's knowledge and with the fervor of one with a burning belief in his cause. A declaration that Indian wars were avoidable was the burden of his message. What was chiefly required to avoid them was to place the management of Indian affairs in the hands of men who understood Indians. It was as simple as that. Three equally simple rules governed the whole area of dealing peacefully with Indians. First, they must be assured of an ample supply of trade goods, with the distribution in the hands of private traders but sensibly supervised by knowledgeable officials to guard against the Indians being cheated. Second, land must be taken from them only after honestly negotiated treaties in which they had received payment that seemed adequate to them. Third, it must be remembered that they enjoyed attention and that therefore they must frequently be invited to conferences, entertained, and given presents. Such a program was admittedly expensive and would require the allotment of much more money to the Indian Department than it had formerly been allowed. But it was not a hundredth as expensive as recurrent Indian wars costing thousands of lives and millions of pounds. So ran his argument.

His hearers were completely convinced. Practically every administrative recommendation urged by Johnson and Croghan was
adopted. In the "Plan for the future Management of Indian Affairs"
announced by the Board of Trade provision was made for a much
more powerful Indian Department operating in a northern and a
southern district under two superintendents and five deputies. In
actual practice this meant that Johnson would be responsible for
Indian relations in the New York-St. Lawrence-Great Lakes area,
Croghan on the Ohio, and Stuart in the south. They were to have
control over all dealings with Indians, including the activities of
traders, and were specially instructed to guard Indian interests in
all land purchases which in every event could only be consummated
by express permission of the King. The already existing Proclamation Line marked the limit beyond which the jurisdiction of provincial governments no longer extended. On the Indian side of the
Line the Indian Department henceforth was to represent imperial
authority.

Croghan was swept up on a tidal wave of that exultation known
only to the man of action who has at last achieved a success for
which he has long struggled. He particularly relished having routed
Amherst. He was writing Johnson: "General Amhirsts Conduct is
Condemned by Everybody and he has been pelted away in the
papers . . . The army Curse him in publick as well as the Merchants . . . in Short he is Nobody heer." And to McKee: "I have
been able to settle the Department of Indian Affairs on a new system . . . The sole management of Indian Affairs and the Regulation
of Indian Trade is invested in the Superintendent and his Agents
independent of the Officers Commanding at any of the posts which
I make no doubt will be no small mortification to some people."

He was too little versed in the intricacies of English politics to
perceive, in the midst of his elation, the fatal flaw in the new plan.
The announcement had been withheld until after Parliament had
adjourned and therefore no money for the moment could be appropriated to implement it. For the time being, Croghan was told, the
expenses of the Indian Department would be met by funds advanced
by the military establishment in America. This, in effect, left final

decision on Indian affairs as much in the hands of the army as before. However, this difficulty was not at first obtrusive. Upon Croghan's return in October 1764 from his personal triumph in London, Gage welcomed him with open arms.

Croghan's providentially timed reappearance offered an opening for that shifting of responsibility which has taken its memorable place in military parlance with the phrase known as passing the buck. If this grandiose new plan, which had so happily already been approved by the politicians in London, to deal with Indians by diplomacy, prodigality, and sweet reason, was at all workable, then here was a chance for Croghan to demonstrate that it was. Gage eagerly pressed upon him £2000 for expenses and £1200 worth of presents and assured him of every co-operation from the army. Croghan as eagerly accepted the challenge. Here, indeed, was a great opportunity to practice and to prove what he so long had preached.

He threw himself into the project with immense gusto but also with a display of self-importance that made him new enemies. He was writing to McKee at Pittsburgh: "You are under no necessity of acquainting any officer what instructions you receive from me . . . You will present my compliments to any gentlemen you please, or none at all as you think proper." His post-London arrogance offended regular officers whose co-operation he needed. But having at last been given the authority, after ten long years of frustration, to do things his way, which he had all along been convinced was the only right way, nothing could swerve him either from his purpose or the method by which he pursued it. He alienated even Bouquet, his old friend and comrade-in-arms, who a month before had been writing Gage, "Mr. Croghan is the fittest Person in America to Transact that Business," but who was now protesting to Gage about the power entrusted "to a man so illerate [sic], impudent and ill bred." Gage declined to interfere. He was too happy to have Croghan relieve him of the fearful burden of dealing with Pontiac.

A more ominous difficulty immediately arose. The frontier objected violently to any proposal to conciliate the Indians. And in rejecting appeasement of their Indian enemy, frontiersmen objected most of all to the practice of trading with them. Few families but had members shot down by Indians armed with guns and gun-powder furnished them by traders. How much more intolerable then was the spectacle of this endless pack train, many horses of which were loaded with costly *gifts* for the very Indians who only the year before had been burning and killing along this same border. The frontier's extreme indignation produced successors to the Paxton Boys who two years before had exterminated the Conestoga and marched on Philadelphia. These new executors of frontier opinion became known as the "Black Boys," since it was their custom some-times to blacken their faces when engaged in their direct action ex-ploits. Croghan's pack train was waylaid on the slopes of Sideling Hill. The Black Boys took care to shoot only the horses and merely to cuff and curse the packers, most of whom were fellow borderers. Sixty-three loads of assorted trade goods that had been intended to smooth Croghan's negotiations with the western Indians were piled and burned. A few packers escaped with their loaded horses to take refuge in Fort Loudon. The frontiersmen pursued and invested the place in open defiance of the English flag and His Majesty's troops. There were parleys and flags of truce and the taking and exchanging of prisoners and other appurtenances of a more formal war. After one skirmish the fort's commander was left tied to a tree. Governor Penn issued proclamations and removed from office the three local justices of the peace who were the principal leaders of the move-ment. Gage placed all regular troops then in Pennsylvania at the governor's disposal to aid him in dispersing the "lawless banditti," as Gage termed them. But the frontiersmen were unimpressed. Or-ders and threats from general or governor were alike disregarded. They continued to patrol the road west. For a time even military dispatches were intercepted and censored. Travelers or packers pro-ceeding westward found a Black Boys' passport more useful than one from Gage or Penn. This was genuine armed insurrection, a harbinger of the greater rebellion against royal authority that was to come just ten years later.

Croghan, who had gone on to Pittsburgh ahead of his convoy, did not permit the loss of his goods to deter him. He borrowed re-placements from local traders, all of whom were naturally eager to forward his enterprise. But his next great difficulty had meanwhile arisen. Before he could so much as start on his thousand-mile journey down the Ohio to beard Pontiac in his Illinois lair he must win the consent of the Shawnee and Delaware. These nearest and most belligerent of all western Indians had ostensibly submitted to Bouquet the autumn before but during the three months that they had had since to reflect upon that humiliation their attitude had stiffened. Their hostages had escaped and returned to them. They were no longer disposed to fulfill their promise to round up and deliver their remaining white captives. They had meanwhile sensed, as had Pontiac, that England's determination to get on with the war had perceptibly cooled. This presumption was supported by everything they could observe. Their nemesis, Bouquet, had withdrawn to Philadelphia and had then resigned altogether from the army. The garrision that he had left at Pittsburgh was not strong enough to do more than hold the fort. There were no signs anywhere that the English were assembling another invading army for the summer campaign season, already so near.

Patiently yet firmly Croghan initiated negotiations with them. The discussions went on through March and April and into May and again and again seemed on the verge of breaking down. But Croghan persisted. Aside from his skill in disentangling the convolutions of Indian thought and speech he had attractive bait to dangle before them which he knew must in time engage their attention. First off, there was the matter of his storehouse full of presents awaiting them if they met him halfway. Indians had an almost compulsive regard for presents. They coveted the physical objects for their intrinsic value but beyond that was the emotional reward of being able to feel that their favor was being courted by the usually domineering white men. They were always as delighted as children around a Christmas tree when the moment came to open the bales of white men's treasures and to distribute among them gold-laced hats, embossed swords, pistols inlaid with pearl, or gilt medallions bearing an inscription describing the wearer as a personal friend of the King of England. The social aspects of a properly conducted peace conference added enormously to the general appeal of the occasion. No matter how long-winded the Indian speeches they were listened to with respectful attention and after the speeches there was always an unlimited amount to eat and drink. Indians, whose ordinary life was so often marked by solitude, hunger, and hardship, were eminently gregarious and eager to embrace the solace of sociability and conviviality. Drunk, happy, and replete, they tended at a peace conference to drift into a state of euphoria in which they forgot ancient distrusts and resentments. That spring of 1765 Croghan expertly played on Indian weaknesses as he nursed and extended his advantage through meeting after meeting. Indian recalcitrance gradually relaxed. He had other baits to dangle more significant than free liquor, whole roast oxen, and silver gorgets. He could point to the Proclamation Line as a guarantee protecting their territory against the continued encroachment of white settlers. And he could promise them that once peace was established the many traders now restrained by the military at Pittsburgh and Detroit would be allowed to carry their goods as far into the Indian country as the Illinois.

The Line did not greatly impress the Indians. They were determined themselves to hold the mountain barrier and had no doubt of their ability to handle the settlers if the army did not interfere. For the last ten years they had been harrying settlers and had found them harder to catch than kill. What did impress them was the promised resumption of freer trade and the assurance that hereafter their dealings with English authority would be in the hands of men like Johnson and Croghan instead of army commanders. Croghan's persistence and earnestness kept gaining ground with them. At a final formal conference on May 8th, attended by more than 500 Shawnee, Delaware, and Mingo, as well as a few visiting Wyandot, agreement was reached. All delivered up their remaining captives. He was able to persuade the Delaware, whose range adjoined the Iroquois, to visit Johnstown to make their peace also with Johnson. And he had so completely won over even the hard-nosed Shawnee that they, as well as the Delaware and Mingo, selected delegates to accompany him down-river and to share with him the perils of his Illinois mission.

How real were those perils was eventually to be demonstrated. Meanwhile a young English officer, unfamiliar with the wilderness and therefore the more eager to attempt the venture, had already braved them. Lieutenant Alexander Fraser, considered qualified chiefly because he could speak French, had been assigned to accompany Croghan as the army's representative with his embassy. Growing impatient with Croghan's prolonged negotiations at Fort Pitt, he determined to go ahead on his own with Francis Maisonville, a Frenchman willing to accept English employment, as guide, and several Fort Pitt soldiers as boatmen. Since Shawnee sanction had not yet been gained, his safety en route depended entirely on his luck. This turned out to be good, then very bad, then good again. Riding the crest of the late March flood water his canoe made the run undetected all the way to the Mississippi. On April 17th he appeared before the astounded St. Ange de Bellerive who had succeeded Neyon as French commandant at Fort Chartres. St Ange had just lived through a similar bizarre experience with Lieutenant John Ross, another young English military emissary, who, accompanied by Hugh Crawford, a trader whose experience with Indians had included a 1763 captivity, had made it overland through the canebrakes from Mobile to the Illinois. The regular army had been so chagrined by its failure to raise the flag at Fort Chartres that commanders were ready to encourage the most harebrained attempt by unsupported individual officers if it promised the faintest chance of so much as a token take-over.

The Indians of the Illinois had with difficulty been persuaded to permit Ross to return, unharmed, down-river to New Orleans. They were daily returning in ever greater numbers from their winter hunting and as they exchanged views their anti-English temper became ever more apparent. Fraser's soldiers were seized and then Fraser himself. One night when there was much drunkenness he was as near death as had been Morris, his predecessor in amateur diplomacy, the previous year. He was saved by Pontiac's personal intervention. The Indian leader listened, patiently and attentively, to Fraser's version of England's peace offer, meanwhile himself repeatedly professing, as he always did, that there was nothing he so much desired as to live at peace with the English, if the English would only permit it. For a day or two Fraser conceived that he was making progress. But whatever his opportunity it passed with the arrival by the Mississippi of a very large convoy of French trade goods. The French were emptying their New Orleans depots before the expected occupation of the city by Spanish authorities. The Indians now had a larger supply of gunpowder than they had had at the outset of Pontiac's War and peace talk became more than ever unpopular. Pontiac insisted, however, on Fraser's being permitted to depart unmolested and the enterprising young man continued his extraordinary journey on down the Mississippi to New Orleans.

Croghan, having finally gained Ohio Indian sanction for his undertaking, set out from Pittsburgh on May 15th. He had no idea what might have happened to Fraser. For the first three weeks of his passage all continued pleasantly uneventful. There have perhaps been few excursions man has ever been privileged to take that could have been more likely to hold him spellbound than a descent of the Ohio in the days when the region was still an undisturbed wilderness. Croghan had often before traveled the first 550 miles of the river, as far as the mouth of the Miami, but he never tired of the magnificent scene. On this passage pages of his journal were filled with his attempts to describe it. The great river wound among wooded hills, each successive bend unveiling another prospect more striking than the last. Herds of deer, elk, and buffalo stood in the shallows, the shining river was animated by unending fleets of ducks, geese, and swans, beneath its surface cruised schools of twenty-pound perch, forty-pound bass, eighty-pound sturgeon, and hundred-pound catfish, the bordering forest was brightened by the scarlet, green, and gold plumage of flocks of parakeets, overhead flew passenger pigeons in such numbers as to darken the sun. The most vivid and lasting impression was of an unlimited primeval fecundity. But along with that was a sense of the incredible loneliness. There were no Indian towns on the river. All had withdrawn to less exposed locations to minimize the dangers of attack in the still smoldering war between Northern and Southern Indians. This loneliness was to continue well into the period twenty years later when thousands of settlers' families began drifting down the river to Kentucky on flatboats. They saw almost as much game and no more people on the banks than did Croghan. In place of the old war among red men there was then the war between red men and white and both races lived well away from the wide river which offered an avenue as inviting to foe as to friend. It was ten years after the founding of Harrodsburg and Boonesborough before there were white habitations on the Ohio below Wheeling, except alongside George Rogers Clark's base of operations at Louisville, and there were never again to be Indian towns on the river.

Croghan's flotilla did little to dispel the primitive loneliness. It consisted of but two small batteaux manned by a handful of white men (one of them his cousin, Thomas Smallman, who only the year before had been a Shawnee captive) and the dozen or so Indian delegates who had volunteered to go along to assure Pontiac of Ohio Indian approval of the mission. In this bold venture a thousand miles into the heart of Pontiac's country Croghan was subjecting his way of dealing with Indians to the severest possible test. His only weapons were his name and reputation, a chest of gold and silver coins, and a few bales of presents. To achieve what he had set out to achieve, the pacification of Pontiac, must otherwise have required in the place of his two barges an armada transporting an army. The silent wooded shores past which he was gliding peacefully must sooner or later have blazed with resistance to an invasion by force.

For all his impatience to get on down-river he paused to land on the Kentucky side a little below the mouth of the Miami to investigate Big Bone Lick of whose marvels he had often heard from Indians. Here at a crossing of two great buffalo traces was a salt spring in the mud around which were imbedded the tusks of mastodons and the huge teeth of other prehistoric animals. Croghan was the first American to have left an account of his fascination with this natural prodigy but he was by no means the last. Nothing so much intrigued every later American pioneer as this deposit of giant bones unless it was the companion enigma of the giant Indian mounds, each covered with trees many hundreds of years old, that dotted the whole Ohio Valley. Contemporary Indians were as much at loss to account for the one mystery as the other. It very much suited the pioneer temperament to accept these twin phenomena as evidence that across this immense land which still presented gigantic rivers, gigantic trees, and gigantic herds of game there once had roamed gigantic animals and gigantic men, for it was assumed that earthworks so enormous as were some of the Indian mounds could only have been erected by a race greater in stature as well as in numbers than the present Indians.

Croghan's swift and peaceful passage continued to and on past the mouth of the Wabash. Each night he camped on the bank, making no effort at concealment and taking care to betray no apprehension. A necessary element in his enterprise was that he must place himself entirely at the mercy of the Indians, as he had had to do so often when a trader, as conclusive evidence of his good faith. He had taken care that word of his coming should have long preceded him and he counted on Pontiac's being at least enough interested to wish to hear what he might have to propose. There remained the very real danger of being assailed by some roving band of irresponsible Indians who might have no more regard for the higher dictates of diplomacy and statecraft than did their rivals in irresponsibility on the white side of the frontier who had burned his convoy. It was this risk that materialized. At daybreak of June 8th, the first anniversary of his memorable meeting with the Board of Trade at what must by now have seemed to him the incredible distance of London, the riverbank encampment of his little expedition was attacked by a war party of 80 Kickapoo.

On account of the diplomatic status of the victims the consequences of the affair immediately took on international proportions. The possible influences motivating the Kickapoo aggression were feverishly debated at every Indian council fire. Upon the issue of the debate hung the whole issue of peace or war. Kickapoo motives had never been easy to assess. The Indian meaning of the name Kickapoo was "standing now here, now there." As a nation they had a long record of moving from place to place and getting into trouble with each successive set of neighbors. They were for the moment much under the influence of the French traders in the Illinois. Their story, when presently they were obliged to account for their action, was that they had been persuaded by these French friends that a war party of Southern Indians led by white men was on its way to attack them. Labored as was this excuse there was some justice, at least, in the attempt to transfer a portion of the guilt to the French. The French in the Illinois had every reason to strive to plant discord between English and Indians. Croghan, always ready to believe evil of his old antagonists, the French, accepted the story. Actually the Kickapoo had been observing his party for some days and were well aware of his identity. Their chief incentive was without much doubt the two boatloads of treasure to be so easily taken. Those bales of trade goods represented a temptation difficult for any Indians to resist.

Two of Croghan's white men and three of the Shawnee delegates were killed by the first Kickapoo volley. The assailants charged into camp, swinging tomahawks. All but three of Croghan's party were struck down, Croghan among them. He later wrote his friend Murray, commandant at Pittsburgh: "I got the stroke of a hatchett on the Head but my Scull being prety thick the hatchett would not enter, so you may see a thick Scull is of Service on some Occasions." The Kickapoo exultation over their easy victory and the amount of plunder they had captured had hardly got under way before it was brought to an abrupt end. The senior Shawnee delegate had been shot in the thigh. Thinking the attackers could only be his lifelong enemies, Southern Indians, he had crawled precipitately off into the brush to hide from them. But when he realized that they were Kickapoo he came limping back. Drawing himself upright, he began most violently to denounce them, assuring them that the Shawnee nation would know how to take vengeance for this criminal assault upon their ambassadors. Those of the Delaware and Mingo delegates who were still able to speak voiced similar strictures.

The Kickapoo were aghast. The possible consequences of having so grossly offended the most aggressively warlike of all Indians were belatedly dawning on them. They became so disquieted that without waiting to pick up all of their booty they set off with their white prisoners on a forced march for their town, Ouiatonon, 430 miles away up the Wabash. The Indian delegates, who had been instantly released with the most abject apologies, loaded their wounded in one of the boats and continued on down-river to present their case to Pontiac. The white men, all but two of whom had been wounded, suffered terribly during their grueling march from hunger, heat, and exhaustion. But Croghan continued to fill his journal with reference to the beautiful meadows, the magnificent forests, the herds of game, to be observed on all sides in this splendid region which had until now unhappily been known only to Indians and a few Frenchmen.

The hurrying Kickapoo paused briefly in the outskirts of Vincennes. Here the French inhabitants congratulated them on their success and meanwhile enriched themselves at Kickapoo expense. Having no idea of the value of specie, the Indians willingly exchanged for trifles handfuls of the gold and silver coins which they had looted from Croghan's strong box. Here also was a Piankashaw town and these fellow Indians took a more jaundiced view of the Kickapoo achievement. They refused to accept a share of the plunder which the Kickapoo hopefully pressed upon them and accused the Kickapoo of idiocy in having committed an outrage which could bring on an intertribal war with the proud and violent Shawnee. Among the Piankashaw were friends Croghan had made in his earlier years as a trader who helped him to buy clothing and horses for which he paid with drafts on the commander at Detroit. But the Piankashaw made no effort to free him. The Indian rule that a captive was the property of the warrior who had taken him was a rule seldom violated.

The crestfallen Kickapoo rushed on with their prisoners to their town at Ouiatonon. Here they bent before the ultimate blow. Their own chiefs denounced them. The arrival of a ceremonial pipe delivered by a Frenchman from the Illinois brought matters to a head. The speech accompanying the pipe was from Kaske, a noted Shawnee chief who had so bitterly disagreed with Shawnee gestures of submission to Bouquet that he had withdrawn from his nation to the Illinois and there attached himself directly to Pontiac. This Kaske, who continued to be noted the rest of his life for his uncompromising enmity to the English and then the Americans, was an interesting figure in his own right. In his personal relationships he exemplified the ferment of conflicting influences working upon the Indian world of Pontiac's time. He had been born in Pennsylvania of a Shawnee mother by a German father and had taken as wife an English girl who had been a captive since childhood. In the message sent with the pipe he called upon the Ouiatonon Indians to prove their determination never to make peace with the English by burning Croghan forthwith at the stake.

By now some dozens of chiefs from the adjacent region, including representatives of the powerful Miami, had hurriedly assembled at Ouiatonon. For the usual Indian inclination to talk, and eat and drink, and then talk some more, there was no time at this council. The threat of Shawnee vengeance loomed starkly, forcing all to recognize the need for an immediate decision. Croghan's own views were invited. He presented them at length with great energy. In many ways it was a repetition, against this vastly different background, of his declamation before the ministers in London. Here, too, he swept all before him. The chiefs were unanimously agreed. He and his companions were released, his captors excoriated, his intercession with the Shawnee requested, and he was assured of safe escort either to Detroit or Fort Chartres, whichever he chose.

Croghan had already begun to realize how bright was the silver lining to the cloud of his misfortune. The attack upon him had greatly strengthened his hand by sowing dissension and arousing new anxieties in the Indian camp. As he later reported, "Had I arrived safe to the Illinois it would not have been in my Power to ... have brought them to reason." He elected to go on to the Illinois to confront Pontiac before the Indian leader had had time to quiet the Shawnee controversy.

After writing reports on the progress of his mission to date to Gage, Johnson, Murray, Capt. John Campbell, who had succeeded Gladwin as commander at Detroit, and Major Robert Farmer, commander at Mobile, he set out with all the principal chiefs who had attended the Ouiatonon council following in his train. He had gone only a few miles before he encountered Pontiac himself on his way to Ouiatonon. The mountain was coming to Mahomet. With Pontiac were, beside his closest personal followers, a number of Illinois chiefs and the still scowling Shawnee, Delaware, and Mingo delegates. It is further testimony to the swiftness of Pontiac's rise to power that, for all Croghan's wide acquaintance among Indians, this was his first meeting with the greatest Indian of his time.

After greetings and polite exchanges of compliments the entire assembly moved back along the trail to Ouiatonon. The two celebrated representatives of their respective races continued to size one another up. Both were impressed but neither was taken in by the other. This was not a meeting of earnest negotiators sincerely committed to making a just peace but of two wary antagonists continuing to grope for fresh advantage. Croghan presently was reporting, "Pontiac is a shrewd sensible Indian of few words, and commands more respect amongst those Nations than any Indian I ever saw could do amongst his own Tribe," but a little later in the same report was adding, "Pontiac and I are on extreme good terms and I am mistaken if I don't ruin his influence with his own people before I part with him." Pontiac, for his part, repeatedly declared, both before and after this meeting, that Croghan had always been the greatest liar of a nation of liars. His estimate was justified in the sense that for ten years Croghan's had been the voice delegated by England to announce innumerable English promises every one of which was soon broken.

This climactic conference which was to determine the issue of peace or continued war was actually an anticlimax. For Pontiac had already made up his mind. The revelation that France, after losing everything east of the Mississippi to England, had ceded everything west of it to Spain had forced him radically to revise his conception of the Indian future. It was obvious that the French could no longer be considered a major element in the Indian situation. The guns and gunpowder upon which Indians depended to exist must presently be available only from the English. This was a harsh fact and the time was fast coming when Indians must make the best of it.

There might never be a better time to start doing that than this year when his followers still considered they had been victorious and this opinion was being supported by the English anxiety to beg for peace. The accident of the Kickapoo attack on Croghan's embassy had been a final spur to hasten his decision. The threat of Shawnee reprisal made it easier to silence the protests of the diehards in his own ranks.

His reasoning, having led him this far, led him on to the indicated last step. There could be no virtue in a grudging half peace. If there was to be peace at all let the English peace offer be accepted so heartily that there was room for the Indians to gain all the rewards that might accompany the reconciliation. Though from this moment on he became outwardly so warm a friend of the English that his followers were shocked, he was under no illusion. On paper the English terms did appear to offer redress of every grievance for which he had fought. But the Proclamation Line recognizing the inviolability of Indian lands he realized was merely another English promise. The Line would hold only if the Indians held it. And the new Indian Department was a pleasant convenience that would merely make dealings with the English more agreeable. In crises to come he knew Indians could no more trust Johnson and Croghan than they could generals or provincial governors. The one decisive element in the situation appeared to him to be the resumption of free trade. In that there could only be an Indian gain. Next year, or the year after, or whenever next came the day Indians must fight, arms furnished them by English traders must make them better able to fight. Having made up his mind Pontiac wasted no time. He readily agreed to accompany Croghan to Detroit and there to conclude a formal peace treaty in the presence of every western nation that originally had answered his call to arms.

The journey from Ouiatonon to Detroit was for Croghan a triumphal progress. Throngs of Indians who had been his friends in his trading days pressed upon him a renewal of that friendship. In town after town English flags which had been kept in concealment for years were brought out and raised as he passed. Captives were hastily collected and turned over to him. At Detroit he discovered representatives of the Lakes nations had already assembled to listen to an Iroquois delegation sent out by Johnson to serve as a diplomatic stopgap until the results of Croghan's Illinois mission had been ascertained. The sudden unexpected arrival of Croghan and Pontiac transformed the occasion from a routine discussion into a decisive peace conference. In late August it culminated in Pontiac's address to Croghan. His peroration was:

"We have all smoked out of the pipe of peace. It's your children's pipe and as the war is all over and the Great Spirit and Giver of Light who has made the earth and everything therein has brought us all together this day for our mutual good to promote the good works of peace, I declare to all Nations that I had settled my peace with you before I came here and now deliver my pipe to be sent to Sir William Johnson that he may know I have made peace and taken the King of England for my Father, in presence of all the Nations now assembled . . . Father: Be strong and take pity on us your children as our former Father did."

For the first time he had apostrophized the English with the term Father. Always before it had been the French who were addressed as Father and the English simply as brothers.

Pontiac's War had ended. However, in those private conversations with Croghan at Detroit at which, as in modern conferences, the real business of the occasion was transacted, Pontiac and every other chief made it clear to him that the basic Indian position with regard to their territory had not shifted. They asserted the French had never been in any sense the owners of Indian land. The French, in their time, had merely been tenants occupying the land temporarily by Indian sufferance. Therefore, ran the Indian argument, in defeating the French the English had in nowise gained title to Indian land. Croghan reported this Indian view to Johnson and Gage. Gage at once repudiated it. There could be no place in any European conception of international relations for an admission of any degree of Indian sovereignty. The Indians could not be considered a nation in the sense that England, France, and Spain were nations. Hence title to the land could not have existed until the French established by right of discovery and occupancy that title which then passed to the English by right of conquest. The Indians whose only former legal status had been that of French subjects had now become by that conquest English subjects. The Indians never accepted this view. But it was the view which, as time went on, was to prevail by the application of superior physical force. When English dominion gave way to that of the United States it continued to prevail and by the same means.

While Croghan was returning eastward by way of the lake route to report his success to Johnson and Gage, Captain Thomas Sterling, commanding a hundred Highlanders, was dropping unopposed down the Ohio from Fort Pitt to Fort Chartres. Croghan had notified Murray that the way was now open and so it proved to be. Thus, at long last, the English flag was raised over the great stone stronghold which itself did not long survive the passing of French suzerainty. Its walls undermined by Mississippi floods, it was abandoned seven years later and its very site soon all but forgotten. After handing over his keys to Sterling, St. Ange and his garrison, accompanied by most of the French inhabitants, crossed the river to take post at St. Louis which had been founded the year before by French traders anxious to escape the coming of English rule in the Illinois.

Croghan, who had so often known public censure, was welcomed upon his return from this last and greatest of his public services by overwhelming public acclaim. The perils and possibilities of his mission had begun to arouse intense interest long before he started. After he had disappeared down the Ohio into the unknown his fate had all through the summer been a subject for discussion rivaling the iniquities of the Stamp Act. The suspense was heightened by the publication of one report that he had been boiled and eaten. When, therefore, the period of anxious waiting was ended instead by the revelation that he had succeeded beyond anyone's wildest expectations the rejoicing was universal. Added to the realization that this worst of all Indian wars was over was the encouragement to hope that Indian peace might now be permanent under this new kind of Indian administration the efficacy of which he had so dramatically demonstrated. The general jubilation took a more realistic turn in the case of most merchants. They were immediately struck by the possible fortunes to be made in the reopened Indian market and as immediately began vigorous preparations to take advantage of the opportunity.

This public acclaim, however, proved to be Croghan's only reward. He discovered upon his return that the Board of Trade's grandiloquent Plan for the Management of Indian Affairs had not progressed beyond its original embryonic stage. No funds had been appropriated nor were any now likely to be. Money to make the plan work still had to be begged from the army. Now that his principal purpose had been served, Gage's welcoming embrace was not nearly so cordial as when he had first returned from London. Croghan himself was forced to admit that he had spent a great deal of money. Gage closely scrutinized his accounts which were in some confusion, as well they might have been after the capture of his goods by Black Boys and Kickapoo, his need to borrow from Pittsburgh traders, and his necessary largess at conferences attended by thousands of Indians. Croghan became so indignant that it took all of Johnson's earnestness to prevent his resigning. For there was still need of his services. At his Pittsburgh and Detroit conferences the Ohio and Lakes Indians had been pacified but the Illinois Indians, who were the farthest away and the most under French influence, were still outside the fold. They continued to exhibit a restlessness that required Croghan's personal attention. Croghan relented and agreed. He went to Pittsburgh, got the rebuilding of twice-burned Croghan Hall under way, and again set off down the Ohio.

That summer of 1766 was seeing a trade boom that was without precedent and that was never again to be matched. Literally hundreds of merchants and traders were rushing their wares over the mountains and on into the Indian country. The traffic was so extensive and so diligently protected by provincial peace officers and Gage's soldiers that the Black Boys despaired of their attempts to stem it. One firm alone, Baynton, Wharton and Morgan, employed 600 pack horses, built 65 batteaux at Pittsburgh, and dispatched westward in one shipment £50,000 worth of merchandise. The Indians, as Pontiac had foreseen, were being inundated by trade goods.

This year Croghan's descent of the Ohio was not so lonely as the year before. With him was a fleet of 17 batteaux, four of which were in his official service and the other thirteen laden with Baynton, Wharton and Morgan cargoes. Again he paused at Big Bone Lick, this time to collect specimens to ship to his friends Shelburne and Franklin in England where the objects excited much interest in scientific circles. At Fort Chartres he had less trouble with Illinois Indians than with Illinois mosquitoes. The iron constitution that had protected him through so many years of excessive hardship at last failed him. He fell victim to the local malaria which was a little later to plague generations of early American settlers along the middle and lower Ohio. When he had negotiated agreements with the Illinois nations similar to those made at Pittsburgh and Detroit and had partially recovered his strength he dropped on down the Mississippi to New Orleans and returned to New York by sea via Havana.

Except for his illness this had seemed the least critical of all his great journeys. He who had had so often to strive for every slightest gain this time had encountered almost no opposition. But he returned to discover that the whole structure of wilderness peace that he had labored so long and so strenuously to erect was already toppling.

XIV

⁊

Stuart II

THE PRINCIPLE of the Line's inviolability had been somewhat
weakened in the north by the government's reluctance to press
England's war against Pontiac to a militarily successful conclusion.
But in the south Stuart so far was succeeding in maintaining the
status quo in a fashion that justified the original hopes of the ministerial framers of the Proclamation. His success in keeping the
peace was based on a coherent policy that was at once bold and
adroit. While keeping the Indians off balance by promoting intertribal dissensions among them he at the same time vigorously protected them against white encroachment.

His task was eased in the immediate emergency created by the
outbreak of Pontiac's War in the north by the timely arrival of English garrisons to take over the former Spanish post at Pensacola on
August 6th and the former French post at Mobile on October 20th.
If during the recent Cherokee War the English regular army had
not impressed Indians with its invincibility in wilderness fighting
it had most certainly impressed them with its willingness to fight
there or anywhere. After the arrival of the first regulars on the
Gulf coast even the most impulsive Indians were disposed to wait

to see how many more might be coming and the interval gave Stuart time to raise other issues which Indians felt a need to discuss before they might decide to act.

Early in the spring he had been directed by the cabinet to summon a general conference of Southern Indians to assure them that English replacement of the French and Spanish on the Florida and Gulf coasts offered no new threat to their security. Stuart used the elaborate preparations for this conference to distract Indian attention from the efforts of French traders to persuade them to emulate Pontiac's outburst in the north. When at length the congress convened at Augusta in November it proved, in its outward aspects, at least, a major diplomatic occasion since it was attended by all three governors of the Carolinas and Georgia. Its scheduled purpose had been to recognize and to celebrate in the south the conclusion of the French War but Pontiac's new war was the ghost at the banquet. After eight days of much earnest talk by both red and white delegates about the virtues of interracial peace and friendship, of much earnest eating and drinking, and of some not quite so earnest appreciation of a somewhat limited distribution of presents, the single tangible result of the conference was a minor land cession by the Creek, whose prior assertion of title had in Georgia extended all the way to tidewater, in return for a white undertaking never to require more land of them. The peace maintained at Augusta remained a most uneasy one. Scarcely were the council cooking fires cold before the war faction among the Creek, led by The Mortar, an aggressively dedicated Creek patriot, had resumed sporadic attacks on the settlements. But for Stuart the conference nevertheless represented a weathering of his first Indian crisis. Pontiac's War, which during that year had risen to such heights of ferocity in the north, had not spread to the south.

The next year, after being shipwrecked en route to St. Augustine, he worked his way westward along the Gulf coast, holding a series of conferences culminating in March 1765 in another general congress at Mobile. The Creek had not ceased to threaten general war or to make intermittent attacks on outlying settlements but Stuart, supported by Gage who had too many demands for troops in the north to want more calls for them in the south, remained patient in his direct dealings with them. By equally prudent collateral maneuvers he kept them confused and preoccupied by instigating Choctaw-Creek hostilities in which the engagements fought far exceeded in numbers engaged and casualties suffered the occasional Creek raids on the settlements. Early in the summer in a carefully staged personal meeting Stuart arrived at an amicable understanding even with The Mortar. Pontiac's War had by now reached a stalemate in the north and the danger of a similar general war in the south was passing. Stuart's greatest remaining problem, for the moment, was the irresponsibilities of the hordes of traders who had swarmed into the Indian country. Control was excessively difficult for they came from all six of the bordering provinces and in each of them local authority made little or no effort to restrain their illegal and unlicensed intrusion. He restored some order by establishing deputies in the main Indian centers of population to guard Indians against the worst trader excesses.

Meanwhile he had had little trouble with his old friends, the Cherokee, but they had, as ever, become involved in troubles of their own. Undismayed by the trials that they had encountered during their attempts to help the English during the French War or by all that they had suffered during their own recent war with the English they had elected again to help the English in this new war by launching attacks against Pontiac's coalition in the north. They had been stirred to this action by £900 worth of presents voted them by South Carolina but so modest a bribe could not have moved them had they not been eager to strike again at their old enemies. A number of Cherokee expeditions conducted raids against Ohio Indian towns and against French traders supplying Pontiac. One of these parties while returning through the mountains along the Virginia border met the fate with which the Cherokee had been made familiar during the French War. It was set upon by Virginia frontiersmen and nine of its members killed. Governor Fauquier, much exercised by the gratuitous outrage, dispatched the always available Colonel Andrew Lewis to apprehend the guilty. He rounded up two of the assailants but they were forcefully rescued by their fellow borderers and no one was ever punished for the murders.

During this period immediately following the Cherokee War there was an interlude in more serious Cherokee affairs that has been given an added interest by its having resulted in a remarkable book. Attakullaculla, with his insuppressible friendliness for everything English, had suggested that the newly made peace between Virginia and the Cherokee might be fostered by the visit of a Virginia officer to the Cherokee country. Young Lieutenant Henry Timberlake volunteered for the possibly perilous mission. He traveled by canoe down the Holston accompanied by an interpreter and by Sergeant Thomas Sumter, later to become the Revolutionary hero for whom Fort Sumter was named. In his tour of the land so pictorially described by Bartram in which other Englishmen had so recently been massacred and burned Timberlake had many excitingly enjoyable experiences which he vividly described in his *Memoirs*.

Upon his return to Virginia he was accompanied by Judd's Friend, next to Attakullaculla and Oconostota the most distinguished of Cherokee chiefs. Fauquier was struck by Timberlake's suggestion that the cause of peace might be further served by escorting Judd's Friend on to England and the governor, somewhat casually as it later turned out, authorized the junket. In London the Cherokee chief and his attendant warriors were greeted with as flattering a reception as had been Attakullaculla a generation earlier. Wherever the Indians appeared they were surrounded by such crowds that they were obliged to stay off the streets. Many of England's most celebrated men called upon them at their lodging. Sir Joshua Reynolds sketched them. They were presented to George III by the same Montgomery who had commanded the English army against which they had so recently fought. One difficulty attended their cosmopolitan experience. Their interpreter had died during the crossing and they were compelled to conduct all conversations, even with royalty, by signs.

Entranced as had been the Cherokee by their social success, for Timberlake the episode represented nothing but grief. He had neglected to draw funds from Virginia in advance. The expense of the Indians' upkeep in London soon exhausted his limited personal means. Sumter took the Cherokee back to America while Timberlake sought to straighten out his financial affairs. He was forced to pawn even his watch to pay his own return passage to America to press his claim for reimbursement. This hope was entirely disappointed. Virginia refused payment on the grounds that the undertaking from the moment he had volunteered to visit the Cherokee country had been "for his own profit and pleasure."

Notwithstanding the debacle of his first effort to improve Anglo-Indian relations he was sufficiently encouraged by the interest of a wealthy Virginia planter to try again. He escorted another delegation of Cherokee chiefs to England so that they might in person present a petition reciting their suddenly multiplying new grievances. The rich planter died, the government declined to recognize the delegates as authorized Cherokee representatives, Timberlake was this time completely impoverished, and the Indians fell into the hands of a carnival operator who exhibited the proud chiefs to the public for an admission fee. Lord Hillsborough belatedly rescued them from the showman, attempted to mollify them by presenting them to the House of Commons, and shipped them off home in the care of two Moravian missionaries. That same year Timberlake died in want and despair a few days before the book describing his adventures had come off the press.

The principal grievance the Cherokee had hoped to bring to the attention of imperial authority in London had been renewed white encroachments on their land. No sooner had the fears aroused by Pontiac's War begun to subside than settlers were again edging into mountain valleys the Cherokee considered theirs. The most disturbing of these infiltrations, even though it was into an area still separated from the nearest Cherokee town by two hundred miles of wilderness, was a southward extension of white settlement from the Valley of Virginia. The basic and apparently insoluble difficulty in this dispute was the diametrically opposed variation in the points of view of the two parties to it. To the settlers the wild land they were occupying was not only unoccupied but unused. That the

Cherokee in their distant towns should presume to claim it seemed totally unreasonable. But all Indians required wide hunting grounds and to the Cherokee they were most decidedly using their land inasmuch as their livelihood depended upon their being able periodically to hunt in it. Indians were often more disturbed by coming upon a white hunter killing game in their territory than by coming upon a new squatter's clearing in a creek bottom. Provincial authorities, though anxious to avoid occasions for a new Indian war, tended to overlook piecemeal intrusions.

Stuart, as soon as he had been notified of the terms of the Proclamation, took the simple position that now that there was a law the one acceptable resolution of every boundary dispute was to observe it. At his every conference with provincial governors he kept pointing to the dictate of the Proclamation. The settlers' trespasses were an offense not only to the Indians but a violation of the King's peace. At his insistence a survey of the Line was instituted and in areas where there could be any doubt its location was marked by a fifty-foot-wide belt of blazed trees. He kept dinning the significance of the Line into the ears of everybody concerned. Land on the Indian side of the Line was Indian and was to remain Indian unless and until Indians relinquished title to a clearly defined portion of it by way of a freely negotiated treaty under the auspices of and with the approval of the English government.

During the first years after the Line's establishment there was among settlers south of Virginia somewhat more disposition to observe it than farther north. The opposing Indians were nearer and more numerous and, however divided they might be on other matters, they were united in their objection to settlers. Their resistance, moreover, was not vitiated by the self-serving interference of Iroquois absentee landlords. And, far from least important, in Stuart they had a champion who watchfully guarded their lawful interests. He honestly believed that the surest way to save the peace was to show as decent a respect for an Indian's legal rights as for a white man's. He took care to strengthen his position as arbiter by constantly referring disputes to London for precise rulings and as a result royal governors who failed to co-operate with him were frequently admonished. In one instance of this firm support from the cabinet Governor George Johnstone of West Florida was relieved after a difference with Stuart.

Various official reports of the time emphasize the extent to which peace and order had been established on the southern border during the early years of Stuart's regime. In 1766 Ensign George Price, commanding at Fort Prince George, was reporting as though it were a matter of course the arrest and imprisonment of illegal settlers. In 1767 James Grant, first governor of West Florida, who had been made a firm believer in the virtue of maintaining peace with Indians by his painful command experiences in the French and Cherokee wars, was reporting that there was no settler beyond the Line in his province and that there would be none while he was governor. The same year Governor James Wright of East Florida was reporting that there were no settlers across the Line and that no Indians had been killed by whites on his border in the past two years. His one complaint was that the Indians harbored runaway slaves.

By a policy based on regard for law, on a practical grasp of wilderness realities, on a willingness to make hard decisions, and on a sympathetic understanding of Indian susceptibilities, Stuart had in the south made a fair start at making the Proclamation idea work. It was in the north that imperial control began first to show premonitory signs of giving way.

Part Three

ॐ

The Gates Unhinged

XV

᪐

The Frontier People II

W HILE CROGHAN was traveling westward down the Ohio, Pontiac was keeping the promise given at Detroit the year before by making his way eastward across the lakes to meet Johnson at Oswego to reaffirm the peace with final formality. Johnson received him with the deepest respect, treated him not as a repentant enemy but as a friend and an equal, addressed him as though he were the one and only spokesman for all Indians. He did not once so much as chide him, however gently, for having caused the loss of so many thousands of English lives.

The astute Johnson was cannily following the course first indicated by Croghan, calculated to "ruin his influence with his own people." It was a policy that soon bore fruit. Indian unity proved less able to withstand the stresses of peace than it had those of war. Every other chief was embittered by the unique favor shown Pontiac. The word that Pontiac had been seduced by the English spread through the Indian world. After Oswego Pontiac began to be regarded less as the great Indian champion than as the great friend of the English. His power waned as swiftly as once it had waxed. The resumption of trade which he had foreseen as a brief interval during which Indians might rearm and regather their forces became instead a kind of vacuum in which each Indian nation considered only its own interests and each Indian his personal advantage.

This Indian relapse into their former disunity came at the very moment they were confronted by a far more deadly peril than had ever before threatened them. They did not at first recognize the new danger for the blow that was already descending was at the hands of the most despised of all their enemies, the white settler. In every war of the past it had been the settlers who had been the easy victims. Attacks on settlements had been half sport, half school for young warriors. The settlers' greed for land had been satisfied only when there were enough soldiers within call. When the soldiers' backs were turned the settlers could be made to flee like rabbits. The real Indian antagonists had always been governors, generals, and armies. With such adversaries they had known how to deal by an alternating resort to war and compromise. They had had occasionally to give ground but it had been a little at a time and generally then only as a result of their own mistakes. The outcome of this last war had seemed to teach that there might no longer be need to give more ground. Therefore they were slow to realize that their doom, so long only foreshadowed, was now upon them.

For in that summer of 1766 merchants and traders were not the only men to be stirred by the opening of new opportunities. A companion stir of excitement ran along the Virginia-Pennsylvania frontier. That far land beyond the mountains had begun suddenly to seem no longer so far. Before the French and Indian War it had seemed a region as distant and mysterious as had America before Columbus. During the French War public attention had been fixed on campaigns in the north between the Hudson and the St. Lawrence. Fort Pitt and Niagara had been the extreme western limits to which people's imagination had extended. But during Pontiac's War their interest had been transported to the farthest reaches of the wilderness. Lonely English garrisons had perished on lonely rivers of which people previously had never heard. It had been like the raising of a curtain to reveal distant, formerly invisible, vistas. By contrast with the Illinois and the Straits of Mackinac the Forks of the Ohio now seemed in the comparative foreground. To the people of the border it had been made to seem nearer by the number of their neighbors who had already viewed the waters of the great river. Twice in two years Bouquet's armies had crossed and re-crossed the mountains, each accompanied by its long supply train. Traders' supply trains were now nearly as long. Scores of men liv-ing along the border had found employment as drivers. Nearly a thousand Pennsylvania and Virginia militiamen and volunteers had accompanied Bouquet to the Muskingum. The mountain barrier no longer seemed the unassailable barrier it had seemed before.

At the same time the Indian danger, by becoming an appalling reality, had become less appalling. Terror, however stark, becomes less stark by repetition. People learn to live on the slopes of a vol-cano. To the man for the first time seeing a pack of howling, gro-tesquely painted savages bursting from the forest, bent on killing him, burning his home, and butchering his family, the sight was a paralyzing spectacle. When witnessed a second and a third time he was still moved to run but this time to run for his rifle. People had observed that in the swiftly passing whirlwind of violence accom-panying an Indian attack some died and others did not. Survival, more often than not, was a matter of chance. It was natural for those who had survived to hold an improved impression of their own luck. Many shared a comforting, though seldom openly admit-ted, assumption that, as with smallpox, one who had lived through a first Indian attack was immune to the next. In any event, harsh experience had taught men realistically to appraise the Indian men-ace awaiting white intruders west of the mountains and as realisti-cally to consider measures by which it might be resisted or escaped. Above all else, there had been the discovery that fear was a more deadly enemy than could be any Indian.

The genuine frontiersman, applying the term to the man at the very edge of the wilderness to distinguish him from his slightly less venturesome border neighbors who lived not quite so near it, was more hunter than farmer. Game supplied much of the food for his family; furs and skins were more readily salable than whatever he could raise in his small clearing. With the rapid increase of population along the eastern slopes of the mountains hunting there became steadily poorer and the storied superiority of the hunting west of the mountains ever more attractive. The common experience was for the man of the family first to cross the mountains alone to hunt and look around. The hunting proved to be as much better as he had been led to expect. But everything else about the country appealed to him, too. Sooner or later he was certain to come upon a spring, or a meadow, or a stand of trees of a size that indicated the richness of the soil, that struck him as a vast improvement over his former location. He was inevitably seized by a temptation to bring out his family and take possession of it. Excited by the announcement of the new Indian peace, some hundreds of frontiersmen began yielding to the temptation.

The 1766 influx of hunters and squatters, most of them, at first, from Virginia, along the Cheat and Monongahela rivers, incensed the Indians and aggravated the officers of the crown whose duty it was to guard Indian interests west of the Proclamation Line. These were rights which had just been reaffirmed by treaties which England had labored to persuade the Indians to sign and which had been hammered out at formal conferences from which the Indian delegates had scarcely had time to return to their towns. Before starting on his last western journey Croghan reported to Gage that the Indians were already so outraged that unless the squatters were promptly evicted "the consequences may be dreadful and we involved in all the Calamitys of another General War." Gage ordered regular troops used wherever necessary to expel the intruders. Governor Francis Fauquier of Virginia and Governor John Penn of Pennsylvania issued repeated proclamations denouncing them and invoking every penalty of the law against them. In London Lord Shelburne, Secretary of State, was writing Gage a peremptory demand that the situation be corrected and the sanctity of the Line be maintained. Murray, commanding at Pittsburgh, dispatched detachments of troops to enforce these several decrees. The squatters were harangued, threatened, and driven bodily from one location after another. Their horses and cattle were seized and their cabins burned. Becoming more and more exasperated by his difficulties in dispersing the trespassers, Murray even sent Indians along with his soldiers to emphasize his warnings that if they did not clear out forthwith the Indians would be permitted to attack them.

There was perhaps a certain hollowness in the efforts of the provincial authorities of Pennsylvania and Virginia to support these expulsion proceedings. The same year that Fauquier was calling upon all intruders from Virginia "immediately to evacuate" and warning them that "they must expect no protection or mercy from government and be exposed to the revenge of the exasperated Indians" the Virginia legislature was providing for the improvement of Braddock's Road to facilitate traffic between Virginia and the Ohio. Pennsylvania was disturbed by the possibility of another Indian war but also disturbed by the revived activities of Virginia's Ohio Company whose designs conflicted so directly with the land interests of the Penn family. Both provinces were having difficulty determining just what attitude to take and just how firmly to take it because both claimed title to the region west of the mountains included in what is now western Pennsylvania. Each privately realized that the eventual establishment of its claim depended primarily on the number of its own citizens it might be able to introduce into the disputed area. The dispute was not to be finally adjudicated until after the Revolution but while it lasted it much accelerated the rate at which the region was settled. There was at this earliest stage, before the relocation of the Proclamation Line by the Treaty of Fort Stanwix, no overt encouragement of settlement west of the mountains by either provincial government. Each merely hoped that, if there were to be illegal settlers, more of them might turn out to be Virginians than Pennsylvanians and vice versa.

But it was not the near connivance of provincial authorities, or the want of enough soldiers completely to patrol the forests, or the hesitation of the Indians immediately to start another war, that accounted for the settlers coming over the mountains. They came because they were the kind of people they had become. They had become people who were unreasonable, unpredictable, uncontrollable. Ten years of war, of unparalleled violence and bloodshed and terror, ten years during which their women and children had been subjected to the same stresses as their men, had changed them. They had become people as different from the docile, law-abiding farmers and craftsmen of their so recent European background as they were separated in distance from those former homes in Wessex, Donegal, or Baden. Most of this change had taken place in the two short years since Bouquet had so mordantly castigated them as weaklings and cowards. The pall of despair, desolation, and death hanging over them had at last become so surcharged that each new aggravation became a spark kindling its own new blaze of rebelliousness. The dubious successes of the Paxton Boys and the Black Boys had spread these flames. Every man, woman, and child on the frontier burned with hatred for all Indians and with scorn for all government. The mountain rampart had become not a barrier but a challenge. The boldest, generally those who had already suffered most, were the first to cross. They came at first with no settled purpose much more coherent than to demonstrate that nobody could stop them. These people were by now a most stiff-necked, headstrong and contrary breed. The King's mandate, terms of treaties, statutes of their own legislatures, proclamations, military regulations, fines, imprisonment, bayonets, hunger, hardship, loneliness, and the certainty of Indian reprisal—all these were thrown into the balance to oppose their coming. And still they came.

Not only did they come but more and more of them were making up their minds to stay. They may have come first to look around. But they liked what they saw. What they liked best about it was the wilderness itself, where a man was free to move about, where he lived by his skill and his wits, where drudgery for wages was unknown, where no man was his master. The forces exerted to expel them but made them the more determined to stay. When soldiers burned their cabins they moved to another creek and built other cabins. They did not wait for Indians to attack them. Indians they chanced to encounter in these forests which by ancient tradition confirmed by yesterday's treaties were Indian hunting grounds they shot on sight. They were rude, vulgar, violent, bitter, cruel, remorseless. They were men able to sleep soundly nights while knowing any dawn might find Indians breaking down the cabin door. They were women who saw husband and children axed in the dooryard and the next day moved in with another frontiersman and began raising another frontier family. They were children who learned how to rip off a scalp at an age other children were learning to read. They were a remarkable people whose like had never been seen before and surely may never be again. They had been made remarkable by the hazards they had already experienced, the horrors they had already known. They had been hit so often that their one overmastering impulse was the instinct to strike back. Every prolonged war has at its end produced veterans who had become so accustomed to the excitement of combat that they were unable to adjust themselves to the monotony of peace. The frontiersmen of 1766 were veterans of a ten-year war of exceptional ferocity. When its end brought an end to the immediate dangers they had barely survived, they of their own volition pursued new dangers. It was a pursuit which was to bring on new wars which were to flame with only momentary interruption for the next twenty-eight years. For among them were more disturbers of the peace and troublemakers than builders of a new society. These first comers to the western wilderness were presently to be followed by steadier and more substantial fellow citizens who were to develop the new country. The first comers were meanwhile to keep pressing onward into the wilderness. They were rebels against restraint and seekers after total freedom. The freedom kept escaping them but their search for it was the hard, sharp edge of the blade that was cutting the way west for their countrymen.

This 1766 breach of the mountain barrier was a turning point in American history to rank with Champlain's antagonism of the Iroquois and England's conquest of French North America. Iroquois opposition delayed the French reach for the Ohio Valley by more than a century and enabled the English tortoise at last to overtake the French hare in the race for the prize. England's victory in the French and Indian War freed the colonies from their former dependence upon England's protection against the French and Indian alliance and led directly to the Revolution. These first few anarchic backwoodsmen, pushing in against unimaginable odds along the

wooded banks of the Monongahela, were now making history in
their turn. They were taking the destiny of a continent out of the
custody of world powers, ministries, military commanders, and
imperial administrators and placing it in the keeping of individual
men who would determine for themselves by their own devices and
according to their own lights what that future was to be. Few as
they were at first, their mere presence was enough to throw his
majesty's ministers' whole program into confusion by raising the
immediate threat of renewed Indian war. Just as the significance
of a military victory may best be judged by considering the consequences had the battle instead been lost, so may the significance of
what these men were doing most clearly be estimated by reflecting
upon how different must most certainly have been the course of
events had they not been doing it. Had events taken the orderly
course envisaged by the framers of the Proclamation Line, had the
Indian Department been undisturbed in its efforts to maintain Indian peace, had the Indians been let alone to take comfort in
re-established supply through officially supervised trading arrangements, had land acquisition been postponed for the future benefit
of officially encouraged land companies, the story would most certainly have been quite a different one.

It was not the actual crossing of the mountains that was in itself
so important. Given the increase in white population on the seaboard, that crossing was bound to come sooner or later. It was the
timing that was important. The presumptuous interference of these
few stubborn men with what can only be considered the normal
course of events came but just in the nick of time. But ten short
years were to elapse between that summer of 1766 and the fateful
July of 1776. By then a few of these interlopers along the Monongahela had tightened their grasp on the Forks of the Ohio and a few
others like them, making a second crossing of the mountains at
Cumberland Gap, were defiantly planting their stockade poles as far
to the west as Kentucky. The advance of these irrepressible people
across the mountains, an advance as outspokenly condemned by a
majority of their own countrymen as by Indians or imperial authorities, fixed the main course of our country's history to this day.

Had they waited for an ever so slightly more propitious moment to make their venture the independence so narrowly won by patriot armies, with the calculating support of France and Spain, must have been an independence limited to the Atlantic seaboard. Had it not been for the existence of these few forest-girt stockades and corn patches west of the mountains the Ohio Valley must at the end of the Revolution have remained at the disposal of England, Spain, and France. These rude and uncouth Frontier People of 1766 were carrying a flag of which no one yet had dreamed.

XVI

༫

Crisis

THE INTRUSION of the few hundred squatters along the Monongahela had forced the dangers inherent in the situation into the
open, exposing every threat in the glare of crisis. Their unwelcome
presence in defiance of the combined will of every other interest
concerned, Indian, imperial, provincial, was an invitation to conflict.
Their coming had brought the final, inescapable moment of truth.

It was crisis first of all for the squatters themselves. They were
threatened with imminent annihilation by the more numerous and
powerful Indians who so bitterly resented their trespass. The next
Indian hunter shot by a squatter or white tree blazer shot by an
Indian could provide the incident to precipitate a new war which
could start with as swift and terrible an onset as had Pontiac's.
For these few settlers west of the mountains there could then be no
hope. They could not look for protection in time either to the reduced garrison of Fort Pitt or to a slow muster of provincial
militia in the east.

And crisis likewise for the nearer Indian nations, Shawnee, Delaware, and Mingo. It was their hunting ground that was being pre-

empted, their honor that was being insulted, their national existence that was being challenged.

And for all Indians. Were the westward advance of white settlement not checked at the physically natural, treaty-sanctioned line of the great mountain barrier where and when might it ever be checked?

And for the government of England. By cabinet decisions, royal decrees, and solemnly negotiated treaties a system had been devised to implement imperial dominion over half a continent. The integrity of the Proclamation Line was its foundation. Was this immense edifice to be overthrown by a few ragged backwoodsmen?

But it was crisis most of all for these backwoodsmen's two million fellow countrymen on the seaboard. Aside from a handful of land speculators few of them were paying the slightest attention to what might be developing in those distant forests west of the mountains. A great Indian war was scarcely ended and there was immediate threat of another but public interest remained centered on ways and means of resisting England's fumbling and diffident proposals to raise in the colonies a portion of the money needed for their defense. No one yet realized how much more than immediate defense was involved.

The crisis slowly deepened. The Indians grimly waited to see what white officials might do to meet their obligations under the treaties. Renewed and more aggressive efforts to expel the squatters were made by the military at Fort Pitt and by provincial authorities. The Indians for a little longer watched and waited. The squatters hung on.

Croghan, upon his return to New York in January of 1767 by way of New Orleans and Havana, was still feeling the aftereffects of malaria. He was greeted by no public acclaim this time. This time he was not only charged with having spent much too much but with having personally profited through favors he had granted traders. Gage cleared him of actual corruption. But, like Bouquet before him, Croghan had had enough. It seemed to him that the greater his services the less they were appreciated just as it had always been true that the sounder his advice the less it had been followed. Again he handed in his resignation. And again Johnson persuaded him to withdraw it. He was needed more than ever. The Indians were becoming so aroused by the appearance of the squatters on the Monongahela that the prospect of another general war was becoming daily more threatening.

Tired and still far from well, he went to Pittsburgh to hold new conferences with the Shawnee, Delaware, and Mingo. He was able at least to distract them for the moment by pointing to the visible efforts being made by the army to evict the squatters. But he re-peated and re-emphasized his warnings to Gage that a new war was inevitable unless something more adequate were done to keep white settlers on their side of the Line. Still weary and half sick he went on to the Scioto to investigate reports that the Indians were calling a great conference among themselves. He learned that the confer-ence had been postponed to the next spring but that all Indian na-tions were exchanging belts with a view to the formation of an Indian confederation. Every Indian realized the need for a united front had become suddenly imperative. For if English authorities failed to expel the illegal settlers, then Indians themselves must do so. He went on to Detroit to assess attitudes among the Lakes In-dians. Everything that he had learned since crossing the mountains had led him to the conclusion that another Indian war was a near certainty. All that was delaying it was the Indian failure so far to hit upon another leader to take the place of Pontiac whose influence had been so much reduced by his willingness to make peace.

In late November Croghan struggled back through the wintry wilderness to Pittsburgh, nearing the end of what was to be the last of his tremendous journeys. He had recovered neither his health nor his spirits. No one was equipped by experience more accurately to appraise the general state of affairs on the frontier and no one viewed it more darkly. He had devoted the most of his life and of his extraordinary energy to the establishment of peace and order in the wilderness. He had had striking successes but each had been but temporary and all was now ending in failure. The three forces upon which peace depended—fair trade, the Indian Department, and the army—were slumping together into ineffectuality at this threatening hour when Indian resentment of the squatters was fast leading to an emergency equal to 1763.

Though the resumption of trade had made encouraging progress in the Great Lakes area, on the Ohio, where Indian relations were most strained, the contrary was true. The great Ohio trade boom of 1766 had within the twelvemonth become a commercial catastrophe. Some of this debacle had been due to a lack of individual judgment and common sense natural to inexperienced traders, some to Indian preference for their former trading association with the French, and some to the high cost of English manufactured articles brought about by the seaboard patriots' nonimportation agreements. But most of it was due to the operation of the simple natural law that water does not run up hill. The flow of the Ohio and the Mississippi ran but the one way. The traders' boatloads of manufactured articles glided to the Illinois with the greatest of ease but to bring back against the current the heavier boatloads of skins and furs received in exchange and then to transport them over the mountains was a task that ate up all the profits. The traders of 1766 were the first to make this discovery that the commerce of the west must flow as naturally as did its rivers to the Gulf, where New Orleans, with its Spanish governors and its French inhabitants, constituted at once the key and the lock to every western enterprise. This natural law was presently to impose a nearly intolerable burden upon the development of American settlement in the west. It was a burden not to be lightened until the invention of the steamboat.

The second force upon which Indian peace depended, the new Indian Department, was being inexorably weakened and the high hopes aroused by its first successes were already fading. It was tied hand and foot by lack of funds, its every intended function stultified by parsimony. There was not sufficient money to hire experienced personnel adequately to regulate the Indian trade, or bestow presents on a scale to mollify Indian resentments, or to set up that imposing façade of authority and generosity which was required to impress Indians. Such money as was furnished was doled out reluctantly by the army which was itself locked in its own strait jacket of governmental economy.

Given the inability of traders and Indian agents to achieve all that had been expected of them, there fell upon the army the responsibility to keep the peace by force. But the army which had not been furnished the resources to deal effectively with Pontiac was being further reduced by the month. It could not field enough soldiers to evict squatters, let alone fight another general war. The cabinet, moreover had already under consideration a program of further and more drastic reduction.

The urge to economize was behind this recoil from wilderness responsibility. And the growing ill will between mother country and colonies was accelerating the process of disentanglement. American resistance to the mildest taxes had exasperated an England which for a time had been prepared, with a great deal of muddling but yet with reasonably good intentions, to maintain frontier peace. The frantic appeals of Gage and Johnson for the money needed to hold the Line and keep the peace fell on increasingly deaf ears. At the distance of London solution to the problem was simple. Let the Indians alone on their side of the mountains. Let the Americans keep to their side, as they were in any event bound to do by the dictate of the King's Proclamation. If the Americans insisted on starting another Indian war then let them fight it. Since they were so bent on handling everything else for themselves they could handle this, too.

With the situation hopelessly deteriorating Croghan could see one consequence more ominous than all the rest. The progressive weakening of the three pacification forces was reopening the whole land question. The Indians were infuriated by the invasion of their hunting grounds by a few hunters and squatters but were as yet becoming only dimly aware of the shadowy and far more numerous array of intruders waiting to come in next. The aspirations of these others were not fixed on a small clearing in a forest but upon land in hundred-thousand-acre tracts. Chief among this gathering host of land seekers were the American veterans of the French and Indian War, the "suff'ring traders," and the land companies. A number of provinces, unable otherwise to reward the war service of their citizens, had in lieu of other payment promised them western lands when and if they could be obtained. The major traders, having failed to secure direct compensation for their war losses, now planned to gain it by petitioning for tracts of western land. The land companies, whose maneuvers to gain fortunes in western lands had necessarily been interrupted by the two wars, were preparing for new and more ambitious moves. Once the imperial enforcement of the Proclamation Line was relaxed, as it now seemed about to be, all of these several invasions were poised to burst into the Indian country.

Of the three looming invasions, the land companies presented the greatest threat because they were able to exert the greatest political influence. In those years between the expulsion of the French and the outbreak of the Revolution no subject so captivated American imagination as the subject of western lands. Pontiac's War and the King's Proclamation had served rather to stimulate than to discourage this interest for it was not modest immediate fortunes but unlimited future fortunes that were envisaged. It was widely realized that Indian military power and the royal edict possibly long postponed the day when the land might actually be had. But meanwhile the land was there and the day must eventually come when it might be possessed. Speculation in these future land values became an American passion. Very many important Americans, including the two greatest of their time, Washington and Franklin, were deeply involved in western land schemes. Franklin represented land companies in Philadelphia and London. Washington was a leading Virginia member of the Ohio Company. In addition he had, as a personal speculation, bought up the land claims of a great number of his fellow veterans of the French and Indian War, confident that they might one day become valuable. With his incisive insight and grasp of affairs, in 1767 he was writing his Pittsburgh land agent, William Crawford, with reference to the Proclamation Line:

"I can never look upon that proclamation in any other light (but this I say between ourselves) than as a temporary expedient to quiet the minds of the Indians . . . Any person, therefore, who neglects the present opportunity of hunting out good lands, and in some measure marking and distinguishing them for his own, in order to keep others from settling them, will never regain it."

Croghan, revolving these signs and portents in his eminently practical mind, came to the same conclusion as had Washington. But he could not wait for the future to be unveiled. It was the explosive present that was still his immediate and personal responsibility. In mid-December he invited the Shawnee, Delaware, and Mingo to another Pittsburgh conference and made another dogged attempt to reassure them. There was, however, nothing that he could say that he had not said before. He could only repeat that the governors of Pennsylvania and Virginia were calling upon their citizens to come back over the mountains and that soldiers from Fort Pitt were trying to drive them back. This could make little impression upon Indians who could see that most of the intruders were still there and that more kept coming. Meanwhile the tension had been accentuated by the growing number of armed clashes. The squatters were continuing to shoot any Indians they encountered in the woods. The Indians were beginning to retaliate by cutting off isolated parties of white men. During the past summer each side had lost upwards of a score in such sporadic aggressions.

Critical as was the situation already, it was given a fearful turn for the worse by the peculiarly brutal murder of ten Indians, four men, three women, and three children, by two white frontiersmen on January 10th. The event occurred not in the disputed region west of the mountains but far to the east, within a dozen miles of the Susquehanna on the fringe of the old white settlement line. The harsh realism of the new frontier attitude was symbolized by the very names of the killers—Frederick Stump and John Ironcutter. The victims were the type of semicivilized, stray Indians who tended to hunt and visit in the area between the Iroquois country and Pennsylvania's northern border. Stump had invited the wandering group into his house, plied them with liquor until they had fallen into a drunken stupor, and then with the help of his servant, Ironcutter, had axed, scalped, and burned all ten. One of the Indian men had been a prominent Seneca and of the Indian wives one had been a Shawnee and another a Delaware. At one stroke Stump had managed to incense not only the already infuriated Ohio Indians but England's chief Indian allies, the Iroquois, upon whose pacifying influence so much depended.

The report of the outrage reverberated through Indian and white worlds alike. An Iroquois delegation descended immediately upon Johnson Hall, indignantly demanding satisfaction. Croghan rushed to Philadelphia where he appeared in person before the assembly. The lawmakers were thunderstruck by his plain speaking. Once it had dawned on them that not only was another Indian war imminent but that this time they could not depend on defense by English armies, they took unprecedentedly prompt action in their own behalf. Support that they had denied Bouquet they now pressed on Croghan to aid him in his last-minute effort to save the peace. The assembly hurriedly enacted a statute imposing the death penalty on all illegal settlers who refused to withdraw from the country west of the mountains and appropriated £2500 for presents to help mollify Indian indignation over the Stump murders. Another £500 was voted to implement a special effort to apprehend Stump and bring him to justice.

Stump was seized by a small group of fellow borderers, who represented a minority of frontier opinion disapproving his action, and deposited in the Carlisle jail. But the great majority of frontier opinion applauded his achievement. Armed frontiersmen marched upon Carlisle and released him by force. He was never brought to trial. Other armed frontiersmen barred the road to prevent the shipment west of the presents furnished Croghan for his approaching negotiations. Even in this extreme emergency frontiersmen were as vehemently opposed as ever to any and every attempt to conciliate the Indians. Frightful as had been their sufferings in the last two wars they hated Indians so passionately that they still preferred another war to any sort of appeasement. It required a strong guard of regular soldiers to get the shipment to Pittsburgh.

Here on April 26th there assembled the last great Indian conference over which Croghan was to preside. The Indians betrayed their inner uncertainties by their willingness to talk after they had been so loudly proclaiming their determination to act. He kept them talking by a judicious distribution of presents and by expatiating upon the new earnestness of Pennsylvania's intention to expel the squatters. Again he managed to stave off immediate war. But his success was almost entirely due to a sudden glaring manifestation of Indian disunity. All Indians had long recognized that formal Indian title to the region between the mountains and the Ohio was vested in the Iroquois. Use of the area as a hunting ground by Shawnee, Delaware, and Mingo had been by Iroquois consent. The Iroquois delegation, instead of supporting the general Indian demand that the squatters be forthwith evicted, stupefied their fellow delegates and undermined the whole Indian position by counseling patience. When the Pennyslvania commissioners invited Indian co-operation in the eviction program the Iroquois remained curiously evasive. Johnson had done his preconference work well. The Iroquois had already sensed the special advantage in prospect for them. Deprived of Iroquois support, the bitterly dissatisfied Shawnee and Delaware withdrew and went home to initiate urgent attempts to draw other western nations into an alliance upon which they could depend.

Indian failure to maintain a united front in this emergency was but a renewed revelation of a basic and immemorial Indian weakness. Through all the years since the white man's first appearance this failure to unite against him had handicapped every Indian effort to resist him. Universal as was the Indian aversion to the white man there had never been for him in his expression of that aversion a zest to equal the satisfaction taken in continuing to victimize an ancient tribal foe. Again and again an Indian nation had, in order to achieve the speedier ruin of a traditional rival, even yielded to the temptation temporarily to assist the white man's conquests. Sioux hatred of Chippewa, Cherokee jealousy of Creek, Chickasaw contempt for Choctaw, Iroquois assumption of superiority to all other Indians, these along with countless other intertribal animosities had persisted and still persisted. Pontiac's brief success in uniting a part of the Indian world had been but limited and regional. The two greatest reservoirs of Indian power, the eastern Iroquois and the Southern Indians, had not been tapped. The continued failure of the Indians to adjust their actions to their true interests, either in this crisis or throughout their past, must be regarded as a fatal flaw in the Indian character. Yet it represents a type of human failure for which there have been many and historic precedents. The most civilized, cultured, and Christian nations of Europe, for one notable parallel, have during a thousand years perpetually taken far more thought to gaining advantage over each other than to the advancing of their common welfare, their common race, or their common faith.

The Indian failure to close ranks was not from want of appreciating the advantages in union. Every Indian was in theory entirely convinced of the imperative need to organize a united Indian resistence. This was the constant topic of discussion at every cooking fire as well as every council that winter and spring. One suggestive example of the earnestness of the Indian impulse to achieve unity was the Cherokee embassy to the Iroquois.

For the past several years both Cherokee and Iroquois had been disposed to negotiate an end to their traditional war, the original cause for which lay so far in the past that it had been altogether forgotten. Both, however, had been put off on one pretext or another by Johnson and Stuart, each of whom was persuaded that the desultory war provided occupation for young warriors who might otherwise get into graver mischief. But Attakullaculla continued to insist and that winter led a delegation of distinguished fellow chiefs on the long journey north to the Iroquois country. Instead of following the Great War Road taken by so many generations of Cherokee warriors he and his fellow delegates sailed in an English man-of-war. Gage received them in New York with great ceremony. Among their experiences in the city was attendance at a performance of *Richard III*. They afterward edified onlookers with a war dance in the street. That spring, amid all the alarms following the Stump murders, they made a peace with the Iroquois at Johnson Hall. A number of Iroquois chiefs then accompanied Attakullaculla to Pittsburgh where he hoped also to resolve Cherokee differences with the Shawnee. But the Shawnee would not listen. Embittered by Iroquois desertion of their cause they were in no mood to accept as friends other Indians who were likewise posing as friends of the English.

As mounting tension that spring exerted increasing pressures upon all parties concerned it was the English government which first gave ground. The growing frontier confusion produced by Indian disunity and indecision was presently made total by formal act of the English cabinet. Soured by American objections to paying any share of the cost, the government determined upon an almost entire disengagement from the responsibilities it had formerly assumed for the maintenance of peace in the wilderness. On March 18th, 1768, while Croghan at Pittsburgh was desperately attempting by the distribution of Pennsylvania's presents to sooth the Indians after the Stump murders and the border mob was marching on the Carlisle jail to free Stump, the full cabinet approved a new policy recommended by the Board of Trade. This new official attitude represented a precipitate retreat from the firm posture assumed in 1763 and 1764. Regard for Pax Britannica was all but disowned. Authority to regulate trade, the chief area of friction, aside from the land question, between the races, was taken from the Indian Department and restored to the several provinces, thereby multiplying astronomically the occasions for dispute. The Indian Department was reduced to an understaffed administrative skeleton, without power to investigate, arbitrate, punish, or reward, thereby depriving it of every opportunity to hold Indian respect. Having so enormously increased the chances for incidents from which wars might develop the new policy next jettisoned the deterrent effect of the regular army's presence in the Indian country. Though yielding to the demands of the politically influential Great Lakes trading interests by keeping small garrisons at Niagara, Detroit, and Mackinac, every other post in the wilderness, including Fort Chartres and Pittsburgh, was ordered abandoned.

In reaching this decision the cabinet's primary motive had continued to seem to be economy at any price. Maintaining the wilderness posts had involved an annual extra cost of £300,000. This had been considered supportable if the colonies could be obliged to pay as much as a third of the amount. When they had instead continued to balk at paying any there had followed the testy cabinet decision to deny them the defense upon which they had appeared to set so little value. A secondary purpose was to gather regular forces in seaboard centers of population where their presence might discourage the growing American inclination to engage in seditious assemblies and riots. A third and unannounced factor, strongly suspected even then, was an underlying feeling in the cabinet that exposing the colonies to a general Indian war with which they must deal themselves might help to restore that sense of dependence on England which had passed with the defeat of the French.

Whatever the purpose the effect was unmistakable. Along a thousand miles of border those implacable enemies, the Indians and the Frontier People, now stood face to face.

XVII

ℰ

Johnson II

To SIR WILLIAM JOHNSON, the great opportunist, the last and greatest of his opportunities had come. He had never been a man to be daunted by the possible consequences of his actions. He had unhesitatingly accepted the command of armies, unhesitatingly invited the risk of battles, unhesitatingly plunged into the most forbidding situations, always with an implicit self-confidence that had fed upon repeated and almost uninterrupted success. When there now fell upon him responsibility for redrawing the map of a continent he accepted it as cheerfully as might a more diffident man an invitation to lunch.

The precipitate negotiation of the Treaty of Fort Stanwix was undertaken with twin hopes on both sides of averting an Indian war in the present and of simplifying the wilderness problem in the future. Both of these objectives were attained but they were attained in a fashion that was the farthest possible from either the intentions or the wishes of either of the two parties to the treaty, the Iroquois Nation and the British Empire. The Iroquois sought to improve their own position at the expense of their fellow Indians and succeeded in the process in bringing upon the whole Indian world, themselves included, consequences more catastrophic than had been produced by any other event since white men had first landed in North America. England sought to strengthen her imperial position in the west at the expense of her colonies and instead set off a train of events which cost the empire a greater loss of territory than did the Revolution.

So reckless and heedless an undertaking could only have sprung from political and economic maneuverings as anomalous and as confused as were the obscure clashes between Indians and squatters in the forests along the Monongahela. There was at no stage and in no sense a meeting of minds. The men who were advocating and promoting the manipulation, cabinet members, Iroquois sachems, royal administrators, provincial commissioners, land speculators, were men of the most diverse views whose aims were in every other respect totally opposed. Among the political figures most responsible for initiating the enterprise two stood out: Lord Shelburne, the minister primarily concerned with American affairs, and Benjamin Franklin, the resident agent in England for Pennsylvania, New Jersey, Georgia, and Massachusetts.

Nothing could have been farther from Shelburne's intention than to take any official step that might seem to sanction American settlement west of the mountains. He had been the chief author of the Proclamation and, although his resistance to expansionism had weakened enough to lead presently to his removal from office, his disposition to maintain the principle of imperial authority had not weakened. As recently as June 20, 1767, he had been writing Johnson, "The settlements lately projected near the Ohio by persons from Maryland and Virginia . . . are so injurious to the Indians, so detrimental to the interests of His Majesty's provinces, and such an audacious defiance of his royal authority repeatedly signified both in proclamations and instructions to his governors and superintendents that they can by no means be permitted."

During the winter, however, Franklin's persistent and persuasive arguments had been increasingly engaging Shelburne's attention. Franklin's pre-Revolutionary political attitude presented a curiously dual aspect. In Philadelphia he was allied with the Quaker majority in an unwearying agitation to obstruct and diminish royal authority. But in London, where though provincial agent he was also spokesman for land company designs, he as unwearyingly sought that augmentation of royal authority upon which those designs entirely depended. His argument gathered sudden weight when he was able to dwell on Indian resentment of the squatter's intrusion. This threat of a new Indian war could not have come at a more awkward moment. The regular army had not yet been extricated from the wilderness. Shelburne was impressed with the necessity of buying a little more time. On January 5, 1768, three months before the announcement of the cabinet's disengagement policy, he authorized Johnson to attempt to distract Indian attention with the purchase negotiation. In the Board of Trade's estimation this was actually a procedure to protect the Indians from settler encroachment since if the land could be bought it would be bought in the king's name and royal authority could thereafter be even more firmly asserted to control or prevent settlement.

Shelburne's consent to the purchase attempt had in London looked prudent enough on paper. But Johnson was a man with an enormously developed talent for taking rope without hanging himself. In this instance he took rope not by yards but by hundreds of miles. He had foreseen the purchase possibility in 1765 and had since then been preparing the minds of his Iroquois intimates. All of his past success had been built on the vigilance with which he had guarded Iroquois interests. Their conception of their interests, most happily for him, had always tended to coincide with his conception of his own. In the situation now developing this coincidence was more apparent than ever. By continuing to humor the Iroquois he and his associates were able personally to profit on an unprecedented scale. Having foreseen the dimensions of his opportunity he moved with swift certainty to take the fullest advantage of it.

All winter, as Croghan had learned on his last journey, the Northern Indians had been exchanging belts and completing arrangements for the assembling of a congress of all Indian nations to organize a confederated resistance to the further extension of white settlement. At Johnson's instigation the Iroquois proposed that the congress be held in their country. The other nations were agreeable since the Iroquois were generally regarded as the senior Indian power. During the summer the more distant delegations journeying to the congress paused frequently en route for preliminary conferences at nearer Indian capitals and these exchanges of views aroused some suspicion of Iroquois intentions but by early autumn more than 3000 Indians had gathered at Fort Stanwix with their Iroquois hosts. It was the greatest Indian congress ever assembled. It had been summoned to co-ordinate Indian resistance. But when the delegates arrived they discovered to their confused dismay that their one function was to witness a complete sellout by the Iroquois of every basic Indian interest.

By the time the congress had convened Johnson and the Iroquois had already made their deal. During weeks of devious, intricate, and secret negotiations they had worked out a complete agreement and there remained only the formality of disclosing to the score or more of lesser Indian nations what the domineering Iroquois had already decided. The essence of Johnson's proposal and Iroquois acceptance had been Indian agreement to a revised definition of the Proclamation Line that permitted along its whole northern section a deviation from the original line of the mountain barrier. In the Iroquois country proper in New York the relocation recognized Iroquois proprietorship in an area extending well to the east of the dividing watershed and in other respects legalistically improved their position. But below the Iroquois homeland the treaty transferred to England the former Iroquois title to all land south of the Ohio River.

Johnson had at first anticipated that the sale would apply only to the critical area between the mountains and the upper Ohio. This had also been the cabinet's understanding and it had taken care specifically to instruct Johnson that the cession should extend only to the Kanawha so that the readjusted Line might then run back up that river to rejoin its original course along the crest of the mountain barrier. The government had intended to countenance no more than a local accommodation to ease a local tension. But the Iroquois, according to Johnson, had refused to recognize any such limitation upon what they might choose to give away. In their anxiety to reaffirm their domination over the other Indians they insisted that the purchase extend on westward along the south bank of the Ohio across Cherokee and Shawnee hunting grounds in the lower valleys of the Cumberland and the Tennessee. After some pious hesitation Johnson took upon himself the responsibility for accepting the Iroquois proposal even though it so completely frustrated the cabinet's purpose in originally authorizing the purchase. At no time had the cabinet regarded the treaty in any other light than as a means of reasserting imperial control over American westward expansion. Instead, the critical area about the Forks of the Ohio had by collusion between Johnson and the Iroquois suddenly been extended all the way into the wilderness of distant Kentucky.

Johnson, realizing the certain need of future political support, had shrewdly invited others to share in the discussions and in the division of the spoils. Andrew Lewis and Thomas Walker came to Stanwix to represent Virginia's western interests. Governor Penn came from Pennsylvania and Governor William Franklin from New Jersey. (New Jersey had no western land aspirations but the province had become a kind of legal haven for various land speculation activities.) Samuel Wharton and William Trent came to Stanwix to further the land designs of the suffering traders. Most Americans, their attention fixed on the taxation quarrel with England, had continued unaware that the great Indian congress was in session. But of the few whose attention instead was fixed on the prospect of winning fortunes in western lands all were there or were represented there.

Former Iroquois sales of distant areas for which they themselves had no use had invariably aroused the bitter resentment of other Indians and had led directly to the 1754-64 decade of frontier devastation. But Johnson was convinced that this time the risk in sight was not so great as the reward in sight. His estimate of the situation proved as astute as had his many earlier appraisals of Indian psychology. To the Iroquois dissipation of Indian interests in the Treaty of Fort Stanwix the other Indian nations were not prepared to interpose an adequate counter. The arrogant Iroquois continued

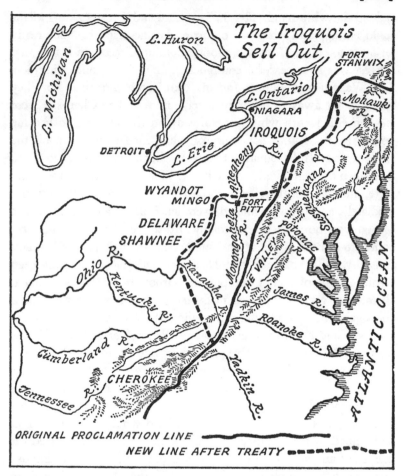

By the Treaty of Fort Stanwix in 1768 the Iroquois and the English government mutually agreed to a re-location of the Proclamation Line of 1763. In addition, the Iroquois insisted upon renouncing their claims to all land south of the Ohio as far west as the Tennessee. In thus expediting the breach of the mountain barrier they hoped to turn the flow of future white settlement away from their country and in the direction of their Indian neighbors. The English ministry declined to accept the cession west of the Kanawha.

to hold the whip hand. The St. Lawrence and Great Lakes Indians could not applaud what was occurring but neither were they ready seriously to object. They were losing nothing directly and their first interest was in a peaceful continuation of their regional fur trade. The Wabash and Illinois Indians were more disturbed but they were too far away to be immediately affected. The Cherokee were too concerned with white men already on the Holston to become excited by the future possibility of white men turning up on the far Kentucky. Indians had not yet yearned, and were never to learn, that when the bell tolled for one it tolled for all. The Shawnee, Delaware, and Mingo, therefore, whose rights were being directly, immediately, and grossly violated, were left isolated and helpless. The Mingo were no more than a colony of displaced Iroquois who were bound to remain obedient and subservient to their parent Iroquois authority. The Shawnee and Delaware had for generations been virtual vassals of their more powerful Iroquois neighbors. What it all came to was that, just as in earlier years the Iroquois had been able again and again to profit by selling Shawnee and Delaware living space and hunting rights in eastern Pennsylvania, they had now managed the same oppressive proceeding west of the mountains.

Consequences of measureless significance were to flow from the Treaty of Fort Stanwix. The results more immediately evident were striking enough:

1. The English government had obtained what it had been most determined to seek. Satisfaction of Iroquois claims had averted the danger of an immediate Indian war. If one came after the English army had been completely withdrawn from the Illinois and the Ohio then the ungrateful colonies must bear the brunt of it that they were felt so richly to deserve. The principle of the Proclamation Line had not been vitiated and to make this point clear the principle was soon to be forcefully reaffirmed in the Quebec Act. The Line had merely been relocated so that instead of running along the crest of the mountains it now ran for an interval along the Ohio River. The land west of the mountains had in no legal sense been laid any more open to settlement than it had been before. Any private or provincial right to take title had been left as firmly as before at the King's disposal.

Franklin, for one, subscribed to this view. Long after the Treaty he still considered the mountains "the real limits of Virginia."

2. The Iroquois gained that renewed recognition of their supremacy over other Indians that their insatiable pride most required. They had gained this gratification at no cost to themselves appreciable to them at the time. In the area nearest their towns their boundary had actually been reaffirmed and their title improved. Neither had their basic motivation been as totally heedless as it came later to seem. Their chiefs who bargained with Johnson and Croghan had for more than a century been accustomed to deal with diplomatic and military realities. By deflecting the prospective pressures of white expansion into the area south of the Ohio they conceived that they had provided a kind of safety valve which would reduce for years to come the threat to their own borders. And as a final though presumably not a decisive consideration, the chiefs who had managed the negotiation had gained the immediate personal reward of being courted by the white commissioners' respectful solicitations together with the privilege of dividing among themselves the purchase price of £10,000, every penny of which was paid exclusively to the Iroquois.

3. The land companies obtained an extinguishment of Iroquois title to the vast tracts that they hoped to acquire between the mountains and the Ohio and the assurance that reducing the immediate danger of Indian war must materially improve their chances of gaining royal approval of these grants.

4. The land grant hopes of the suffering traders were raised for the same reason and to the same degree as were those of the land companies.

5. The veterans whose expectations had been so often and so long delayed were given reason for feeling that there was now less reason for longer delay.

6. Johnson and his principal associate, Croghan, ostensibly won most of all. The recent swift decay of the Indian Department's importance and the new imperial policy of wilderness disengagement which so unquestionably foreshadowed freedom of action on the frontier had convinced both that the time had come to look to their

own interests. This each proved abundantly able to do. They might still be considered Gatekeepers in the sense that as Indian agents they still represented imperial authority west of the mountains. But theirs from now on was only lip service and Croghan was soon to resign in order to devote himself entirely to land-development projects. What immediately transpired was that their generous and grateful Iroquois friends granted Johnson and Croghan 200,000 and 100,000 acres respectively in New York and at the same time re-affirmed a shadowy early grant of 200,000 acres made to Croghan on the Ohio.

7. The other Indian nations directly involved, the Mingo, Delaware, and Shawnee, suffered, on the other hand, more by the treaty than they could have by a losing war. The Mingo and Delaware were obliged to relinquish their hunting rights between the mountains and the Ohio along the western reaches of the old mountain line and to foresee an early advance of the white frontier into an area 200 miles nearer their towns. Having suffered as had the Delaware and Mingo, the Shawnee had also been confronted by a sudden, stunningly unexpected, new threat to their favorite hunting ground in Kentucky.

Aside from land speculators almost the only Americans of the time to take a personal interest in the treaty negotiations were the New England missionaries to the Iroquois. Two of them, David Avery and Jacob Johnson, attended the sessions at Fort Stanwix to protest privately, publicly, and by formal written petitions to Johnson and the several governors and commissioners. They vigorously opposed the projected treaty and conducted an active agitation among their Iroquois adherents, urging them to oppose it. It was their boldly announced view that the Indians were being led to surrender rights essential to their temporal welfare and that the surrender was bound to lead to future hostilities which would, among other catastrophes, stultify the propagation of the gospel among them. Johnson, writing to Gage, bitterly denounced the missionaries' interference, accused them of serving New England land interests, and summed up his version of the episode with the remark, "I treated them with silent contempt."

Despite his scorn of the missionary conscience, Johnson had certain lurking qualms of his own about his Fort Stanwix achievement. He had long posed as the friend and champion not only of the Iroquois but of all Indians. He could not remain unaware of how crushing if not mortal a blow he had dealt the Indian cause. In a letter of March 22, 1769, to Gage, after he had had time to ponder what he had accomplished, there was a distinctly apologetic note. "For my part I could not see any ill consequences or impropriety," he wrote. "If it had not been done the Virginians would nevertheless have pushed settlements there." He did not live quite long enough to become equally aware of how crushing a blow he had dealt England's cause in the west.

Lord Hillsborough, who had succeeded Shelburne by becoming England's first Colonial Secretary, was deeply displeased by the treaty's terms and sternly reprimanded Johnson for exceeding his authority. He was particularly exercised by Johnson's having disobeyed his instructions to limit the cession to the Kanawha. Even from the immense distance of his office window in London Hillsborough could see how many new difficulties had been brought into view. He took the position, and clung to it during the next four supremely critical years, that the "two capital objects" of the Proclamation were to confine the colonies to territory where they could be kept "in a due subjection to and dependence upon the mother country" and where they would be "within the reach of trade and commerce" of Great Britain.

Johnson's defense was that the Iroquois had been so insistent upon the westward extension that unless he had acceded there could have been no treaty. This explanation Hillsborough was forced, however grudgingly, to accept. The English army was being withdrawn from the west and the former threat of war must in whatever event be at least temporarily averted. But the Privy Council's ratification of the treaty was delayed until July, 1770, and was even then most reluctant. "It is not, however, His Majesty's intention," warned Hillsborough, "that the settlement of His subjects should be carried beyond the Boundary of Virginia." He coldly withheld approval of the immense Iroquois grants made to Johnson and Croghan and threw the whole weight of his influence against approval of the land company and suffering trader petitions.

In the south Stuart struggled valiantly to restore some sort of order in the boundary chaos created at Stanwix. In the January 5th order authorizing Johnson to attempt the purchase Stuart was instructed to consider the Kanawha the new future line between the Cherokee and Virginia. The projected purchase, in the Board of Trade's view, was to represent merely a local bulge to the westward about the Forks of the Ohio. Except for this one aberration the Line was to continue to hold to the crest ridge of the mountains. Stuart restrained provincial authorities by frequent appeals to ministerial authority and negotiated patiently with his old Cherokee friends who trusted him. As a result, at the Treaty of Hard Labor, he was able to gain Cherokee assent to a new boundary running from Fort Chiswell on New River in a straight line to the mouth of the Kanawha. The Proclamation Line was thus again for the moment continuous. In the south it followed the mountain barrier. Below the southern end of the Valley of Virginia it veered northwestward to the Ohio, then ran up the Ohio to Kittanning, then made a great circuit to the eastward to encompass the Iroquois country.

Johnson had in effect forced his government to accept the treaty by presenting them with a fait accompli. Grudging as was the cabinet's eventual ratification it could not very well be withheld without accepting frontier defense responsibilities the ministry had determined to relinquish. But there remained for Johnson the problem of requiring the western Indians also to acquiesce. This was not so easy a matter as jostling the distant and flabby-willed cabinet. The Shawnee, who had been most offended, were continuing to make the most earnest efforts, under their principal chief, Cornstalk, probably the most able Indian of his time, to organize an Indian coalition to oppose the Anglo-Iroquois alliance. Conference after conference was held on the Scioto at which Indian delegates from near and far debated the extent to which Indian security was threatened. The full impact of Cornstalk's appeal was blunted, however, by the progressive evacuation of the English regular army. It was the presence of English garrisons in the wilderness that had been the primary cause of Pontiac's War. Their withdrawal now from every post south of Lake Erie and west of the mountains, including even the great bases at Fort Chartres and Fort Pitt, had relieved Indian apprehensions of England's aggressive intentions. There seemed now so much less to fear since most Indians were confident that with the army out of the way they would have as little difficulty dealing with settlers as in 1755 or 1763. Even so, there was still room to argue that the time to stop the white advance was now, at the mountain barrier, and Cornstalk's persistence in this view began to find support from the same intransigent faction among the Seneca that had joined Pontiac.

Johnson's counter to this latest Indian attempt at united action was calculatingly to promote intertribal Indian animosities. With some help from Stuart he encouraged the Cherokee to consider renewing their traditional war with the Shawnee. The trade-loving Lakes Indians were prompted to plant mutual suspicion among the various delegations at the Scioto conferences. The Iroquois were persuaded to instruct their delegation to denounce and then openly to threaten the Shawnee. "It is a disagreeable Circumstance," Johnson was writing Hillsborough, "that we must either agree to permit these people to Cut each others' Throats or risque their discharging their fury on Our Traders & defenceless Frontiers . . . but Common policy and our own Safety required it." Hillsborough was disturbed lest this policy seem "irreconcilable with the principles of humanity." He could not deny the gravity of the danger, however, and agreed that "therefore the King, however unwillingly, cannot but approve of your . . . making the security of His subjects and the Peace of the Frontier the principal Object of your attention." This squeamish approval was accompanied by one last sanctimonious regret: "But it would be most pleasing to His Majesty if it could be attained without encouraging the Savages in their barbarous attacks on each other."

In this new Indian crisis in which there was greater need of Indian unity than ever before, Pontiac, the great advocate of Indian unity, played no part. He had made no effort to regain the influence that he had lost so swiftly when he had made his peace with the

English. Having been convinced by the French downfall that Indians had no other recourse than to endeavor to get along with the English he was resolved to make the best of it. In 1768 he was writing Jehu Hay at Detroit: "I have no complaint whatever against the English. It is only my young men who have shamed me . . . by the insults they have made me, saying that I was never a chief." There was nevertheless some fear that in this hour of Indian need Pontiac might emerge from his seclusion to vitalize Indian resistance by again raising his standard. Had there been any such chance it was removed by his death in April of 1769. He was assassinated by an obscure Peoria Indian in the street of Chaokia in front of the Baynton, Wharton and Morgan store. His assailant fled and motive for the attack remained a mystery. The local French promptly charged that the murder was arranged by English traders and speculators who feared Pontiac might oppose their plans to establish a colony in the Illinois.

Hillsborough's distrust of the treaty continued and deepened. "Every Day discovers more and more the fatal Policy of departing from the Line prescribed by the Proclamation of 1763," he was writing Johnson in 1772. The great Iroquois land cession, he declared, "instead of being attended with Advantage to this Kingdom and Security to the Colonies is now likely to have no other Consequence than that of giving a greater Scope to distant settlements, which I conceive to be inconsistent with every true principle of Policy, and will most probably have the effect to produce a general Indian War."

Johnson, however, persisted, on the whole successfully, in his time-tested efforts to keep the Indians confused and disunited. On July 11, 1774, in the course of dissuading the Seneca and Delaware from supporting the Shawnee in their war with Virginia he was addressing their delegates at Johnson Hall with his customary ardor. In the midst of his harangue he collapsed, apparently from the heat and overexertion, and died within two hours. Death came at a merciful moment for him, before he could begin to guess how much the world as he had known it was to change. Within the same twelve-month his every achievement of a lifetime of achievement had been swept away.

The Treaty of Fort Stanwix marked in the truest sense of the phrase the end of an era. The tremendous outburst of energy which had characterized England's expulsion of France from North America had been succeeded by as sweeping an ebb tide of indecision and irresolution. The English government had remained convinced of the imperative necessity of restraining settlement to the area east of the mountains until such time as the westward advance might be supervised, Indian rights guarded, and wilderness peace maintained. But it had at the same time become unready to pay any part of the price required. Its every measure had been half-hearted, its every move vacillating, its every responsibility evaded.

The west was about to pass into the keeping of firmer hands.

XVIII

❦

The First Crossing

ONE HUNDRED AND SIXTY-TWO YEARS had elapsed since the first English-speaking colonists had landed on the coast of North America. In the interval they had found firm lodgment along the full length of that coast from Maine to Georgia, in the process dispossessing Dutch and Swedish rivals and the original Indian occupants. Welcoming immigrants and importing slaves, their number had steadily increased until it had passed the two-million mark. Yet so far they had continued to face eastward toward the old world from which they had come, their commerce, even with each other, was seaborne, their every political, economic, and cultural interest was interwoven with England's, and they remained an outlying fringe on the rim of the Western European community. Now had come the moment when for the first time Americans were to become truly Americans by beginning to turn instead to face westward. This was the most important moment in American history after Jamestown. No American then living, or who has lived since, but has been supremely affected by it.

We, the legatees of that prodigious venture, have tended to take our great legacy for granted. That all came out so well has led to the comfortable assumption that it could not have come out any other way. Even our school children have long been taught the doctrine of manifest destiny. According to this interpretation of our early success as a people the first crossing of the mountains was a sure-footed setting out along a wide and inviting avenue leading to certain greatness for the young nation, which in that year 1769 was yet unborn and even unconceived, and thereafter the continued westward movement of our forefathers was irresistible and inevitable.

It is true enough that it did prove to be irresistible but nothing could be farther from the truth than that it was inevitable. Manifest destiny referred to a much later state of mind and the phrase itself was not coined until after the first crossing of the eastern mountain barrier had been followed by a crossing likewise of the Mississippi, and then of the far western mountains, and long after this continuing westward march had made the weak young nation a giant in size and strength. The first white men to become genuine settlers in the western wilderness by bringing their families with them were sustained by no such comforting glimpse of the future. The most that they could see was that they were embarking on a course that could hardly have been more uncertain and more hazardous. Every early settler was aware that the risk he was inviting amounted to the risk of his life and of the lives of his family. Even were the Indian danger to be for the time postponed there was in his first year the ever-present threat of starvation.

Neither was he sustained by the thought that he was an empire builder. There was nothing about his struggle to survive to make him aware that his success or failure in it was to govern the westward extension of the dominion of a country which did not yet exist. When it did exist he was still slow to become conscious of the historic role that presently was to appear his. He was too concerned with getting his stockade erected in time to be too concerned with the establishment of a relationship with the country he had left which he was much more inclined to regard as his former country. He long continued to feel cut off from his fellow countrymen in the east by distance, the contrary flow of his commerce, and his well-founded conviction that they were indifferent to his fate. That the process led eventually to the coalescing of the violently dissatisfied western settlements into semi-independent new states adhering to the still new United States was far indeed from inevitable. It was much nearer a miracle.

There were few enough evidences of this eventual miracle in the circumstances surrounding the first crossing of the mountains in 1769. Every eventuality then foreseen indicated an entirely contrary course. The men who had engineered the Treaty of Fort Stanwix had known exactly what they wanted. They were eminently practical, extraordinarily capable, politically influential, and well acquainted with the frontier. They had powerful friends, amounting to associates, in Indian council houses, provincial statehouses, and at court in London. They had every reason to expect to gain what they wanted and the last thing that they wanted was a sudden disorderly rush of free settlers. What they did want were grants of land so far from the old frontier, so exposed to Indian threat, so susceptible to governmental regulation, that the eventual introduction of settlers could be managed for the profit of the legally recognized proprietors of the grants.

Progress toward achievement of these grandiose designs was impeded, however, by their very number and magnitude. In the limited area between the Kanawha and the mountains the vast tracts that they sought necessarily overlapped. Competition among the rival promoters was unavoidable. Most prominent among these competitors were the old Ohio Company, the Indiana Company in which most of the suffering traders had pooled their interests, and Croghan, who besides his claims as a suffering trader had the enormous private grant on the Ohio deeded to him by his Iroquois friends. The competitive situation was further complicated in 1769 by the maneuvers of the two adjacent provinces, Pennsylvania and Virginia. The Penn family took the position that the treaty had placed the territory ceded by the Iroquois at Pennsylvania's disposal. Virginia took the contrary view that it was instead within the borders of Virginia. There was initiated, as a result, the long and violent dispute between the two provinces that at times verged on civil war. This surely

represented confusion enough but there was more. All of these competing and conflicting claims rested on the legalistic basis of the
Iroquois cession. But that had been made to England and before the
title of any of the claimants could be established the cabinet's approval had to be obtained. The Proclamation was still in effect and
title to land west of the mountains still depended entirely upon the
King's sanction. The cabinet played an excruciatingly painful cat-
and-mouse game with the petitioners. For long it withheld support,
then promised its assent, then withheld approval again. No single
grant west of the mountains was ever legalized.

Four figures towered above all others in this aggressive quest for
private fortune in western lands: Washington, Franklin, Croghan,
and Samuel Wharton. Washington's terse instruction to his western
agent, Crawford, was "my plan is to secure a good deal of land" and
he pursued his aim by successive private petitions for grants, by
buying up veterans' claims, by political activity both within and
without the Ohio Company, and by making personal explorations
and surveys on the Ohio. Franklin took a participating interest in
every new land company design, even in the most distant and far-
fetched of all, that of the Illinois Company, and continued to serve
as the petitioners' untiring advocate in England. Croghan used his
Indian, trading, and administrative associations so effectively that
he became, briefly, the greatest of all potential proprietors, nurtur-
ing, before his debtors again overtook him, claims to more than
300,000 acres on the upper Susquehanna and the upper Ohio. Samuel
Wharton, Philadelphia merchant and senior partner in the great
wilderness trading firm of Baynton, Wharton and Morgan, during
his four-year residence in London as representative-in-chief of the
suffering traders labored diligently to undermine the governmental
objections to the land grants and became at length so adept at wield-
ing political influence that he was able to overthrow cabinet ministers.

The principal claimants had recognized almost at once that their
one hope was swiftly to compose their own differences. The Grand
Ohio Company was speedily formed as a kind of catchall to include
everybody's expectations and thereby to disarm anybody's opposition.

Within the broad scope of this new conglomerate petition there was room for the old Ohio Company, the Indiana Company, Washington, Croghan, and for even the 200,000 acres promised Virginia's veterans by Dinwiddie in 1754. But cabinet approval was still denied and for three years the petitioners petitioned in vain. Hillsborough remained fixed in his conviction that western expansion represented a threat to imperial security. By adroit maneuvers Wharton enlisted political support through offering participation in prospective profits to enough influential Englishmen to bring about Hillsborough's downfall in 1772. The way now seemed open to cabinet approval. Croghan was exultantly writing to Johnson, "by the best accounts I can lern, the limits of the new grant will contain thirty od millions of acres and the office will open att 10 (pounds) Sterling per hundred and a half penny per acre quitrent which will make a handsome division."

Reiterated assurances of forthcoming cabinet approval led to an explosive mushrooming of the project. Hillsborough's downfall had removed active ministerial opposition even to the formerly denounced extension west of the Kanawha. The ardent promoters envisaged the erection of a new colony stretching along the south bank of the Ohio from east of the Kanawha to west of the Kentucky, free of the political control of either Virginia or Pennsylvania, in which they could maintain undisturbed management of the distribution of land. The new province won the cabinet's preliminary approval and so nearly approached reality as to be named, as once had been Virginia, in honor of the Queen of England. It was christened Vandalia in romantic tribute to Queen Charlotte's reputed descent from the ancient Vandals. Thus there seemed to be about to be a Fourteenth Colony on the very eve of the Revolution which was to cost England the original Thirteen. However, at the last moment, when the hopes of the promoters had reached a peak and their prospects of unlimited fortune appeared secure, the cabinet roused to take a sharper look at the project in the light of multiplying American manifestations of rebelliousness. This seemed on more mature consideration hardly the time to encourage American expansionism. Approval of the conglomerate land grants was again withheld. Instead, by the passage of the Quebec Act in 1774 supervision of most of the western wilderness was placed in the hands of the Governor-General of Canada. The promoters and speculators associated with the Grand Ohio Company, with its offspring, the Walpole Company, and with the whole Vandalia project, were left with nothing to show for all their years of effort and expense.

But the collapse of the land companies' vast balloon had not been solely due to the shifting opinions and reversed decisions of England's cabinet and parliament. Had the imperial government instead formally and finally approved the grants the outcome would not have been greatly different. For the land itself was being in the meantime taken. The Frontier People were entering upon their inheritance. Like Johnson they had seen their opportunity and they had wasted even less time in seizing it.

News of the Treaty of Fort Stanwix had caused a profound stir along the border. The extraordinary Iroquois cession was assumed to mean that Indian peace was likely for at least a year to come. For people inured to the shocks and alarms of the wars of the so recent past this was a long enough look to be granted into the future. What might come the year after could be faced when it came. The opportunity was now. The hunters and squatters of 1766 had shown the way. In the spring of 1769 Forbes' Road and Braddock's Road, which formerly had known only the passage of armies and traders' supply trains, were lined with loaded farm wagons, trudging families, plodding livestock. These were not hunters and squatters, expecting only to camp for a season before moving again or scurrying back. These were people on their way to build homes, to raise crops, and to improve the land of which they were taking possession. They crossed the mountains by the two famed military roads and fanned out to inspect and select homesites of their choice on the banks of the Monongahela, the Youghiogheny, the Loyalhannon, the Allegheny, and the Ohio itself. By midsummer of 1770 five thousand of them had made the crossing. In another three years their number had swelled to 30,000. This already storied land about the Forks of the Ohio was the key to the west. For the last twenty years it had been fought over by armies, world powers, and hordes of savages.

This pushing and unruly throng of self-willed newcomers was now undertaking to make it theirs.

Their sudden coming had been as much resented by every other interested party as it would have been before. The King's Proclamation had not been lifted, the Indians were still outraged, the land companies claimed the land that was being pre-empted. To none of these assertions of prior rights did the stubborn intruders pay the slightest attention. For possession of the locations they were choosing they depended at first solely on the fact of their occupation and then on the fact that they stood ready to defend their occupation whether challenged by governors, generals, Indians, or land agents. But their boldness was rewarded. They were not challenged. The Treaty of Fort Stanwix which had been planned with so much Machiavellian care to benefit others had served instead to benefit them and only them. Though the time was soon to come when they would be challenged, when they were to be obliged to fight, and suffer, and endure, to hold their new homes, they were first given a brief breathing spell. The King's soldiers at Fort Pitt were too few to attempt the ejection of so many and were in any event presently altogether withdrawn. The enraged Indians, even though relieved of the need to take into account intervention by the army, were too preoccupied with their own intertribal dissensions to attempt immediately to expel the unwelcome newcomers. The frantic land companies were themselves as yet only claimants, were armed with no physical means to enforce their wishes, and remained helpless to interfere.

On the other hand the two provinces from which the settlers had erupted, Pennsylvania and Virginia, leaped to their support in order to support their own rival claims to the region. Pennsylvania's assembly had not so long before declared the mountains the province's western boundary and as recently as the year before had decreed the death penalty for settlers west of them. But now Pennsylvania hastily opened a land office and made active official efforts to legitimatize the titles of her migrating inhabitants. Virginia as eagerly smoothed the way for her settlers. Much legal confusion naturally resulted from this duplication of asserted jurisdiction. The early settlements passed swiftly from communities in which there was no formal law whatever to communities plagued by rival codes, complete with competing courts, sheriffs, and tax collectors. The end effect, however, was not oppression but license. Settlers who failed to gain title recognition from one could appeal to the other. Many took advantage of the situation to ignore either jurisdiction. There was a tendency in each community for local public opinion to rule. Improvements were recognized as the property of the man making them and in practice this principle soon evolved into a tacit recognition of his permanent ownership of the land upon which they had been erected. Even the status of the earliest illegal settlers, the hunters and squatters against whom imperial and provincial authority had fulminated so thunderously, was accepted as constituting an established right of prior occupation and thus they profited by their original brazen flouting of that authority. Through all the tumult and contention of this sudden mass migration the one rule that prevailed was that each settler must decide his problems for himself. Responsibility fell not upon government or even upon society but upon him. If sufficiently determined he was able to take and hold what he wanted. There was no room amid such conditions for the weak or the timid. Those who were easily discouraged soon retreated to their former homes in the east.

Though these first settlers to cross the mountains were not subjected immediately to the violent trials of war this cannot be construed as a reflection upon the boldness of their venture. They could not know when they came that they would not be required to fight for their right to stay. The year before a general Indian war had been universally accepted as imminent. Every former effort to settle west of the mountains, beginning with Gist's in 1754, had been a blood-drenched failure. The fearful depredations of Pontiac's War were still too recent not to remain an appallingly fresh memory. His warriors then had swept eastward over the mountains while in this western country toward which settlers now were streaming the few hunters and farmers clustered by permission about Fort Ligonier and Fort Pitt had survived only by taking refuge within the walls. Those military sanctuaries were now being dismantled and for defense the new settler could from now on depend only on himself and his neighbors. This thought was continually impressed upon him. From the seat of his wagon as he traveled westward he could see the ashes and graves left by his predecessors.

But even though, as it turned out, he was spared an immediate general war his other difficulties were shattering enough. The size of the 1769 migration soon exhausted the available game and food supply. Hundreds starved before they could raise a first crop. Overshadowing every other deterrent was the basic realization pressing upon every man's spirit that literally every other man's hand was against him and that whatever he got was to be his only if he were able to take it and then to hold it. Light is thrown on the necessary resolution of these first western settlers by the comments of observers at the time. In the course of discussing their bare-faced usurpation of land-company claims, Washington in the journal of his Ohio tour of 1770 wrote, "how difficult it may be to contend with these people . . . is easy to be judged from every day's experience of land actually settled." In 1772 Crawford was writing Washington: "There are such numbers of people out now looking for land, and one taking another's land from him. As soon as a man's back is turned another is on his land. The man that is strong and able to make others afraid of him seems to have the best chance as times go now."

As Washington and Crawford were wryly noting, these were a very special kind of people. Each was so fiercely individualistic that as a class they defy description by generalization. Perhaps their extraordinary qualities may be brought into clearer view by tracing briefly the experience of one of the representative families among them. The Zane brothers, Ebenezer, Silas, Jonathan, and Andrew, were among those who crossed the mountains in 1769 to look for land that suited them. They found a spot they liked on the very bank of the Ohio at the mouth of Wheeling Creek, the site of the present city of Wheeling, West Virginia. They cleared it, built houses, barns, and stockade, planted a corn crop, and the next year brought out their families. Their station was the westernmost and by far the most exposed of all western settlements and was to remain so for many years to come. It was divided only by the river from country that was to remain Indian country until the late 1780's. As an isolated outpost of the white frontier it was always the first to be struck by Indian attack. But the Zane brothers had not wandered ignorantly into dangers of which they had been unaware. They were of a family that had long known the frontier. Their father, William, had been a Philadelphia Quaker who had withdrawn from the Society of Friends upon marrying outside the sect and had then settled on the South Branch of the Potomac deep in the Virginia mountains when that had been a site more isolated than was the new Zane location in 1769. In 1755 William's place had been overrun in the Indian invasion following Braddock's defeat and for the next five years he had been an Indian captive. During Pontiac's War his youngest son, Isaac, was taken at the age of nine.* Isaac grew up among Indians, took a Wyandot wife, and lived as an Indian the rest of his life. He contrived, however, to avoid conflict with whites except in one instance when during a chance wilderness encounter one of his Indian daughters was shot by a white militiaman. The brothers Zane held to their new location with never-wavering resolution. It was the almost perpetual target of Indian raids and was three times formally besieged. During these twenty years of conflict every member of the family had personal experiences which found a place in frontier annals. The most noted of these was an exploit of the youngest sister, Elizabeth. Home on vacation from school in Philadelphia, she was present during the last siege. The defenders ran short of ammunition. Divesting herself of her outer clothing for greater ease in running, Elizabeth raced from the stockade to Ebenezer's house where was stored a reserve supply, and got back safely through a hail of Indian bullets with a keg of gunpowder. As she and her brothers had foreseen, the Indians had been so startled by a woman's sudden dash into the open that they had first hesitated to shoot and then had shot too hurriedly to take certain aim. Andrew once leaped from a 70-foot cliff to escape pursuing Indians. On another scout he was not so fortunate. This time the Indians killed him. Silas survived all the sustained border fighting of the Revolu-

---

* Not to be confused with the contemporary Isaac Zane who was one of the largest landowners in the Valley of Virginia.

tion only to be killed in ambush in the renewal of Indian wars in 1785. Jonathan was of all the brothers the most expert woodsman and was much sought after as guide by commanders of expeditions against Indians. When frontier peace came at last he became active in opening up for others the wilderness in which formerly he had been able himself to keep alive only by his superior skill and cunning. He built the first road into the interior of Ohio, operated ferries, and founded a number of towns, among them the present city of Zanesville, Ohio. The record of this one family thus becomes the record of a whole frontier from the first daring venture into the forest to the final era of building roads, mills, schools, and churches.

Hundreds of such families as the Zanes were coming over the mountains this year and the next and the year after as the Frontier People, prepared and hardened by unexampled adversities, suddenly and instinctively recognized their great opportunity. They had come from Pennsylvania and Virginia but they were not taking possession for Pennsylvania or Virginia. All were subjects of the King but they were not taking possession for England. They were taking possession for themselves. It only became apparent thirteen years later that this was providentially to turn out to mean that they were taking possession also for the United States.

XIX

༄

The Frontier People III

THE CHANGE IN FRONTIER TEMPER first perceptible in 1766 and unmistakable by 1769 was a metamorphosis as complete as the
transformation of the worm in the cocoon into a winged creature of
the air. The misery-haunted inhabitants of the border who had
formerly been the perpetually harried victims of seemingly implacable circumstance had suddenly begun instead to see themselves as
the appointed masters of their own fate. There had been an altera-
tion in their outlook, their deportment, and their every attitude. A
change so remarkable, and one with so direct a bearing on the whole
country's future, deserves some attempt at a closer examination.
The phenomenon was apparent everywhere along the frontier but
nowhere was it so clearly apparent as in that isolated section of the
frontier in the Valley of Virginia. It was here that the people of the
border began first fully to recognize their identity as a separate people and to realize that every relief or advantage they sought was to
be gained only by their own exertions.

Nothing contributed more to this new frontier spirit of which the
Valley had become the cradle than did the simple and basic fact of
the Valley's geographical conformation. The two-hundred-mile long

north-south trough was flanked on the side of the wilderness to the west by the massive bulk of the main Appalachian range and separated from the older part of Virginia to the east by the Blue Ridge. With heights rearing against the sky to the east as well as the west the early settler in the Valley was from the first impressed with a sense that he was cut off from all help except his own. Another consequence of the Valley's conformation was the distance settlers were required to cover to reach their new homes. Occupation began at the northern end of the narrow trough and thereafter all later settlers were obliged, as the occupation pushed southward down its length, to make longer and longer sorties from their former homes. This was in striking contrast to the case in Georgia, the Carolinas, Pennsylvania, and New York where the frontier was edged westward a farm's width at a time while each new settler remained still in close contact with his former neighbors. In the Valley it was the more common experience for settlers moving southward to take twenty-, thirty-, and fifty-mile jumps. By such long moves away from every former association they were ever more sharply impressed with the fact that thenceforth they might count solely and entirely on themselves.* A third consequence of the Valley's geography was its bearing on its inhabitants' military situation. It could have been so swiftly settled in the first place only because it was an area on the Great War Road between the Cherokee and Iroquois countries and therefore was unoccupied by Indians. The nearest Indian towns were the Cherokee far to the south on the Tennessee and the Shawnee even farther to the northwest across the Ohio. Only in its extreme northern end was the Valley adjacent to the great invasion routes and major battlegrounds of the French War and Pontiac's War. Therefore English regular armies which assumed the major responsibilities for frontier defense in New York, South Carolina, and Pennsylvania were never drawn into the Valley. Yet the Valley was

* As an adjunct to these long moves the covered wagon came here into general use nearly a century before its more famous heyday on the far western plains. In one year more than a thousand wagons were counted on one Valley road. Daniel Boone's Quaker father, for one example, traveled by wagon with his family and household effects in one move of more than five hundred miles from the Susquehanna in Pennsylvania down the Valley and on to the Yadkin in western North Carolina.

The Valley was the source and focus of frontier energy which led to the settlement of the upper Ohio, the Holston, and Kentucky between 1769 and 1775. From the north end of the Valley it was 140 miles by Braddock's Road to the Forks of the Ohio in Pennsylvania, from the south end, 135 miles over the Allegheny Divide to the mouth of the Watauga in the Holston, and 437 miles over the Wilderness Road to the Falls of the Ohio in Kentucky.

The long, narrow corridor of the Valley, shut off by mountain ranges from earlier populated Virginia to the east and the wilderness to the west was ideally suited to the development of a totally self-reliant frontier culture. Settled largely by Germans and Scotch-Irish crossing the Potomac from Pennsylvania, the occupation of the Valley proceeded from north to south with a momentum that carried on beyond to the Yadkin, the Holston and the Kentucky.

sufficiently susceptible to attack by war parties filtering through the mountains from the northwest to suffer frequently and bitterly. Having no other recourse than to make an unaided stab at their own defense the settlers steadily learned to make an increasingly resourceful one. Thus in nearly every respect its geography made the Valley a nearly perfect school for frontiersmen.

Next in importance after geography among the influences developing this frontier's self-dependence was the composition of its new population. First to come in at the northern end were Germans from Pennsylvania who by 1740 had settled much of the Shenandoah section of the Valley. The next wave was largely Scotch-Irish, also from Pennsylvania. They swarmed down the middle and into the southern end of the Valley and, swerving slightly eastward along the James, eventually kept on into North Carolina. Meanwhile, movement directly westward from Virginia, except for a few outstanding men who became the new frontier's natural leaders, was largely limited to ex-redemptioners, recently arrived overseas immigrants, and a scattering of native Virginians of the least substantial sort. The disconformities in the populations on either side of the Ridge included religious as well as economic and social contrasts. Most of the new settlers were Lutherans, Presbyterians, or various sects of dissenters who had as little sympathy with Virginia's established Anglican church as they had in common with Virginia's ruling oligarchy of great landowners. This lack of common interests had little if any impact on the older, more prosperous, and more populous portion of Virginia but it served greatly to intensify the settlers' feeling that they were cut off, that they were a people set apart, and that they must cope with their own problems according to their own lights and in their own way.

A final major influence bearing upon the new spirit of self-reliance on Virginia's frontier was Virginia's county system. By the terms of Virginia's original charter the province's territory was described as extending westward to the shores of the Western Ocean, then supposed to lie just west of the Blue Ridge. As the settlement line pushed slowly inland from tidewater to piedmont, Virginia had formed new counties to meet the ordinary needs of local government. When the new settlements began to develop west of the Blue Ridge far from Virginia's centers of population but still in a region assigned by her charter to her jurisdiction, the simplest response to the problem of local government was to continue to incorporate new counties. The first two, Frederick and Augusta, were enormous, with western and northwestern boundaries considered to extend indefinitely inland across not only the mountains but the Ohio as well. As the new settlements increased in population the two gigantic counties were subdivided, Frederick spawning Berkeley and Dunmore, and Augusta, Botetourt and Fincastle. As a result the new settlements gained prompt and practical experience with the conduct of their own political affairs. The new settlers were in most locations strangers to each other upon arrival but they were obliged to learn quickly to work together. Absorbed as they were in the task of clearing land, building homes, feeding their families, and fighting off Indians, they were required as well to lose no time in appraising their neighbors in order to select among them the more likely candidates for such posts as sheriff, militia commander, magistrate, and surveyor. The demands of self-government were made the more pressing by the dangers to which every community was constantly exposed.*

Yet these several forceful influences tending to foster the unique self-reliance that came first to characterize the Virginia frontier could have served no sufficient purpose had the people of that frontier not been able to rise as individuals and as communities to the extraordinary occasion. That they were able to rise to it with such eventual success was in large part due to the appearance among them of equally extraordinary leaders. As on every other frontier these leaders were of two widely contrasting types. There were first the rare men who had been gifted with that natural and instinctive aptitude for woodcraft that made them able to compete in the wilderness with Indian woodcraft and who along with that aptitude were endowed with an inclination to put it perpetually to the test. Then there were

---

* Virginia's proliferating county system by which new ones were formed along her western frontier as rapidly as the number of new settlers warranted was the direct forerunner of the later process by which western communities were admitted as new states in the union.

the few early settlers who were inevitably elevated in the esteem of their neighbors by obvious attributes of character, education, ability, and personality which fitted them to plan, to organize, to command, and to accept responsibility. The Valley was notably fortunate in the number and quality of both of these types of leaders.

The accomplished woodsmen were of first importance in the earlier days of each new settlement. Their acquaintance with the country had enabled them to guide the newcomers to the location, their hunting skills helped to keep the community fed, and their wary ranging served to watch and warn against Indian threat. Their equanimity in moments of crisis as much as their experience and their marksmanship constituted a new settlement's first line of defense. Their importance diminished as the settlement became more firmly established. By then most had of their own volition gone on to newer and more exposed locations. Before the French War such roving hunters and adventurers had made themselves familiar with the mountains to the west of Virginia. After that war they were exasperating Bouquet with their excursions into the forbidden forests of the upper Ohio. The violence of Pontiac's War had scarcely subsided before they were hunting, trapping, and spying out the land as far west as Kentucky. Wherever they went, whether returning briefly to the settlements to recount what they had seen or pushing on deeper than ever before into the wilderness, they were the inveterate enemies of all Indians and Indians returned the compliment by hating their kind even more bitterly than they did settlers. They had by now become the forever famous long hunters. Daniel Boone became the most noted of them but he was only one of many. Among others as well known at the time were John Selling, James Knox, Casper Mansker, Anthony and Isaac Bledsoe, Elisha Walden, Henry Skagg, Stephen Sewell, Jesse Hughes, Michael Stoner, and Simon Kenton. It was these wilderness wanderers who together pointed the way west.

The leaders of the second type have attracted less attention since but at the time they exerted an even more impressive influence upon the frontier's defense and extension. They were the stubborn and solid builders of new communities which were already becoming new counties and were soon to become new states which were to form the larger part of a new nation. Devoted primarily to the development of their own land they were possessed by the mingled vision and common sense to recognize the necessity of devoting themselves as well to the affairs of their neighbors. Every interest on the frontier was perforce a common interest. Each was a border Cincinnatus, called often from his plow to the public service. The new community, in casting about to fill its need for sheriff, judge, militia commander, surveyor, felt so strongly its need that it invariably picked not the man most willing to serve but the man all recognized as the most able to serve. Its survival depended upon how well it picked. This imperative need for leadership was met on Virginia's frontier by men whose qualities within their field matched the capacity for leadership of that great array of senators, generals, and presidents later furnished the nation by Virginia's dynasty of great landowners. To notice only a few, selected almost at random from that roll of honor:

Andrew Lewis. His father, John, having fled Ireland after having killed his Ulster landlord, had become the first settler in the Valley. His younger brother, Charles, most gallant and beloved of all border commanders, was killed at the Battle of Point Pleasant. Growing to manhood amid the rigors, hardships, and dangers of the frontier he from his youth exhibited an innate readiness for authority and command. His career, like that of the frontier he served, was marked for years by frustration, defeat, and disaster. Yet so forceful was his personality that never did his fellow frontiersmen waver in their trust in his leadership. He commanded a company and was wounded at Fort Necessity. He commanded the unfortunate Sandy Creek expedition and the Virginians at Grant's defeat before Duquesne where he was himself captured. After being exchanged the frontier continued to recognize him as unhesitatingly as before as its senior and most capable militia commander. He served in the Cherokee War and with Bouquet on the Muskingum while during all the intervening years he had been chiefly responsible for organizing the frontier's defense. It was only after twenty years of campaigning that there came his first experience with success at the head of his

Virginians in their fierce battle with the Shawnee at Point Pleasant.

William Preston. Brought to the frontier as a child, upon his youthful acquaintance with the wilderness was superimposed a more formal education by a Presbyterian minister. His ability so early attracted the attention not only of his neighbors but of the authorities at Williamsburg that at the age of 23 he was a member of the Virginia delegation sent to treat with the Indians at Logstown in 1752. At the outbreak of the French War he was engaged in the distribution of ammunition for frontier defense and was present at the famous Indian attack on Draper's Meadows which resulted in the death of Colonel James Patton and the storied Ingles-Draper captivities. Throughout the French War and Pontiac's War he was a mainstay of frontier defense, commanding rangers, building forts, and serving as county lieutenant, colonel of militia, high sheriff, judge, and surveyor. It was under his supervision that the extraordinary surveys of Kentucky were made in 1773 and 1774 and he was a principal organizer of the Point Pleasant expedition. His father had been a ship's carpenter who had become one of the Valley's earliest settlers after having eloped with his captain's sister. His son became a governor of Virginia.

William Christian. His father, Israel, a Manxman, settled in the Valley in 1740 where William was born in 1742. At the age of twenty he was commanding a company in the Cherokee War. As the settlement line moved southwestward he moved with it, successively establishing new stations on the most exposed outer fringe where defense was a perpetual problem. He took a prominent part in the organization of Fincastle County west of New River, represented the new county in the House of Burgesses, and commanded the Fincastle regiment in Dunmore's War. The story of his life literally paralleled the history of the frontier of his time. He was born on the frontier and lived always on it by moving continually westward with it until he was killed by Indians in Kentucky in 1786. He had married Anne Henry, sister of Patrick Henry. All of his surviving five daughters married prominent frontiersmen, thus carrying on the family tradition of frontier leadership.

William Fleming. He was educated as a physician at the University of Edinburgh, became a naval surgeon, and saw much active service, as an incident of one campaign being imprisoned in Spain. Coming to America early in the French War he accepted a commission as ensign-surgeon in Washington's regiment guarding the Virginia frontier. He served with Forbes and in the Cherokee War. Fascinated by his border experiences, he became himself a settler in the Valley and in 1763 married Anne, William Christian's daughter. He commanded the Botetourt regiment at the Battle of Point Pleasant where he suffered terrible wounds from which he never entirely recovered. Though his strength was permanently impaired he was thereafter concerned with frontier defense and served as state senator, as acting governor of Virginia during Cornwallis' invasion, and as high commissioner seeking to unravel the enormous confusion into which Kentucky land titles had fallen. His death in 1795 was an aftereffect of his Point Pleasant wounds twenty-one years before. His literate and most articulate letters and journals throw an absorbing light not only on his times but on the man who wrote them.

Evan Shelby. Here was a man capable of becoming an outstanding border leader in both senses of the term. He was an able and responsible commander as well as a skilled and crafty woodsman. Born in Wales, he came to America as a boy and was immediately drawn to the frontier where he soon made himself a master of his new and strange environment. He was a scout with Braddock and commanded a company with Forbes. For a time after the French War he engaged in the Indian trade but in 1771 at the age of fifty-one he for the first time became a settler, selecting an advanced location on the Holston that made his station a defense outpost for this exposed flank of the frontier. He served with distinction in the Point Pleasant campaign and his long wilderness experience well fitted him for that leadership during the border wars of the Revolution which culminated in his appointment as general of Virginia militia. He left very many descendants among whom was a son who became the first governor of Kentucky.

These are but a few instances suggesting the kind of men who were furnishing a vitality of leadership which was preparing the

frontier for its imminent leap hundreds of miles westward to the
far center of the Mississippi Valley. But this supremely dramatic
achievement must have remained as impossible as it then had seemed
to be had not there been followers to measure up to these leaders.
These, the unrecorded and unnamed rank and file of the border
people, were in their own way as extraordinary as their standard
bearers.

In 1774 the frontier, extending from the Mohawk in New York to
the Savannah in Georgia, still ran east of the original Proclamation
Line except for the bulge toward the Fork of the Ohio and one other
much smaller intrusion along the Virginia-North Carolina border.
Along it in scattered, raw, new settlements and homesteads lived a
heterogeneous population of Germans and Scotch-Irish, somewhat
fewer English, and a sprinkling of Welsh and Huguenot French.
Of the settlers over thirty years of age many more had been born
in Europe than in America though by now there was growing up a
whole generation that had been born on the frontier. Whatever their
origins all had been long enough subjected to the same hardships
and dangers to have begun to develop among them more similarities
than dissimilarities. The extreme rigors of a common environment
were forcing them into a common mold. They might have come
from different backgrounds and still speak in different tongues but
all were alike in that they were wretchedly poor, lived in log huts
or brush shacks, scratched a bare subsistence from a half-cleared
corn patch, reared very large families, and hated their Indian enemies
to the west with only a little more virulence than they hated their
more fortunate countrymen to the east. The trait held most universally in common was a fierce dissatisfaction. Any horizon beckoned since beyond it must await a situation which however dubious
must prove happier than the one in which they now were fixed.
Their one great and shining reward was a sense of personal freedom.
However miserable their lot they had sought it of their own volition
and they were free to move on in search of another whenever they
so elected.

From the earliest days of the frontier when supercilious seaboard
residents had first begun to call them "back-country people" they had

been regarded with a perplexed mingling of derision and contempt as a folk too slow-witted to step back from the blows falling upon them. No sophisticated observer who had paused long enough to take any note of them but had been struck by their miseries, vulgarities, and barbarities. Bouquet had called them "vagabonds" and "scoundrels" and Gage "banditti." But Lord Dunmore described their particular peculiarities with somewhat more perception when in the course of presenting his celebrated defense to his ministerial critics he wrote:

"But My Lord I have learnt from experience that the established Authority of any government in America and the policy of Government at home, are both insufficient to restrain the Americans; and that they do and will remove as their avidity and restlessness incite them. They acquire no attachment to Place: But wandering about Seems engrafted in their Nature; and it is a weakness incident to it, that they Should forever immagine the Lands further off are Still better than those upon which they are already Settled. But to be more particular: I have had, My Lord, frequent opportunities to reflect upon the emigrating Spirit of the Americans Since my Arrival to this Government. There are considerable bodies of Inhabitants Settled at greater and less distances from the regular frontiers of, I believe, all the Colonies. In this Colony Proclamations have been published from time to time to restrain them. But impressed from their earliest infancy with Sentiments and habits, very different from those acquired by persons of a Similar condition in England, they do not conceive that Government has any right to forbid their taking possession of a Vast tract of Country, either uninhabited, or which serves only as a Shelter to a few Scattered Tribes of Indians. Nor can they be easily brought to entertain any belief of the permanent obligation of Treaties made with those People, whom they consider as but little removed from the brute Creation. These notions, My Lord, I beg it may be understood, I by no means pretend to Justify. I only think it my duty to State matters as they really are."

For all the penetration of his analysis Dunmore missed their most significant characteristic. The Frontier People had come to possess the most essential virtue that can be possessed by any people

—fortitude. The longer and more severely they suffered the less ready they were to yield to their adversities. This quality was perhaps most eloquently epitomized by one of their own number in a 1774 letter written William Preston by Arthur Campbell, who had himself once been carried into captivity by Indians when a boy of fifteen. Referring to the uncertain fate of John Floyd, a young schoolteacher then engaged in surveying beyond the mountains in an area being overrun by Shawnee, Campbell wrote: "I am very uneasy about my Friend Floyd: I hope he is only in Danger."

XX

❦

The Great Crossing

THE FIRST AMERICANS to look beyond the mountains for the fulfill-
ment of their expectations called themselves Men of the Western
Waters. No allusion could more clearly emphasize how complete
had been the readjustment of their every major interest. By western
waters they meant streams which flowed westward toward the Mississippi instead of eastward into the Atlantic. There were not yet
wagon roads, canals, or river steamboats and they were committing
themselves to a separation from old associations as radical as had
they or their fathers in making their original move across the Atlantic. Travel from the new homes they were seeking back to the
cities of the seaboard would become a longer and more arduous
journey than from those cities back across the Atlantic to Europe.

The western waters nearest to the very early frontier were in a
unique area. On account of comparative ease of access it amounted
to a southern extension of the Valley of Virginia and was to be
reached not by travel west but by travel south. Yet its streams
flowed westward. The crestline of the Alleghenies, elsewhere so
unmistakable, took here a jog to the east while at the same time
losing much of its prominence. By a kind of geographical accident,

here the real mountain barrier lay far to the west of the actual divide, for two of the greatest rivers of the west, the Tennessee and the Kanawha, rose inside this angle side by side. Each had eroded the head of its watershed until its upper tributaries had penetrated into a region well to the east of the main bulk of the Appalachian range. Divided only by steep but narrow and easily surmountable ridges, their headwaters were interlaced with each other's and with those of the eastward flowing Roanoke and James. A man on foot or horseback found awaiting him a rough but readily passable route when seeking to reach the upper Roanoke, whether he came southward down the Valley or westward from tidewater, and from the Roanoke on he was separated only by local watersheds, each to be crossed in a short day's journey, from New River, flowing northnorthwest into the great Kanawha, and, successively, beyond, the Holston, Clinch, and Powell, flowing south-southwest into the Tennessee. This singular region with its paradoxical centrifuge of rivers and its even more paradoxical distortion of the mountain barrier was to assume a strategic importance in the western movement second only to the Forks of the Ohio. But this importance was late in becoming apparent.

The first Englishmen of certain record to enter it and thus to be first to stand on western waters were Thomas Batts and Robert Fallam in 1671. They crossed the piedmont, scaled Blue Ridge, turned down the Valley, and just beyond the next ridge came to their astonishment upon a westward flowing river. They called it the Great River. Later Virginians called it New River. So long had seemed its discoverers' journey from the then westernmost Virginia settlements that they imagined that they might have approached the Western Ocean. They measured the river for tidal rise and fall and brought back the story that they were certain that they had caught a distant glimpse far down its valley of waves and sails.

It was another three quarters of a century before the first settlers appeared on New River. They were introduced under the sponsorship of James Patton, the great forerunner of Virginia's first generation of great expansionists. He was an English sea captain who had made more than a score of Atlantic crossings with shiploads of

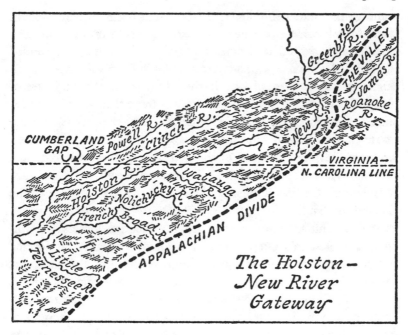

The Holston —
New River
Gateway

Here in what is now southwestern Virginia and northeastern Tennessee, the narrow mountain valleys produced a breed of frontiersmen of
truly heroic stature. New River was a projection of the Valley of Virginia but the people of the Holston faced single-mindedly westward. It
was men from the Holston who founded Kentucky and Tennessee during the same years they were fighting off the Cherokee, winning King's
Mountain, and riding with Marion, Morgan and Rickens.

At the foot of the Valley of Virginia nature had providentially arranged a narrowing of the mountain barrier of historic importance.
New River became the first westward flowing stream to be discovered
by the Englishmen Thomas Batts and Robert Fallam in 1671, and its
banks the site in 1748 of the first English settlement west of the Appalachian Divide: William Ingles'. After the border pressures of the
French War and Pontiac's War had relaxed, the New River crossing
became after 1766 the main gateway for the sudden settlement of the
Holston that became a tide sweeping on to Kentucky and Tennessee.

immigrants and redemptioners. Becoming at last fired with a desire himself to become a part of this beckoning new world to which he had brought so many others, he persuaded the same Governor Gooch of Virginia who made the first Ohio Company grant to assign him 120,000 acres of land in the wilderness to the southwest of Virginia's then frontier. His venture was more than a land speculation for he proposed to take personal charge of the grant's development and himself to introduce actual settlers. In 1748, continuing to extend his colonizing, he established two seventeen-year-old Irish youths, William Ingles and John Draper, on New River. Their station became the first English settlement on the western slope of the Allegheny divide.

Patton's initiative and success led to a sudden increase in Virginia's interest in western lands. The Ohio Company was formed by northern Virginians whose attention was fixed on the northwest and the Forks of the Ohio. Central and southern Virginians formed the Loyal Company to investigate the possibilities to the more remote southwest. Dr. Thomas Walker, whose intellectual and scientific attainments commanded the widest respect and who was later to become the guardian of the young Thomas Jefferson, took active lead of this new enterprise. Instead of confining his promotional efforts to political and financial activities in Williamsburg and London he went into the wilderness to see for himself what kind of land and how much land might be available. The Company had been granted 800,000 acres but to find anything like that amount of accessible land beyond the already settled or pre-empted portion of Virginia was far more of a problem than to coax the grant from Virginia's complacent government. To look for it up the Kanawha to the northwest was useless. The river wound for hundreds of miles through deep gorges in rugged mountains and finally joined the Ohio too close to the towns of Indians under French influence to suggest this as an appropriate site for a settlement. To look southwestward down the Tennessee was equally inadvisable since any move in that direction must at once offend England's uncertain friends, the Cherokee, and soon thereafter get into country to which North Carolina had a stronger claim. There was therefore nowhere to look but west and this Walker did. In 1750 he set out with five companions on his famous exploring journey, crossing the Holston, Clinch, and Powell rivers, picking up the Great War Path used by Cherokee and Shawnee warriors in their attacks on each other, and keeping on to the discovery of Cumberland Gap. By now he had put what he had hoped was the principal part of the mountain barrier behind him yet there seemed nothing but more mountains and even wilder wilderness beyond. In April he erected the first log cabin to be built by white men in Kentucky as a token that he had come not merely to look but to possess. Continued circling to the north and northeast disclosed, however, only more of these densely thicketed and nearly impassable mountains. In July he struggled back to Staunton, having found no land beyond the Gap worth his company's attention. One item in his report, however, stirred many pulses. He wrote: "We killed 13 Buffaloes, 8 Elks, 20 Deer, 4 Wild Geese, about 150 Turkeys, besides small game. We might have killed three times as much meat, if we had wanted it."

Meanwhile the little settlement on New River, named Draper's Meadows for John Draper's father, George, who had failed to return from a hunting trip, continued modestly to flourish. William Ingles married John's sister, Mary, and founded a family whose absorbing adventures dramatically illustrate, because they chanced to be recorded in some detail, the kind of stresses to which every frontier family of the time was subjected. Draper's Meadows was overwhelmed by the first Indian attack of the French War to strike the Virginia frontier. On July 8, 1755, the day before Braddock's disaster on the far off Monongahela, a Shawnee war party swept in upon the little settlement. James Patton himself was present, being engaged, with the aid of young William Preston, in distributing a fresh supply of ammunition to the more outlying stations. He was then 63 but the old sea captain was as fiercely vigorous as ever. He cut down two Indians with his broadsword before being borne down by numbers. In the sudden desperate confusion of the attack Ingles and Preston both escaped death, each fortunately spared for an ensuing lifetime of service to the frontier.

Mary Ingles and her two children, four-year-old Thomas and two-year-old George, were among those carried off by the Indians. The third day after her capture she gave birth to a baby girl but managed nevertheless to keep up with the war party during its three-hundred-mile return over the mountains to the Scioto. Three months later she came to grips with her fearfully difficult decision. Determined to return to her husband, she realized any attempt to escape was hopeless with an infant in arms. She therefore left the baby behind in a Shawnee salt-making camp at Big Bone Lick and after weeks of starving and freezing made her way through the winter wilderness back to Virginia.

Though Mary bore her husband four more children and Ingles' station became one of the most substantial on the Wilderness Road she never ceased to brood over the baby girl she had abandoned. During the next ten war years both parents were continually absorbed in the duties and demands of frontier defense but both likewise were continually oppressed by the thought of their captive children. Nothing was ever heard of the fate of the little girl but eventually they learned that George had failed to survive the first year of his captivity. Ingles never relaxed his efforts and the year of the Fort Stanwix Treaty he finally succeeded in locating and ransoming Thomas. Seventeen by now, Thomas had forgotten every word of English and had become a complete Indian. For a time after his return to his parents only constant watchfulness restrained him from escaping back to the Shawnee. Educated by a no less distinguished tutor than Dr. Thomas Walker, he eventually became reconciled to life among the whites, set up a place for himself, and married. After another fourteen years he suffered exactly as had his father. His home was burned in a 1782 Indian attack in which his wife in her turn was carried off.

Such afflictions as these suffered by the Ingles family were common on the southern Virginia frontier during the repeated attacks and perpetual threat of attack of the French War, the Cherokee War, and Pontiac's War. During this ten-year-long strain the frontier did not advance. It did well to hold its own, which it did on the whole, aside from withdrawal from some of the outlying and more exposed stations. The demands of continued conflict provided, meanwhile, a training school for woodsmen, for local militia, and, above all, for citizen commanders destined to meet the greater demands to come. It was a hard school. Men who were not quick to learn were no longer quick.

With the restoration of a troubled peace in 1765, the southwest Virginia frontier first rebuilt and then began to contemplate the new land beyond New River. The first to venture westward were the long hunters. Most were but dimly aware of the immense service they were about to perform. They were chiefly impelled to see country they had never seen before. At first they hunted across the Holston, the Clinch, and the Powell. But Cumberland Gap, discovered by Walker 15 years earlier, drew them like a magnet. They passed through it and roamed on westward, hunting, trapping, marveling at the height of the cane and the number of buffalo, until the more venturesome had emerged from the last mountains into the beautiful lowland valleys of central Kentucky. Most of those restless wanderers have remained nameless. But one of them has given his name to an era. Though Daniel Boone had been preceded by many others, his own first excursion into Kentucky in 1767 was noteworthy as a preparation for later achievements. Accompanied by Samuel Harrod and Michael Stoner, he passed through the Gap and wintered in the same thicketed maze of eastern Kentucky mountains which had so disillusioned Walker. But so far Boone was looking for room to hunt not to plant and he was more attracted than dismayed. In 1769 he went back, this time accompanied by John Finley,* an old ex-trader whose stories of the Kentucky country had excited Boone when the two had served together with Braddock. Finley had not seen Kentucky since in 1752 he had for a few weeks had a trading post there but he still remembered vividly what he had seen there. Boone and his companions, who included his brother, Squire, roved for almost two years across Kentucky, exploring, hunting, trapping, becoming in the course of their wanderings as familiar with the enchanting Blue-

---

* Historical references to Boone's friend have ranged in spelling from Finley to Findley to Findlay. His own version when he signed his name was "Findlay."

grass as with the Barrens or the Wilderness. For years the Shawnee had been increasingly disturbed by these insolent invasions of their favorite hunting grounds by white hunters. As yet unwilling themselves to accept sole responsibility for breaking the peace they contented themselves for a while with catching as many of the interlopers as they could, confiscating their arms, horses, traps, and furs, scolding them, threatening them, and turning them loose. Boone and members of his party were twice captured and plundered. The Shawnee chief's grimly succinct advice to them is recorded as: "Now, brothers, go home and stay there."

Tales of the wild paradise in Kentucky brought back by long hunters stirred the imagination of their stay-at-home neighbors. On the southwestern Virginia frontier practical attention was so far, however, too intent on the immediately adjacent valleys of the Holston, the Clinch, and the Powell to be as yet seriously distracted by a prospect so far, however fair, as Kentucky. But any advance across even this nearest threshold was ostensibly denied them. By the terms of the Proclamation, which defined the western limit of legal settlement as the line of the watershed dividing eastward and westward flowing rivers, even the twenty-year-old settlements on New River were illegal. Virginia was appealing to the cabinet for some adjustment of this manifest injustice. The cabinet declined to budge, ruling that there could be no exceptions and that the New River settlers must withdraw. But the King's ministers were far off and concerned with many other problems. The settlers were right there on the ground and concerned with but this one. They sat tight. Those who had been tenants merely ceased paying their quitrents. The cabinet relented enough to consent to the New River settlers remaining, providing the consent of the Cherokee could likewise be obtained.

Stuart undertook to negotiate this question with the Cherokee and they readily agreed in 1768 to the Hard Labor line which left the New River settlements on the Virginia side. The cabinet accepted this solution but decreed that under no circumstances were there to be further grants west of the Proclamation Line. This disapproval was never relaxed and the governors of Virginia were

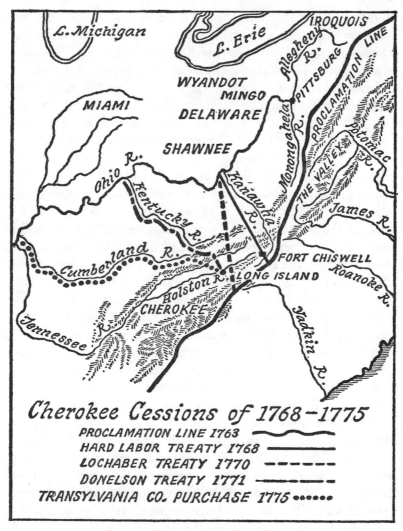

Cherokee Cessions of 1768-1775

PROCLAMATION LINE 1763 ————
HARD LABOR TREATY 1768 ————
LOCHABER TREATY 1770 – – – –
DONELSON TREATY 1771 —·—·—
TRANSYLVANIA CO. PURCHASE 1775 ••••••

The Cherokee yielded to the same temptation as the Iroquois when the two agreed to a westward adjustment at the Proclamation Line. They, too, hoped to funnel the flow of future white settlement away from their homeland. The English government declined to accept any of these cessions except that marked by the Line from the mouth of the Kanawha to Fort Chiswell.

repeatedly and sternly instructed to conform to the injunction. But the wave of frontier excitement produced by 1768's promise of at least temporary Indian peace, which had led to the rush of settlers to the upper Ohio, stirred a similar reaction in southern Virginia and western North Carolina. There was an immediate pressing by bolder borderers into the inviting valleys of the Holston and the Clinch even though this was regarded at the time as all but certain to draw Cherokee attack. That they were violating English law concerned them least of all.

Stuart was fully prepared to hold the Line and to protect Cherokee interests but his intentions were frustrated by the Cherokee themselves. Their older and more influential chiefs, including particularly Attakullaculla and Oconostota, had on their visit to the Iroquois in 1768 been deeply impressed by the dexterities of Iroquois statecraft. The Iroquois had contrived to guard their own borders by turning the tide of white advance off to the west. The Cherokee proposed now to do the same in their sphere. Without regard for Stuart's advice they began offering the Virginians even more than the Virginians were asking. The successive Lochaber and Donelson lines, revising the boundaries between Virginians and Cherokee, each readily if not eagerly approved by the Cherokee, were like gates swinging open, inviting white settlers to push westward toward Kentucky rather than southward toward the Cherokee homeland. As a result, settlers were able to occupy, unresisted, the upper valleys of the Holston and Clinch and to begin to trickle into the Powell. Their number swelled so rapidly that in 1772 the new county of Fincastle was formed to conduct the affairs of Virginians living west of New River. This advance and the coincidental advance of settlers into western Pennsylvania at the other end of the active frontier were like the two horns of a crescent, each aimed at Kentucky. Cherokee policy had combined with Iroquois policy to dump the entire burden of Indian resistance to white encroachment upon the shoulders of the forsaken Shawnee. It was the ensuing lodgment of American frontiersmen in the middle of the Mississippi Valley, however limited and precarious a lodgment at first, that was to sever the main Indian defense line, frustrate every imperial purpose of England and Spain, and make the new United States a continental power almost from the date of birth.

But these were distant prospects to those frontier leaders, farsighted as they were, who in 1773 made the actual decision to undertake at once the occupation of Kentucky. The stupendous difficulties lying in wait were far more visible. Kentucky was very far away indeed and to be reached from the existing frontier only by a passage of hundreds of miles through an unbroken wilderness inviting Indian attack at any mile or any hour. It had been but eight years since Gage and Bouquet had concluded that such a passage was a task too difficult for a fully organized professional army. The westernmost settlements from which the long leap must be launched, on the Monongahela and the Holston, had been themselves so recently occupied that people had as yet scarcely begun clearing their land and were in many cases still uncertain whether they were in Pennsylvania, Virginia, or North Carolina. They already had problems too many and too pressing to have attention to spare for an entire new set of problems. Their greatest need was a pause to consolidate gains that had already been made too fast. But with that willful self-assurance that was a frontier characteristic so new nobody yet recognized it, it was nevertheless determined to reach straight away for Kentucky.

Ironically enough, the groundwork for the move was laid by Lord Dunmore, the new Governor of Virginia, whose official duty it was to prevent it. In this new frontier crisis, exactly as had his predecessor, Dinwiddie, in the frontier crisis of 1753, he ignored his government's instructions and confounded his government's policy. Most royal governors had accepted their posts in the hope of improving their private fortunes. Most had instead become involved in tedious and protracted disputes with provincial assemblies who objected to every exercise of executive authority. Dunmore was no exception in this respect, for in 1773 Virginia was seething with rebelliousness. But he was at the same time able to please at least those relatively few Virginians who were directly interested in western lands. His support of their designs, which we may infer may have included some of his own, violated cabinet directives to an extent made possible only by the length of time required for the transmission of official dispatches to and fro across the Atlantic. His arbitrary pronouncements had effect during the many weeks before a cabinet veto could arrive and meanwhile his acts were beyond recall. He was also shrewd enough at the outset to foresee that it would be safe to oppose the Vandalia project, which offended eastern as well as western Virginians since if it became a reality it must constitute a barrier cutting Virginia permanently down to the size of other provinces. His political perspicacity on this score was demonstrated by the cabinet's ultimate rejection of the project.

Dunmore's chief western interest was concentrated on the anarchic situation occasioned by the Pennsylvania-Virginia dispute over the upper Ohio. The flood of settlers pouring into the area was daily adding to the confusion and continually inviting intervention. Gage was still issuing proclamations calling upon illegal settlers wherever located to "quit these countries instantly and without delay" but words alone, however official, carried now even less weight than they ever had before. Fort Pitt had been abandoned and dismantled in 1772 and with it the last physical vestige of imperial authority west of the mountains had vanished. Dunmore went himself to Pittsburgh, proclaimed the area a part of Virginia to be designated the District of West Augusta, appointed Virginia justices, and privately encouraged his principal supporter, Dr. John Connolly, Croghan's nephew, to raise the standard of civil war, if necessary, to maintain Virginia's claim. Further to encourage his supporters he offered to grant them land anywhere, including Kentucky. The cloud on his authority to do this, cast by the fact that the cabinet had repeatedly and specifically forbidden it, did not trouble the men who rushed to accept. They were not men who held authority in high regard.

Dunmore's arbitrary display of energy at Pittsburgh was to have but passing effect. It was not Virginia but Pennsylvania which was presently to establish claim to the region. But in the Holston and Clinch settlements of Fincastle County, three hundred miles away, there were effects which were never to pass. William Preston had been born on the frontier, had grown up with the frontier, and had fought in all the wars of the frontier. He was now county lieutenant and county surveyor. The latter office was if anything the more important. Nothing except survival was more important on an advancing frontier than acceptable surveys of new land being claimed. They were not important as efforts to establish title under the laws of Virginia or of England, since so far all titles west of the Proclamation Line remained invalid. They were important in that they were required to provide a clear designation of each man's claim in order to mitigate boundary disputes with adjoining claimants. Preston seized with instant vigor the opportunity opened by Dunmore's extravagant offer of grants. The western boundary of Fincastle, Virginia's newest county, was presumed to extend indefinitely westward. Preston claimed the authority, as Fincastle's surveyor, to order and to supervise surveys in Kentucky while at the same time denying the legitimacy of surveys made there by any other authority than his. The little group of extraordinarily vital and vigorous local leaders of Virginia's southwestern frontier had suddenly determined not only that Kentucky must be forthwith preempted but that they themselves must take command of the process. Control of events was not to be left to land companies, or royal governors, or infinitely distant cabinet ministers, but was to be taken by the frontier and exercised in the frontier's own interests. This was a position they were about to prove themselves abundantly able to maintain.

They realized, moreover, that whatever was to be done had to be done immediately. The excuse provided by Dunmore's grants might soon pass. He was certain soon to be suppressed or recalled by his indignant superiors in London. There was still every prospect that even sooner the projected province of Vandalia would be set up, thus erecting a permanent barrier of prior claims, unsympathetic officials, and politically powerful influences to every aspiration of the Virginia frontier. Under less pressing circumstances a much more cautious program would have been indicated. So precipitate a thrust as deep into the Indian country as Kentucky would without the slightest doubt bring on an Indian war. But the other threats left no time for discretion. There was literally no time to lose. None was.

In 1773 the previous invasion of Kentucky by long hunters was succeeded by a new invasion by surveyors. Guided and guarded by long hunters with previous experience with the country, they ranged across Kentucky with their chains, compasses, and little red flags, selecting and marking the more attractive tracts. The outraged Shawnee sought to discourage them as they had formerly the hunters. Many were despoiled and later in the year a number of the more persistent were killed. But like the long hunters they were not to be discouraged.

Not all of these 1773 surveyors were subject to Preston's supervision. Thomas Bullitt, for one, had advertised in newspapers of Pennsylvania as well as Virginia for volunteers to accompany him. To Preston's even greater dissatisfaction Bullitt paused on his way down the Ohio to treat with the Shawnee for permission to conduct his surveys. Other parties were led by William Thompson, James Finley, James Harrod, James Smith, and James McAfee. But Preston began soon to gather the reins more firmly into his own hands. Later in the year he organized a larger and more formal surveying party under John Floyd which was to make a more complete and authoritative survey superseding the earlier piecemeal ventures.

None of these surveys was clothed with any authority more substantial than Preston's assertion that as surveyor of Fincastle County his jurisdiction extended indefinitely westward. No one making them imagined the surveys were establishing titles of any legal validity. But the frontier had by now well learned that actual occupation could be depended upon to lead to practical possession. What the surveyors were achieving was to select and designate prior claims to land for the benefit of themselves, of their frontier friends, relatives, neighbors, and associates still east of the mountains, and of a select few figures of political and economic influence whose support and sympathy were worth enlisting. Among this latter group were Washington, Patrick Henry, Colonel Richard Byrd III, and John Connolly.

Daniel Boone, for his part, saw no compelling virtue in fooling with or waiting for surveys. On the road to possession occupation in person was in his view a longer step than pre-emption on a map. In late September he started for Kentucky with forty-odd actual settlers, some of them his former neighbors from the Yadkin and others his more recent neighbors from the Clinch. The risks confronting and the hopes animating the little expedition were precariously balanced but fully understood. So far the Shawnee had been kept isolated by the diplomatic maneuvers of Johnson and Stuart and the self-serving intertribal machinations of the Iroquois and the Cherokee. Boone's risk was that the Shawnee had by now been made so desperate that they might feel compelled to go to war even though they must fight alone. His hope was that they might continue to hesitate until he had had time to build a stockade in Kentucky. If they gave him that much time he counted on being able thereafter to hold it. The Shawnee were not long in dispelling every doubt. They attacked him before he had reached Cumberland Gap. Among the five whites killed were Boone's son, James, and Henry, son of William Russell, a Fincastle justice and an outstanding leader of Clinch River settlers. The Shawnee had served grim and unmistakable warning. Were the Virginians to keep on coming at Kentucky then they must expect war.

Boone, somewhat reluctantly, turned back. He was not so much perturbed by Shawnee hostility, which he had more than half expected, as he was by his uncertainty about the Cherokee attitude. The Shawnee attack on the Cherokee side of the mountains suggested progress toward an understanding between these traditional enemies. The more than two-hundred-mile-long trail over the mountains to Kentucky was an incredibly perilous line of communications at best. Were the Cherokee to support Shawnee resistance by attacking its Virginia end it must become an impossible one. There had been recent indications that such a development was far from impossible. For the last three years persistent Shawnee delegations had been seeking better relations with the Cherokee and beseeching them to realize that the Shawnee cause against the whites was a common Indian cause. A lively faction among the Cherokee, particularly among the younger warriors, had begun to agree with this point of view.

After the Cumberland Gap attack on Boone, frontier leaders made urgent representations to the Cherokee, demanding to know their intentions. It presently became evident that the peace faction, headed by Attakullaculla, was still in control of their councils. With Cherokee neutrality assured, at least for the moment, Preston ordered Floyd to proceed. As soon as spring made wilderness travel feasible the advance into Kentucky was to be resumed and the Shawnee challenge to be accepted. The frontier began to prepare for the coming war. The Frontier People had come a long way since the days they had cowered in despair awaiting the succor of an English regular army. They were now boldly seeking a war and proposing when it came to wage it unassisted.

The winter was filled with alarms which each week became more strident. The fierce animosity between the races led people almost to welcome every rumor of trouble. The long frontier with its isolated farms and stations offered innumerable opportunities for local provocations, altercations, and incidents. The nearer Cherokee and Mingo who had promised neutrality were more often involved than the more distant Shawnee. By 1774 the frontier was more than ever disposed to feel that any and every Indian was after all just another Indian. Reports of instances of whites killing Indians and Indians killing whites flared like heat lightning along the border.

The Shawnee dispatched delegations to other nations in one last frantic effort to rally support. But in the north the Iroquois more sternly than ever admonished the Mingo and Delaware to stand aside, in the south the opinion of the peace faction among the Cherokee that Cherokee interests were not involved continued to prevail, and in the west the Miami and Wyandot offered the Shawnee no support more tangible than their profound sympathy. A Shawnee delegation came also to Pittsburgh to remind Alexander McKee, Croghan's successor as Deputy Superintendent, that this white encroachment below the Kanawha was a flagrant violation of solemn treaties and a repudiation of every assurance offered them under the Proclamation. It was McKee's official duty to listen. But he had been stripped of the power to offer redress. He could only agree with the justice of their protests, condole with them, and counsel them to remain patient.

The Pennsylvania-Virginia territorial dispute was serving all that late winter and early spring to heighten every other border tension. Connolly announced that he had been commissioned Virginia's commander on the Ohio by Dunmore, called up the Virginia settlers of the area for militia service, and erected a stockade on the ruins of Fort Pitt which he called Fort Dunmore.* Rival Pennsylvania officials placed Connolly under arrest but his Virginia militia forced his release. Since the Virginia militia constituted the only even partially organized military force in the region, Virginia partisans were able to establish Connolly's temporary supremacy and to harass, imprison, maltreat, and expel Pennsylvania sheriffs and justices. The Shawnee had been sufficiently observant to be by now making a distinction between the settlers from the two provinces and to be asserting that only the Virginians were their enemies. Connolly, for his part, was equally aware that an Indian war would improve Virginia's position in the boundary dispute with Pennsylvania. He circulated reports along the Ohio frontier advising all settlers to prepare at once to defend themselves and declaring that the long-threatened war with the Shawnee had to all intents and purposes already begun. Anxious to assure the safety of the sympathetic Pennsylvania traders residing in their towns, the Shawnee conducted them to Pittsburgh with a Shawnee escort commanded by Cornstalk's brother. In spite of its having been engaged in a mission committed to saving white lives, Connolly attempted to seize and then to assault the escort. The Shawnee were only saved from this turbulent militia by the sagacity of Croghan and McKee in contriving to smuggle them out of Pittsburgh and back to their country.

Cornstalk still hoped to keep his nation out of a war which he well realized must surely be lost if fought without allies. But he

---

* Among all the vexations Dunmore was inflicting upon his government the sharpest reprimand given him was for having presumed to re-establish a fort which the King had abandoned.

was also being forced to realize that the one alternative was abject surrender. For that portentous spring of 1774 the ever more imminent threat of war produced no slackening in the compulsive surge of the white frontier toward Kentucky. Floyd's expedition made its way down the Ohio and resumed the provocative surveys. James Harrod conducted a party of actual settlers to Kentucky where they began the erection of the houses of Harrodsburg, destined soon to be the capital of Kentucky. George Rogers Clark, then only twenty-two but within three more years to become the greatest of all frontier leaders, was camped near Zane's Station with another party of 90 settlers on their way to Kentucky who were lingering there only while they decided whether to go on or first to strike a warning blow at the nearest Shawnee. War had by now become without doubt inevitable before the summer was over but it was precipitated immediately by an instance of white brutality even more shocking than had been the Stump murders.

On the west bank of the Ohio River, near the present Steubenville, Ohio, there was a small Mingo village presided over by a jovial, middle-aged subchief whose Indian name was Tachnechdorus. He was better known to his many white friends as Logan. Most other Indians of the region had long since withdrawn into the interior of Ohio but this handful of Mingo were not alarmed by their proximity to the white frontier since they were a colony of the Iroquois who were as clearly recognized as allies by Virginia and Pennsylvania as by England and their chief, Logan, had for long been as clearly recognized as a staunch friend of the whites with whom all of his life he had lived in close and amiable contact. Logan's mother was a Cayuga and his father had been a Frenchman who after having been captured as a child by Oneida had grown up to become an important Iroquois chief. Logan had formerly lived on the Susquehanna and had taken his white name as a mark of his attachment to James Logan, the Quaker Indian agent and later governor who for half a century had been much respected by all Pennsylvania Indians. During the French War and Pontiac's War Logan had clung to his white loyalties at so great a risk to his life that he had finally been forced to flee to Philadelphia for refuge.

Just across the river from the Mingo village was a white settlement usually known as Baker's Bottom inasmuch as its principal edifice was a bar kept by Joshua Baker. Its inhabitants were grimly aware of their exposed location at the very edge of the Indian country but their relations had been amicable with their immediate Mingo neighbors who had been accustomed often to paddle across the river to trade, visit, or drink. Baker's wife had a cow and frequently gave Mingo women milk for their children. Connolly's warning that the frontier must prepare at once to defend itself roused among the settlers that ferocious antipathy to all Indians with which from childhood all border people had been imbued. As was the case with the Paxton Boys and the Conestoga their implacable attention became fixed on the nearest Indians. When four of the Mingo, two unarmed men and two women, came unsuspectingly across the river they were made drunk and butchered. Five more Mingo who came at intervals to inquire what had happened to the others were shot down before they could get out of their canoes. Among the nine dead were Logan's mother, brother, sister, and several cousins.* Strapped to his sister's back, and surviving, was the infant son of John Gibson, then a trader and later a Revolutionary colonel, a judge, and secretary of Indiana territory.

The bereaved Logan fiercely renounced his lifelong partiality for whites. His vengeance was terrible. Gathering about him a band of his previously neutral Mingo which was soon joined by numbers of ardent young Shawnee who had become impatient with Cornstalk's inaction, he began his extraction of an eye for an eye. He did not attempt a single invasion. Instead, he divided his fol-

---

*In his celebrated lament for his slain kin, which has possibly been somewhat refined in translation, in one version by so skilled a pen as Jefferson's, but which still represents substantially the burden of his oration, Logan accused Michael Cresap of the murders. But Cresap has been absolved by the direct and detailed testimony of George Rogers Clark who affirmed that Cresap that day was fifty miles from the murder scene and engaged instead in persuading Clark and his followers to abandon their projected foray against the Shawnee.

lowers into small packs which were directed to lurk in the wilder
ness until they could descend by surprise upon isolated farms and
outlying settlements. No tactic could have been more cruel or more
effective or more nearly impossible to counter. His stabbing attacks
were scattered from the Allegheny to Cumberland Gap so that the
frontier was terrified from end to end and at no point could the
inhabitants feel that they might not be the next to suffer. Logan
later said that he himself halted his depredations after he had personally killed 13, which according to his count was the number of
his relatives, friends, and acquaintances the whites had killed that
spring, but his followers pretended to no such restraint. The frontier's recent advance across wide expanses of new country had left
it sprawled, disorganized, and most difficult to defend. Soon thousands of these new settlers were in flight. Most sought refuge in
the nearest larger settlement but many of the fainter-hearted kept
on eastward across the Monongahela and even across the mountains.
The frontier now had the war that it had so deliberately sought.

The government in London was perhaps not too disturbed that
the Americans should have a border war which it could be hoped
might distract them from their seditious concern with petitions,
protests, and riots but was nevertheless incensed by Dunmore's
many irresponsibilities. In the colonies, however, there was little disposition to regard it as an American war and less intention of becoming involved in it. Everybody who did not live on the frontier,
which included nineteen out of every twenty Americans, charged
those who did live there with having forced the war on the inof-
fensive Indians. American abhorrence of the Logan murders was
universal but the bitterest public denunciations were directed at
Dunmore and the principal frontier leaders, in that order. Pennsylvanians asserted that he with the connivance of such fellow con-
spirators as Connolly and Preston had fomented Indian trouble to
aid Virginia in tearing away the western portion of their province.
Tidewater Virginians were no better pleased. They charged that
the same combination had embarked upon an indefensible land-
grabbing program for their personal profit which could prove of no
conceivable benefit to the province as a whole. Most patriot leaders

from Charleston to Boston accused Dunmore of engaging in a
Royalist plot to embroil the colonies in an Indian war in order to
draw American attention away from their just quarrel with George
III and his ministers. All in all the conviction of seaboard people
was all but unanimous that the frontier should be left to stew in
its own juice. Pennsylvania's assembly declined to call up a single
company of militia, though a grudging allowance was made for the
hiring of a hundred rangers to assist in the defense of some of
Pennsylvania's more exposed settlements. At Williamsburg the
House of Burgesses was nearly as much opposed to the appropriation of defense funds. Dunmore's sole recourse in the emergency
which he had done so much to bring on was to call up the militia
of the frontier counties which amounted to notifying them that
they could expect no help.

All along the more exposed edges of the frontier people were
either fleeing or "forting," as they termed the hasty resort of the
inhabitants of each neighborhood to the nearest community stockade for refuge and mutual defense. Fincastle County was beset
in addition to its general defense problem by two other concerns.
The first was that the increasingly restless Cherokee might enter
the war, an apprehension that had been deepened by the recent
peculiarly gratuitous murder by one Isaac Crabtree * of an inof-
fensive Cherokee visitor, commonly known to the whites as Cherokee Billy, while the victim was innocently observing an afternoon
of horse racing at a Watauga settlement. The second was fear for
the fate of their surveyors scattered through Kentucky who might
not yet have realized how much more dangerous their situation
had suddenly become.

With regard to the Cherokee threat it could only be trusted that
they would swallow this last provocation, as they had so many others, since there was no possibility of appeasing their wrath by
penalizing Crabtree. On any frontier it was regarded as utterly
irrational to consider punishing a white man for any injury, in-

---

* Crabtree's hatred of Indians had been intensified by his having been with
Boone's party during the attack in which young James Boone and Henry Russell
had been killed by Indians.

cluding murder, done an Indian. But something could be done about the surveyors. Daniel Boone and Michael Stoner were dispatched to search Kentucky for them. The two combed the Kentucky wilderness as far as the Falls of the Ohio and in two months returned safely after dodging Indians during the most of an 800-mile journey.* They had been in time to warn many of the surveyors. A few had already been killed, but some escaped by canoe down the Mississippi, and most of the others were able to get back over the mountains. Harrod's party broke off their construction of Harrodsburg and marched to the Holston where they enlisted in a body in the frontier army then being organized. By midsummer there was not a white man left in Kentucky.

For Dunmore, with a war on his hands for which his government, his province, and public opinion everywhere held him chiefly responsible, there was no alternative to getting on with it as best he could. This turned out most unexpectedly to be very well indeed as a consequence of a development nobody then was prepared to believe possible. First reports of fleeing settlers had indicated another sad repetition of the helpless frontier panic that had followed the outbreaks of the French War and Pontiac's War. But there was something different about this 1774 frontier and how great was that difference was about to be demonstrated. It presently became apparent that many more people were forting than fleeing and that instead of waiting for help they were themselves already preparing to strike back.

Having no semblance of a regular army at his command and having been refused by his assembly the appropriation that would have permitted him to mobilize the militia of eastern Virginia, Dunmore's campaign plans were necessarily limited to whatever use could be made of the totally untried and most sketchily organized frontier militia. His only thought at first was of defense. He directed the militia of the northern Virginia frontier to construct a fort on the

* As evidence of how deep-seated by now had become the frontiersman's land-seeking impulse, Boone paused near Harrodsburg amid all the dangers of his journey to mark a claim and build a cabin on it to signify the land had become his property.

Ohio at Zane's Station and the militia of the southern frontier to march up the Kanawha to construct another fort on the Ohio at the mouth of that river.

In the north the task was simplified by the existence of wagon roads, nearby settlements, and an available food supply. The northern commander, Major Angus McDonald, whose previous military experience as a sergeant under Bouquet had included an attempt to expel the trespassing "vagabonds" of 1762 in this same region, was able promptly to obey his instructions. The new fort was called Fort Fincastle since it was just far enough west to be within the far-flung boundaries of Preston's Fincastle County. But more was to come of the maneuver. Contingents of frontier militia were seldom so much commanded by their officers as were their officers by the opinions of their men. Infuriated by the continued depredations of Logan's raiders, the 400 militiamen of McDonald's command held angry meetings and voted to move from defense to offense. Dropping down-river in bateaux and canoes, McDonald marched ninety miles into the wilderness and burned several of the nearer Shawnee towns after encountering no resistance beyond some scattered sniping and skirmishing. The Shawnee were fully able to have overwhelmed so small a force as McDonald's, as they were soon to prove, but they declined to give battle. Cornstalk was well aware that a rout of McDonald could not become a victory that could win a war. He was still casting about desperately but unsuccessfully for the support of allies to enable him either to strike back hard enough to deter white aggression or at least to negotiate from a position of strength. McDonald's frontier militia withdrew to the Virginia side of the Ohio, delighted with their success and animated by a new confidence in their prowess. They had some reason to feel pleased with their temerity. Theirs had been the first offensive engagement undertaken by an independent frontier force since Armstrong's Kittanning raid eighteen years before in 1756. Aside from having demonstrated the new frontier resolution, the campaign was perhaps chiefly significant for having provided George Rogers Clark with the first military experience of his memorable career.

The southern commander, Colonel Andrew Lewis, was confronted by an infinitely more formidable task. Among his problems was almost every classic difficulty known to military science. He was undertaking to march his army 200 miles through forested mountains and keep it fed and supplied over a lengthening line of communications made by the nature of the terrain peculiarly susceptible to disruption in order to seek battle with an enemy in the heart of that enemy's country. Meanwhile his main base, together with the homes and families of his men, was exposed to an ever more serious threat of Cherokee assault which must be made even more likely by the departure of the majority of its defenders. Possibly not least among his burdens was the oppressive memory that in every former campaign in which he had commanded he had encountered disaster. If so he did not permit this thought to swerve him a hairsbreadth from his purpose.

Almost his only element of strength, aside from his own indomitable spirit, was the stature of the men who rallied to his standard. Not until the days of a Scott, a Grant, or a Lee, was an American commander to be blessed with such an array of supremely qualified lieutenants. His colonels, William Preston, Charles Lewis, William Christian, and William Fleming, were men whose outstanding capacities were rivaled only by those of his junior officers, among whom were James Robertson, Evan Shelby, Arthur Campbell, William Ingles, Benjamin Logan, Daniel Boone, William Russell, John Field, James Harrod, William Cocke, John Floyd, Matthew Arbuckle, Valentine Sevier, and James Ward.* Upon his muster rolls were most of the greatest names in frontier annals.

Dunmore's astonishing proposal that quotas of the militia of Augusta, Botetourt, and Fincastle counties, representing respectively the middle Valley, the southern Valley, and the new southwestern frontier, be organized into an expedition to make the infinitely difficult Kanawha advance to the Ohio was taken under consideration

---

* In view of his exceptional ability as woodsman and scout, Daniel Boone, much to his regret, was left behind to assist in guarding the Clinch River settlements during the expedition's absence. Preston, Campbell, and Cocke also remained to supervise defense of the denuded border. James Ward, who was killed at Point Pleasant, had a brother, John, who had been a captive since childhood and whose body was discovered among the Shawnee that had been killed by James' Company.

by the frontier's local leaders. At first glance it seemed to border on the fantastic to expect a crowd of untrained and unequipped settlers, not all of whom had guns and no one of whom had more than enough powder to do a little hunting, to make such a march into the Indian country as had only been made before by a Braddock, a Forbes, or a Bouquet with a regular army supported by artillery, wagon trains, and ammunition by the ton. Everybody, moreover, was aware that nobody could command the services of a single militiaman. All that was possible was the suggestion that a man might feel like volunteering, after he had been able to persuade himself that this was at least a halfway rational project. There was as little respect for another man's opinion on this side of the frontier as on the Indian side. But the more people thought about it and talked about it the more most warmed to the idea. In the course of attempting to arrive at a decision the military commanders of each community undertook an exchange of letters with their fellow commanders which resembled on a smaller but equally vital scale the exchange of views and news undertaken by the contemporary committees of correspondence in the course of attempting to hit upon the most effective means by which patriots might resist the impositions of the King's ministers. It presently became apparent that the frontier consensus favored any move to hit back at their Indian tormentors. But in one respect they differed with the governor. No one could see the use in making so great an effort just to build a fort. What was much preferred was to keep on across the Ohio until the Shawnee, together with any other Indians who might side with them, could be met and fought on their own ground. Augusta and Botetourt began at once to muster their regiments and to wrestle with the so much greater task of arranging for their supply while in the field.

Upon Fincastle's county lieutenant, Preston, fell the heaviest burden of all, for his southwestern border was more exposed to Indian raids and was increasingly threatened by the possibility of a general Cherokee attack. It was for Preston to attempt to decide how many men must be retained for home defense before allotting men to the expeditionary force and for each man who volunteered for distant service to decide if it was really his duty to leave his family for his neighbors to guard. Uppermost that summer in every responsible settler's mind was the dread that meanwhile, in some sudden gust of panic, the whole frontier might be abandoned, as had so often happened in former wars. Some inkling of the resolution with which people were facing up to this danger may be gained from extracts from messages being exchanged by Preston and his local commanders:

The frenzied labors of emergency stockade building were touched upon in a July 13th note from William Russell on the Clinch which closed with, "Pray excuse haste, my Hands are so sore at work about the Fort, I can scarcely write." James Robertson was writing from Watauga on July 26th, "Onless you send Some men down the Case will be Bad So that I must stay with (no) more than Six men unless I kill part and tye the Other. I Expect we will have a war amongst our Selves without that of the Indians." The tension continued and on September 25th, when the expeditionary army was already hundreds of miles away, William Cocke was getting off a circular letter to Holston inhabitants, saying, "I would therefore advise and Request you not to Give the Indians one foot of Ground for by Flying we not only make them Sensable of Our incapasity to Receave them but give up our property for their surport." On September 29th Arthur Campbell was more confidently reporting to Preston from the Holston, "I have had the good fortune notwithstanding the late alarms occasioned to keep the people from flying the country." That there was still anxiety on the Holston was indicated, however, by George Adams' message of October 4th, "Amunition is very scarce With us Which is ye ocasion of abundanc of Feare." On October 6th Campbell was remarking dryly on his defense supervisory difficulties, "The most of the people in this Country seem to have a private plan of their own for their own particular defense" and was adding a grim footnote, "The Boy that was scalped is dead, he was an extraordinary example of patience and resolution to his last, frequently lamenting 'he was not able to fight enough to save his mammy.' "

In spite of these preoccupations with immediate border defense

Fincastle had furnished nearly three hundred men for the Kanawha expedition in response to Preston's July 20th call for volunteers: "Our Cause is good; & therefore we have the greatest Reason to hope & expect that Heaven will bless us with Success in the Defense of ourselves & families against a parcel of murdering Savages. Interest, Duty, Honor, self preservation and everything which a man ought to hold Dear or Valuable in Life ought to Rouze us up."

Light is thrown on the realities involved in raising a contingent of volunteers on this already beleaguered border by the experiences of James Robertson, the future founder of Tennessee but now concerned with the defense of Watauga of which he had been one of the earliest settlers. Robertson had been taught to read and write by his wife but his having come so late to learning had not inhibited the vigor of his expression. In responding to Preston's call to arms he wrote, "Since rec'd your letter I have been continually on Horse Back amongst the People. I will get 18 or 20 men Ready to start Thursday Evening or Friday morning." The next day he was writing a shade less confidently, "I thought to get them march'd today but it was not in my power. Some had grain to put up . . . Pray sir if Possible Procure me a Quire of Paper as I cannot get one Sheet." By August 11th his troubles were multiplying: "I have had a Severe Spell of a Great Cold and the worst tooth Ache that ever was." The next day he reported: "This morning Our Scouts met with a Couple of Poor Little Boys between this and Bluestone that made their Escapes from the Indians Last Tuesday night about midnight . . . I had A thought of Seting home next Monday but I wont Atempt it untill I See if we Can Rub up these Yalow Dogs A Little. I supose my helpless famyly is in Great fear and Indeed not without Reason . . . N.B. Sir I have been in the greatest misery Ever any felow was in. Since last Monday with A pain in my Jaw one of my Eyes Has been Shut Up Ever Since and has hardly Either Eat or Slept I Declare." By September 1st he was already late for the army rendezvous and his aggravation was again centered on his difficulties with his detachment of volunteers: "I gather them all Together Saturday and Pretends to make A Draft by your Orders I tell them, and dont want to Concern with any that has famylys, but Only

these Hulking younge Dogs that Can be well Spar'd." Still, by
September 12th he was well enough satisfied and even a little proud:
"I thought it was meerely Impossible to do it in the time and I am
sure there is not Such an Other Company for the Quaintyty of men."
He and his little band of neighbors had arrived and were now a
part of the army.

The commander of that army, Andrew Lewis, was tough, cold,
stern, and with a look about him to shake even the most truculent
frontier volunteer. His driving insistence on conformance and performance had given the bold outlines of reality to a project which
had in the beginning seemed as unlikely a military enterprise as
could well have been imagined. By September 1st his shuffling, el-
bowing, brawling rabble of volunteers had begun to behave enough
like an army to be achieving an orderly rendezvous at Camp Union
on the Greenbrier and on the 7th he was able to begin his northward march over the mountains.

Two days before the First Continental Congress had assembled.
The last glimmer of imperial influence was fading from the frontier
scene. Johnson, Pontiac, and Bouquet were dead. Croghan, his last
bright dream of fortune ended, was beginning to drift into a penniless and invalid obscurity. By the next spring patriots would have
exiled Stuart. The frontier arena had been cleared of every figure
who formerly had dominated it. To take the place of its one-time
masters the frontier had bred sons of its own to take command.
Their readiness for this sudden presumption to self-sufficiency was
now to be tested by the conduct of this homespun and buckskin
army, the first of all frontier armies, which with every step of its
northward march was setting precedents and establishing traditions.

Christian with the larger portion of the Fincastle regiment had
been enough delayed by the greater distance to be covered and by
his border's special difficulties to be the last to arrive at the rendezvous. As a result, much to his men's disgust, he was given the duty
of guarding the convoy. Lewis partly reassured them with the promise that he would give them time to catch up with the main army
before he crossed the Ohio into the Shawnee country. No regular
officer but must have fallen in a faint if confronted by the demand

that he prepare plans for the supply and security of such an army on such a march through such a country. Former armies marching into the wilderness had paused to build roads over which wagon trains could be dragged and had still found the supply problems all but insoluble. But the problem of supplying this army was solved almost in passing by men who by long frontier experience had learned to adapt and to make do. Beef was driven on the hoof over the steep mountain trails and flour was transported by an ingeniously alternating use of pack horses and of canoes which were constructed as needed. The army's security en route was as imperturbably maintained. Cornstalk's reconnoitering parties shadowed the march, kept constant track of its progress, sniped at stragglers, and watched for chances to stampede the horses. But this was not an army with masses of slow-moving regulars to offer fat targets. It was rather an army so lean, active, and alert that it was never safe to stray within a long gunshot of it.

Lewis kept on north through the Kanawha gorges and over the wooded ridges and on October 8th camped on the Ohio to await the arrival of Christian and his convoy guard. Here in a hollow tree was found a letter left there by scouts * from Dunmore's army and soon Lewis was able to exchange repeated messages with the governor. For Dunmore had before the end of August been so impressed by the vigorous response of the frontier to his originally forlorn call to arms that he had decided himself to take the field. Marshaling the militia of the northern Virginia frontier, he had started down the Ohio in boats and canoes with 700 men while another body of 500 under Major William Crawford, † Washington's land agent, marching overland, crossed the Ohio at the mouth of the Hockhocking. Reassembling his army, Dunmore dispatched orders to Lewis to make haste to join him and began slowly to advance into the wilderness toward the main Shawnee towns on the Scioto.

Cornstalk had closely observed this formidable convergence of

---

* Two of these messengers were frontier figures then fast friends but soon to gain fame of the most contrary sort—Simon Kenton and Simon Girty.

† In 1782 after a disastrous rout of his command by Wyandot and Shawnee he was captured and burned at the stake to cap one of the most dramatically tragic episodes in frontier history.

white armies advancing upon his country. The last faintest hope of
support from other Indian nations had faded. His nearest and
friendliest neighbors had remained as unmoved by the Logan murders and now by these white invasions as had the self-centered
Iroquois or the self-hypnotized Cherokee. He was left with no alternative to war but submission. Yielding at last to the importunities
of his warriors he chose war as the lesser evil. Having finally decided
to fight he struck shrewdly, swiftly, and with terrible force. Concluding the more sensible way to deal with an enemy so superior
in total numbers was to assail it in detail, he determined to destroy
Lewis before he could join Dunmore or had himself been joined by
Christian. Crossing the Ohio in canoes and rafts with 800 warriors
the evening of October 9th, he planned to storm Lewis' camp the
morning of the 10th.

The attacking Shawnee were as confident as they were enraged
and determined. The force that they were stalking was in their
estimation not a real army but a mere aggregation of settlers and
they had learned by long experience that settlers were more often
quailing victims than serious antagonists. So certain were they of
an easy victory that in their battle plan they had posted warriors
along the banks of both rivers to dispatch white fugitives who might
try to escape by swimming.

Two hunters out at dawn to shoot turkeys detected the presence
of the advancing Shawnee while they were still a mile from camp.
One was shot but the other got back with the alarm. Most of the
men being awakened by the sudden shrilling of fifes and rattle of
drums had never before been on a battlefield. For weeks they had
been talking of the day they might at last come to grips with the
Indians. Now they were realizing with a stabbing intensity of com-
prehension which they could not possibly have foreseen that not
only the day but the very hour was upon them. The veteran Lewis
well understood how critical was that moment. He had all too often
before seen untried men break, men who had seemed in all outward aspects as bold as these. He knew that the issue of the battle,
the fate of his army, and, perhaps, the outcome of the war could be
decided in the next few minutes. Inexperienced soldiers were never

prepared for the shocking violence of the first blast of enemy gunfire.

He ordered his two colonels, William Fleming and Charles Lewis, to lead detachments of 150 men each out to meet the Indian advance with a view to determining its strength. It proved strong enough to throw back and for a time to threaten to destroy the reconnaissance force. The initial collision with the Indian onrush was made the more dismaying by the almost immediate fall of both colonels. Charles Lewis was killed and Fleming suffered wounds observers considered mortal.

The howling Shawnee rushed forward, certain that the recoil must become a rout and then the familiar panic. But the frontier militia did not break. Their retreat was slow, they fought stubbornly for each foot of ground that they were forced to give up, and they kept their line intact. To the astounded Indians these no longer seemed settlers. They seemed rather to be white warriors as resolute in battle as the most dedicated red warrior.

Lewis ordered out fresh companies to thicken and lengthen his battle line. Finally the Shawnee advance was stemmed. For hours the struggle continued with unabated ferocity while the issue appeared to tremble in the balance. These were adversaries who for generations had visited nightmarish miseries upon the other and on this field they were giving vent to animosities bred in them from the cradle. On the thicketed slopes and in the swampy bottoms the battle lines were interlocked, often at hand to hand, and the fighting was at all times so close up that each side was continually yelling taunts, threats, and imprecations. In later accounts of the battle both belligerents paid the highest tribute to the other's extreme aggressiveness. The Indian warrior caste was committed to courage in combat by training, experience, and immemorial tradition. The frontiersmen had had no such tradition. They were founding one that day.

By noon it was the Indians who were beginning, almost imperceptibly at first, to give way. Painfully, foot by foot, the whites recovered the ground that they had lost. But only darkness put an end to the battle. From dawn to dusk the brutal testing of one another's will to fight had continued without quarter offered or sought.

It had been a conflict as desperately sustained as at Bushy Run but there had here been one great difference in that this new kind of borderer had proved himself as adept at woods fighting as his Indian antagonist. Again, as at Bushy Run, the two forces were about equal in number, roughly 900 whites to 800 Indians. White casualties ran to a quarter of the number engaged and the Indian losses were probably as many.

That night Cornstalk withdrew across the Ohio while Lewis built breastworks to shelter his wounded. Tactically the battle had been a draw but strategically it was an overwhelming Indian defeat. Cornstalk's only hope had been to crush Lewis as Braddock had been crushed, with the chance that panic might seize the frontier, Dunmore feel compelled to withdraw, and other Indian nations be so impressed that they must rush to join the victors. Instead, he could now only look forward to the junction of Christian, Lewis, and Dunmore and his own hopeless inferiority from then on. The war was already over. He presented himself to Dunmore with an unqualified appeal for peace.

In the resulting Treaty of Camp Charlotte the significant clause was a Shawnee acknowledgment of the white man's right to Kentucky. In its first war the frontier had failed to punish the Indians as it had been hoped they might be punished but it had won the new land it had sought to win. This opening of its own way west had come at the last possible moment for with the outbreak of the Revolution the next year that opportunity must otherwise have been lost, perhaps forever.

Historians have fixed the name Dunmore upon this war between the Shawnee and the Virginia frontiersmen. It would be difficult to find one more inapt than that of an English governor for a conflict which was so intrinsically and essentially American and which produced results so detrimental to every English interest. It was a war provoked by frontiersmen, waged by frontiersmen, and won by frontiersmen for the sole benefit of frontiersmen. In striving for what they alone wanted they won much more than they then realized. Far broader vistas were opened by their victory than the way to Kentucky. It provided an example suggesting to all Americans the possibility of a self-sufficiency such as the frontier had discovered, a reminder that patriots everywhere could without professional aid plan and organize means of defense and, if need be, raise an army, feed an army, lead an army. The lessons learned at Point Pleasant were instructive on wider fields than the coming series of desperate frontier wars. There were not only veterans of Point Pleasant at Vincennes, Piqua, and King's Mountain. There were also men who had learned on that field and on their way to it at Saratoga, Brandy-wine, Cowpens, and Yorktown. Washington, who had known Lewis since Lewis had served with him at Fort Necessity, was so impressed with his conduct of the Point Pleasant campaign that in 1775 he proposed Lewis be made commander-in-chief of the Continental Army.

The war with the Shawnee had scarcely been won before the men who had been harried from Kentucky were back there again. Clark, rushing down the Ohio to Kentucky in the earliest spring of 1775, found them everywhere. That impetuous young man was fired with an enthusiasm for the new country that was presently to make him the frontier's greatest champion, to save Kentucky for Virginia, and to win the entire northwest for the United States. The Harrod brothers and their hardy companions had already returned to re-occupy Harrodsburg on March 15th and to make it the first perma-nent settlement in Kentucky. By mid-April Benjamin Logan was building his station near the present Stanford and Isaac Ruddle his on the South Fork of the Licking.

So far the frontier's advance over the mountains into Kentucky had proceeded under the umbrella of a pretended regard for at least a shadow of legality. The initial occupation of Kentucky had been a flouting of the laws of England but had paid lip service to the laws of Virginia. The first settlers in Kentucky were able to con-sider themselves outlying communities of Virginia's Fincastle County. The presumption of Virginia's jurisdiction had rested origi-nally on the terms of Virginia's charter, had been denied by the Proclamation, and had then in practical effect been reasserted by the military success of Virginia's frontier militia under the nominal command of Virginia's royal governor in compelling the Shawnee to acquiesce in the occupation. But now the frontier was to take its longest and, measured by the magnitude of the consequences, by far its most significant step. After toiling so far over wild mountains to find new homes in a distant wilderness, men who had ventured so boldly were as boldly to assert that their right to the land that they had taken was inherent in them and in their act of taking, that this right was in no way dependent upon the laws under which they formerly had lived, whether provincial or imperial, and that with that right was included the inseparable right to govern themselves in their new situation.

As with so many of the greatest developments in man's progress, this great step was taken in the beginning almost by accident and certainly in the most awkward manner possible. Richard Henderson was a prominent North Carolina lawyer, with a taste for adventure, great determination, soaring imagination, and an intense interest in western lands, who was oppressed by Virginia's apparent monopoly beyond the mountains. Being a lawyer he cast about for a legal loophole in that monopoly and conceived that he had found one. He gathered about him associates possessed of sufficient capital, organized the Transylvania Company, and hired the most celebrated frontiersman within reach, Daniel Boone, to be the project's field manager. With £10,000 worth of presents as bait he lured the Cherokee to a conference at Sycamore Shoals on the Watauga to listen to his proposal that the Cherokee sell to him their title to their ancient hunting grounds between the Kentucky, the Cumberland, and the Tennessee. Four years before, in running the Donelson line, the Cherokee had readily made over to Virginia such claim as they had to land east of the Kentucky. Henderson was now asking them to make over to him their claim to land west of the river but with the distinction that he was seeking to make it a more solid transaction by offering a substantial consideration. Whatever the status of the Cherokee title Henderson was clothed with no authority from the government of either his province or the empire to accept the transfer of that title to his company yet it was upon this curious transaction alone that he was expecting to found the whole future of his project. His undertaking was as violently denounced by Governor Martin of his own province as by Governor Dunmore of Virginia. Martin termed the Henderson group "an infamous Company of land Pyrates."

The Cherokee were impressed by the cabinful of presents and by the attendance at the conference with Henderson of such men as Daniel Boone, James Robertson, and John Sevier. They were also astounded. The land that they were being asked to sell had already been sold by the Iroquois at Fort Stanwix in 1768, had been cleared of Shawnee interference by the Virginians in the so recent war, and had from the earliest times been claimed by the Virginians, insofar as in Indian estimation white men could ever properly lay claim to any land. Their own hunting privileges in that rich region had once been valued but this proposal now to pay them for something they had already decided to relinquish fitted precisely with their own more recent policy of hoping to funnel white aggression away from their country and off to the west. Every aspect of the proposal seemed to favor grasping such an unexpected and unaccountable windfall. That they continued for many days to hesitate and quibble was only because of their reluctance to include in the purchase a right of access that did impinge upon land nearer their towns.

Old Attakullaculla, still dominant in Cherokee councils, as usual took the lead in recommending compliance with white desires. But the deal was not to be consummated without objection. His own son, Tsugunsini, better known as Dragging Canoe, a stalwart, six-foot warrior who had become head man of a village in his own right, towered over the tiny, shriveled figure of his eighty-year-old father and gave voice to the most violent protest. The impression he made on the white men present they were never to forget. His face was fiercely strong and given an added ferocity by the scars of smallpox and his deep voice was resonant with emotion. He declared his people could be making no greater mistake than to continue to sell land or in any way to continue to tolerate white encroachment and that he, for one, would never again submit to yielding another foot of it. He was to make his word good. During the many bloodstained years immediately to come no name was to be made more dreaded along the frontier than his. But that day the older chiefs prevailed and on March 17, 1775, Henderson's purchase along with his purpose was achieved.

Daniel Boone had not lingered at the conference after the first day. Already he was cutting the trail through Cumberland Gap that was to become known as the Wilderness Road and on through the region of laurel-tangled ridges and cane-choked gorges beyond which was to all who later traversed it to be known as The Wilderness. His trail-clearing party of 30 men was twice attacked by Shawnee, with a loss of three killed and a number wounded. Among the Shawnee there were many confirmed dissenters who, like Dragging Canoe and his followers among the Cherokee, were determined never under any circumstances to make peace with settlers. Boone kept on and on April 15th began the construction of the station which became known as Boonesborough. Later in the summer he brought out his wife, Rebecca, and their daughters who on September 6th became the first white women to set foot on the banks of the Kentucky. That same month the women of the McGary, Hogan, and Denton families arrived at Harrodsburg. There remain many contemporary references to how much more sedate soon became the formerly unrestrained behavior of the men on this newest frontier.

Henderson, meanwhile, had closely followed Boone with another forty settlers, arriving at Boonesborough the day after Concord and Lexington. He could have had no way of knowing that the Revolution had begun but he had come to Kentucky to sound in this far wild a kindred clarion call. The real basis upon which were founded his expectations for his land company was now revealed. He proposed to persuade the still fewer than two hundred settlers in Kentucky to declare themselves a political community separate from and independent of the provinces from which they had come and to proclaim their intention henceforth to govern themselves. In response to his summons eighteen delegates from the four Kentucky settlements assembled on May 23, 1775, at Boonesborough in the shade of a gigantic elm which Henderson feelingly described as "this divine tree." However material were some of the advantages he planned to gain for his company, there were phrases in his opening address to the Boonesborough Convention which compare not too

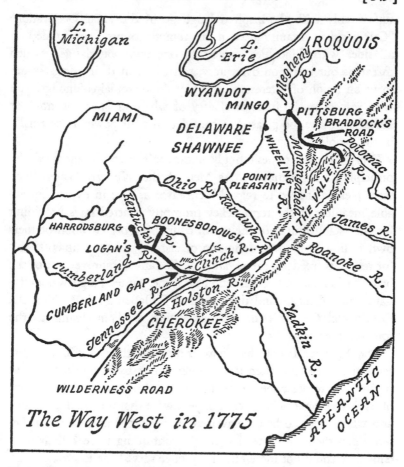

The Way West in 1775

From the Valley of Virginia the settler had his choice of the Wilderness Road in the south or Braddock's Road in the north. The central route via the rugged gorge of the Kanawha was impassible on account of Indian opposition at the mouth of that river.

unfavorably with the inspired language of the great Declaration: "Our peculiar circumstances in this remote country, surrounded on all sides with difficulties, subject to one common danger, which threatens our common overthrow, must . . . in their effects secure to us an union of interests . . . If any doubt remains amongst you with respect to the force or efficacy of whatever laws you now, or hereafter, make, be pleased to consider that all power is originally in the people."

Every delegate unhesitatingly and wholeheartedly endorsed the principle of independence. As Men of the Western Waters they were pleased indeed to regard themselves as free in every conceivable meaning of the term. They promptly enacted laws providing for the establishment of their own courts, the organization of their own militia, their own definition of crimes and punishments, and for religious freedom, preservation of the range, improvement of the breed of horses, and conservation of game. James Hogg was designated their delegate and dispatched to Philadelphia to petition the Continental Congress for the recognition of Transylvania as the fourteenth colony.

The Frontier People had now completed their mission, in the sense that they had taken the position which by having been taken in time was to prescribe their country's size and the federal structure of its government. They were not yet aware that they had a country and when they did become aware they remained as centered as before upon their own interests. But in continuing to seek their own ends they could not more effectively have served the interests of the new nation. Their fierce determination to seize land for themselves in the face of whatever privation and peril was to confer upon their country a nearly immediate dominion it could not without them have dreamed of gaining for generations. Their equally fierce insistence upon their own freedom of action was to force upon the national government acceptance of that most successful of all political devices, the progressive admission to the union of new and equal states, which was to lead to a growth more rapid and vigorous than has ever been achieved by any other nation. These immeasurable gifts were made the more precious by their cost to the givers in

dangers and sufferings even more painful than any they had already
survived.

The independence proclaimed at Boonesborough was beat upon by
many storms, many of which were of the westerner's own making.
The founding fathers in congress at Philadelphia were intellectually
intrigued by the strangely moving cry from a far wilderness but
were too preoccupied with the need to maintain a united front
against the King's ministers to consider for a moment risking a possible offense to Virginia. In Kentucky the inhabitants who had
cheered Henderson were soon disillusioned by the realization that
Henderson's company proposed to levy quitrents and began talking
instead of a republic as free of Transylvania as of Virginia or the
King. Clark, the loyal Virginian, strenuously advocated a nominal
reacceptance of their Fincastle County link with Virginia and in
1776 the suddenly looming threat of a general Indian war gained
him a hearing from his fellow settlers. Next, by his almost single-
handed exertions, he persuaded a reluctant Virginia assembly to recognize Kentucky as another of its counties and after much more
argument to advance him five hundred pounds of gunpowder without which the settlers must have been unable to defend themselves
that first grim winter of the war in the west. Though this was a
temporary return to the Virginia fold the seed planted at Boonesborough did not wither. Through all the vicissitudes of the ensuing
years of violence the westerners never retreated from their insistence
upon their freedom of action. They exerted pressures upon the central government that were at times carried to the point of threatening to secede or to turn into the outstretched arms of Spain, France,
or England. Eventually they won their point. Kentucky was admitted as a state in 1792 and Tennessee in 1796. The United States had
followed the frontier over the mountains.

This tremendous event had been made possible by the westerners'
ability, meanwhile, to hold against incredible odds to their isolated
lodgment in the center of the Mississippi Valley. Scarcely had the
original handful of settlers cut their stockade poles when war burst
upon them. For them the Revolutionary War did not end after a
mere seven years of travail. For them the war flamed on for another

thirteen years after Yorktown. Their Indian enemies, made finally aware of the virtues of concerted action, supplied from English arsenals, supported by corps of Tory rangers, attacked them from every quarter. Spain shut off their commerce. Their own leaders lent themselves to Spanish, French, and English conspiracies. The first federal troops to come to their aid came only toward the end of the twenty-year-long war and then only to suffer repeated humiliating defeats. Still, with the resolution bred in them by past trials the new Frontier People, the westerners, hung on. Having dared to cross the mountains they dared to stay and they gathered from their very adversities fresh energy for their next prodigious spring all the way to the Pacific.

Actions presenting so great a contrast to the ordinary course of human behavior indicate the power of the impulse that had gripped them. They had been moved to advance, not once, not occasionally, but again and again, into dangers as terrifying as any man can ever know. They had been sustained to endure such trials by more than a mere craving for land. They had caught a glimpse of a more complete freedom. They were people who truly valued freedom. They had come from stocks which had already set upon freedom a sufficient value to cross an ocean to a strange far land in pursuit of it. In the new world they had found a scene still cluttered with bond service, quitrents, class distinctions, legalistic inequalities. Glowing in the sky over the dark wilderness beyond the promise still beckoned. The complete freedom they sought may have continued to elude them but the reward of seeking it had not.

Bibliography

Among reasonably available published material dealing with the pre-Revolutionary American frontier are the following:

Abernethy, Thomas Perkins. *Western Lands and the American Revolution.* New York, 1937.

Adair, James. *History of the American Indians.* London, 1775. Reprint (Samuel Cole Williams, ed.). Johnson City, Tenn., 1930.

Alden, John R. *John Stuart and the Southern Colonial Frontier.* Ann Arbor, 1944.

Alvord, Clarence Walworth. *The Mississippi Valley in British Politics.* 2 vols. Cleveland, 1917.

Alvord, Clarence Walworth, and Bidgood, Lee. *First Explorations of Trans-Allegheny Region by the Virginians.* Cleveland, 1912.

Ambler, Charles H. *George Washington and the West.* Chapel Hill, 1936.

Annals of the West. Ed. by James H. Perkins and J. M. Peck. St. Louis, 1850.

Bailey, Kenneth P. *The Ohio Company of Virginia.* Glendale, Calif., 1939.

Bakeless, John. *Daniel Boone.* New York, 1939.

Bartram, William. *Travels.* Philadelphia, 1791. Reprint (Mark Van Doren, ed.). New York, 1940.

Billington, Ray Allen. *Westward Expansion.* New York, 1949.

Blair, Emma Helen. *The Indian Tribes of the Upper Mississippi Valley and Region of the Great Lakes.* 2 vols. Cleveland, 1911.

Bond, Beverly W. *The Foundations of Ohio.* Columbus, 1941.

Brebner, John Bartlet. *Explorers of North America.* New York, 1933.

Brown, John P. *Old Frontiers.* Kingsport, Tenn., 1938.

Buck, Solon J. and Elizabeth H. *The Planting of Civilization in Western Pennsylvania.* Pittsburgh, 1939.

[353]

Butterfield, Consul. *Washington-Crawford Letters*. Cincinnati, 1877.

Charlevoix, Pierre F. X. de. *Journal*. 2 vol. London, 1761. Reprint (Louise Phelps Kellogg, ed.). Chicago, 1923.

Clark, George Rogers. *Papers*. Ed. by James Alton James. 2 vols. Springfield, Ill., 1912 and 1926.

Clarke, T. Wood. *The Bloody Mohawk*. New York, 1891.

Collins, Richard H. *History of Kentucky*. 2 vols. Covington, Ky., 1877.

Connell, Brian. *The Savage Years*. New York, 1959.

Cotterill, Robert S. *History of Pioneer Kentucky*. Cincinnati, 1917.

Cotterill, Robert S. *The Southern Indians*. Norman, Okla., 1954.

Crane, Verner W. *The Southern Frontier*. Ann Arbor, 1929.

Croghan, George. *Journals*. Extensive selections in Vol. 1, *Early Western Travels*. Reuben Gold Thwaites, ed. Cleveland, 1904-07.

Cuneo, John R. *Robert Rogers*. New York, 1959.

Darlington, Mary C. *History of Colonel Henry Bouquet*. Pittsburgh, 1920.

Darlington, William. *Christopher Gist's Journals*. Louisville, 1898.

Dillon, John G. *The Kentucky Rifle*. Washington, D.C., 1924.

Doddridge, Joseph. *Notes on the Settlement and Indian Wars of Virginia and Pennsylvania*. Wellsburg, 1824. Reprint (Alfred Williams, ed.). Albany, 1876.

Downes, Randolph C. *Council Fires on the Upper Ohio*. Pittsburgh, 1940.

Dunbar, Seymour. *History of Travel in America*. 4 vols. Indianapolis, 1915.

Filson, John. *The Discovery, Settlement and Present State of Kentucky*. Wilmington, 1784. Reprint (Willard Rouse Jillson, ed.). Louisville, 1929.

Franklin, Benjamin. *Writings*. Albert Henry Smyth, ed. 10 vols. New York, 1907.

Gage, Thomas. *Correspondence*. Ed. by Clarence E. Carter. 2 vols. New Haven, 1931-33.

Griffis, William E. *Sir William Johnson*. New York, 1891.

Halsey, Francis Whiting. *The Old New York Frontier*. New York, 1901.

Hanna, Charles A. *The Wilderness Trail*. 2 vols. New York, 1911.

Hart, Freeman H. *The Valley of Virginia in the American Revolution*. Chapel Hill, 1942.

Haywood, John. *Civil and Political History of Tennessee*. Nashville, 1823. Reprint Nashville, 1891.

Heckewelder, John. *History, Manners and Customs of the Indian Nations*. Philadelphia, 1819. Reprint (William C. Reichel, ed.). Philadelphia, 1876.

Heckewelder, John. *Narrative of the Mission of the United Brethren*. Philadelphia, 1820. Reprint (William Elsey Connelley, ed.). Cleveland, 1907.

Hennepin, Louis. *New Discovery*. London, 1698. Reprint (Reuben Gold Thwaites, ed.). Boston, 1901.

Henry, Alexander. *Travels and Adventures*. New York, 1809. Reprint (James Bain, ed.). Boston, 1901.

Hodge, Frederick Webb. *Handbook of the American Indians*. 2 vols. Washington, D. C., 1907-10.

Hornaday, William T. *Extermination of the American Bison*. Washington, D.C., 1889.

Hulbert, Archer Butler. *Historic Highways of America*. 16 vols. Cleveland, 1902-05.

Hunt, George T. *The Wars of the Iroquois*. Madison, Wisc., 1940.

Hutchins, Thomas. *Topographical Description*. London, 1778. Reprint (Frederick Charles Hicks, ed.). Cleveland, 1904.

James, James Alton. *Life of George Rogers Clark*. Chicago, 1928.

Jillson, Willard Rouse. *Pioneer Kentucky*. Frankfort, Ky., 1934.

Johnson, Sir William. *Papers*. Ed. by James Sullivan and Alexander C. Flick. 9 vols. Albany, 1921-39.

Johnston, J. Stoddard. *First Explorations of Kentucky*. Louisville, 1898.

Kenton, Edna. *Simon Kenton*. New York, 1930.

Kenton, Edna (ed.). *The Indians of North America*. 2 vols. New York, 1927. (Selected extracts from the Jesuit Relations.)

Kercheval, Samuel. *History of the Valley of Virginia*. Winchester, 1833. Reprint Woodstock, 1850.

Kincaid, Robert L. *The Wilderness Road*. Indianapolis, 1947.

Koontz, Louis Knott. *Robert Dinwiddie*. Glendale, Calif., 1941.

Lahonton, Louis-Armand. *New Voyages to North America*. London, 1703. Reprint (Reuben Gold Thwaites, ed.). Chicago, 1905.

Lewis, George E. *The Indiana Company*. Glendale, Calif., 1941.

Long, John. *Voyages and Travels*. London, 1791. Reprint Vol. II, *Early Western Travels,* (Reuben Gold Thwaites, ed.). Cleveland, 1904.

Long, J. C. *Lord Jeffrey Amherst*. New York, 1933.

Mayer, Brantz. *Logan and Cresap*. Albany, 1867.

Mooney, James. *Myths of the Cherokee*. Washington, D.C., 1900.

Morgan Lewis H. *The League of the Iroquois*. Rochester, 1851. Reprint (Herbert M. Lloyd, ed.). New York, 1904.

Morris, Thomas. *Miscellanies in Prose and Verse*. London, 1791. Abridged reprint in Vol. I, *Early Western Travels* (Reuben Gold Thwaites, ed.). Cleveland, 1904.

New York. *Documentary History*. Ed. by E. B. O'Callaghan. 4 vols. Albany, 1850-51.

New York. *Documents Relative to Colonial History*. Ed. by E. B. O'Callaghan and J. R. Broadhead. Albany, 1856.

Pargellis, Stanley M. *Lord Loudon in North America*. New Haven, 1933.

Parkman, Francis. *Montcalm and Wolfe*. 3 vols. Boston, 1904.

Parkman, Francis. *Conspiracy of Pontiac*. 2 vols. Boston, 1907.

Peckham, Howard H. *Pontiac and the Indian Uprising*. Princeton, 1947.

Pennsylvania. *Archives*. Ed. by Samuel Hazard. 12 vols. Philadelphia, 1852-56.

Pennsylvania. *Colonial Records*. Ed. by Samuel Hazard. 16 vols. Philadelphia, 1852.

Pennsylvania. *Frontier Forts*. Report of Commission to Locate Sites. 2 vols. Harrisburg, 1896.

Pittman, Philip. *European Settlements on the Mississippi*. London, 1770. Reprint (Frank Heywood Hodder, ed.). Cleveland, 1906.

Pound, Arthur, and Day, R. E. *Johnson of the Mohawks*. New York, 1930.

Ramsey, J. G. M. *Annals of Tennessee.* Charleston, S.C., 1853. Reprint Kingsport, Tenn., 1926.

Riegal, Robert E. *America Moves West.* New York, 1930.

Rogers, Robert. *Journals.* London, 1765. Reprint (F. F. Hough, ed.). Albany, 1883.

Rogers, Robert. *Concise Account of North America.* London, 1765.

Roosevelt, Theodore. *The Winning of the West.* 6 vols. New York, 1889-96.

Sargent, Winthrop. *History of Expedition Against Fort Duquesne.* Philadelphia, 1856.

Savelle, Max. *George Morgan, Colony Builder.* New York, 1932.

Severance, Frank Hayward. *An Old Frontier of France.* 2 vols. New York, 1917.

Smith, Richard. *A Tour of Four Great Rivers in 1769.* New York, 1906.

Smith, William. *Historical Account of Bouquet's Expedition.* Philadelphia, 1766. Reprint Cincinnati, 1907.

Stone, William L. *Life and Times of Sir William Johnson.* 2 vols. Albany, 1865.

Thwaites, Reuben Gold. *Early Western Travels.* 32 vols. Cleveland, 1904-07.

Thwaites, Reuben Gold, and Kellogg, Louise Phelps. *Documentary History Dunmore's War.* Madison, 1905.

Timberlake, Henry. *Memoirs.* London, 1765. Reprint (Samuel Cole Williams, ed.). Johnson City, Tenn., 1927.

Turner, Frederick Jackson. *The Frontier in American History.* New York, 1920.

Turner, Frederick Jackson. *The Significance of Sections in American History.* New York, 1932.

Volwiler, Albert T. *George Croghan and the Westward Movement.* Cleveland, 1926.

Walton, Joseph S. *Conrad Weiser.* Philadelphia, 1900.

Williams, Samuel Cole (ed.). *Early Travels in the Tennessee Country.* Johnson City, Tenn., 1928.

Washington, George. *Diaries.* Ed. by John C. Fitzpatrick. 4 vols. New York, 1925.

Washington, George. *Journal.* Ed. by Joseph Meredith Toner. Albany, 1893.

Withers, Alexander Scott. *Chronicles of Border Warfare.* Clarksburg, W.Va., 1831. Reprint (Reuben Gold Thwaites, ed.). Cincinnati, 1895.

INDEX

INDEX

Abercrombie, James, 88, 116
Adair, James, 130, 144
Adams, George, 338
Albany, N.Y., 7, 103, 105, 111, 151, 226; Congress of (1754), 110, 111; militia of, 108
Algonquin Indians, 151
Aliquippa, Queen, 55-56, 68
Allegheny Mountains, 6, 48, 62, 92, 178, 313
Allegheny River, 32, 56, 109, 171, 179, 295
Amherst, Jeffrey, 9, 10, 11, 13, 24, 82, 83, 99, 116, 123, 125, 140, 143, 160, 227; in Pontiac's War, 173-74, 175, 176, 177, 206-07, 225
Appalachian Mountains, 16, 18, 19, 54, 67 n., 128, 302, 314
Arbuckle, Matthew, 336
Armstrong, John, 197, 335
Attakullaculla, 133, 136, 138, 139, 142, 145, 248, 273, 322, 328, 347
Aubry, Charles, 94, 118, 119, 120, 121
Aughwick, 60, 67, 73, 80
Augusta County, Va., 305, 336, 337
Avery, David, 284

Baker, Joshua, 331
Bartram, William, 248; quoted, 131-32
Batts, Thomas, 314, 315
Baynton, Wharton and Morgan, 243, 244, 288, 293
Beaujeu, Daniel Hyacinth de, 75, 76, 77
Bedford, Fort, 6, 48, 90, 91, 95, 96, 178, 224
Bellerive, St. Ange de, 232, 242
Berkeley County, Va., 305
Bienville, Celeron de, 56, 58, 63
Big Bone Lick, 234-35, 244, 318
Black Boys, 229, 243, 260
Black Watch regiment, 177
Bledsoe, Anthony and Isaac, 306
Bloody Bridge, English defeat at, 188-90
Blue Ridge Mountains, 35, 52, 302, 304, 305
Boone, Daniel, 30, 306, 320, 326, 328,

336 and n., 347; as field manager of Transylvania Company, 346; in Kentucky, 319, 327, 334, 348; Shawnee attacks on, 327, 348
Boonesborough, Ky., 234, 348, 351
Botetourt County, Va., 305, 336, 337
Bouquet, Henry, 7-11 passim, 23, 83, 85, 89, 91, 93, 94, 169, 230, 257; Bradstreet denounced by, 214; at Bushy Run, 182-84; commissioned as brigadier general, 220; Croghan criticized by, 228; death of, 220-21; discipline valued by, 214; expeditions led by, 86-87, 174, 175-84, 211, 215-16; at Forks of the Ohio, 97; Indians cowed by, 218; letter to Harris, 204-05; military career of, 87, 88; as naturalized English citizen, 220; Pennsylvania government's attitude toward, 176, 214; in Pontiac's War, 174-84, 208, 226; in quarrel with Virginia, 220; in road dispute, 91-92; settlers dragooned by, 99; terms of, in peace talks with Indians, 217
Boyd, Rhoda, 218
Braddock, Edward, 7, 24, 25, 30, 112; expedition of, 71-78; Indian allies visited by, 73; routed by Indians, 77-78, 112
Braddock's Road, 63, 91, 92, 93, 259, 295, 315
Bradstreet, John, 94, 208, 211-16 passim, 223
Brant, Joseph, 50, 110
Brant, Molly, 107, 110, 122, 124
Bull, Fort, 88
Bull, William, 143, 145
Bullitt, Thomas, 326
Bunker Hill, 115
Bushy Run, 180; Bouquet's victory at, 182-84
Byrd, Richard, III, 326

Cahokia, Ill., 33, 164
Campbell, Arthur, 312, 336 and n., 338
Campbell, Donald, 160, 186, 238

Canachquasy, 56 and *n.*

Canada, 12, 13, 14, 58, 89, 102, 103, 154; capitulation, 82, 122, 164, 223

Canajoharie Indian conference, 117

Canajoharie, William of, 110

Carlisle, Pa., 7, 48, 176, 177, 178, 215, 226, 271

Caroline, as William Johnson's wife, 107, 109

Cartier, Jacques, 37

Catawba Indians, 73, 144

Cayuga Indians, 31, 117, 191

Champlain, Lake, 89, 102, 114

Champlain, Samuel de, 31, 32

Charleston, S.C., 126, 129, 133

Charlevoix, Pierre François, quoted, 28

Chartres, Fort, 33, 48, 164, 208, 213, 222, 223, 232, 238, 244; English flag raised over, 242; withdrawal from, 274, 287

Cheat River, 258

Cherokee Indians, 34, 73, 89, 129, 272, 280, 282, 302, 316, 317, 327; cessions of, in 1768-75, 321; costumes of, 135; English aided by, 136-38, 247; English in wars with, 12, 140-45, 245, 307, 308, 309; fraternization with Fort Loudon garrison, 134-36; frontier people's attack on, 247; frontier people threatened by, 333; games of, 135; grievances against settlers, 249-50; Henderson's conference with, 346-47; hostility to French Indians, 132, 134; and Iroquois, 273; London visited by, 248-49; matriarchal society of 135; policy on white encroachment, 322; power of, 130-31; pro-English influence among, 133, 136; and Shawnee, 273-74, 287, 327-28; Stuart's admiration of, 136; towns of, 131, 134; towns destroyed by Grant, 144-45; and Treaty of Fort Stanwix, 286; and Treaty of Hard Labor, 321; wars of, 12, 132-33, 136-38, 140-45, 245, 307, 308, 309

Chestnut Ridge, 5, 64, 67 and *n.*, 93, 179

Chickasaw Indians, 34, 129, 132, 144, 272

Chippewa Indians, 33, 39, 123, 148; Mackinac captured by, 165-68; in

Pontiac's War, 157, 166 *ff.*; Sioux as enemies of, 168, 272

Chiswell, Fort, 286, 303

Choctaw Indians, 34, 129, 132, 146, 247, 272

Christian, William, 308, 336, 340, 341, 344

Christie, John, 169, 170, 171, 177

Clark, Daniel, 50

Clark, George Rogers, 234, 330, 331 *n.*, 335, 345, 351

Claus, Daniel, 124, 125

Clinch River, 314, 317, 319, 320, 322, 327

Clinton, George, 107

Cocke, William, 336 and *n.*, 338

Concise Account of North America, A, 148 *n.*

Conestoga Indians, 201; murder of, 202, 229

Congress of Albany (1754), 110, 111

Connolly, John, 50, 324, 326, 329, 331, 332

Continental Congress, 19, 340, 350

Contrecoeur, Pierre de, 67, 68, 74, 75

Cornstalk, Chief, 286, 287, 329, 335, 341, 344

County system, Virginia, 304-05

Coytmore, Richard, 139, 140

Crabtree, Isaac, 333 and *n.*

Crawford, Hugh, 232

Crawford, William, 269, 293, 298, 341

Creek Indians, 34, 129, 130, 132, 142, 146, 193, 246, 247, 272

Cresap, Michael, 331 *n.*

Cresap, Thomas, 62, 63

Croghan, George, 7, 8, 9, 11, 23, 26, 47, 138, 268, 278, 340; arrival in America, 50, 51; at Aughwick, 60, 67, 73, 80; bankruptcy of, 60, 224; at Big Bone Lick, 234-35, 244; Bouquet alienated by, 228; in Braddock's expedition, 73, 76, 78; daughters of, 50; as Deputy Superintendent of Indian affairs, 81, 224; at Detroit peace conference, 240-41; French threat perceived by, 60, 73, 78; frontier people opposed to, 228-29; and Gage, 223, 228, 238, 241, 242, 243, 258, 265, 266; Gist befriended by, 63; home built by, 53, 54; on Illinois mission, 231, 233-35, 238-40; illness of, 244,

Logan, Chief, 330, 331, 332
Logan, James, 330
Loudon, Fort, 12, 89, 134-36, 141, 143, 144, 145; invested by frontier people, 229; surrendered to Cherokee, 142
Loudon, Lord, 88, 116
Louisville, Ky., 224
Loyal Land Company, 26, 316
Loyalhannon, 6, 93, 94, 95, 295
Lyman, Phineas, 115
Lyttleton, Fort, 224
Lyttleton, William Henry, 139, 140, 143

McAfee, James, 326
McDonald, Angus, 335
McDougal, George, 160
McKee, Alexander, 224, 227, 228, 238, 329
Mackinac, Mich., 24, 31, 33, 59, 153, 274; captured by Indians, 165-67
Mackinac, Straits of, 32, 169, 256
Maisonville, Francis, 232
Manhattan, bought from Indians, 9
Manifest destiny, doctrine of, 291
Mansker, Casper, 306
Maps, 2, 25, 36, 66, 281, 303, 315, 321, 349
Marion, Francis, 144, 145
Marquette, Jacques, 32, 129; quoted, 27
Martin, Governor, 347
Maryland, 25; Indian raids on, 79
Maumee River, 34, 48, 163, 212
Men of the Western Waters, 313, 350
Menominee Indians, 33, 168, 169
Metai secret society, 148
Mexico, 18
Miami, Fort, 163, 164
Miami Indians, 34, 56, 57, 58, 59, 164, 238, 328
Miami River, 7, 26, 34, 48, 56, 109, 233
Michigan, Lake, 32, 163, 169
Michigan (schooner), 160, 186, 187, 190
Middle Ground, 35
Minavana, 166
Mingo Indians, 55, 60, 73, 74, 216, 220, 231, 236, 264, 266, 270, 272, 282, 284, 328, 330; murder of, 331; in war with frontier people, 331-32
Mississippi River, 16, 17, 18, 25, 27, 31, 32, 33, 49, 151, 164, 208; Charleston traders at, 129; Fraser's journey to,

232; French posts on, 152, 164; frontier people at, 351
Missouri River, 54
Mitchell, John, 25
Mobile, Ala., 130, 174, 238, 245
Mohawk Indians, 31, 104-05, 106, 107, 108, 113, 117, 144
Mohawk-Ontario portage, 88
Mohawk-Oswego route to Lake Ontario, 30
Mohawk River, 48, 71, 102, 104, 105, 106, 155, 310
Monckton, Robert, 112
Monongahela River, 32, 56, 63, 75, 78, 99, 179; frontier people at, 258, 262, 295, 323
Montcalm, 24, 88, 116, 149
Montgomery, Archibald, 86, 89, 140, 141, 142, 248
Montreal, 31, 33, 39, 169
Morris, Thomas, 213, 232
Mortar, The, 193, 246, 247
Mortier, Abraham, 9
Moultrie, William, 144
Mounds, Indian, 234-35
Mount Johnson, 105, 106, 110, 124, 125
"Mover," 44
Murray, William, 220, 236, 238, 242, 258, 259
Muskingum River, 7, 26, 34, 48, 56, 162, 216, 218, 223, 257

National Road, 64
Necessity, Fort, 67 n., 69, 73, 74, 75, 78, 110, 307, 345
Negroes, 103, 127
Nemacolin, 63
Nemacolin's Path, 56, 64
Neutral Ground, 35
New England, 112, 129; French threat to, 72, 102
New Jersey, 203, 280
New Orleans, 17, 49, 50, 115, 151, 152, 210, 232, 233, 244; as key to trade, 267
New River, 286, 314, 315, 316, 317, 319, 320
New York province, 10, 31, 48, 49, 72, 81, 102, 112, 203, 244, 302; Cherokee visit to, 273; colonial assembly of, 19, 72, 108; Dunbar's retreat to, 78; early settlements in, 104; French-